UTB

W0386869

Eine Arbeitsgemeinschaft der Verlage

Böhlau Verlag · Wien · Köln · Weimar
Verlag Barbara Budrich · Opladen · Farmington Hills
facultas.wuv · Wien
Wilhelm Fink · München
A. Francke Verlag · Tübingen und Basel
Haupt Verlag · Bern · Stuttgart · Wien
Julius Klinkhardt Verlagsbuchhandlung · Bad Heilbrunn
Mohr Siebeck · Tübingen
Nomos Verlagsgesellschaft · Baden-Baden
Orell Füssli Verlag · Zürich
Ernst Reinhardt Verlag · München · Basel
Ferdinand Schöningh · Paderborn · München · Wien · Zürich
Eugen Ulmer Verlag · Stuttgart
UVK Verlagsgesellschaft · Konstanz, mit UVK/Lucius · München
Vandenhoeck & Ruprecht · Göttingen · Oakville
vdf Hochschulverlag AG an der ETH Zürich

Dirk Siepmann/John D. Gallagher/
Mike Hannay/J. Lachlan Mackenzie

Writing in English: A Guide for Advanced Learners

2nd revised and extended edition

A. Francke Verlag Tübingen und Basel

Dr. Dirk Siepmann is Professor of English Language Teaching at Osnabrück University.

John D. Gallagher B. A. is Lecturer in Business English and Business French at Münster University.

Dr. Mike Hannay is Professor of English Language at the Vrije Universiteit Amsterdam.

Dr. J. Lachlan Mackenzie is Honorary Professor of Functional Linguistics at the Vrije Universiteit Amsterdam.

Bibliografische Information der Deutschen Nationalbibliothek

Die Deutsche Nationalbibliothek verzeichnet diese Publikation in der Deutschen Nationalbibliografie; detaillierte bibliografische Daten sind im Internet über http://dnb.d-nb.de abrufbar.

2., überarbeitete und erweiterte Auflage 2011
1. Auflage 2008

Internet: http://www.francke.de
E-Mail: info@francke.de

Einbandgestaltung: Atelier Reichert, Stuttgart
Satz: Informationsdesign D. Fratzke, Kirchentellinsfurt
Druck und Bindung: CPI – Ebner & Spiegel, Ulm
Printed in Germany

UTB-Band-Nr.: 3124
ISBN 978-3-8252-3600-7 (UTB-Bestellnummer)

Contents

Preface to the Second Edition

This second edition includes a number of additions to the original text. First, Chapter 3 of Module II has a new Section 8 which describes the basic principles for coordinating and listing pieces of information, as well as presenting solutions for the frequent problems that writers have in this area of sentence construction. Second, Chapter 2.4 of Module III has been expanded to include more material on existential clauses and how to use them. And thirdly, Chapter 3.2 in Module I now highlights the main differences between German-style and English-style introductions.

In addition to the new material, references have been updated where necessary and a number of typographical errors have been corrected. The contributions of Hannay and Mackenzie were partially financed by the research project INCITE09 204155 PR (Autonomous Government of Galicia) and FFI2010-19380 (Spanish Ministry of Science and Innovation).

July 2011 *The authors*

Preface

One of the most obvious facts about the world we live in is that the written word is everywhere. Every day, more and more people across the globe are being confronted with other people's writings and are being called upon to produce writing themselves, in their private lives and above all in their professions. Furthermore, as the internationalization of our world continues, so we all are increasingly being faced with the tasks of reading and producing texts in languages other than our own. In particular, the dominant role of English in global communication makes it essential that skill in writing English should be part of the stock-in-trade of all educated people, wherever they live.

At German-speaking universities, most departments understandably demand that written work should be submitted in German: this places fewest communicative barriers between teachers and students and also fosters the German language as a medium of scholarly discussion. In departments of

English and in a growing number of science faculties, however, students are being required to do an increasing amount of their written work in English, and other departments outside the Arts faculties, too, are gradually coming to accept work submitted in English. This development may arise from a desire to train German-speaking students to practise communicating in the academic lingua franca or it may form a response to the growing number of visiting students from other countries whose German is not yet sufficient for academic writing. It is to all students who need to write term papers in English, for whatever reason, that this book is primarily addressed. We trust that it will also be of assistance to senior academics who wish to publish in English. Last but not least, it may offer fresh insights to professional writers and editors as well as to teachers and students in the senior years of the *Gymnasium* (grammar school).

The reader may justifiably wonder what is new about this book. After all, there is already a plethora of style guides, composition textbooks and self-help Internet sites giving advice on professional or academic writing in English. This book is different in at least two respects. Firstly, while we do offer advice on how to write effectively, our advice is not based on any prescriptive notions of what constitutes a 'good' text. Rather, we attempt to offer objective insights into those features of English academic text that may pose problems for the German-speaking writer of English. To take just one example, some style guides intended for native speakers set out fairly rigid rules on nominalization, claiming that texts will be easier to understand if the writer uses as few nominalizations as possible. However, as close observation of academic text will show, the situation is far more complex. One reason is that nominalization is a standard feature of academic language; this is just as true for English as for any other European language. As a result, budding academic writers who are anxious to join the academic community have no alternative but to use nominalizations in conformity with academic norms. Another reason is that the choice between a nominal and a verbal construction often depends on context. In the following sentence, for example, the noun *supersession* is clearly preferable to its verbal equivalent *supersede,* whose use would make the sentence far longer and more complex. This is because the verbs *advocate* and *expect* take different complements (e.g. *advocate that* + subjunctive, *expect that* + *will*-future):

> Most of those who advocate or expect the **supersession** of capitalism by socialism have a strong sympathy with the idea of socialism and, indeed, call themselves socialists. (Robinson 1980: 141)

Similar observations could be made about countless other points we discuss in this book. In each case, rather than providing prescriptive rules, we aim to provide strategies and exercises designed to help our readers cope with the twin demands of effectiveness and conformity to discoursal norms. The assumption throughout is that a reader who has insight into language, and more specifically into the interplay between function and form, will be able to make the right choices at any particular juncture in a text.

Intimately connected with this is a second feature that sets *Writing in English* apart from general textbooks on writing: it is geared specifically towards the needs of German-speaking readers. We base all our observations on authentic student and native-speaker texts from various sources, some of them electronic, and we draw on a wide range of research literature, some of which deals with cross-linguistic and cross-cultural difference. We are confident that this corpus-driven approach has allowed us to describe deviation and error in students' interlanguage with greater precision than is the case in textbooks which are aimed at a more general audience. In this sense, the present book will be helpful not only to non-native writers, but also to native editors struggling to correct fully formulated texts submitted by German-speaking authors.

It may appear from the foregoing that this book adheres to what Lea and Street (2000) have dismissively dubbed the 'study skills' methodology rather than the, to them less reprehensible, 'academic socialization' and 'academic literacy' approaches. According to Lea and Street, the study skills methodology focuses on "attempts to 'fix' problems with student learning" and treats these as "a kind of pathology". However, we have no qualms about drawing our readers' attention to 'surface features' like appropriate text structure and grammar because, as Raimes (1983, quoted in Grabe and Kaplan 1996: 31) puts it, "many of our students ... cry out for rules, for something concrete to monitor their performance with".[1] What Lea and Street seem to forget is that many advanced second-language writers already have a reasonable command of general writing strategies in their first language and that these usually transfer positively to the second language (Grabe and Kaplan 1996: 241). Their main worry, therefore, is not the assertion of their 'identity' in the teacher-learner relationship. What they are really concerned about is the fact that they cannot attain 'writing power' and cannot become members of the academic discourse community before they have mastered the rudiments

1 As should be clear from the preceding paragraphs, we are fully aware that rules are not the only thing students need. The most important thing is an understanding of the linguistic regularities underlying rules.

of their second language, any more than in traditional societies an apprentice was able to wield influence within his guild before becoming a master craftsman.

Part of any induction into a community (in our case, the community of academic writers in English) involves learning the ropes and discovering what is allowed and what is disallowed. Accordingly, we accord attention to the major subgenres between which many students in today's modular education have to shuttle and discuss the important matter of plagiarism. In response to the complaint, echoed in Lea and Street (2000), that teachers have tended to abuse their position of power to impose inconsistent and idiosyncratic requirements, we will provide teachers with a set of accepted practices which they and their students can rely on (at the risk of casting ourselves as authority figures!).

Having ourselves published articles and books in languages other than our own, we are painfully aware of the formidable difficulties associated with writing in a foreign tongue. The non-native writer needs to invest extra time and effort in what is already a lengthy research and publication process. This has led German and other non-English academics to suggest that texts written "for a majority of non-English readers by a majority of non-English authors" do not need to be "fully idiomatic" (Dressler 1977: 4; cf. also Carli and Ammon 2008).

We do not find this line of argument particularly convincing. Since "everything is idiomatic in language" (Hausmann 1997; this informs our Module III), we have to write idiomatically if we want to be understood. We communicate by means of form-meaning pairs such as words (*pen*), phrases (*make a claim, blind spot, spill the beans*) and larger chunks of text whose usage has been arbitrarily established in prior communication. Thus, the word combination 'make a claim' could theoretically mean 'invent a claim', but there is a convention which assigns it the meaning 'utter an assertion'. There is, of course, nothing that prevents foreign-born writers from using 'make a claim' creatively to mean 'invent a claim'; the snag is that their (unidiomatic) use of the word combination is certain to be misinterpreted by both native and non-native speakers of English. At worst, such a strategy results in texts that are "literal translations from the language of the author concerned, and the reader most competent to unravel the meaning is the one who can first translate them back into that language" (Snell-Hornby 1982: 84).

There is thus a very weak case for norm infringements. Once you start turning a blind eye to them, it is difficult to say where to draw the line. But there is also a pedagogic reason for our uncompromising stance on conformity to the norms applied by native users. This is the age-old insight that the lower you set your sights, the less you will ultimately achieve; if we abandon the aim of attaining (near-)nativeness and full idiomaticity, competence levels will continue to slide downwards. Throughout this book we have therefore done our utmost to help our readers to express themselves in clear and idiomatic English.

It is this concern with idiomaticity which also fuels our understanding of what a 'good' English text is. We do not view Anglo-American style as being in any way 'superior', and agree with Pöckl (1995) that British and American writing gurus may be guilty of "naïve Anglo-American ethno- or glottocentrism" when they compare their own writing norms with those of other cultures ('contrastive rhetorics').[2] Pöckl points out that almost all British and American researchers in contrastive rhetorics tend to use positive terms ('linear', 'symmetrical') for 'Anglo-American' style, whereas their descriptions of foreign discursive conventions appear to be loaded with negative implications ('non-linear', 'asymmetrical', 'incoherent'). That such a view is partial should be obvious; inverting the black-and-white dichotomy, we might state with equal plausibility that German texts, by virtue of their digressiveness, are versatile and multi-faceted, whereas Anglo-American writing is repetitive and colourless. Equally, German text structure might be likened to that of a "staircase" or "spiral" (Pöckl 1995: 103) leading the writer through ever more complex stages of reasoning to the conclusion. Viewed from this perspective, English academic style will appear like a walk across a monotonous plain.

While the terminology of Anglo-American contrastive rhetorics is undeniably infelicitous, European critics like Pöckl seem to forget that the late Australian researcher Clyne (1987), for example, does not see German 'Exkurse' in wholly negative terms. In his view such digressions have discernible and useful functions – such as familiarizing the reader with a theory or providing historical background. This does not mean, however, that such passages should simply be transplanted into English-language texts!

Where Pöckl (1995) clearly goes astray is in his charge that native English readers are ethnocentric because they are allegedly loath to plough through articles that violate Anglo-American norms. Just as foreign-language conversation classes aim to enable learners to function adequately in the target community through adherence to social and linguistic conventions, so it seems only natural to expect non-native writers to try to meet readers' expectations for a natural-sounding text.

2 The discussion in this and the next three paragraphs is closely based on Siepmann (2006).

The question of readers' expectations also brings aesthetic concerns to the fore, concerns which have received insufficient attention in writing manuals. Under the twin pressures of teamwork and time constraints, many students (and even professional academics) neglect even to revise their papers before submission (Pöckl 1995: 105), let alone respond to the exigencies of good style (Chargaff 1986: 108). Unlike many of our contemporaries we believe that careful revision and stylistic honing are integral to the writing process, and in the present book, chiefly in Module IV, we have striven to offer some guidelines on stylistic matters.

Implicit in the foregoing is our belief in the value of language awareness, focus on form, and strategy training – a belief rooted in the growing empirical evidence of the need for consciousness-raising among language learners. Numerous studies have shown that learners fail to notice many important language features unless their teachers resort to some kind of focus-on-form intervention (cf. Norris and Ortega 2000 for a meta-analysis of over 40 studies comparing focus on forms, form and meaning). In this book we therefore discuss a number of lexico-grammatical and textual features of English academic writing which learners tend to overlook, such as – to mention two arbitrary examples – the delicate interplay of formal and informal style or the expression of circumstance by means of subject noun phrases rather than prepositional phrases. We also attempt to provide a reactive focus on form by analysing errors made by our students and other writers with a German-speaking background. As James (1998: 241ff.) argues on the basis of Tomasello and Herron's 'garden path' studies, error commission is not irreversible, and systematic correction of errors may yield better results than the often vain attempt to forestall errors.

In other words, we assume that students can learn from their mistakes. But this is obviously not the whole story, for, taken to its logical extreme, such a position would mean that "the more errors we make, the faster we will learn" (James 1998: 242). As stated above, we believe that students should be encouraged to avoid errors in the first place. Profiting from the leisurely pace at which most academic writing is produced, they ought to reflect on their behaviour as writers and try to make controlled use of the expressive resources of modern English. Wherever feasible, we therefore offer our readers a wide variety of effective strategies for producing fluent texts, such as strategies for planning and revising overall text organization, strategies for combining sentences and strategies for building noun phrases or collocations. We also take due account of the empirically proven interplay between writing and translation at the word or phrase level (cf. Königs 1990, Smith

1994), for many learners with a German-speaking background continue to think in their mother tongue while they are planning their English texts, and they often jot down German words and phrases which they try to render into English at a later stage in the writing process. This is only too natural, since German-speaking students – including students of English – still do a lot of their reading in their mother tongue, thereby picking up subject-specific terminology and phraseology mainly in German.

The instructional strategies we have used in compiling this book have proved their effectiveness (cf. Zimmermann 1985; Marzano, Pickering and Pollock 2001). The book is organized in such a way as to accommodate various approaches (e.g. cover-to-cover reading or dipping into individual modules). The index will meet the needs of readers who require information about individual words, stereotyped expressions or questions relating to the writing process, and the glossary provides definitions of most of the technical terms we employ. Each module contains an introduction and an advance organizer in addition to chapter and strategy summaries. We highlight similarities and differences between English and German and analyse typical specimens of more or less effective writing; and wherever possible, we use graphics or tables to make complex subject-matter more accessible. We also provide ample opportunities for practice, including exercise keys, on the accompanying website (utb-mehr-wissen.de); as Hinkel (2004) points out, "the learning of many L2 academic skills, such as writing, reading, vocabulary, and/or essay editing, is largely a solitary activity", and interaction with us as authors (by reading this book or attending our classes) cannot replace actual practice at writing.

Our lasting gratitude goes to the hundreds of students whose work we have read and corrected over the years and whose thoughts have found their way into many of our examples. The contributions of Hannay and Mackenzie were partially supported by the Spanish Ministry of Education and Science within the project "A comparative perspective on the grammar-discourse interface in English, with special reference to coherence and subjectivity", no. HUM2007-62220.

Dirk Siepmann/John D. Gallagher/Mike Hannay/J. Lachlan Mackenzie

References

Carli, Augusto and Ulrich Ammon (eds) 2008. *Linguistic inequality in scientific communication today = AILA Review 20.* Amsterdam: Benjamins.

Chargaff, Erwin 1986. How scientific papers are written. *Fachsprache* 8: 106–110.

Clyne, Michael 1987. Cultural differences in the organization of academic texts. English and German. *Journal of Pragmatics* 11: 211–247.

Dressler, Wolfgang U. (ed.) 1977. *Current trends in textlinguistics*. Berlin: De Gruyter.

Grabe, William and Robert B. Kaplan 1996. *Theory and practice of writing*. London: Longman.

Hausmann, Franz Josef 1997. Tout est idiomatique dans les langues. In Michel Martins-Baltar (ed.), *La locution entre langue et usages*. Fontenay/Saint-Cloud: ENS Editions, 277–290.

Hinkel, Eli 2004. *Teaching academic ESL writing: Practical techniques in vocabulary and grammar*. Mahwah, NJ: Lawrence Erlbaum Associates.

James, Carl 1998. *Errors in language learning and use: Exploring error analysis*. London: Longman.

Königs, Frank G. 1990. *Beim Übersetzen schreibt man - übersetzt man auch beim Schreiben? Ein psycholinguistisch orientierter Vergleich zweier fremdsprachlicher Produktionsprozesse bei fortgeschrittenen deutschen Spanischlernern*. Bochum: Post-doctoral thesis.

Lea, Mary R. and Brian V. Street 2000. Student writing and staff feedback in higher education: an academic literacies approach. In Mary R. Lea and Barry Stierer (eds), *Student writing in higher education: new contexts*. Buckingham: Society for Research in Higher Education and Open University Press. Excerpted in: Hyland, Ken 2006. *English for academic purposes: An advanced resource book*. London: Routledge, 119–123.

Marzano, Robert J., Pickering, Debra J. and Jane E. Pollock 2001. *Classroom instruction that works: Research-based strategies for increasing student achievement*. Alexandria VA: ASCD.

Norris, John M. and Lourdes Ortega 2000. Effectiveness of L2 instruction: A research synthesis and quantitative meta-analysis. *Language Learning* 50: 417–528.

Pöckl, Wolfgang 1995. Nationalstile in Fachtexten? Vom Tabu- zum Modethema. *Fachsprache* 17: 98–107.

Robinson, Joan 1980. *Further contributions to modern economics*. Oxford: Blackwell.

Siepmann, Dirk 2006. Academic writing and culture: An overview of differences between English, French and German. *Meta* 51: 131–150.

Smith, Veronica 1994. *Thinking in a foreign language. An investigation into essay writing and translation by L2 learners*. Narr: Tübingen.

Snell-Hornby, Mary 1982. English language courses at German universities: Cinderella or Sleeping Beauty? *Neusprachliche Mitteilungen* 35(2): 81–87.

Zimmermann, Günther 1985. Selbstlerngrammatiken im Fremdsprachenunterricht. In Zimmermann, Günther and Elke Wißner-Kurzawa (eds), *Grammatik: lehren – lernen-selbstlernen*. München: Hueber.

Introduction

For most people it is difficult to produce effective writing in a foreign language. Writing well can be hard work even in your native language, but it can be especially daunting to write in a second language such as English. You cannot always trust your intuitions about word order and word choice, as you usually do in your mother tongue, and it may take considerable time and effort to organize your text in a sensible way. At least in the initial stages, what you can write will lag behind what you want to write, and you are bound to make mistakes. However, all these difficulties are by no means insurmountable, so that you should not worry too much if you do not produce a polished text at the first attempt.

What this book does is provide you with a framework for developing the skills that will allow you to produce that polished text. More specifically, it gives you an understanding of what it takes to produce a successful academic text in English, including the following:

- organizing ideas so as to provide a clear focus for the text;
- designing the text to fit in with genre conventions;
- shaping sentences that fit the context and allow the important information to stand out;
- using lexico-grammatical combinations to ensure idiomatic phrasing;
- using the lexical constructions which are characteristic of academic argumentation;
- choosing formulations in keeping with what is generally understood as academic style.

Being able to do all these things means that you have developed a considerable discourse competence. Accordingly, our aims in this book can be seen in the context of the relevant communicative competences described in the Common European Framework of Reference (CEFR, 2001). We give you much of the support needed to develop your writing skills from the B range in the CEFR framework up to the C range, which encompasses the levels of proficiency and mastery. The central notion here is discourse competence (CEFR, 2001: 123), which embraces all the activities listed above.

The development of your discourse competence goes hand in hand with the development of linguistic competences, the most important of which are lexical and grammatical competences. In this book we provide a lexical and grammatical description of the major features of written academic English, identifying the key elements of the repertoire that you will need to attain proficiency (level C1) and indeed mastery (level C2) in writing. Broadening your linguistic repertoire will mean that you gradually overcome any sense of linguistic limitation that you might have. We also aim to make writing a more conscious and controllable activity for you by focusing throughout the book on areas of English where German learners are known to have problems; in addition, for each major area of writing we formulate practical guidelines and strategies that will help you produce more effective text. If you understand and appreciate why one way of saying things is more appropriate and more effective than another way, then you will be able to develop control over your writing.

The four modules

To give you an idea of the subjects we address, let us look at some typical problems in producing effective text. First consider this introduction to a student essay on 'youth unemployment', paying particular attention to the final sentence:

> ***Solving youth employment, a complicated issue***
> Graduation day is a milestone in a person's life. Years of hard work are finally rewarded with a slip of paper which promises a great future. This slip of paper will guarantee a good job; at least, that is what teachers and parents have always been saying. In reality, however, things turn out to be a little more complicated than people seem to think. Many graduates optimistically start applying for jobs, but soon discover that finding work in today's job market is not as simple as they were made to believe. After a few unsuccessful applications many soon begin to feel disappointed and redundant. Their dreams of making it in the world are shattered, and a number of them simply give up trying. **This shows that youth unemployment is a very serious and growing problem, a problem with many aspects, none of which should be overlooked when trying to find a solution**.

The first thing we see in this introduction is that the text is actually about graduate unemployment rather than youth unemployment, but what is of perhaps greater concern is the final sentence, which should provide the basic thesis to be developed in the rest of the essay, but does not do this very effectively. First, the opening to the sentence, *This shows that [...]*, suggests that the sentence functions merely to conclude an argument, not that it will be the launching pad for several paragraphs of further text; in fact, it is not at all clear where the essay will go from here. Second, no evidence has been provided, even implicitly, for the claim that youth unemployment is actually growing, which means that the final sentence is not even an effective summary of what has been argued so far. What is more, the picture that does emerge from the introduction is of the emotional consequences for the young people concerned. But it is not at all clear from the text that these are the aspects that need to be taken into account – neither the title nor the final sentence of the introduction suggests that it is the emotional state of young, highly educated but unemployed people that is going to be the focus of the essay. All in all, it appears that the introduction has not been adequately thought through, and the reader may be excused for not wanting to read on.

How to go about preventing problems like these is the subject of **Module I**. Module I is called ***Text organization*** and is about text design, thematic organization and logical ordering. It takes you through the process of planning and sets out basic features of text design for different kinds of paper that you may have to write. Details are given on such matters as the formulation of your title, the structure of paragraphs, patterns of argumentation, and means of referring to other writers.

Constructing a framework for your text is one thing. Fleshing it out is quite another. This brings us to the construction of sentences, which are the basic building blocks of text. Consider the following example:

> The purpose of this paper is to examine in depth the impact of Berlin's home care programs for the elderly. Here the degree to which functionally disabled elderly people receive badly needed help is a central question.

This short excerpt from the opening to a paragraph is not particularly reader-friendly. The second sentence has a rather long subject which presents new information, and the reader is informed that this is going to be a central question. However, given the opening sentence we may assume that it is the writer's intention here to actually announce one of the central questions. In that case it would make for a more effective text if the information presented by the grammatical subject were to appear at the end of the sentence, which is the normal position in English for focused information. The problem can be easily solved by switching the information around. Here are two options, the second of which makes use of a special presentative construction, which is a handy device in academic text.

> A central question here is the degree to which the functionally disabled elderly receive badly needed help.

> Of central concern here is the degree to which the functionally disabled elderly receive badly needed help.

Both these formulations have the advantage that the initial element sets up a close semantic link with the notion of 'examine' from the previous sentence, thus leading to greater cohesion than in the original formulation.

This example shows that effective sentence building is not only a matter of creating sentences which are grammatically correct, but also a matter of organizing the flow of information so that it fits into the context. What you need in order to produce this more effective piece of writing is first of all the grammatical competence to construct this particular clause pattern in the first place, and secondly the discourse competence to use it at an appropriate point in your text. All of this is the subject of **Module II**, which is called ***Building effective sentences.*** Underlying the principles for clause and sentence construction which we propose in this module is a view of language which assumes that the linguistic choices available to language users can best be understood in terms of the functions they perform in communication.

When we go a further level down from the clause we come to the word level. Here it is our aim to describe the most important factors affecting word choice and crucially the combination of words in academic text. We will see that the choice of appropriate and effective vocabulary is not a matter of filling slots in sentences with words and expressions that you may, for example, pick up from a dictionary. In fact, such free choice among lexical elements is rarely available, and possible choices differ widely from one language to another. The non-native writer therefore needs an acute awareness of the pitfalls involved in combining English words and in translating lexical items from German into English. The German word combination *(eine) Qualität* + *gewinnen* is a case in point because neither the noun *Qualität* nor the verb *gewinnen* can serve as a basis for translation. The following sentence by a German writer of English shows interference with the German collocation and needs to be completely rephrased:

?In the computer age challenges have gained a new quality …

Here a more natural English sentence would be *The challenges facing us in the computer age are of an entirely different kind*. This treatment of lexical matters is the subject of **Module III,** which is called ***Lexis and grammar.*** The module is strongly contrastive, and contains a host of strategies for making your written English more idiomatic.

Now consider, as our final problem, the following stretch of text, in particular the use of the first person singular in the expression *I think*:

> For instance, the official and unofficial names of computer systems or applications, or everything else that has to do with IT (Information Technology) is often related to the use of acronyms or playing with words. For that reason **I think** it could be useful to have always a look at some important and distinguished sources of knowledge in general [...]

There are several points in an academic text where the writer may justifiably feel the need to come to the foreground and use the first person form to announce his/her presence. In general, however, it is advisable to let the content do the talking, as it were, and adopt more indirect methods for expressing one's position with regard to the content. In this case, it is doubtful whether the use of *I think* adds anything to the text. Indeed, one might argue that the expression *it could be useful* implies that the writer thinks it could be useful, in which case *I think* is redundant, and can be omitted. The resulting formulation is rhetorically more powerful.

This use of the first person relates to what may be generally called 'academic style'. A detailing of academic style, and of the principles of language use such as clarity and concision which have a bearing on how readers experience the texts they read, is the subject of the final module, **Module IV**, which appropriately enough is entitled ***Style***.

Writing strategies

Taken together, the four modules of this book aim to build up your knowledge of text design and extend your linguistic repertoire in areas which are particularly relevant for developing discourse competence in the area of academic writing. Our main concern is to enable you to gain a better understanding of the operations involved in producing effective academic texts in idiomatic English. However, the transition from understanding to action is difficult to make. Of great importance here is that you use the time made available by the relatively slow communicative process of writing to apply the strategies we recommend. That is why each module proposes a number of useful strategies, such as strategies for getting started, for building complex sentences, for avoiding mistakes in word choice, and for being concise, to name but a few.

In addition to the specific strategies, we recommend the following general strategies which will help you with your first essays.

1. **Write in English from the start.** Do all your writing, even your roughest drafts, in English, using words and structures with which you are already familiar or of which you have compiled a list for the writ-

ing task at hand. If you can think of a particular word or phrase only in German, just note it down and translate it later. Strategies for translating and paraphrasing concepts which elude you are discussed in Module III.
2. **Think of your reader.** As well as having something interesting to say, you need to make yourself fully understood. Take time to stand back and look at your text through the eyes of a potential reader. Will s/he be able to understand what you have written?
3. **Do your writing in stages.** When you work on an essay or a paper, divide the task into small subtasks. And start early!
4. **Reread and rewrite.** Rarely will you get it perfect the first time in German, let alone in a second language. Make a habit of re-reading what you have just written. At the paragraph level, for instance, ask yourself the following questions:

   - **Will the reader understand what this sentence actually means?**
   - **Is this sentence relevant to the topic of the paragraph?**
   - **Is this sentence adequately linked to the preceding one?**
   - **Will the reader be interested in what I have said in this paragraph?**

5. **Revise** your finished text carefully. Consult dictionaries, grammars, the Internet or your teacher to find answers to specific questions about the English language.

Using the book

This book is intended for advanced learners of English who have a desire to improve their academic writing skills by broadening their lexical and grammatical repertoire and by achieving a fuller understanding of how these linguistic resources can be put to effective use. Inevitably, then, we assume that users of the book have a keen interest in language in general and a basic knowledge of English grammar and grammatical terminology in particular. For instance, you will be expected to remember from your school days such basic terms as 'subject' and 'present perfect'. Less basic terms than these are included in the glossary at the end of the book.

Our general recommendation for tackling the book is not in any way surprising. The best place to start is the beginning, and then it is advisable to move from module to module in succession. It is only when the modules are taken together that you can form a picture of the organizational and linguistic competences that allow the writer to produce effective academic texts in English. There is also a basic logic to the ordering of the modules, starting with matters of global text organization and step by step homing in on smaller linguistic units. However, each module is very much self-contained and can therefore be studied independently. For instance, if you are happy about your text planning skills, and your tutor is too, but you have been advised that your English is not very idiomatic, then you might wish to study Module III independently. It goes without saying that we provide cross-referencing in order to point out where important subjects are treated in a different context in another module.

We have developed a range of exercise material to fit in with the goals of the book. A number of exercises give you practice in identifying and using relevant lexical and grammatical constructions; other exercises invite you to identify and reformulate incoherent and unidiomatic stretches of language, as well as formulations with stylistic shortcomings; yet others take German as a starting point and require you to translate sentences into English. All these exercises are available online at the publisher's website (utb-mehr-wissen.de). We have included exercise keys which where relevant give detailed feedback on suggested formulations. This allows you to enhance your understanding of what makes one formulation more effective than another.

Although this book gives you a solid base for developing your writing skills in English, it cannot possibly provide you with all the support you need to become a masterful writer. Wherever possible, we have therefore suggested other sources of information on problems that you will encounter, including vocabulary books, dictionaries, and Internet sources. In particular we recommend that you buy at least one recent unabridged bilingual dictionary (*zweisprachiges Großwörterbuch*) and a new edition of a monolingual learner's dictionary (*einsprachiges Lernerwörterbuch*). There are five learner's dictionaries to choose from: *Cambridge Advanced Learner's Dictionary; Collins Cobuild English Dictionary; Longman Dictionary of Contemporary English; Macmillan English Dictionary;* and *Oxford Advanced Learner's Dictionary.* Make sure that you indeed buy the largest, unabridged versions of these dictionaries.

Module I

Organizing ideas into text

Introduction

This module introduces you to the main type of text (or genre) this book will train you to produce, the term paper. You will learn how the production of a term paper involves three types of process: a range of preparatory activities, the actual writing, and then the essential afterwork, i.e. various stages in which you revise and adapt your text. Writing a term paper calls upon many different skills. It requires thought, creativity and awareness of academic norms. If you want to write a successful term paper, you should not delay but start as soon as it has been assigned.

This module consists of four chapters. Chapter 1 starts by giving some background to the notion of a term paper and then sets out the various steps in the planning process, explaining how that process interleaves with the actual writing of the paper. The chapter assumes that you will be preparing your paper on a computer and goes into the various advantages of doing so, as well as some of the perils of which you should be aware.

Chapter 2 starts off by distinguishing between the two major types of term paper, concentrating on their relevance for work in a Department of English: the literary and the linguistic modes. This distinction has wider relevance, corresponding to the scholarly essay and the scientific article respectively. The chapter goes on to discuss quotation and paraphrase: you are told how and when to quote and to paraphrase, and how these techniques differ from one mode to the other.

Chapter 3 gives you advice about the writing process, showing you how to formulate the title, the introduction, the body and the conclusion of your term paper. The paper should be divided into sections: the introduction and conclusion each represent one section, but the body will consist of several sections. Within a section, there are various paragraphs. Chapter 3 also explains various ways of building paragraphs in English.

Chapter 4 is concerned with all the many activities that still have to be done after you have finished writing your paper. It contains hints on how to edit it in order to get rid of any imperfections, and also on how to format the paper to satisfy the requirements of an academic submission.

Chapter 1

The term paper: gearing up to start writing

The main points of this chapter are these:

- Writing a term paper in English gives you practice in using the norms of English academic prose.
- A term paper is an example of an argued text.
- The preparation of a term paper involves a complex interaction of planning, writing proper and editing.
- Planning should be done in English and involves six phases.
- You should use a word-processing computer program to plan, write and edit your term paper.
- Using a computer has many advantages but also poses several dangers.

1.1 The term paper as an argued text

The term paper (*wissenschaftliche Hausarbeit*) that will be the main focus of this book is a type of argued text which has a well-established place in the academic life of German, Austrian and Swiss universities (cf. Kruse 2006). This chapter is concerned with how you can best prepare yourself to write effective and successful term papers in English. Our recommendations are based upon general norms that apply throughout the academic world, and more particularly at German-speaking universities. You should be aware, however, that each university, and each department within each university, has its own specific rules and regulations for the appearance, length and content of term papers, and these should be consulted in addition to the general guidelines given here.

The term paper is of course an educational text in the sense that the end product is not actually intended for independent publication. Nevertheless, students are expected to write term papers as though[1] they were to be published. This is motivated by the status of the term paper as a training ex-

[1] On the 'as though' status of the term paper, see Pieth and Adamzik (1997).

ercise.[2] The intention of academic institutions in making this requirement of you is that the experience of researching and writing a text of this kind should prepare you to write longer, more complex texts later in your education, with a particular view to your final dissertation; and ultimately, the experience should make the transition to actual publication smoother. This book is conceived with the same ambition and has a similar preparatory function, since the skills you acquire by working with it will be beneficial for all the argued texts you will have to write in the future; and these skills are to a considerable extent also transferable to any texts you may write in German or other languages.

You will be writing in English and not simply making an English-language version of a text that could have been written in German, had the requirements been different. A substantial body of research (conveniently summarized in Siepmann 2006) has shown that outwardly comparable texts in English and German have very different internal properties, arising from differences in 'intellectual style' and educational traditions. One of the purposes of this module (see particularly Chapter 3) is to introduce you to the typical properties of texts written in English. Among these are (a) the assumption that it is primarily the writer's rather than the reader's responsibility to ensure that the text succeeds in imparting information and ideas, for example by being very explicit about the coherence and overall structure of the text; (b) the tendency for the writer in English to pursue a single line of argument, without digressions or variety in how s/he communicates with the reader (without the array of different "text acts" found by Sachleber 1993 in German texts); and (c) a preference for a particular type of paragraph structure, which almost always starts with a topic sentence announcing the scope of each paragraph.

The term paper belongs to a particular category of texts, the category of argued texts. An *argued text* has two major functions: it presents information (the expository function), and it takes a stand on that information (the more narrowly argumentative function). Argued texts are not only found in academia. Business reports, newspaper editorials, ecological surveys, histories, biographies, many of the more demanding texts you may have to write in your lives all involve that crucial mix of exposition and argumentation. Narrative and descriptive texts have different functions, of course, and less formal texts such as letters or e-mails will not be as rigorously constructed

2 The additional instrumental value of writing in acquiring proficiency in syntax has been emphasized by Weissberg (2000).

as a term paper. Nevertheless, mastery of the argued text can make an enormous contribution to your general writing skills, since the principles of organization we will be discussing return, relaxed and adapted to various degrees, in all text types.

The term paper is so called because it is usually produced at or towards the end of a term (or semester). It arises from a teaching-learning situation and allows you as a student to show what you have learned from a course of instruction, how you have reacted to that material and what you can do with it. Very often, before you sit down to write it, you will be able to discuss the subject of your term paper with your adviser, who will help you to focus on a subject that is neither too broad nor too narrow. In almost all cases, however, the final choice of the subject of your term paper will be your responsibility.

1.2 The three processes of planning, writing proper and editing

A piece of text as complex as a term paper cannot be composed at one sitting. The actual process of composing text (what we will call the *writing proper*) implies two other processes, which precede and follow the writing proper respectively: *planning* and *editing*. In general terms, planning inevitably precedes writing proper, since you cannot start to produce text without having first thought about what you want to write about. Likewise, the editing must generally follow the writing proper. After all, if editing involves reading your own work critically and making changes, there must already be a text there for you to modify. Research into how writing actually occurs (Flower and Hayes 1981) has shown, however, that this picture is too simple: skilled writers actually allow the three processes to overlap in time, with planning, writing proper and editing all involved during the same session at the computer.

As your text gradually takes shape, you will often notice that certain elements of your original plan no longer seem as appropriate as you thought before; they will need to be revised or even rejected. What is more, the writing process itself often stimulates new ideas, and their relevance to the original plan continually needs to be assessed. As a result, planning and writing proper will often overlap. This is no less true of writing proper and editing. Every writer is simultaneously a reader of his/her own work, and as soon as you have written something, even a single sentence, you will inevitably go back and monitor whether you have succeeded in expressing your true communicative intentions. Editing may even overlap with planning. As you read your draft self-critically, you may decide that reformulation is not enough, but that the entire plan you started with has to be amended. Back to the drawing board! The result, of course, is that lengthy sections of your work will have to be rewritten. The processes of planning, writing proper and editing therefore need to be seen as cyclical:

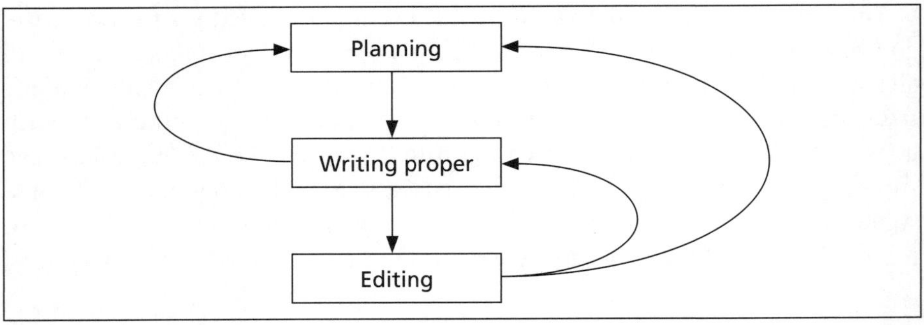

Figure 1

In practical terms, it is very important that you reserve enough time for the preparation of your term paper and that the period of time you assign to this work be divided into separate phases for planning, writing proper and editing. We know from experience that it is above all the time needed for editing that students tend to underestimate. You should try and have the pre-final version of your paper ready at least four days before the submission date. Leave it for a day or two, and then return to it, reading it almost as though it were someone else's work. This will give you just enough distance to be able to assess its true value and then, on the final day before the deadline, to make the final adjustments that are necessary. See Chapter 4.

1.3 Making the plan

A major part of your preparation of a term paper involves *planning*. Making a plan is the first stage of any writing project. At school you will already have heard how important it is to draw up a plan before starting to write. We strongly recommend that you plan as much of your text as possible in English, since planning is all about taking all the disparate sources of your knowledge – your reading, your research, but also your own ideas, and your attitudes and feelings about the subject matter – and transforming these into language items that correspond to your communicative goals. If you do a substantial part of this planning in German, you will be creating all sorts of problems for yourself: you may develop ideas that are beyond your knowledge of English; or you may run into difficulties of translation that will make your text sound foreign. Planning in English will also help you to get into the mind-set of writing in an international language. This may affect the communicative choices that you make, for example in not selecting examples that are only comprehensible to native speakers of German. After all, if you are writing in English, you have to assume that your reader will have the general knowledge of an average academic user of English.

We realize, of course, that asking you to do not only the writing of your term paper but also the thinking behind it in English is a tall order. In German-speaking countries, English is still very much a foreign language, not (yet?) having acquired the status of a second language that it enjoys in Scandinavia and the Low Countries, where almost all the background reading done by students is in English. Research has also shown that in practice most students do not succeed in suppressing their native tongue when trying to write in another language; however, the native tongue is then, according to Zimmermann's (2000) findings, being used for inner reflections on what to write rather than for pre-formulating sentences for subsequent translation (cf. also Königs 1989 and Smith 1994). Nevertheless, and especially if you are studying English as part of your course and you are writing about some aspect of the English-speaking world,[3] you should make every effort to treat the entire experience of preparing, thinking about, writing and editing your term paper as an 'all-English island'.

It is useful to conceive planning as consisting of six steps, each of which takes you a little nearer the point when you can begin to produce text:

1. generating the content
2. grouping and selecting points
3. establishing a perspective
4. determining an intention
5. dividing the material into sections
6. entitling sections and paragraphs

We will now discuss each of these steps in turn.

Generating the content

The first step basically involves deciding what to write about. When you start working on a term paper, your major fear is probably going to be that you will simply not have enough ideas. After all, the expectations are high: at *Bachelor/Proseminar* level the text may have to be 12 to 15 pages long, and at

---

3 Friedlander (1990) finds that planning in L1 correlates with better L2-essays about L1-topics and that planning in L2 correlates with better L2-essays about L2-topics.

Master/Hauptseminar level sometimes even twice as long. If your term paper is an expansion of a class presentation (*Referat*) you will already have a basis; but if the paper is about something new, you will have to construct your plan from scratch. Of course you have your class notes and your (possibly quite vague) ideas about what might be interesting, yet almost certainly not enough for your purposes.

The subject matter of your term paper may be determined by your tutor, who has indicated that it should be about some particular aspect of the material studied in class; either all the members of the class will have to write about the same subject, or the subject will be divided over named students, each dealing with a specific aspect. Alternatively – and this is most often the case – it will be up to you personally to settle on a topic, with the only requirement being that it should be related to the subject of the class. Here, too, there are different options: an overview of the field, a comparison of opposing viewpoints, an analysis of some phenomenon (a literary work or a set of linguistic data), a historical survey (for example of a literary movement or a school of linguistics) – the possibilities are endless. Almost every assignment will send you back to the class reading list, but no matter how much reading you do, that will not generate the content of your term paper.

There is a solution to this problem, and it lies in *interacting*:

Interact with yourself: Conduct an argument about the material with yourself and make notes about your inner dialogue, jotting down ideas, hunches, examples, anything that occurs to you.

Interact with others: Brainstorm with fellow students (preferably in English); if your own viewpoint is already beginning to crystallize, then others' reactions will give you a good impression of the stronger and weaker parts of your argument.

Interact with written documents: Treat your background reading (books, journals, encyclopedias, online scientific articles) as a resource, as raw material that you can use for your own purposes; don't copy screeds of text or summarize the entire document, but plunder the documents for ideas that inspire or enlighten you. Try as much as possible to consult sources written in English.

Interact with the Internet: The treasures of the web are easily accessible, but beware! Not all the information is reliable and much of it has no scholarly basis; web pages come and go; and, above all, do not let the apparent anonymity of the net fool you into copying text from web pages (this is a form of plagiarism, see section 1.4).

Generating the content is not just a matter of developing ideas, of course. You should already be preparing yourself for the linguistic challenges that lie before you. As you consult your sources, observe the specific vocabulary used by the writers. Do not just make a list of isolated words but note down the constructions in which they appear. Notice, too, the use those writers have made of the typical expressions found in academic prose. Without copying these expressions too literally, allow yourself to absorb the turns of phrase that characterize argued texts. (Module III will give you detailed help with these tasks.)

Grouping and selecting points
Once you have assembled the jumble of ideas that will form the basis for your term paper, you can move to the second step, grouping and selecting. Grouping involves finding connections among the various ideas you have generated. The ideas that have lots of connections to other ideas (high-density linkage) will be prominent in the text that ultimately results from your planning. Those that have only a few connections (medium-density linkage) will need to be considered carefully: which of these are really essential, which can already be dropped at this stage? Finally, the ideas with little or no connection to others (low-density linkage) may now appear to be whimsical or dispensable; on the other hand, with a little more thought and development, they may be joined up to the emerging structure. Having grouped the ideas according to the density of their linkage to other ideas, you should now select which are relevant and which are not. Naturally, you will feel a natural resistance to jettisoning the results of your hard work, but if you conclude that certain ideas are simply not appropriate for your purposes, out they must go.

Establishing a perspective
The result of grouping and selecting is well structured and easy to survey. It is now time to add dynamism to the static overview you have created by establishing what perspective you are going to take on the matter. If you are working within a theoretical framework, your perspective will already have co-determined both the preceding steps; if you are not, this is the moment at which to decide how you wish to approach the material you have examined. Will your study be theoretical or empirical? Qualitative or quantitative? Diachronic or synchronic? Informed by political, religious, moral beliefs or 'objective'? Answer to questions like these (exactly which questions you ask of yourself depends upon the field and the subject of the term paper) will help you to decide which ideas to take as a starting point and which will be postponed to the Body sections of the text.

Determining an intention

Whereas the previous step answers the question 'Where am I coming from?', the next step answers the question 'Where do I want to get to?' This step, which we may call determining an intention, is crucial to good planning. You may not yet know what the conclusion of your term paper will be, but you must have a good idea of what you want to achieve. Do you want to present only one side of an argument, or give equal voicing to both sides? Can you achieve your aims by theoretical argument alone, or will you also need examples? Do you want to persuade your reader of your viewpoint, or is a dispassionate description of the situation enough? The decisions that you make at this stage will be essential for the Introduction of your term paper. They also form the basis for the decisions that you now go on to make.

Dividing the material into sections

The fifth step in planning, that of dividing the material into sections, involves creating the basic framework on which to construct the term paper. The double outcome of this step will be a working title and a provisional structure for the Introduction and the Conclusion. In Chapter 3, we will explain how to formulate an effective title. As far as the Introduction is concerned, what you need to do at this stage is to determine how it will reflect your perspective and your intention (the results of steps 3 and 4); and as for the Conclusion, you need to map out how it will respond to the expectations created by your Introduction. In a well-structured term paper, the Conclusion should offer answers to all the questions raised in the Introduction.

Many writers are tempted at this point to go ahead and actually produce a final or pre-final version of the Introduction. After all, the material is already available: what is to stop you from writing it out? Our general recommendation is to resist this temptation and to postpone the actual formulation of the Introduction until the entire remainder of the text has been written (in pre-final form). The reason is that an Introduction is always an introduction-to: you can never be sure what exactly to include and what exactly to omit till you know what you are introducing the reader to. Many Introductions which are perfectly adequate as textual units fail, because they do not prepare the reader for what is to come or offer information that is not relevant to the Body of the text. And the same goes for Conclusions. A simple rule of thumb runs as follows:

PLAN your Introduction, then your Conclusion, and then the Body of your text
but
WRITE the Body of your text, then the Conclusion, and only then the Introduction; and then find the best possible title

Entitling sections and paragraphs
The final planning step returns you to the outcome of step 2, grouping and selecting. Now that you know what will be going into the Introduction and Conclusion, you can begin to construct the sections and paragraphs of the Body of the paper around the points with high-density linkage, i.e. the major ideas. For a term paper of 4,000 words, for example, we may assume that the Introduction and Conclusion will run to some 1,000 words in total (i.e. approximately 500 words each), leaving 3,000 for the Body; and for shorter and longer papers, this 25%:75% ratio can be retained. A 3,000-word Body could quite naturally fall into three roughly equal sections of more or less 1,000 words each; and each section will comprise on average some five paragraphs of approximately 200 words. Now, for each section, you should devise a heading, and also headings for each of the component paragraphs; if your material is rich enough to allow it, you can already allocate more detailed points to specific paragraphs.

The result of these six steps is a framework which is the result of creative thinking, and self-critical pruning, which derives its dynamism from a clear perspective and well-articulated intention, and which is divided into logically ordered sections, with appropriate plans for the Introduction and Conclusion. If you take a document like this (often known as a *Gliederung*) to your adviser, you can be very sure of a constructive, helpful response.

1.4 Using a computer

It goes without saying, perhaps, that a large part of your planning (and all of the subsequent stages of writing proper and editing) should be carried out with the aid of a word-processing program on the computer. Next to your computer, you will of course also have written notes from class, piles of quotations from the library, and all sorts of other jottings. In addition, if you find it useful to develop mind maps to generate ideas (where the ideas are grouped radially around a central notion), these are much easier to diagram on paper. In any case, as your term paper begins to take form, do not hesitate to lay out your plan on the computer. You can print it out for your adviser and even pin it up on your wall so that you can always see the bigger picture. In this way, once the structure for the term paper has been approved, possibly after some adaptation, the already existing structure merely needs to be fleshed out with text. For this purpose, the word-processing program's 'outline view' facility is invaluable.

The advantages of electronic preparation (and indeed submission) of term papers are overwhelming. For one thing, your term paper will look, and feel, professional; for another, you can avoid ever losing your precious work by regularly saving your work to the hard disk and additionally availing yourself of the online 'remote back-up' offered by most internet providers these days. We strongly recommend readers of this book to take full advantage of the computer resources now available and to continually develop their keyboard skills and their knowledge of the potential of word-processing programs. Here are some of the facilities offered by word-processing programs:

Spellchecker
All contemporary word-processing programs have a spellchecker. Make sure that you set the checker to the form of English (UK, USA, etc.) which is your own preference or which is required by your teachers. Do not rely blindly upon the spellchecker, however, since it will not discover words that you have spelled wrongly to look like another possible word (e.g. *then* misspelt as *than*, or vice versa).

Grammar checker
Many programs also have a grammar checker. This should be used with even greater caution, since such checkers work with linear patterns rather than a true hierarchical analysis of grammatical structures. Nevertheless, they are very often helpful with errors of agreement, especially between subject and verb, and may draw your attention to overuse of certain constructions, such as the passive or very long sentences. Similar comments apply to the writing enhancement software currently available as a plug-in to word-processing programs.

Thesaurus
Another useful resource in such programs is the thesaurus (a list of synonyms, sometimes with antonyms – words of opposite meaning). Used together with a good monolingual dictionary, this can help you with your lexical choices (see Module III).

Hyphenation
Hyphenation programs can be used to break long words at the end of lines at appropriate places. The rules for hyphenation are quite different in English and German, so if you do activate such a program (which is usually optional), ensure that you are using one for English.

Translation
Translation programs should be avoided. If you can't think of the right English word for a particular notion, we suggest you don't rely on a translation program to render the German word, since the programs typically have only one equivalent for each word.

Readability
A number of programs now offer readability calculations, including average sentences per paragraph, average words per sentence, etc. You may find it useful to have the Flesch Reading Ease[4] of your text calculated. The lower the score, the more difficult your text will be to read; for an academic text of the type you are writing, you should aim for a score between 30 and 60.

Word count
If you have to write a certain number of words, the word count facility will let you know how well you are advancing. And whether or not your paper must come to a certain number of pages, the program's pagination facility should be applied.

More generally, word-processing programs, which make moving or deleting material so easy, are very much to be welcomed, since they positively encourage writers to experiment with different formulations and to edit their own writing critically. In fact they make it possible for planning, writing proper and editing to merge into one structured enterprise.

Another major advantage of writing on the computer is that the word-processing program can run together with other support programs. In fact there is an entire *electronic workbench* available to the contemporary writer. Here are some resources that are of enormous benefit:

On-line dictionaries
A number of faculties make major on-line dictionaries, monolingual and bilingual, available to their students; otherwise, such dictionaries are available on CD-ROM. In addition, the OneLook facility at http://www.onelook.com gives free access to hundreds of on-line dictionaries and glossaries; fairly reliable on-line German-English internet dictionaries are to be found at http://dict.leo.org and http://dictionary.reverso.net. You should, however, make sparing use of dictionaries. Consult them above all to check that your sense about the meaning of a word or expression is correct. If a German word oc-

4 Flesch Reading Ease is calculated as $206.835 - 1.015 \times (\text{total words} \div \text{total sentences}) - 84.6 \times (\text{total syllables} \div \text{total words})$.

curs to you as you are writing and you discover that its dictionary equivalent in English is a word you don't know, it is dangerous to assume that the English word will be used in the same contexts (cf. Module III, Chapter 3.1).

Concordancers
These are programs which are primarily designed for linguists wishing to retrieve language data from corpora (large bodies of text) – and indeed they have been used in preparing this book. These programs are also available for writers who wish to know which words and expressions regularly collocate with one another (cf. Module III, Chapter 3.2). You can either apply a concordancer to a corpus of your own choosing or even use WebCorp http://www.webcorp.org.uk to concordance the entire Internet (but then remember that not everything written in English on the web is by native writers and that there is no guarantee of grammatical correctness, even with native writers!). In addition, there are a number of corpora of English that are on line. Here are some that you can consult very easily, all using the same concordancer:

The British National Corpus at http://corpus.byu.edu/bnc/
The BYU Corpus of American English at http://www.americancorpus.org/
The *Time* Corpus (from the American magazine *Time*) at http://corpus.byu.edu/time/

Applying a concordancer to such corpora will help you test whether certain collocations in your draft have been used by native writers.

On-line grammars
These should be used with great caution; at present no on-line facility offers the thoroughness and reliability of printed grammars. Moreover, most on-line grammars are oriented to native speakers and thus answer rather different questions from those that you will be likely to ask.

On-line style guides
Style is too subtle to be handled via an on-line program (cf. Module IV), but one useful site is the European Commission Style Guide currently at http://ec.europa.eu/translation/english/guidelines/documents/styleguide_english_dgt_en.pdf. Beware of ancient style guides now available on the internet (because their copyrights have lapsed!): much of their advice is no longer relevant, or even correct.

In addition, use of the computer also gives you access during writing to a range of programs such as spreadsheets and databases compatible with the word-processor as well as programs for statistics, graphics, text analysis, etc.; these programs can be used in parallel with the word-processor. Particularly relevant for academic writing is the availability of reference management software such as EndNote or the open-source Zotero; these programs can be used for the automatic creation of bibliographical references according to the citation style demanded. An increasing number of universities are now making EndNote or similar facilities available, under licence, to their students and staff.

A final advantage is that the computer also offers parallel access to the enormous resources offered on-line by academic libraries and archives. All leading scholarly journals are now available both in print and on line. Downloading on-line versions is quicker and cheaper than photocopying, and also makes certain that the original will be quoted accurately. In addition, a huge range of literary, cultural and historical texts from previous centuries are now available through various digital libraries. Since these texts may contain errors of transcription or may not reflect the latest editorial insights, they should be used sparingly, and always with the best printed edition open on your desk; nevertheless, their availability makes searching with a concordancer easy and attractive.

For many writers, both experienced and inexperienced ones, this electronic workbench is complemented by the use of search engines, which allow them to consult the vast resource known as the World Wide Web. In 1.3 above, we mentioned "interaction with the internet" as an important source of inspiration for writers as they generate content for their texts. There are, however, a number of problems and dangers to which we must draw your attention.

Non-academic sources

One thing that the advent of the Internet has not changed is the requirement that term papers should quote only scholarly sources, i.e. sources that contain information that has gone through all the various checks that academic editors and publishers apply. Most of the information on the Internet is not subject to such verification, including on-line encyclopedias like Wikipedia, and therefore may not be quoted in an academic work such as a term paper. An exception may be made for scholarly journals which apply all the usual reviewing procedures but are only available in electronic form, such as the Erfurt-based electronic journal of English studies *EESE* (http://webdoc.gwdg.de/edoc/ia/eese/eese.html) or *Constructions*, the web-based journal of Construction Grammar (http://www.constructions-online.de). If you do find interesting information on the Internet that derives from scholarly sources, you should track down those sources and quote them only.

Term papers for sale

Through the Internet, certain firms make available (at a considerable fee) ready-made term papers, written – it is claimed – by PhD-holding writers. It will be clear that anyone making use of these facilities and presenting work bought from these firms as though it were his/her own is committing fraud. The widespread misuse of internet search engines for this purpose – after protests from universities – led a major search engine company to discontinue advertisements for such firms in May 2007, extending a policy already applied to advertisements for dangerous drugs, prostitution, weapons, etc. Buying your way through education in this way is illegal; if you are caught at it, you will be liable to prosecution.

Plagiarism

The apparent anonymity of the net may encourage students who are short of inspiration to simply cut and paste text from a webpage into their term paper. This dishonest practice, which is a form of plagiarism (i.e. the intentional theft of other people's written work and the ideas it contains), has sadly reached such epidemic proportions in certain educational institutions that these institutions have now hit back by (a) requiring that all term papers be submitted in electronic form and (b) also submitting all papers to an automatic plagiarism check before they are passed to the academic staff. Each university has developed its own response to plagiarism, behaviour which is both self-defeating – since the plagiarist learns nothing valuable from the experience – and unfair, since it disadvantages students who work honestly. Suffice it to say that this book is not written for students who plagiarize. (We return to plagiarism in Chapter 2.2, where we discuss how to take account of other relevant texts through quotation and summary without falling foul of the anti-plagiarism regulations.)

Collusion

The Internet now offers programs such as GoogleDocs that make it possible for more than one person to work together on a text. Whereas these programs are invaluable for many professionals who have to compose texts for business purposes with colleagues in other cities or even other countries, they may not be used for the preparation of term papers. Each term paper must be fully planned, written and edited by the one person whose name appears on the cover sheet – unless your teacher has expressly given permission for multiple authorship of a term paper. If you clandestinely work together with another person on your term paper, you (and the other party) are guilty of collusion, an offence that is just as serious as plagiarism.

1.5 Conclusion

To conclude this chapter, we should make some comments about the relationship between background reading and the writing process. It is a characteristic of academic writing that it should take account of the existing literature, whether to benefit from the insights of earlier research, to find fault with preceding studies, or to provide a model for one's own work. In practice, you may find that this aspect of the whole project takes up so much time that not enough remains for the complex processes associated with writing set out in this chapter. In every field of science and scholarship, academic production is growing at ever faster rates, so that even experienced researchers have the greatest difficulty in keeping up, even in a very narrowly specialized area.

In Chapter 2, we suggest that your term paper should include, in the Orientation section of your Introduction, a survey of the literature, but that this survey should only cover those works that are immediately relevant to your purposes. Gone are the days when term papers consisted mostly of the review of the literature, followed by the briefest account of the writer's own position! But how are you to make the selection of what to read and what of your reading to include?

The answer again lies in the integration of processes. Just as planning – writing – editing is not simply a chronological sequence, so reading – researching – writing should also not be seen as a temporal succession of three separate activities. All three are bound together in a nexus that means you will be reading, researching and writing more or less at the same time. Not only will your reading influence your research, but the development of your research will suggest new readings, which in turn will affect the research; and the experience of writing, i.e. communicating your research to others, will tend to affect your own understanding of your work and frequently cause you to discover shortcomings that need to be repaired. The result is the same kind of toing and froing between reading, researching and writing as we observed for the processes within writing.[5]

---

5 See, for the "co-implication" of reading, research and writing, Kwan (2008). See also Fabb & Durant (2005: 4), who point out that "[w]riting helps you understand what it is you will need from the books you read; the notes you take will be much more focused as a result".

Chapter 2

Different types of term paper: Two models

The main points of this chapter are these:

- There are two major types of term paper, the essay and the mini-article.
- Usually, literary analysis takes the form of an essay, while linguistic analysis is reported in a mini-article.
- When incorporating the views of other scholars into your text, you must either quote or paraphrase.
- In both cases, you must give your sources; otherwise you are committing plagiarism.
- Each type of term paper has its own conventions for quoting and paraphrasing.

2.1 Term paper as essay or as mini-article

All term papers are highly structured texts, with a clear division into Introduction, Body and Conclusion, with additional subdivisions within the Body, and with strict requirements for bibliographical references. In addition, there are a number of demands concerning the formatting and physical appearance of term papers which have to be met by all submissions (see Chapter 4.2). Having said that, we must emphasize that there is an enormous variety across institutions in the German-speaking world and across disciplines in the extent to which the structure of the term paper must be made explicit.[6] At one extreme, we find the term paper as *essay*, with no overt division into sections and a strong preference for no content footnotes, i.e. only footnotes that give references to literature quoted or paraphrased; at the other extreme, we find the term paper as *mini-article*, with explicit division into numbered sections, sometimes with set headings, and free use of footnotes. The term-paper-as-essay is encountered above all in disciplines such as history, literary studies, philosophy and theology, while the term-paper-as-mini-article is the norm in psychology, sociology, economics and most branches of linguistics. Between

6 In social psychology (Hutz 1997) and sports science (Trumpp 1998), for example, German scholars have remained averse to abandoning their culture-specific patterns of writing.

the two extremes, we find a range of intermediary forms; you should consult your teachers and your department's website to discover which is appropriate for each term paper you submit. If you are studying English language and literature, for example, you may well have to employ two forms, one for your linguistic and the other for your literary term papers!

In order to exemplify the two forms, we will take as our models the norms that are generally applied in the academic study of English literature and those characteristic of work in English linguistics, respectively. These can be applied, *mutatis mutandis,* to other disciplines as well. It is not our task in this book to help you produce better literary or linguistic analysis; our recommendations apply only to the processes that will ultimately lead to a physical product of which you can be proud. Before we progress to separate discussions of literary and linguistic term papers, we will first consider a phenomenon which is common to all kinds of term paper, namely reference to other texts through quotation and paraphrase.

2.2 Quotation and paraphrase

Every academic text offers a balance between its author's own argument and references to texts written by other authors. This is one of the trickiest aspects of academic writing, since you can be marked down for making too little reference to relevant published material but you will also be faulted for being too dependent upon such material if the result is that your own argument does not emerge clearly.

The central point to bear in mind is that quotation, although essential for an academic text, should always remain subservient to the argument of that text. In a literary essay, for example, you will quote a passage from a work of literature only if it provides persuasive evidence for the point you are making. In general terms, you must assume when writing a literary analysis that the reader is already familiar with the work you are discussing. (Although this is inevitably not always the case, literary scholars abide by this convention.) You therefore do not need to cite the original in order to make observations about plot, character, style, etc. You only quote from the work under analysis if you are making a point that would most likely have escaped the casual reader. By quoting a passage, you are in effect asking the reader of your essay to reread that passage in the light of the argument you are making.

Similarly, in linguistic analysis, where there is no 'primary text' as such but language data (of whatever type), you quote only data that is crucial for your argument. Let us imagine that you have examined the occurrence of a particular grammatical phenomenon in a corpus and, as a result of counting, observed certain statistical trends; these have been presented in tables containing frequency of occurrence under particular conditions and calculations of statistical significance. Under these circumstances, it would be impossible (and undesirable) to quote all the data examined. However, in order to clarify your procedure and to draw the reader's attention to difficulties of analysis or interesting exceptions to the trends you have observed, it is entirely acceptable to quote and discuss individual pieces of data. Normally, linguists do not quote more data than is required to make the point; and it is never acceptable to introduce data into your text without discussing its particular relevance. Much the same applies to work in other linguistic traditions, where the author him/herself devises the data (typically from his/her native language) as examples of particular syntactic, morphological or phonological structures; here, too, no more data needs to be 'quoted' than is required to make the author's argumentative point.

When citing the words of other scholars who have published on the same subject as you are discussing, you need to bear in mind that direct quotation is applied predominantly, although not exclusively, when you disagree with another scholar. Then it is a matter of quoting a crucial passage which you can then show to be ill-founded in some way: for example, it may be inaccurate in its analysis, internally contradictory, or in some respect incomplete. You owe it to your reader, of course, to make perfectly clear why you are dissatisfied with the passage you quote. Quotation without discussion is taboo in academic writing.

Avoid triumphantly quoting authors who adopt the same position as you. If you are tempted to do so, you must at the very least develop such a quotation in a new direction not anticipated by the author quoted. From time to time, however, it may be permissible to quote a source that supports your own position, in apposition to your own point. Thus, you can state something relatively uncontroversial, for example about the role of Universal Grammar in language acquisition, and then add something like:

> As Chomsky (1980: 34) puts it, language acquisition is interpreted as the "growth of cognitive structures along an internally directed course under the triggering and partially shaping effect of the environment".[7]

[7] Quoted, with minor adaptations, from Smith, Kenny. 2003. *The transmission of language: models of biological and cultural evolution*. University of Edinburgh: PhD dissertation, p. 11.

where the quotation is from a prominent authority and is particularly succinct or elegant; in this way, the quotation remains subservient to your argument.

Whenever you introduce a quotation, it is essential that you clarify the contribution of that quotation to your purposes. The principal way of doing this is to integrate it into the syntax of a larger sentence, using the content of that sentence to indicate the status of the quotation. Here are some examples of how to do this:

> Newmeyer (1998: 189) claims that all the distributional peculiarities of *there* "follow from the lexical semantics of *there* and the pragmatics of its use".[8]
>
> Carlson defends the position that "the natural world is essentially aesthetically good".[9]
>
> As Kanaganayakam points out, each essay is imbued "with a deep awareness of the fluidity of margins."[10]

The way you introduce the quotation will indicate to the reader how you stand with respect to its content. To endorse a quotation, you can use expressions such as *emphasize, make clear, agree, acknowledge, point out, report* or *mention*; to prepare the reader for your disagreement with a quotation, use verbs like *claim, argue, assert, allege, contend, state, suggest, postulate* or *believe*, all of which allow you to be respectful to the other party without giving your approval to their position. It is important in any case to realize that a quotation can never clinch an argument. However eminent a scholar may be, a quotation from his/her work will never *prove, show* or *demonstrate* anything, and these verbs should be scrupulously avoided.

Too many quotations will disturb the flow of your text. Luckily, there is an alternative to quotation, namely *paraphrase*, where you carefully reformulate the argument of another scholar in your own words, without using much if any of the original formulation. An advantage of paraphrase is that it allows you to save space by reducing what may be a lengthy argument, too long to quote verbatim, to a few words. Another is that you can integrate it into your own argument by using introductory expressions, just as with quotations: *Smith's argument that* PARAPHRASE allows space for you to disagree; *Smith's ex-*

8 Adapted from Aarts, Bas. 2004. Modelling linguistic gradience. *Studies in Language* 28(1). 1–49, p. 12.

9 Adapted from Godlovitch, Stan. 1998. Valuing nature and the autonomy of natural aesthetics. *British Journal of Aesthetics* 38(2). 180–197, p. 187.

10 From McCall, Sophie. 2007. Review of Chelva Kanaganayakam, *Moveable Margins: The Shifting Spaces of Canadian Literature. Canadian Literature* 194. 95–97, p. 95.

planation that PARAPHRASE does not. Finally, there is the possibility of adding evaluative expressions, as in *Smith's surprisingly Freudian argument that* ... or *Smith's cogent and convincing explanation that* ... .

Both quotations and paraphrases must be acknowledged. Although this is perhaps self-evident for quotations (since you will want to indicate where the material between quotation marks came from), it is no less true of paraphrases, since in both cases you are alluding to the intellectual work of others. It is important to emphasize that the reader of an argued text will always assume that any statement that is not acknowledged as coming from a third party is a statement by the author him/herself. Analysts of academic texts have sometimes described them as being "polyphonic" (Fløttum 2005), i.e. as involving many voices, like a choir. The reader must be able to distinguish your voice from all the other 'singers'. The important thing to realize is that even accidental failure to mention the source of words or ideas borrowed from other authors may open you to the charge of plagiarism (cf. Chapter 1.4). So check for every sentence you write that the reader will be entirely clear whether its content is yours or expresses someone else's opinion or results.

As has been said, paraphrases have the advantage of being well integrated into the flow of the ongoing text. Quotations will always remain more salient, but may be subdivided into two types, integrated and non-integrated quotations. Where you wish to quote a passage that is shorter than three full lines, you should integrate it into the running text, as part of a sentence, surrounded by double quotation marks, as in:

> ... James's flamboyantly avowed responsiveness to sensory impressions, and his understanding of aesthetic pleasure "not as idealist contemplation but as practice indissolubly entangled in social experience."[11]

Traditionally, as in the preceding example, if a quotation ends a sentence, the full stop is included within the quotation marks; nowadays, this is increasingly being seen as illogical, with a preference for the punctuation of the embedding sentence to be criterial, as in:

> ... the critics assert that "jazz, like language, is a system of signs".[12]

Notice that if the passage you quote itself contains a quotation, that quotation should appear between single quotation marks, i.e. the structure is "... '...' ...".

---

11 Adapted from Halliday, Sam. 2006. Helen Keller, Henry James, and the social relations of perception. *Criticism* 48(2). 175–201, p. 177.

12 Adapted from Smyter, Sofie de. 2007. Michael Ondaatje's *Coming Through Slaughter*: Disrupting Boundaries of Self and Language. *English Studies* 88(6). 682–698, pp. 684–685.

Where the length of the passage quoted is three full lines or more, the quotation is not integrated but presented without quotation marks, indented, and optionally in a smaller typeface, and both preceded and followed by a blank line (note that this format is also employed for quotations in verse). The introductory text often ends in a colon, as in:

> HCF's hypothesis appears to be a radical departure from Chomsky's earlier position that language is a complex ability for which the human brain, and only the human brain, is specialized:
>
> > A human language is a system of remarkable complexity. To come to know a human language would be an extraordinary intellectual achievement for a creature not specifically designed to accomplish this task. A normal child acquires this knowledge on relatively slight exposure and without specific training. He can then quite effortlessly make use of an intricate structure of specific rules and guiding principles to convey his thoughts and feelings to others, arousing in them novel ideas and subtle perceptions and judgments (Chomsky 1975: 4).[13]

If you are quoting at such length that a non-integrated quotation is called for, then clearly you must ensure that you provide sufficient discussion to justify its appearance as a very visible interruption to the continuity of your text.

On certain occasions, you may feel the need to adjust the quotation in some way to make it fit better into your text. You must only do this if the adjustment is innocuous (for example to expand a pronoun that would otherwise be uninterpretable). You may also wish to reduce a quotation by leaving out parts you consider less relevant (as long as you leave out nothing essential). Added material should be placed between square brackets; omitted material is replaced by three dots. The following examples show adjustment and reduction respectively; in the first example the verb *laugh* must be made finite in the syntactic context and therefore is adjusted to *laughs*:

> And while Adonis straightforwardly "loves" hunting, he does not simply "scorn" Venus – as grammatical parallelism would have him do – but rather "*laugh[s] to* scorn" her [my emphasis, LS].[14]

> ... quoting Ella Shohat's suggestion that postcolonialism concerns itself with "continuities and discontinuities . . . on the new modes and forms of the old colonialist practices".[15]

13 Adapted from Pinker, Steven and Ray Jackendoff. 2005. The faculty of language: What's special about it? *Cognition* 95. 201–235, p. 204.

14 Shohet, Lauren. 2002. Shakespeare's Eager Adonis. *Studies in English Literature* 42(1). 85–102, pp. 85–86.

15 Adapted from Mishra, Vijay and Bob Hodge 2005. What was postcolonialism? *New Literary History* 36. 375–402, p. 375.

As we can see from the first of the preceding examples, it is also possible to emphasize a particular section of a quotation – provided there is corresponding discussion of that particular item in your text – by placing it in italics, followed by the phrase [my emphasis] (in square brackets), optionally followed by a comma and the author's initials in small capitals. If parts of the original quotation are in boldface or italics, this must be preserved in your quotation without further comment.

Finally, if there is a mistake in the quotation (a misspelling, a typographical error or a grammatical blunder), do not correct it but stick to the original and add [*sic*] – the Latin word for 'just like that'. By the way, you should never 'correct' American spelling to British spelling or vice versa; respect the orthographic preference of the original writer.

You may on occasion wish to quote a passage in German, or in some other language than English. If you do so, you should provide either a translation into English after the quotation or a full paraphrase within your discussion of the quotation.

Here are some further pieces of advice about quotation:

No quotes from footnotes
If at all possible, do not quote from footnotes; and if you quote a passage that contains a footnote, silently omit the footnote in your quotation.

Always quote from the original
If you wish to use a passage quoted in secondary literature, check in the original whether it has been correctly quoted (and that the sense of the original has been preserved). Only if the original is absolutely unavailable should you give the reference, as in:

> "we still do not appreciate as fully as we ought ... the importance of narrative schemes and models in all aspects of our lives" (Culler, as quoted in Reid, 1992: 1)[16]

Avoid quoting oral communications
On occasion, you may wish to quote something your lecturer has said in class or something that a fellow student has suggested to you. Very sparing use should be made of this possibility, which should be shown as follows (where p.c. = personal communication); note this is the only context in which academic titles are used:

---

16 Adapted from Funnell, Warwick. 1998. The narrative and its place in the new accounting history: the rise of the counternarrative. *Accounting, Auditing and Accountability Journal* 11(2). 142–162.

(Prof. Dr. Hans Heinrich Müller, class lecture, University of Göttingen, 21 February 2008)
(Sabine Giger-Büchel, p.c.)

2.3 The literary essay

The great majority of literary essays (to use the term normally applied to term papers in literary studies) arise from a class situation in which a literary work, or more typically several works, have been subjected to close analysis from one or more points of view. The literary essay gives the student an opportunity to display his or her understanding of the concepts, analytical techniques and/or historical contexts that have been the subject of the seminar, usually by applying these either to the study of an entire literary work not discussed in class or to some hitherto undiscussed aspect of a literary work which has already been partially analysed. Literary scholars make a sharp distinction between primary and secondary literature, and students are expected to show in their writing that they are thoroughly and critically familiar with both. *Primary literature* covers the work under analysis and also other relevant literary work which it may be relevant to mention; the broader term 'primary material' covers other artistic products (pictorial, filmic, musical, etc.) which may be related to the primary literature. *Secondary literature* refers to published (non-literary) work by scholars of literature (critics, theoreticians, etc.) and possibly by academics in other fields; it is called 'secondary' because it involves interpretation or evaluation of the original, primary materials.[17] The art of writing a literary essay involves developing a sense for the optimal balance between treatment of primary and secondary literature. Your own essay, of course, is itself a – probably modest – contribution to secondary literature; and the more secondary literature you read, the better you will develop a sense for its norms.

The genesis of a literary essay involves a kind of alternation between primary and secondary literature. Everything starts, of course, with the primary text and with some (hopefully inspired) hunch you may have about that text. The next stage involves discovering whether your hunch has already been treated in the secondary literature, and how. This experience will likely lead you to consider other primary texts referred to by literary critics, and possibly how these have been interpreted in secondary works, until you can

17 We also recognize 'tertiary literature', such as encyclopedias, which involve the distillation of information, often in simplified form, that is derived from primary and/or secondary literature. Tertiary literature should generally not be quoted in academic essays, since it is typically intended for popularization of scholarly findings.

formulate a more precise version of your hunch, a true research question. This then becomes the guide to the enquiry of your essay: the Introduction will explain the background to this research question, with appropriate references to discussions in the secondary literature; the Body will set out the arguments that provide the elements of an answer to the research question; and the Conclusion will indicate what answer you give to the question, on the basis of the argument developed in the Body, possibly also specifying why the question cannot be answered unequivocally or which parts of the question remain unanswered.

On this basis it will now be possible for you to elaborate a provisional outline for the entire essay, which should if at all possible be discussed with your adviser before you proceed. The outline should contain, in the form of hierarchically organized headings:

- the research question and a list of relevant secondary literature (to be developed into the essay's Introduction)
- major arguments towards an answer to the research question (to be developed into the essay's Body), with titles of relevant secondary sources
- likely outcomes of the argument, open ends, and unanswered subquestions (to be developed into the essay's Conclusion)

On the basis of this outline, your tutor may suggest further secondary literature; and you yourself can deepen your understanding of scholarly traditions and insights by mining the library. Useful tools that can help you find relevant material are:

- ABELL – Annual Bibliography of English Language and Literature, 1920–
- ABES – the Routledge Annotated Bibliography of English Studies (relaunched in 2007)
- MLA – the Modern Language Association International Bibliography
- YWES – the Year's Work in English Studies

Most of these will probably be available on-line through your university computer system, and each of them will point you towards pertinent resources in the university library.

When consulting secondary literature, you should work with your (revised) outline, linking each secondary work you read, and possibly wish to quote, to a point in your outline. This is a good way of ensuring that you remain in control of the entire process, and that your readings and quotations are subservient to your argument. As you progress, so you should note down carefully all the documentary information about each source that may be needed for your bibliography (ideally using reference management software such as Endnote or Zotero). Normally this will include:

- the full names of all authors/editors
- the full title and subtitle (if any) of the work cited
- the place of publication and the name of the publisher
- the year of publication

In literary essays (unlike linguistic term papers, cf. 2.4), it may be permissible for you to include works in your bibliography which you have not cited but which nevertheless have contributed to your thinking.

It is essential that any quotations from either primary or secondary literature you wish to include are completely accurate. If you decide to paraphrase rather than quote, be very careful that your rewording is fair to the original author. More generally, you should be certain that you understand the scholarly context from which any idea you wish to incorporate in your essay is taken. By quoting someone 'out of context', you may be distorting their argument or misrepresenting their contribution to ongoing debates. The evaluator of your essay will be interested to know how well you understand how the various scholars you quote relate to each other in the academic world. If it is relevant to do so, you should refer explicitly to disputes in literary and critical theory, showing how opposing viewpoints lead to different interpretations of the literary work under examination. One simple way to do this is to ensure that you deal with the authors of secondary literature in chronological order, noticing who quotes whom, and whether these quotations are critical or approving.

Perhaps the most important point to bear in mind is that the literary essay, even though it inevitably deals with such matters as narrative, character, human nature, etc. remains an argued text. There is no single correct view about a text; any view is valid for which evidence can be found. The central role of argumentation means that there is no point in summarizing the plot (which your reader is assumed to know already). It also means that the order in which matters are treated in your essay need not correspond with that of the original work, but is dictated by your argumentative purposes.

Referring to other texts in literary essays is done through documentary notes. These notes, which, given the possibilities of contemporary word-processing programs, should always be formatted as footnotes, are sufficient in themselves to lead the reader economically and unambiguously to the reference source. Nevertheless, a bibliography is also required at the end of your essay: it not only provides the reader with an alphabetic overview of the works cited, but also allows you to provide complete details, for example an unabbreviated title or a subtitle omitted from the notes. If you are not using reference management software, you should still get your word-processing program to generate the form of the notes: the footnote function will automatically add a superscript arabic number at the point where you wish to add the note – always after any punctuation! It will also open a position at the bottom of the current page where you can write your note. For a product the length of a term paper, it is normal to have the numbers run through the entire work; for a book-length publication such as a dissertation, you may wish to start numbering again for each chapter. The following suggestions will cover the majority of references; for specific problems not dealt with here, see the *MLA Handbook for Writers of Research Papers* (7th edition, New York NY: Modern Language Association, 2010).

Each note starts with the author's name (or authors' names), spelled and ordered exactly as the author him/herself spells it, and followed by a comma. Authors like A.S. Byatt – she uses exactly that form – should not have their full names added, and *noms de plume* such as George Eliot should be respected. References to an edition should indicate the editor's name, followed by ed. (or eds[18] if there are more editors); references to a work in an edition, however, should begin with the name of the author, with the editor's name mentioned after the title. Here are some examples (with later information omitted):

> Derek Pearsall, …
> Ralph Hanna III and Traugott Lawler, eds, …
> N.F. Blake, 'Caxton's Second Edition of the *Canterbury Tales*', in *The English Medieval Book: Studies in Memory of Jeremy Griffiths*, eds A.S.G. Edwards, Vincent Gillespie and Ralph Hanna, …

If your footnote corresponds to a paraphrase rather than a quotation, then the author's name should be preceded by 'See' (or the contraction 'Cf.' from the Latin *confer* 'compare'); see the next example below.

The next element of the note is the title of the work cited. The title and subtitle are given in full unless they are particularly lengthy, in which case they may be abbreviated, or in the case of a cumbersome subtitle, omitted – one could for example omit the subtitle in the preceding example; the bibli-

---

18 Some people prefer to spell the contraction eds without the final full stop, reasoning that "s" is the last letter of the word that has been contracted (editors); this is the policy we follow in this book.

ography will restore full details. If the work cited is a book, the title and subtitle should be italicized. The title of an article, a poem or a short story is not italicized (unless it contains a title, as in the preceding example) and should appear within single quotation marks. All the words in the title except prepositions, conjunctions and articles are capitalized. Notice that the names of sacred works (the Bible, the Qur'an, etc.) are never italicized; neither are the names of series or editions, nor the chapters of a book.

The title and subtitle are followed by the publication details in round brackets. For a book or an article in a book, the brackets contain the place of publication, followed by a colon, the publisher, a comma, and the date, as in:

> See Matt Ridley, *Nature via Nurture: Genes, Experience, and What Makes Us Human* (New York: Harper Collins, 2003).

It is normal not to mention the name of the publisher for works published prior to 1918, although post-1918 editions of primary works originally published before that date do require mention of the publisher. Very often, you will want to quote work that was published in past centuries but has recently been reprinted; in such cases, you give the date of the first edition followed by a semicolon and then the publication details for the modern edition. If you need to specify which edition you have consulted, you place a corresponding raised numeral before the year of publication. If you are quoting from a particular page, rather than alluding to the work as a whole, place a colon after the closing bracket and then the page number. Here are a couple of relevant examples:

> Jane Austen, *Emma* (1816; Harmondsworth: Penguin, 1988).
> John Donne, *Poetical Works*, ed. H.J.C. Grierson (London: Oxford UP, ^{2}1933): 319.

As in the latter example, you should use the shortest unambiguous form of the publisher (UP for University Press).

Where you are citing an article in a journal, the title is followed by a comma and then the name of the journal, italicized, immediately followed by the volume number of the journal (not italicized) and the year of publication in round brackets; this is followed by a colon and the page references. Where the journal is well known, for example *TLS*, you need not give the full title *Times Literary Supplement*; if you use an abbreviation, ensure you use the abbreviation recognized by the journal's editors. It is useful (but not obligatory) to give the issue number (many journals have several issues *per annum*); this helps your reader find the electronic version of the journal. It is normal to contract the final page number if that number is above 100; redundant numbers are omitted. Thus we find 91–99, 395–401 and 923–1003, but 1123–29 and 1608–774, where the latter two are understood as 1123–1129 and 1608–1774.

In quoting from a poem, you should give the line number (preferably without addition of l. or ll.) only if the poem is non-stanzaic and is appreciably longer than a sonnet. In quoting from a play, the following formula applies:

> [title: capital roman] comma [act: roman small caps] comma [scene: roman lower case] comma [lines: arabic (with contractions if applicable)]
>
> e.g. *As You Like It*, II, vii, 136–49.

It often happens that you need to refer more than once to the same work. The first reference note is then given in full, but later notes are abbreviated to a minimum of information compatible with being unambiguous. Here is an example of a full note, followed by acceptable abbreviations of a later note; whichever style of abbreviation you choose, stick to it:

> Stefano Rosso, 'Postmodern Italy: Notes on the "Crisis of Reason", "Weak Thought", and *The Name of the Rose*', in Matei Calinescu and Douwe Fokkema, *Exploring Postmodernism* (Amsterdam/Philadelphia PA: Benjamins, 1987): 79–82.

Rosso, 'Postmodern Italy', 83.	[surname and abbreviated title]
Rosso, in Calinescu and Fokkema, 83.	[surname and surnames of editors]
Rosso, in *Exploring Postmodernism*, 83.	[surname and title of book]

It is very old-fashioned to use such Latin contractions as *ibid.* (lit. 'the same place') or *op.cit.* (lit. 'the work cited (above)'). However, the Latin *passim* (meaning 'throughout') is a useful way of indicating that the subject matter is found regularly throughout the work you are referring to, and not on particular pages.

The bibliography, which appears as the last item of your essay, is an alphabetical list of all the work cited in the footnotes accompanying the preceding text. In certain contexts it is also permissible to include works that you have consulted but not actually quoted. Where relevant, you should divide your bibliography into Primary Works and Secondary Works, ordering each alphabetically according to the family name of the authors and editors.

Whereas the constituent parts of the reference note are separated by commas, with bibliographical references, we find full stops, except that the author and the title of an article are separated by commas. The correct order is illustrated by the following examples:

Lee, Dorothy H., 'The Quest for Self: Triumph and Failure in the Works of Toni Morrison'. In Mari Evans, ed., *Black Women Writers: A Critical Evaluation*. Garden City NY: Anchor, 1984. 346–59.

Plato. *The Works of Plato*. Tr. Benjamin Jowett. Ed. Irwin Edman. New York NY: Random, 1928.

2.4 The linguistic mini-article

The argued text in linguistics comes in two major varieties, depending upon the nature of the work that is being reported. On the one hand, we have qualitative studies, which cover such options as a detailed case study of a particular linguistic problem or an evaluative overview of an area of research. Qualitative studies tend to ask 'why and how questions': why does a set of data show a certain pattern of grammaticality and ungrammaticality; how has the expression of negation changed over the centuries; how has the applied linguistics community reacted to Krashen's 'monitor hypothesis'? On the other hand, we have quantitative studies, which – as the name suggests – inevitably involve some element of counting. Quantitative studies divide into two major types: the experimental and the non-experimental. The former give an account of a linguistic experiment or questionnaire, while the latter report on corpus research, i.e. the extraction of quantifiable trends from large bodies of language data. Quantitative studies thus tend to ask 'what questions': what were the subjects' reaction latencies under various experimental conditions; what are native speakers' attitudes to immigrants' accents in English; what are the most frequent collocates of a particular verb? Let us consider the latter, quantitative type of term paper first.

The form of a linguistics term paper of the quantitative type tends to conform to the divisions found in argued texts from other predominantly quantitative disciplines such as sociology and psychology. This entails dividing the text into sections, with the following numbered major headings:

1. Introduction
2. Background
3. Data
4. Results
5. Discussion
6. Conclusion
7. References
8. Appendices (optional)

Texts that are set up in this way report on research that has been conducted prior to the writing process and their structure reflects the ideal progress of a research project. The first section (Introduction) explains in general terms the framework in which the work is placed and justifies the overall relevance of the question that will be asked. The second section (Background) provides the scholarly setting for the work, giving a critical overview of all relevant previous studies and distilling from these one or more hypotheses, the validity of which has been tested in the research. The third section (Data) describes the data that has been used, whether that data has been derived by experimentation or by detailed inspection of a corpus. The numerical results are not mentioned until the fourth section (Results), which gives nothing more than a statement, often with numerical findings, of the outcome of the research. The assessment of the repercussions of the results is postponed until the fifth section (Discussion), which should link back to the Background section, showing how the research has contributed to the ongoing scholarly debate described there. The sixth section (Conclusion) deals with any difficulties encountered in conducting or assessing the research and sets out various suggestions for future work. After the References, it may be necessary to add Appendices with further detail about the data, questionnaires, or any other matter which is so substantial that it would disrupt the smooth flow of the text.

The qualitative linguistic term paper does not have a pre-formatted structure. Rather, it is the nature of the argument that will determine the structure of the Body sections. Whereas with quantitative studies, the term paper is a write-up of research conducted before the writing process, with qualitative studies the writing is to a large extent itself the research. What is valued here is above all the excellence of the argumentation. Given the principles adopted by the author (and set out in the Introduction), is the argument logically compelling? Have convincing examples been provided of the points being made? Is the data well described? Does the argument contribute to linguistic theory? These are the kind of criteria a reader will use to assess qualitative work in linguistics.

Whereas in quantitative work, the majority of the discussion of the literature will be found in the Introduction and Background sections, in qualitative work the engagement with other scholars' work tends to be found throughout the text, since the author is in constant argument with positions taken by other scholars. The art lies in inventing a structure that will make a strong argument for your position, while making fully explicit how it relates to the positions taken by others. In this way, you will not only make your own point, but also show that you understand how the academic field in which you are working is organized.

When you quote, paraphrase or summarize work by other authors in a term paper about linguistic subjects, you give the full information about each publication in an alphabetically organized section called References at the end of your paper. At the point where you name the source in the text, you give a briefer indication, called a *textual reference*, containing either two or three pieces of information which will be expanded as a *full reference* in the References section (this technique is known as Harvard referencing, since it was first used by a Harvard professor in 1881). The textual reference contains just enough information for the reader to be able to quickly locate the full reference in the alphabetical list. The following suggestions are to a large extent inspired by the Unified Style Sheet for Linguistics Journals recently adopted by many academic journals in linguistics (see http://linguistlist.org/pubs/tocs/JournalUnifiedStyleSheet2007.pdf, consulted 1 March 2011).

Let us first consider the textual reference. It consists of an indication of the author, the date of publication and very often the number of the page(s) you are quoting or paraphrasing. When referring to an author, you give his/her family name only: note that in certain cultures, this may not be the last name. Where you refer to a work by two authors, both family names are given, linked by an ampersand (&); where the work has three or more authors, give the name of the first author only, followed by et al. (short for Latin *et alii* 'and others'). If you wish to use authors' names in the genitive case, then *'s* is attached to the last name only. Here are some examples:

> Boland (1999) sets up a set of hypotheses concerning the order of acquisition of adverbs.[19]

> Goddard & Wierzbicka's (2002) presentation of the Natural Semantic Metalanguage …

> … the Norwegian tendency to avoid indefinite new referents in clause-initial position, noted by Faarlund et al. (1997).[20]

The name is followed by the date of publication in round brackets. If your quotation or paraphrase relates to more than one work by the same author, the dates are separated by a semicolon. If you cite more than one work by

---

19 Adapted from: Butler, Christopher S. 2004. Corpus studies and functional linguistic theories. *Functions of Language* 11(2). 147–186, p. 169.

20 Adapted from: Hasselgård, Hilde 2004. Thematic choice in English and Norwegian. *Functions of Language* 11(2). 187–212, p. 200.

the same author from the same year, a letter of the alphabet (starting with a) should be added to the date. Here is an example:

> Wierzbicka (2002a; 2002b) deals with cultural scripts in Russia and Australia respectively.

If you are not quoting or paraphrasing a particular passage but evoking an entire work, you can then limit yourself to author and date, as in the preceding example. But every time you quote directly from an author or paraphrase a segment of his/her book or article, you must indicate the page(s) which you are quoting or paraphrasing. This is done by placing a colon after the date, followed by the page numbers; these should always be given in full. Here is an example:

> According to Haase (1991: 168–171), grammaticalization operates in the first instance as a constraint ...[21]

The name of the author in all the examples given above was integrated into the text. However, there is an alternative, which applies when you are writing about ideas rather than individuals. In this case, both the name and the date (and possibly the page reference) occur within brackets, and not integrated into the syntax of the current sentence, as in:

> ... the meaning of a word is mapped from one semantic domain (the source domain) onto another (the target domain) (Lakoff & Johnson 1980; Croft 2000: 240).[22]

The list of full references, entitled References, forms a separate (unnumbered) section at the end of your term paper. It is a list of all and only all the works you refer to in your text, including any notes. It is ordered alphabetically according to the family name of the author. Each new entry starts at the left margin; if the entry takes up more than one line, the second and all subsequent lines should be indented (creating what is called a 'hanging paragraph'). Here is an example:

> Grimshaw, Jane. 1990. *Argument structure*. Cambridge MA: MIT Press.

As will be apparent from this example, each entry consists of four parts: (a) the author or editor's name; (b) the date of publication; (c) the title; (d) de-

---

21 Adapted from: Matras, Yaron & Jeanette Sakel. 2007. Investigating the mechanisms of pattern replication in language convergence. *Studies in Language* 31(4). 829–865, p. 833.

22 Adapted from: Petré, Peter. 2006. The prefix *be-/bi-* as a marker of verbs of deception in late Old and early Middle English. *Belgian Journal of English Language and Literatures* 4 (New Series). 109–127, p. 119.

tails of the publisher. Each of these parts ends with a full stop. Let us consider each in turn.

In the case of a single author, provide the family name, followed by a comma and all remaining names as given in the title of the work cited. (Linguists' traditional habit of reducing all given names to initials has been abandoned in the Unified Style Sheet, since this practice is not appropriate in all cultures.) Names that involve *von, van, de* etc. should be alphabetized according to the upper-case name, with the patronymic preposition appearing after the other given names. In the case of two authors, the second author's name should be given in the order 'given name' 'family name', preceded by an ampersand (&). With three or more authors, do likewise, but with the ampersand preceding only the last name. Here are some examples:

> Marle, Jaap van. 1985. *On the paradigmatic dimension of morphological creativity*. Dordrecht: Foris.
>
> Huddleston, Rodney & Geoffrey Pullum. 2001. *The Cambridge grammar of the English language*. Cambridge: Cambridge University Press.

If an editor is involved rather than an author, you should insert the formula (ed.) or (eds) after their name, as in:

> Horn, Laurence R. & Gregory Ward (eds). 2004. *The handbook of pragmatics*. Oxford: Blackwell.

The date should indicate the year of first publication. If a book has been reprinted, it is the date of original publication, not of the reprint that should be indicated (since a reprint involves no changes to the original text). If a book has been revised, however, it is the date of revision that should be given.

As with textual references, if you refer to more than one work by the same author from the same year, the corresponding letter should be appended to the date:

> Wierzbicka, Anna. 2002a. Russian cultural scripts: The theory of cultural scripts and its applications. *Ethos* 30(4): 401–432.
>
> Wierzbicka, Anna. 2002b. Australian cultural scripts – *bloody* revisited. *Journal of Pragmatics* 34(9): 1167–1209.

The title should be given in full, including any subtitle. If you are referring to a book, the title must be italicized; if not, the title is not given any special treatment. You should use capitals only for the first word in the title, unless they are justified on other grounds (e.g. a German title with all nouns capitalized, or the name of a language in the title).

If there is a subtitle, it should be included, italicized if you are referring to a book and with the first word capitalized, after the title and separated from it by a colon. Sometimes, the subtitle does not further specify the content of the book, but indicates for example the occasion of the book's publication, as with *Festschriften* and conference proceedings. In such instances separation by a full stop is preferable. The title of a book may be followed by a specification of the series in which the book appeared and the book's number in that series: this is not italicized and is capitalized according to the specifications of the publisher. If the book quoted is not the first edition, the number of edition in the form '2nd edn.' should be given after the title. Here are some examples illustrating these points:

Lakoff, George & Mark Johnson. 1999. *Philosophy in the flesh: The embodied mind and its challenge to western thought*. New York NY: Basic Books.
Napoli, Donna Jo & Judy Anne Kegl (eds). 1991. *Bridges between psychology and linguistics. A Festschrift for Lila Gleitman*. Hillsdale NJ: Lawrence Erlbaum.
Steen, Gerard J. 2007. *Finding metaphor in grammar and usage* (Converging Evidence in Language and Communication Research 10). Amsterdam & Philadelphia PA: Benjamins.

Where the work referred to is an entire book, the entry closes with a specification of the place(s) of publication, a colon, and the name of the publishing company. Mention all the locations of the publishing company, linking them with an ampersand (&), as in the preceding example. Avoid redundant specifications like Verlag and Press, except where this might cause confusion, as with, for example, Cambridge University Press. Places of publication in the USA are followed by a comma and an indication of the state, using the standard postal abbreviations (FL for Florida, MA for Massachusetts, etc.; even if this means that you write New York NY). Note that place names should always be given in the accepted English form, i.e. Munich, not München; The Hague, not Den Haag.

Where you are referring to an article which is a chapter in a book, the preferred format for such references is as follows: In + name(s) of editors in normal order + (ed.) or (eds) + comma + title in italics + comma + page references, followed by place of publication and publisher, for example:

Holme, Randal. 2003. Grammatical metaphor as a cognitive construct. In Anne-Marie Simon-Vandenbergen, Miriam Taverniers & Louise J. Ravelli (eds), *Grammatical metaphor*, 391–416, Amsterdam & Philadelphia PA: Benjamins.

Where the work referred to is an article in a journal, the name of the journal follows the title of the work, italicized and with all nouns, verbs, adjectives and adverbs capitalized – this unequivocally shows its status as a journal. The title of the journal is immediately followed by the volume number, a full stop, and the page references. The volume number may be followed by the issue number in round brackets (most journals have several issues per volume). Certain regular, typically annual, publications like *Chicago Linguistics Society* or the *Annual Review of Cognitive Linguistics* are treated as though they were journals (i.e., the editors are not mentioned). Here is an example:

Langacker, Ronald W. 2001. Discourse in cognitive grammar. *Cognitive Linguistics* 12(2). 143–188.

There is an increasing trend towards electronic publication. If a work referred to is only available electronically, it is permissible to indicate the URL (Uniform Resource Locator) of the website, typically starting, in the position otherwise occupied by journal information, with http://. This should be followed by the date of consultation. For an electronic journal, give both the journal reference and the URL of the website. See the following examples:

Harder, Peter. 2006. Recursion in a functional-semantic grammar. http://harder.ansatte.hum.ku.dk/publications/ (20 January 2008).

Lemmens, Maarten. 2006. More on objectless transitives and ergativization patterns in English. *Constructions* 1. http://www.constructions-online.de (20 January 2008).

Unpublished dissertations are treated as if they were books. In place of the publisher, give the name of the university at which the dissertation was defended.

Linguistic data may be presented in three ways:

Tables and appendices
If you have a large amount of well-structured data, it may be laid out in tabular form either as interruptions to the running text or, if the data does not need to be consulted intensively to follow the text, in an Appendix (or in a numbered series of Appendices) appearing at the end of your term paper. The tables should be numbered in capitalized roman numerals (Table I, Table II, etc.) and provided with a title; the number and the title should be placed under the table.

In a running sentence
Individual morphs, words or short sentences may be quoted in the ongoing text. These are given without quotation marks, and must be italicized. The

first word of sentences quoted in this way should be capitalized. Here are a couple of examples:

> The suffix *-er* is added to verbs such as *bake* to form agentive nouns.
> The most natural answer to the question *How did Florence put away the glassware?* has the manner adverbial in clause-final position.

Morphemes quoted in the running text should appear in small capitals, and not italicized:

> Classical Latin *legit* 'he/she reads' realizes the morphemes LEG- 'read' + PRESENT + 3RD PERSON + SINGULAR.

As will be clear from the preceding example, morphs, morphemes, words and sentences from languages other than Modern English should be immediately preceded by the name of the language in question and immediately followed by an indication of the meaning (a 'gloss'). The meaning is not underlined, but written in lower case surrounded by single quotation marks.

Semantic, syntactic or phonological features are enclosed in square brackets (e.g. [+animate], [HEAD], [+coronal]). Phones, i.e. speech-sounds, are also enclosed in square brackets, according to the conventions of the International Phonetic Alphabet (e.g. [k]). Phonemes (or sequences thereof) are preceded and followed by obliques and, if more than one language or language stage is being discussed, should be preceded by an indication of the language (stage) in which they have phonemic status. Example:

> Unlike French /k/, RP /k/ is aspirated in syllable-initial position.

A full set of phonetic symbols ready for incorporation into a text is available online at http://languagelink.let.uu.nl/tds/ipa/index.html.

As numbered items

Longer data items such as entire sentences and texts are presented in a manner similar to non-integrated quotations, but with the difference that each item is numbered. The conventions require that the number should not be indented and should precede the data item, which is thereby effectively indented; the number is enclosed in parentheses. The numbering should be continuous throughout the entire text (although it is permissible to start at (1) again in a new chapter, say in a longer work such as a dissertation). Optionally, lower-case letters may be added after the numbers, but still inside the parenthesis, to indicate pieces of data that belong together; upper-case letters may be used to represent the participants in a dialogue. Some examples will make this clear:

A rather similar kind of alternation between the second and third possibilities is found with a word like *only* in English:

(8) a. Fred has only published two articles.
b. Fred has published only two articles.[23]

... the semantic-syntactic requirement of a subject has to be satisfied by the context, which may be linguistic:

(5) A. How's Bertha today?
B. Ø Doesn't look too well, I'm afraid.

It is difficult, then, to describe initial word absences categorically as "not dependent on linguistic context".[24]

As will be clear from these examples, the sentence preceding the data ends with a colon; it may also contain some sort of cataphoric marker such as *as in, such as*, or *following*.

As mentioned above, data from languages other than Modern English should always be provided with a gloss in Modern English. If the items' morphological or syntactic structure is at issue, they should also be further elucidated by means of an interlinear gloss (with no quotation marks). This gloss is called interlinear because it stands between the data items and their idiomatic translation into English. Its use involves breaking the words down into morphemes by means of the insertion of hyphens and glossing each morpheme separately. Where a portmanteau morph realizes more than one morpheme, the morphemes are connected by full stops in the interlinear gloss. The elements of the interlinear gloss should be positioned immediately under the relevant words in the data item (through the use of tabs). The internationally most respected instructions for interlinear glossing are those given in the Leipzig Glossing Rules http://www.eva.mpg.de/lingua/resources/glossing-rules.php, which include an extensive list of appropriate abbreviations for morphemes. Here is an example of a Latin sentence:

(16)	Puell-a	mens-am	vid-et
	girl-NOM.SG	table-ACC.SG	see-PRES.3SG.IND
	'The girl sees the table.'		

The purpose of numbering data is to allow easy reference in the text to what are often quite lengthy and intricate data items. In principle, items are pre-

23 Adapted from: Vincent, Nigel. 1999. The evolution of c-structure: Prepositions and PPs from Indo-European to Romance. *Linguistics* 37(6). 1111–1153.

24 Adapted from Thomas, Andrew L. 1979. Ellipsis: The interplay of sentence structure and context. *Lingua* 47. 43–68.

sented only once; however, if renewed reference is made in the text to data which first was mentioned several pages earlier, it is courteous to the reader to present the data again, employing the original numbering and indicating in the text that the data is being 'repeated here for convenience'.

Your evaluation of the grammaticality of the data may be relevant. This is indicated by means of starring. The conventions employed by J.R. Ross in his PhD thesis *Constraints on variables in syntax*, p. 40, n. 9,[25] are those to which the majority of linguists still adhere:

> I will occasionally wish to designate more than two degrees of acceptability; when I do so I assert that I find sentences prefixed with an asterisk are completely unacceptable; those prefixed with a question mark followed by an asterisk are only barely acceptable, if at all; those prefixed with a question mark are not fully acceptable; and those with no prefix are completely acceptable.

Here are some examples:

(46) ?I hate that you are always so greedy.
(47) ?*This is the malt that the rat that the cat killed liked.
(48) *That it is unnatural is obvious for Icarus to fly.

The asterisk is also used in historical-linguistic work to indicate reconstructed forms:

> Both Latin *dens* 'tooth' and English *tooth* can be derived from the same Proto-Indo-European root **dent-*, which may itself be connected with Proto-Indo-European **ed-* 'eat'.

25 (Available from http://dspace.mit.edu/bitstream/1721.1/15166/1/14704247.pdf.)

Chapter 3

Title, Introduction, Body and Conclusion

The main points of this chapter are these:

- The term paper divides into sections, each with its own heading.
- The first section is the Introduction, the last is the Conclusion, and the intermediary sections form the Body.
- Your term paper should carry a title that satisfies various requirements.
- There are conventions for how to structure the sections of a term paper.
- There are also various possible structures for the paragraphs that make up sections.
- The entire paper, and the sections within it, and the paragraphs within them should all have forward dynamics.

3.1 The Title

Your term paper must have a title, which appears prominently on the cover sheet (cf. Chapter 4), with all the nouns, verbs, adjectives and adverbs capitalized. Since the title contains the first words your reader will see, it is particularly important that you devote attention – as one of the final steps in preparing your *Hausarbeit* – to selecting the best possible title. It is the 'shop window' of your text and should therefore catch the reader's eye, inviting him/her to open your work and to engage with it. But it must not make false promises: the ideal title tells readers exactly what they may expect from the text it introduces.[26] For this reason, your title should never simply be a repetition of the assignment that has been prescribed: rather, it should prepare the reader for your views and for your reaction to the challenge of that assignment.

---

26 For the importance of an effective title in "prevent[ing] a paper from being discarded and ensur[ing] that it addresses the right audience", see Soler (2007: 90).

Titles perform two functions: they evoke the context within which your term paper has been written; and they announce the specific topic that will be dealt with. It is therefore a good idea to ensure that your title contains two elements, one corresponding to each of these functions. We will call the former the Frame (the general area to be dealt with) and the latter the Theme (the sub-area you will be focusing on). The reader's interest is awakened by the Frame; it is stimulated by the Theme.

An effective way of structuring titles is to begin with the Frame, followed by the Theme as a subtitle, with these two elements separated by a colon (:). Here are a couple of examples:

Provocative and Unforgettable: Peter Carey's Short Fiction[27]
Hedges: A Study in Meaning and the Logic of Fuzzy Concepts[28]

Another possibility is to start with the Theme and then contextualize it with the Frame. Such titles are generally less forceful than the previous type of title, but they have a descriptive coolness which is suitable for the argued text. They do not involve a subtitle, but rather link the Theme to the Frame using a preposition such as *of* or *in*, all within the context of one noun phrase (NP):

Parts of Speech in Generative Grammar[29]

The following title gives a Theme within a Frame which itself is placed in a larger frame:

The Directionality of Conversion in English[30]

Sometimes the Frame refers to two ideas, and the Theme is the relationship between the two. Then the Theme can be left implicit by simply presenting the two elements of the Frame, linked by *and* ($Frame_1$ and $Frame_2$):

James Joyce and the Development of Interior Monologue[31]

Where the relationship between $Frame_1$ and $Frame_2$ is not obvious, the title may be more effective when that relationship is mentioned as a subtitle:

Mary Shelley and Edward Bulwer: *Lodore* as Hybrid Fiction[32]

---

27 Adapted from the title of an article by Margarete Rubik (2005) in *European Journal of English Studies* 9(2). 169–184.
28 The title of an article by George Lakoff (1972) in *Chicago Linguistics Society* 8. 183–228.
29 The title of an article by Joseph Emonds (1987) in *Linguistic Inquiry* 18. 613–632.
30 The title of a book by Isabel Balteiro, published in 2007 by Peter Lang, Berne.
31 From the title of an article by Derek Bickerton (1968) in *Essays in Criticism* 18. 32–46.
32 The title of an article by Richard Cronin (2000) in Michael Eberle-Sinatra (ed.). *Mary Shelley's Fictions*. Houndmills: Macmillan & New York NY: St Martin's. 39–54.

As will have been clear from the examples given, titles are typically Noun Phrases (NPs).[33] This has two major advantages. Firstly, NP titles are neutral, unlike full sentences, which express judgments, and it is not the function of a title to make a judgment, but to announce a subject. Secondly, the NP is both short and expandable: it is the perfect medium for striking a balance between brevity and clarity (or in Soler's terms, "informativity and economy", 2007: 97).

What has been said about titles also applies to headings, if you are writing a term paper of the type that requires the component sections (and their subsections) to have headings. Headings are typically even shorter than titles, and may even consist of one word; here too, NPs are the norm.

Whereas titles of linguistic works tend to give a straightforward presentation of the content that is to follow, in literary essays, the title "characteristically sets out to attract the reader through a kind of verbal flirtation, enticing the reader with suggestive and tantalizingly enigmatic hints of the delights that follow" (Haggan 2004: 313). Haggan goes on to warn that "in some cases, where this is carried to the point of obfuscation, it may be pertinent to ask whether this may actually result in turning the reader away in frustration instead of attracting him", giving (2004: 310) the example of the title

Manifest Domesticity

which heads an article on women's writing about the home in 19th-century American literature; the title is a pun on the expression 'Manifest Destiny', the doctrine that the United States was 'manifestly' destined to expand from the Atlantic to the Pacific Ocean. This kind of verbal sleight of hand is very difficult to pull off; we recommend that you write titles that are both understandable and appealing.

3.2 The Introduction

The term paper consists of a number of sections (*Abschnitte*), two of which have a special status: the Introduction and the Conclusion. We will here deal with the Introduction, saving the treatment of the Conclusion until after our discussion of the Body sections below.

Although the Introduction is obviously the first section of the term paper, many skilled writers – as we recommended in Chapter 1 – in fact prefer to write the Introduction last, once they know exactly what they are going to be introducing. Whether you follow this advice or not, you must ensure that

---

33 This is confirmed by Soler's (2007: 96) examination of 570 titles from leading journals.

your Introduction fully prepares the reader for what it is to follow. Having reached the end of the Introduction, the reader must feel entirely confident that the following Body sections will grow organically from what s/he has read and that the Conclusion will provide answers to the questions raised in the Introduction.

The Introduction has a preparatory function. It provides the background information that the reader will require if s/he is to make sense of the remainder of the text. This means that, as a writer, you have to be particularly sensitive to what your reader may be expected to know already and what will be new to him/her. For a student writing for a professor, this may be a very difficult question: the best policy is to act as though you were writing for a fellow student of the same level of knowledge as yourself.

The Introduction is also an invitation to the reader to enter the discourse world evoked by your text. This means that you are well advised to start from shared knowledge, leading your reader gradually into new territory. In this way you will help your reader to get used to your point of view. It will also make your reader more willing to accept the purpose of your text as a valid one – even though it may be a purpose s/he personally disagrees with. This means that an Introduction has both a *cognitive* function, in providing the information that the reader will need to make sense of your argument, and a *rhetorical* function in persuading your reader to be interested in your point of view and in whetting his/her appetite for the intellectual fare on offer.

There is thus a fairly sharp contrast between German-style and English-style introductions. German introductions tend to neglect the rhetorical function, focusing on the 'facts of the matter', while English introductions tend to be more persuasive in nature, following a clear sequence of rhetorical moves. Whereas German introductions usually leave a great deal of information implicit on the assumption that an audience of experts can read between the lines, filling in missing links on the basis of their world knowledge and their knowledge of text types, English introductions take a more explicit and reader-friendly approach often grounded in common-sense ideas about reality; there are no gaps or discontinuities in the argument (see, for example, Hinds 1987, Bachschmidt 1999, Thielmann 2009: 76–77). Our advice for writing introductions, therefore, is to make liberal use of linking words such as *however, therefore, since* or *as*, advance organizers (*there are two ways of viewing … One is … Another is …*) and anaphoric pronouns such as *this* (*this procedure*), *these* and *such*.

The Introduction, entitled simply Introduction and numbered "1.", should amount to approximately one-eighth of your text, i.e. about 500 words in a

4,000-word term paper, or correspondingly more for a longer paper. It is not normal to break an Introduction into subsections. A 500-word Introduction should be divided into a number of paragraphs (for the internal structure of paragraphs, see 3.3 below). We suggest – merely as a guideline – that you divide your Introduction into four paragraphs (of roughly 125 words each) as follows (note that paragraphs never have a heading, so these names are merely mnemonic):

Topic paragraph
Orientation paragraph
Thesis paragraph
Organization paragraph

The Topic paragraph introduces the subject matter of the term paper; the Orientation paragraph explains your stance on the subject matter; the Thesis paragraph sets out the particular research question to be addressed in your paper; and the Organization paragraph briefly indicates how the rest of the paper will be structured. If you are writing an essay-style term paper (cf. Chapter 2), then the same advice applies, but without the heading '1. Introduction'.

Topic paragraph
The Topic paragraph is geared to establishing common ground between you and the reader. The information given here should be comparatively uncontroversial, based on facts rather than opinions, and also should be relatively non-technical in its vocabulary. The purpose of this paragraph is to win your reader's good will (Latin *captatio benevolentiae*); a striking example of the phenomenon you are discussing will therefore often work well here. Although it appears immediately after the title, the Introduction should read like a fresh start, and never refer back in any way to the title. Particular attention should of course be given to the very first sentence, since this is the reader's initial confrontation with your text: a badly formulated beginning can create a negative impression that nothing can put right.

Orientation paragraph
The Orientation paragraph is where the Introduction achieves its primary function, that of providing all the background necessary for the understanding of your argument. This is where you clarify which particular aspect of the subject matter described in the Topic paragraph you have chosen to address and from what angle you will be approaching it, but without yet formulating an exact research question. It may also be appropriate to state which areas

you will be unable to deal with. If you have a particular ideological and/or scholarly commitment, indicate that here: whether you are taking, let us say, a feminist view, or the standpoint of Systemic-Functional Linguistics. This is also where you can refer to the major works of background literature that are relevant to your undertaking, either works that have influenced your thinking or works that you disagree with, or both. Resist the temptation to mention all the secondary literature here: in modern argued texts in English, it is normal to introduce references to other works only where they are pertinent to the ongoing argument.[34] If you need to refer to a lot of background literature, then the Orientation paragraph may be expanded into two or three paragraphs, but remember not to deal with more secondary literature than is relevant for your purposes.[35]

Thesis paragraph
The Thesis paragraph is where you clarify the question that will be addressed by your term paper. It culminates in the *thesis statement*, which occupies a crucial position in the text. In certain kinds of term paper the thesis statement may take the form of an explicit hypothesis, i.e. an assertion that such and such will be found to be true; the rest of the text is then dedicated to testing the validity of this hypothesis. In other term papers, the thesis statement may be less formal, but still will define the scope of the Body sections. It makes a commitment to the reader, creating expectations that s/he will want to see fulfilled. This also means that the thesis statement should imply rather than pre-empt the discussion that is to follow; and it certainly unwise to give away your conclusions at this stage. Aim to intrigue your reader with a suggestive thesis statement; motivate him/her to continue reading and to delve into your argument.

Organization paragraph
The final Organization paragraph gives the reader an idea of how you are going to set about exploring the implications of the thesis statement in the Body sections of the term paper. It should be kept as brief as possible, since you do not want to lose the dynamism built up in the previous paragraphs with a lengthy piece of 'housekeeping'. The purpose of this paragraph is thus,

34 In addition, the literature review "is often strategically employed by researchers to assert, *inter alia*, their disciplinary identities and alignments with specific groups" (Kwan 2008: 54).
35 It should be observed that this approach to background literature is strongly associated with writing in English. Writing in German is more tolerant of extended treatment of theory, historical background and polemic with other authors (Clyne 1997), especially in the language sciences (Oldenburg 2002).

as the name suggests, to indicate concisely and accurately how the argument will be articulated across the following sections.

3.3 The Body sections

The Body of your term paper (i.e. the entire paper minus the Introduction and Conclusion) should be divided into a number of sections. In a 4,000-word text, you could for example opt for four Body sections of approximately 750 words each (numbered 2. through to 5., if numbering is required). One or more of these sections may be – if this is justified by the subject matter – divided into subsections (numbered 2.1 and 2.2, for example), but we recommend caution: subsections with fewer than three paragraphs should be avoided. The headings of each Body section should be a brief announcement of its content; never use the expression 'Body section' in such a heading.

The division of the Body into sections should reflect the logic of the argument. In planning your term paper, you grouped your ideas into various clusters (cf. Chapter 1.3): the sections of the Body now represent the translation of those clusters into organized language. The ordering of the sections should create a sense of *forward dynamics*. The reader should be, as it were, taken along on an intellectual journey, leading from the starting-point of the thesis statement to the destination guaranteed by the prospect of the Conclusion. The journey may not always follow a straight path, but the reader should never lose the sense that s/he will ultimately arrive. For this reason, the route should be properly signposted. Among the signposts that you should erect are well-chosen section headings that capture the essential content of their section, an indication at the end of each section of the direction to be taken in the next and/or a few words at the beginning of the next section on how it relates to the previous one. If you are writing an essay-style term paper (cf. Chapter 2), there will be no headings or any other formatting of the text indicating section breaks; in such essays, the textual signposts are even more important.

The actual direction taken by the Body sections will of course be dictated by the communicative ambitions of the writer. In quantitative linguistic term papers, as we saw in Chapter 2.4, the sequence of Body sections is fixed (Background – Data – Results – Discussion); but in all other types of paper it is the argument itself that determines the content and sequence of sections. In any case, it is vital that there should be an identifiable, coherent pattern.

One possible type of ordering of Body sections is chronological. If you are presenting a subject that lends itself to a historical treatment, such as a number of works by the same author or a particular debate in literary or linguistic theory, then chronology offers you an attractive principle. However, if you are focusing on the contemporary situation in some field, which inevitably has arisen from various historical developments, the Body may be organized according to quite different, non-historical, principles.

These principles may be more abstract, having to do with relationships between ideas and concepts. One major principle is that of opposition, which will be particularly relevant in a term paper in which you are considering the advantages and disadvantages of a theoretical proposal. Here the Body may consist of a number of sections dealing with the advantages, followed by a roughly equal number dealing with the disadvantages. The reverse order is equally possible. Which ordering you choose will be determined by your Conclusion: the notion of forward dynamics dictates that you first deal with the position you oppose and then the position you support. This then leads naturally into the Conclusion, where you confirm your preference for the second position. An advantage of the opposition principle is that both sides of the argument get an equal hearing. Where there are more than two positions, you will again do well to order them according to increasing acceptability.

In other term papers, you may be presenting only one side of an argument. This involves you in presenting various pieces of evidence for your Conclusion, each in its own section. The question now arises of how to order these in the text – how you classify and organize your material is one very important way in which you can establish control as a writer and persuade your reader of your viewpoint. You may be tempted to begin with your best argument, and then to present the less persuasive ones in the remainder of the Body. The drawback of this procedure is that although the Body will have a strong start, the overall impression will be anticlimactic and will go against the notion of *forward dynamics*. The reverse strategy is usually also ineffective, since beginning with the weakest argument, even if you admit that it is not strong, will be likely to undermine the reader's confidence in your ability to persuade him/her. So what is generally the best policy is to start with the second-strongest argument, then continue with your weaker ones, and to end with the very strongest. In this way your chances of winning your reader over to your viewpoint are increased by the strong impression made by the first-presented argument; the final argument should then carry the day, with a very natural lead-in to a powerful Conclusion.

However you decide to structure the Body of your term paper, never forget the notion of gradual, incremental build-up. If you find that in one of the early sections you have to refer forwards to later sections to explain certain notions, this is probably a sign that you have not yet found the ideal order. If in one or more of the later sections you feel the need to explain certain basic notions that really should have been explained in advance, then you again need to reconsider the sequence.

3.4 Paragraphs within the Body sections

All the sections in the Body consist (as do the Introduction and Conclusion) of a number of paragraphs (*Absätze*) – as mentioned above, we recommend a minimum of three per section (*Abschnitt*) or subsection (*Unterabschnitt*). Each paragraph presents a coherent set of sentences that together make a contribution to the ongoing argument. The structure of the paragraph is designed to guarantee both its inner coherence and adequate connection to the preceding and following text.[36] The paragraph is recognizable by being indented, and by nothing else: paragraphs should not be additionally separated by a blank line. Note that the first paragraph of each section or subsection of your text should not be indented: its initial position in the section is enough to identify it as a paragraph.

Just as the entire term paper has a tripartite structure (Introduction – Body – Conclusion), so the individual paragraph, too, is composed of three parts, generally known as:

Topic sentence
Elaboration
Climax sentence

Topic sentence

The foundation of every paragraph is the initial sentence, the topic sentence. This sentence performs a dual function. Firstly, it announces what the rest of the paragraph will be about, and indeed a paragraph will be coherent to the extent that all the sentences in that paragraph fall under the scope of the topic sentence. Secondly, it relates the paragraph as a whole to the surrounding text, especially to the preceding material. The central section of the paragraph consists of several sentences and is known as the elaboration of the topic

[36] Kaplan (1980), in his seminal paper, observed that in English paragraph development the thought patterns which English-speaking readers appear to expect are "dominantly linear"; while paragraph development may be discursive, it is never digressive.

sentence; this is the part of the paragraph that offers the most information and has its own forward dynamics. The final sentence is known as the climax sentence: it may be explicitly linked to the topic sentence, but is never a mere restatement of the latter. Rather, it serves to make clear the 'cognitive gain' of the paragraph and may, where appropriate, point ahead to the topic sentence of the next paragraph. The structure of the paragraph may thus be visualized as in Figure 2:

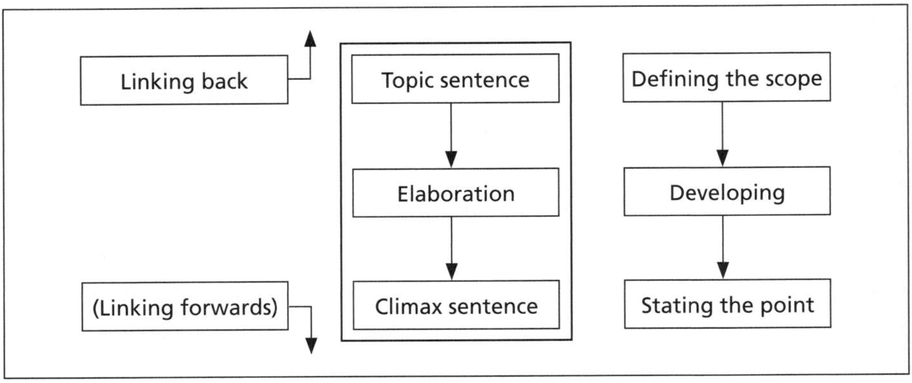

Figure 2

Elaboration and climax sentence

We may distinguish various types of elaboration. Depending on the content and communicative goal of the paragraph, it may be one of seven types:

1. spatial elaboration
2. temporal elaboration
3. analytical elaboration
4. deductive elaboration
5. inductive elaboration
6. dialectical elaboration
7. enumerational elaboration

Spatial elaboration

Spatial elaboration is found in paragraphs whose goal it is to describe some aspect of reality, especially the spatial configuration of things and places. Such paragraphs typically have a topic sentence that introduces the location, an elaboration that takes the reader on an imaginary journey around the area being depicted, and a climax sentence that identifies some point as being of particular importance for the ensuing text. This kind of elaboration is not frequently encountered in argued text, and will therefore not be dwelt on longer here.

Temporal elaboration
Temporal elaboration is used where various pieces of historical evidence are adduced for the claim made in the topic sentence. This type of elaboration is appropriate, for example, if you are giving a brief, paragraph-length presentation of the development of an author's work or the sequence of activities carried out in an experiment. Just as the Body as a whole can show chronological sequencing, so the paragraphs within it should give the succession of events in the order of their actual occurrence in time. This means in practice avoiding paragraphs in which you describe one event and then another, earlier event, introduced by some such formula as "This was after …". In a paragraph with temporal elaboration the climax sentence should present the historical high point of the period under discussion.

Analytical elaboration
Analytical elaboration occurs where the topic sentence presents a generalization and the following sentences serve to validate, particularize, exemplify or specify that generalization. In the Discussion section of a term paper, one might find a topic sentence such as *The results of the analysis demonstrate that the first hypothesis was not borne out.* This statement must then be justified with sentences such as *Although there was a small tendency for the subjects to use the subjunctive mood where predicted, the tendency was not statistically significant* or *Five of the sixty subjects displayed the predicted behaviour in their answers to the questionnaire, but the remaining fifty-five either displayed non-predicted behaviour or failed to answer the relevant questions.* The paragraph might then climax in a provisional conclusion like *It would appear, therefore, that the hypothesis, despite being grounded in existing findings, does not paint a true picture of the subjects' linguistic behaviour.*

Deductive elaboration
Deductive elaboration is found where the topic sentence makes some assertion that, at least at first sight, has some obvious validity and where the elaboration teases out the logical consequences of that assertion. A topic sentence like *Language is a vital tool of human communication* would then be followed by sentences such as *Any study of language must therefore take account of its role in communication* or *Attempts to deal with linguistic phenomena without addressing the intentions of language users are doomed to failure.* In such a paragraph, the climax sentence will take the form of a conclusion to the argument presented in the elaboration, e.g. *It follows that every effort should be made to elaborate a functional*

theory of language. This conclusion can then be taken in the following paragraph as a basis for further argumentation.

Inductive elaboration

Inductive elaboration, by contrast, occurs when the topic sentence makes some claim whose validity is not immediately apparent. Consider the following paragraph:[37]

> It might be said that every poem is ultimately a poem about writing poetry. The manifestation of idea in a form is itself a new and never repeated enterprise each time. This is no less true for Frost. While it would be a violation of his artistry to force a poetics reading on every poem, one need not read far in his work to find points where form, metaphor, and idea coalesce in such a way as to suggest certain things about the act of writing poetry. As is the case with "Mowing," "The Oven Bird" also is such a poem. The concluding lines in particular suggest this, but from the outset there are clues similar to those given in "Mowing." The bird, for example, is the creator of the song; the listener, however, perceives his or her own meaning in the song. The hints are indeed given by the physical setting in which the song occurs – both in the natural setting and the way the poem is "set."

The initial sentence of this paragraph tentatively (*It might be said …*) makes a generalization, which is certainly not obviously correct; surely poems are also 'about' love, death, hope, etc.? After the author concedes that the generalization (*a poetics reading*) may not always be appropriate for Frost, two poems are adduced as evidence for the claim, and particular examples are given from one of them. The following paragraphs of the original text give several more examples of the author's claim about Frost's poetry, for which reason the paragraph shown above lacks a climax sentence.

Dialectical elaboration

Dialectical elaboration is appropriate where a paragraph presents an opposition in a nutshell. Here the topic sentence (plus possibly one or two further sentences) presents the 'thesis', i.e. the proposition to be discussed. The elaboration then offers the 'antithesis', i.e. the counterargument. The climax sentence then contains the 'synthesis', i.e. a resolution of the opposition that still preserves something of both sides of the argument. Thus, in an essay on English as an international language, we might find a topic sentence such as *Many people in Europe consider English to be the natural language of choice for international conversations*. Possibly after a sentence or two developing this 'thesis',

[37] Adapted from: Timmerman, John H. 2002. *Robert Frost: The Ethics of Ambiguity*. Lewisburg PA: Bucknell University Press.

we could imagine an 'antithesis' introduced by *Nevertheless, there are many parts of Europe where other languages fulfil this function*. The following sentences would exemplify this counter-assertion, leading to a climax sentence that reconciles the two viewpoints, for example *EU policy, which calls for all citizens to master two foreign languages without specifying which, allows for a range of choices without stifling the primordial position of English.*

Enumerational elaboration

Enumerational elaboration, finally, is encountered in those paragraphs in which the topic sentence serves above all to quantify the points that are made in the elaboration. Consider the following example (from which all the references to sources have been removed to increase readability):

> Antinucci and Miller attributed this pattern of use to children's immature conception of time. However, this strictly cognitive explanation is no longer held by anyone. This is because, first of all, even before their second birthdays many children do on some occasions clearly refer to past situations with activity verbs that have no current perceptual manifestations. Secondly, in a number of comprehension experiments in which children must choose the picture that best depicts a present tense, past tense, or future tense utterance regardless of aspect, they perform well from a relatively early age. And thirdly, a number of studies on second language acquisition have shown that second language learning children and adults also use tense-aspect marking in the same biased way as young children, and they presumably are not cognitively immature.[38]

What we find is a topic sentence (the second sentence of the paragraph) that rejects the claim reported in the first sentence. The remainder of the paragraph gives three reasons for the author's assertion: these are indicated by *first of all, secondly* and *thirdly*. Enumerational paragraphs often lack a climax sentence, and this example is no exception. See also Module III, Chapter 4.4.

Three points need to be made about these seven types of paragraph elaboration. (This is clearly going to be an enumerational paragraph!) Firstly, not all well-written paragraphs can be neatly assigned to one of the seven classes. One reason for this is that paragraph divisions may be inspired by other considerations than the logical properties of the argument. Since there is a preference for paragraphs in English academic texts to be neither too long nor too short and all roughly equal in length,[39] it regularly happens that we break

38 Adapted from: Tomasello, Michael. 2006. Acquiring linguistic constructions. In Deanna Kuhn & Robert Siegler (eds,), *Handbook of Child Psychology: Cognitive Development*. New York NY: Wiley. 255–298, p. 280.

39 Since German writing generally has a greater focus on content than on form (Clyne 1987), there is greater tolerance of paragraphs of uneven length.

a paragraph with a long elaboration into two normal-length paragraphs or that we link a very short paragraph to an adjacent larger one. Secondly, all the seven techniques listed can be applied at the higher level of the section: thus we can also have analytical, deductive, inductive, etc. sections. Thirdly, any one text should ideally show a range of different types of elaboration. By varying the internal structure of your paragraphs, you can subtly keep your reader motivated to read on; a succession of paragraphs, all with the same structure, will inevitably have a soporific effect. What you especially need to retain from the classification is that the structure and content of the elaboration is determined by the status of the topic sentence and that a paragraph will often seem incomplete without a climax sentence that represents a significant addition to the preceding argument.[40]

Let us conclude this section with a brief analysis of two body paragraphs. Consider the following paragraph from an (admittedly now rather dated) monograph about Germany:

> German literature since 1945 can be said to fall into three main periods. First was the time of the so-called 'literature of the ruins', when writers were painfully struggling to come to terms with their experiences of the war and of Nazism and were groping towards new values. This was followed by the left-wing political commitment of the 1960s, a period of angry disillusion with Germany's materialistic and conformist new society. Then since the early 1970s writers have been retreating again from public and social themes into their private worlds of individual feeling, nostalgia and *Innerlichkeit* (inwardness). The first two of these periods produced at least two novelists of major world rank, Heinrich Böll and Günter Grass, as well as a number of other significant writers such as the poet and critic Hans Magnus Enzensberger, the novelist Martin Walser, and the playwrights Peter Weiss and Rolf Hochhuth. The third period has been much less distinguished. (Ardagh 1990: 258)

This paragraph shows a clear example of temporal elaboration, with a high degree of coherence. Ardagh develops the initial topic sentence step by step, setting out facts in chronological order, and never pausing to comment on irrelevancies. The elaboration consists of two parts. In the first, Ardagh describes in general terms the three periods mentioned in the opening sentence; in the second, he makes value judgments about the principal literary representatives of the periods in question. Note that the coherence of the text is underlined by words and word-groups which serve as cohesive devices:

40 It should be noted that paragraphs with topic sentences and climax sentences are characteristic features of English prose. Paragraphs in German academic writing tend to be more tolerant of digressions from the strict discipline suggested in this section.

first, this was followed by, then, the first two of these periods, the third period. The formulation of the last sentence of the elaboration is pithy and also functions as a 'sting-in-the-tail' (and polemic) climax to the paragraph.

We move on now to examine a second paragraph from published work:

> There is a considerable literature on machine translation (e.g. Booth, 1967) but at least since Bar-Hillel (1964) there is fairly general agreement that computers will not be much used for translation (except in restricted areas such as meteorology) in the foreseeable future; they are already of incalculable assistance to terminologists in compiling glossaries and bilingual dictionaries. Melčuk's work on MT (e.g. in Booth, 1967) has thrown light on translation procedure. (Newmark 1981: 10)

The most noticeable feature of this paragraph is its lack of coherence. It satisfies none of the elaboration patterns set out above and seems to present the author's random reading notes rather than to develop a line of argument. It contains four pieces of information: (1) the existence of a considerable literature on machine translation; (2) fairly general agreement that computers will not be much used for translation; (3) computers' incalculable importance for compiling glossaries and bilingual dictionaries; (4) the relevance of Melčuk's work for translation procedure.

Since the author's main focus is presumably on machine translation, unit (3) does not belong in this paragraph and should be omitted. Secondly, the close connection between units (1) and (4) (as well as the repetition of the reference to Booth 1967) indicates that (4) should be placed immediately after (1) in order to enhance the coherence of the paragraph. Our extract could perhaps be initially rewritten as follows:

> There is a considerable literature on machine translation (MT); of particular importance is Melčuk's work on translation procedure in MT (Booth, 1967). At least since Bar-Hillel (1964), however, there has been fairly general agreement that in the foreseeable future computers will not be much used for translation (except in restricted areas such as meteorology).

The result is coherent in that the first part of the first sentence now functions as a topic sentence, which is specified after the semicolon by the highlighting of Melčuk's work. The second sentence presents something of a counterargument, or at least a deflation of the positive tone of the topic sentence. This suggests a dialectical elaboration. However, the paragraph offers no synthesis, and thus remains incomplete. What emerges from this analysis is that the entire planning of the paragraph was faulty.

3.5 The Conclusion

The Conclusion is the last part of your term paper. Too often, the Conclusion reads like an afterthought, like an obligatory addition to an argument that has already been completed. In fact, the Conclusion should be the high point of the text.[41] In the daily practice of academics, who are confronted with many argued texts every day on top of their other responsibilities, they are forced to limit their reading of articles and reports to the minimum. In making a preliminary assessment of the relevance of a text, they often take in no more than the title, something of the Introduction, but in any case they do read the Conclusion, since it is there that the relevance of the text for its readership is most powerfully enunciated. The purpose of the following paragraphs is accordingly to offer some advice on how to write effective Conclusions, formulated in such striking, forceful terms that they leave a lasting impression on the reader.

If the function of the Introduction is to lead the readers *into* your argument, that of the Conclusion is to lead them back *out* again, changed in some way. The Conclusion is therefore the prime location to discuss the implications, practical and/or theoretical, of the argument that has gone before. It is therefore insufficient for a Conclusion to be a simple restatement or summary of what has already emerged from the Body sections. Rather, it should continue the forward dynamics of the text as a whole. In addition, if the Body sections have offered cool, objective argumentation, the Conclusion gives you the opportunity to clarify your personal opinion about the matter at hand.

The Conclusion (which – if your term paper is of the type that uses headings – must be appropriately numbered and entitled Conclusion or Conclusions) should generally represent one-eighth of the entire text, being roughly equal in length to the Introduction (i.e. some 500 words in a 4,000-word term paper). This provides enough room for everything the Conclusion has to do and also ensures that it is likely to be shorter than any of the Body sections. After all, the Conclusion is a continuation of the text rather than an independent argument.

The Conclusion is likely to consist of more than one paragraph. One possibility is a sequence of three paragraphs, as follows:

Transition
Repercussions
Envoy

41 Hemingway is said to have rewritten the concluding section of *Farewell to Arms* 39 times before he was satisfied with it.

Transition

The Transition paragraph serves, as the name suggests, to make a smooth and convincing modulation from the Body sections to the Conclusion. Transitions should, if at all possible, not be mere summaries of the argument, since summaries are backward-looking and therefore bring the forward dynamics of the text to a grinding halt. The most effective Transitions are those that succeed in distilling the impression that you would like the reader to derive from the entire preceding argument.

Beware of falling into the trap of providing a conclusion to only part of the argument. In a text that presents, equally and fairly, two sides of an argument, both sides should be mentioned here, even if you go on in the Repercussions to express your favour for one side. If you have constructed the Body of the text in such a way that the final section contains the most important point you wish to make (as we have recommended), ensure that the Conclusion does not simply develop that final point.

The first sentence of the Transition paragraph (i.e. the first sentence of the Conclusion) needs special care. Avoid linking this sentence to the preceding text with such words as *so, therefore, thus* or *however*: these are simply too light to carry the cognitive link between Body and Conclusion. It is also quite unnecessary to use expressions such as *in conclusion, to conclude, by way of conclusion, to sum up*, etc.; they are unsubtle and redundant. What we would suggest, however, is that you insert words such as *certainly, clearly, indeed, arguably, undoubtedly* into that first sentence; judiciously deployed, these have the effect of intimating agreement between the reader and the writer. Here are some examples:

> A good deal of progress has been made towards determining the order in which the poems were written, but clearly much remains to be done.

> The results have undoubtedly shown our initial hypothesis to be justified; yet why were the results not even more clear-cut?

Repercussions

The reason why we give the name Repercussions to the core of the Conclusion is connected with the relation between the text and the reader. Your intention is to leave the reader in some way changed or influenced by what s/he has read. The reader will typically be interested in the practical implications of your argument: "Yes, you have persuaded me of your standpoint, but what does it mean for me and my life?" This gives you an opportunity to emerge from behind the screens of scholarly distance to express your own take on the matter at hand. In this way, you can use the Conclusion section to consider the real-life repercussions of what you have claimed, possibly indicating the lessons that can be drawn from past errors or making suggestions for the elimination of present abuses. If the reader feels that these follow naturally from a well-presented argument in the Body sections, s/he will be more likely to be persuaded and possibly even affected in his/her everyday actions.

Remember that the word *conclusion* in English has two senses: 'ending' (*Abschluss*) and 'deduction, judgment, insight' (*Folgerung, Erkenntnis*). It is definitely the second sense that should be uppermost in your mind as you plan, write and edit the final section of your term paper. This will remind you that summarizing is not enough. The Conclusion gives you a chance to draw your personal deductions from what you have found. In principle, using the same reference works and other sources of information, two authors could very well come up with very similar Body sections; where they will differ is in the conclusions that they infer from the information that has been assembled, because each writer brings his/her own perspective to bear.

No term paper, no academic article, no book is ever the 'last word' on the subject it deals with. Certain aspects are inevitably left out of consideration, for example because the author has no access to relevant information, or simply if limitation on research time and/or the length of the text have not permitted a fuller treatment of the matter. One possible function of the Conclusion is to indicate honestly, and never apologetically, the inadequacies of the argument.

Envoy

The final paragraph of the Conclusion (and of course the final paragraph of the entire term paper) should make a resonant and, if at all possible, positive impression on the reader. For this reason, we call it the Envoy, a term taken from the analysis of poetry: etymologically, it means the final text segment you send the reader away with. Pay particular attention to the very last sentence. Try to write one that can stand by itself, without leaning on preceding sentences for its interpretation. In particular, aim to put a word or phrase in sentence-final position that has positive, active connotations.

Chapter 4

Getting the paper ready for submission: Editing and formatting

The main points of this chapter are these:

- Every term paper should be thoroughly edited before being submitted.
- You should edit your text at three levels: the macro-level, the meso-level and the micro-level (in that order).
- You must ensure that your term paper satisfies the formatting requirements of the department you are submitting it to.
- The end product should look attractive and tidy, but not too ornate.

4.1 Editing

Every term paper needs to be thoroughly edited before being submitted. It is important that you reserve enough time for this, preferably letting a day or two pass between completing your assignment and editing it. This is because editing involves adopting a kind of split personality. While remaining the writer of the text, as an editor of the text you are primarily a reader, putting yourself in the shoes of the person who will ultimately be the recipient of the text. And you are not just any reader: you must be the most critical, nit-picking reader your text could ever encounter. As an editor, what you are doing is attempting to anticipate every difficulty a reader might possibly have with what you have written.

As is well known, perfect communication between two human beings is achieved very rarely, if ever. The fact that there is physical and temporal distance between writers and their readers makes it all the harder to communicate intentions unambiguously. Add to that the problem that the English language is not your native tongue, nor perhaps that of your audience, and the problems mount up. Your only hope is to formulate your ideas so accurately and transparently that the anticipated readership is most likely to understand your text in the way you would wish. Communication theorists have pointed out that this involves (at the very least) satisfying four requirements (known as Grice's maxims),[42] which boil down to the following recommendations, adapted to the writing situation:

42 For the original formulation of the maxims see Grice (1975).

- Offer the reader neither more nor less information than s/he needs (Maxim of Quantity)
- Give the reader an honest and well-argued account of your beliefs (Maxim of Quality)
- Stick to the point, without digressing into side-issues (Maxim of Relation)
- Formulate your ideas in a straightforward, understandable way (Maxim of Manner)

Of course there are special circumstances in which you may wish to deviate from these precepts, but bear in mind that you will then be asking your reader to do the additional work of noticing what you are doing and figuring out why – perhaps your intention is to be ironical, tongue-in-cheek or amusing. These are tricks that are notoriously difficult to bring off in a foreign language!

The purpose of editing, then, is to revise a pre-final draft in such a way that the chances of misunderstanding will be minimized. Many inexperienced writers, even those who accept the necessity of editing in principle, find this a very difficult and painful thing to do – even to the extent of abstaining from doing it at all. You may well feel that hacking away at the text you have produced in the sweat of your brow is almost like cutting into your own flesh. Particularly if you are the kind of writer who waits for inspiration and then pours out his/her thoughts in one volcanic eruption (not our ideal, as our ironic formulation should make clear!), you may resist the suggestion that every word and every turn of phrase should be weighed and tested against other formulations. Whereas the 'volcanic' technique seems time-efficient and often does produce dynamic, fluent text, the drawback is that authors of this kind are writing primarily to satisfy their own urge to create rather than to communicate their ideas to other people. As a result, there is a real risk that the text will end up pleasing only the writer and will remain impenetrable for the reader. Hence our recommendation, no matter what your personal style of writing, to reserve sufficient time and energy for editing.

It has often been said that there are (at the extremes) two kinds of writers: the Mozarts and the Beethovens. Mozart was reputed never to alter a single note that he committed to paper, whereas Beethoven is said to have agonized over every phrase, filling countless notebooks with musical experiments before pronouncing a work completed. Be this as it may, taking Mozart as your model does not exonerate you from being self-critical. As was pointed out in Chapter 1, the three processes of writing (planning, writing proper and editing) need not follow one another in time. What Mozart was able to achieve was a fusion of the three processes in time: as the formal perfection of his compositions shows, he did not avoid the artistic and communicative responsibility of self-critical reflection on his work, even as he produced it.

Editing involves reviewing your work at various levels. Our suggestion is that you initially edit your work separately at each level; as you get more experienced in editing, you may be able to edit for two, and ultimately for all three levels at one pass. The levels will be known as the macro-level, the meso-level and the micro-level.

Macro-level editing

At the macro-level, you are looking at the text as a whole and at the relations between its major components (the sections). Here you check your general impression of the entire text. Does the Introduction provide all the information necessary to understand the Body sections? Conversely, do the Body sections fall within the scope of the thesis statement enunciated in the Introduction? Do the central sections lead plausibly to the Conclusion? Does the Conclusion succeed in adding to the outcome of the Body sections? Important questions at this level concern whether the reader is liable to find the text as a whole both pleasing and persuasive. Is it stylistically unified (an important question if the text has been written at several sittings)? Is there needless repetition? Have the key terms been used consistently? Do I adopt a steady viewpoint? Does the reader get a clear understanding of what I want to say?

Meso-level editing

Having convinced yourself that the text is indeed attractive and effective at the macro-level, you then move on to the meso-level, considering each individual section and the paragraphs it contains. Here you verify that each section works as a unit. Have I ensured that the first paragraph is not indented and all following paragraphs are? Are the paragraphs of roughly equal length, or do I need to redistribute the information? Do the paragraphs have a recognizable topic sentence, and does that topic sentence really define the content of what follows within the paragraph? Look at the elaborations (central parts) of the paragraphs, too. Have I given sources for everything I have quoted or paraphrased? Have I been factually accurate? Have I produced relevant evidence for my claims? Will my reader be able to follow my argument without re-reading or checking back to earlier sections? Can I do anything (reformulation, repunctuation, etc.) to ease my reader's interpretation task?

Micro-level editing
Micro-level editing covers all the various aspects of the final tidying-up of your text before you print it for submission. This is the all-important stage at which you remove those irritating little errors that can so easily undermine a reader's otherwise positive impression of a text. Are there typographical or orthographical errors (the computer can help here)? Have I avoided all the typical pitfalls for the non-native writer (errors of collocation, of formality, of preposition usage, false friends, etc.)? Have I respected the punctuation conventions of English? Are there remaining grammatical errors within my clauses (errors of agreement, complementation, word order, choice of modal verb, form of adverbs, noun phrase structure, etc.)? Have I made optimal use of clause-combining techniques and options for information ordering in the clause?

If your department publishes a set of explicit assessment criteria, i.e. a statement of how the person who will be grading your work is supposed to come to his/her decision, then you should certainly also consider how well – in your opinion – your work satisfies those criteria. The same applies to any list of learning outcomes, which indicate what you are supposedly able to do as a result of having attended the course in question: ask yourself to what extent your term paper shows that you have attained those outcomes.

4.2 Formal requirements

The term paper has to satisfy a number of formal requirements which vary in detail from university to university and even from department to department. Nevertheless, the following guidelines give a good example of how to proceed.

We are here assuming that you will be required to submit your term paper on paper (as the name of this genre suggests!). There is admittedly an increasing tendency towards recommending or even demanding electronic submission of papers, but even then the requirements are generally identical to those for paper submission. For all truly paper submissions, it is in any case essential that all the pages should be of the same size, DIN A4, and printed on one side only.

The term paper begins with a cover sheet, which should contain all or most of the following information (certain universities may require you to give this information, or part of it, in German):

- the name of the university and the department
- the title (and subtitle, if present) of the term paper in boldface, and clearly distinct from the other information

- the name of the author(s), followed by their postal address, telephone number and e-mail address
- the name of the programme (e.g. English Language and Literature)
- the level of the course (*Fachsemester*)
- the title of the course (*Lehrveranstaltung*) and the semester in which it was given
- the name of the course instructor (*DozentIn*)
- the module the course belongs to and the number of ECTS credits available
- the date of submission

If your text is of the type that contains headings (cf. Chapter 2), the second page will give a complete listing of headings in your term paper. This should be entitled Table of Contents and give the numbers (preferably arabic, optionally roman) and names of all the headings and subheadings in the paper, with the starting page of each at the right margin. These should be ordered with the headings flush left, and subheadings indented; if you have divisions within subheadings, these should be further indented. This page may be followed, if required, by another page entitled List of Abbreviations, containing an alphabetically ordered list of the abbreviations used in your paper, with a parallel column explaining all the abbreviations.

You now progress to the text, which – if it has headings – will start with the heading Introduction. The text should be both left- and right-justified and surrounded by margins large enough to leave space for your tutor's/marker's comments. The suggested margins are: 4 cm left, 2.5 cm right, 3 cm top and bottom. The pages should be numbered in arabic numerals, with the first page of your text numbered as page 1 – the title page, table of contents and list of abbreviations do not get a page number. For the text itself, choose a font that is easily readable (Times New Roman is a popular choice) and a font size that is easy on the eyes: 11 or 12. The headings can be larger (13 or 14) and set in bold type; they are separated from the following text by a blank line. The spacing between lines should be 1½. Footnotes should be set at the same font size as the main text, but with single spacing. Your word-processing program will automatically generate the horizontal line between the main text and the footnotes.

Remember that the first paragraph of each section or subsection is not indented; all subsequent paragraphs are indented; we suggest that you set the indentation to 1.25 cm. You are recommended to record all these settings, or the departmental requirements if they deviate from them, as a 'style' in your word-processing program: this will save you having to redo the settings for every term paper you write. Notice that tables, figures, diagrams and maps should be added to your text and positioned such that the reader will easily follow the relation between each table etc. and the prose discussion thereof.

Once you have completed the text, you add the remaining sections, two at most. Your term paper will end, in the case of a literary term paper, with the Bibliography, or in the case of a linguistic term paper, with the References (see Chapter 2); these may optionally be formatted with single line spacing. Both these sections simply continue the pagination of the preceding text. However, if you have Appendices, these should appear after all other the parts of the term paper, including the Bibliography/References and also continuing the pagination. Make sure there is a perfect correlation between the references in your text and those in the bibliography.

Each copy of the whole product (some departments require you to submit two copies) should be stapled together in the top left-hand corner as one unit. It is unnecessary and indeed undesirable for you to embellish your term paper with any of the flourishes or curlicues made available by contemporary computer technology. Resist any temptation to add photographs of the authors you are discussing, to make use of 'artistic' fonts or indeed to add anything to your text that is not strictly necessary for the scholarly argument you are making. We would also strongly recommend that the term paper is not inserted into a plastic folder (unnecessary and damaging to the environment); printing on recycled paper, white or off-white, is quite acceptable, and clearly advisable (but check with your tutor to find about their personal preferences).

Bibliography

Ardagh, John 1990. *Germany and the Germans*. London: Penguin.

Bachschmidt, Patrick 1999. Construction de l'argumentation dans l'article de recherche en mécanique, différences entre discours du francophone et de l'anglophone. *Asp* 23–26: 197–207.

Clyne, Michael 1987. Cultural differences in the organization of academic texts: English and German. *Journal of Pragmatics* 11: 211–247.

Fabb, Nigel & Alan Durant 2005. *How to write essays and dissertations: A guide for English literature students*. 2nd edition. Harlow etc.: Pearson Longman.

Fløttum, Kjersti 2005. The self and the others: Polyphonic visibility in research articles. *International Journal of Applied Linguistics* 15(1): 29–44.

Flower, Linda & John R. Hayes 1981. A cognitive process theory of writing. *College Composition and Communication* 32(4): 365–387.

Friedlander, Alexander 1990. Composing in English: Effects of a first language on writing in English as a second language. In Barbara Kroll (ed.), *Second language writing: Research insights for the classroom*. Cambridge: Cambridge University Press. 109–125.

Grice, Paul H. 1975. Logic and conversation. In Peter Cole & Jerry Morgan (eds), *Syntax and Semantics* 3, 41–58. New York: Academic Press.

Haggan, Madeline 2004. Research paper titles in literature, linguistics and science: Dimensions of attraction. *Journal of Pragmatics* 36(2): 293–317.

Hinds, John 1987. Reader versus writer responsibility: A new typology. In Ulla Connor and Robert Kaplan (eds), *Writing across languages: Analysis of L2 text*. Reading, MA: Addison-Wesley. 141–152.

Hutz, Matthias 1997. *Kontrastive Fachtextlinguistik für den fachbezogenen Fremdsprachenunterricht: Fachzeitschriftartikel der Psychologie im interlingualen Vergleich*. Trier: WVT.

Kaplan, Robert B. 1980. Cultural thought patterns in intercultural education. In Kenneth Croft (ed.), *Readings on English as a second language*, Cambridge: Winthrop. 399–418.

Königs, Frank G. 1989. *Beim Übersetzen schreibt man – übersetzt man auch beim Schreiben? Ein psycholinguistisch orientierter Vergleich zweier fremdsprachlicher Produktionsprozesse bei fortgeschrittenen deutschen Spanischlernern*. Habilitationsschrift, Univ. Bochum.

Kruse, Otto 2006. The origins of writing in the disciplines: Traditions of seminar writing and the Humboldtian ideal of the research university. *Written Communication* 23 (3): 331–352.

Kwan, Becky S.C. 2008. The nexus of reading, writing and researching in the doctoral undertaking of humanities and social sciences: Implications for literature reviewing. *English for Special Purposes* 27: 42–56.

Macheiner, Judith 1995. *Übersetzen: Ein Vademecum*. Frankfurt am Main: Suhrkamp.

Newmark, Peter 1981. *Approaches to translation*. Oxford: Pergamon Press.

Oldenburg, Hermann 2002. *Angewandte Fachtextlinguistik. 'Conclusions' und Zusammenfassungen* (Forum für Fachsprachenforschung 17). Tübingen: Narr.

Pieth, Christa & Kirsten Adamzik 1997. Anleitungen zum Schreiben universitärer Texte in kontrastiver Perspektive. In Kirsten Adamzik, Gerd Antos & Eva-Maria Jakobs (eds), *Domänen- und kulturspezifisches Schreiben*. Frankfurt am Main: Peter Lang. 31–71.

Rodman, Lilita 1996. The pragmatics of non-adverbial *there*-clauses in scientific articles. *Forum of the Linguistic Association of Canada and the United States* (LACUS) N° 23: 657–663.

Sachtleber, Susanne 1993. Textstile in der Wissenschaftssprache. In Hartmut Schröder (ed.), *Fachtextpragmatik*. Tübingen: Narr, 61–79.

Siepmann, Dirk 2006. Academic writing and culture: an overview of similarities and differences between English, French and German. *Meta* 51: 131–150.

Smith, Veronica 1994. *Thinking in a foreign language: An investigation into essay writing and translation by L2 learners*. Tübingen: Narr.

Soler, Viviana 2007. Writing titles in science: An exploratory study. *English for Specific Purposes* 26: 90–102.

Thielmann, Winfried 2009. *Deutsche und englische Wissenschaftssprache im Vergleich. Hinführen – Verknüpfen – Benennen*. Heidelberg: Synchron.

Trumpp, Eva Cassandra 1998. *Fachtextsorten kontrastiv. Englisch-Deutsch-Französisch* (Forum für Fremdsprachen-Forschung 51). Tübingen: Narr.

Weissberg, Bob 2000. Developmental relationships in the acquisition of English syntax: Writing vs. speech. *Learning and Instruction* 10 (1): 37–53.

Zimmermann, Rüdiger 2000. L2 writing: Subprocesses, a model of formulating and empirical findings. *Learning and Instruction* 10 (1): 73–99.

Module II

Building effective sentences

Introduction

In this module we move away from the higher units of organization within the text and descend into the paragraph, where the basic unit of text is the sentence. In terms of text construction, it is at sentence level that grammatical structure and information structure come together into one complex process: information has to be organized, or packaged, into grammatical units. We are going to look more closely at the patterns of informational organization which are found in English sentences, and academic English in particular. You should see the module as a kind of 'grammar for writing'.

There are four chapters. In Chapter 1 we start off by looking at how the context of academic writing affects the basic shape of sentences, and then proceed to introduce the central notions of information packaging and sentencing. An understanding of what is involved here will help you to get to grips with the task of building sentences which are appropriate in written academic text, and help you develop control over the writing process.

Chapter 2 concentrates on information packaging in the simple clause, and looks at the range of construction types which English offers to express ideas in such a way that what has to stand out does indeed stand out, and at the same time in such a way that the information fits naturally into the linguistic context. In Chapter 3 we take a detailed look at the complex sentence, presenting a set of techniques for subordinating one piece of information to another. Finally, Chapter 4 turns to punctuation. The readability of complex sentences is strongly dependent on a correct and also strategic use of punctuation, and the punctuation choices which you make reflect the informational and rhetorical relationships between the different units of the complex sentence. It is for this reason that we have chosen to go into detail on punctuation in this module, rather than treat it more summarily under, for instance, the heading of style.

All in all, this module is not only concerned with helping you develop your skill at deploying grammatical constructions, but you should also see it as an attempt to support your developing discourse competence. A good writer has a fully-fledged grammatical repertoire, and can use the formal options available in a grammatically correct fashion, but this expressive power is only valuable if the writer can use these options appropriately. This means that you need to have insight into the communicative effect of each grammatical choice: the effect on textual coherence, as well as the effect on meaning in terms of highlighting or backgrounding particular pieces of information.

Chapter 1

Basic issues in sentence construction

The main points in this chapter are these:

- Sentences are best seen as orthographical-rhetorical units consisting of one or more clauses.
- An effective clause is organized such that the information which is presented first follows naturally from the previous context and also prepares the reader for what is still to come.
- An effective clause is organized such that it is immediately clear for the reader what constitutes the most important piece of information. This information normally occurs in clause-final position.
- An effective complex sentence is one which clearly shows the relative weight of individual ideas and which clearly expresses the meaning relationships between these different ideas.

This chapter is a general introduction to the module. It starts off by discussing what we understand by the notion 'sentence' in the present context (1.1), and it goes on to present two further notions which serve as valuable foundations for understanding what makes sentences effective in a given context. The first of these notions is information packaging, which relates to the organization of information within the clause ('Teilsatz') and the choice of grammatical construction (1.2). The second is sentencing, which has to do with rhetorically oriented decisions which determine how you combine clauses into sentential units (1.3). The other chapters in this module elaborate on these two notions.

1.1 Sentence construction

Sentences are the building blocks of your paragraphs. But what, for current purposes, actually constitutes a sentence ('Satz')? It is essential that you see the sentence in two very different, but ultimately related ways. Most straightforwardly, it is an orthographical unit that is clearly identifiable by a capital letter at the beginning and a full stop at the end.[1] What is equally important in the present context, however, is its status as a rhetorical unit; that is to say, a sentence is a segment of text comprising one or more units of information which together constitute a specific and relatively independent step in fulfilling your communicative aim at the level of the paragraph. The orthographical definition says something about the form of the sentence, while the rhetorical definition says something about the status of the sentence in terms of your communicative intentions.

The orthographical-rhetorical sentence can have different grammatical forms. What we will call the simple sentence ('einfacher Satz') basically consists of one independent clause (also called 'Satz', or 'Hauptsatz', in German) with a finite verb, as in the following example:

> Writing is an important skill.

However, we include under the heading of simple sentence those cases where a constituent either itself consists of a clause or otherwise contains one, as is the case with the relative clause in the following example:

> Writing is a skill **that can be learned**.

The relative clause here is what we call 'embedded' ('eingebetteter Satz') (see Chapter 3.1.1 for more detail).

Alternatively, the sentence may be more complex, consisting of two or more clauses which are combined in some way. For the purposes of this book we will use the term 'complex sentence' ('zusammengesetzter Satz'). Here is an example:

> What is more, when you look at language under a microscope, you can see it changing almost as you watch it: words and phrases, pronunciations and rhythms become widely imitated at astonishing speed. (McCrum et al. 1986: 11)

In the part up to the colon, this sentence first has two subordinate clauses, then the main clause, then another subordinate clause; after the colon there is another main clause. The different ways of constructing complex sentences will be discussed in Chapter 3.1.1.

---

1 Actually, this is not rigid enough as a formal definition, because it does not take account of sentences ending in question marks or exclamation marks, nor does it recognize that capitals are used for proper nouns and titles, and that stops are used for abbreviations (cf. Greenbaum & Nelson 2002: 13).

Finally, a sentence may not even contain a full clause, in which case we talk of a sentence fragment or a non-clausal sentence ('Satzäquivalent'). Consider the following example, in bold print:

> If large numbers come from bright regions and small numbers come from dark regions, then large number equals white equals snow and small number equals black equals coals, right? **Wrong**. The amount of light hitting a spot on the retina depends not only on how pale or dark the object is but also on how bright or dim the light illuminating the object is. (Pinker 1998: 7)

Although *Wrong* does not constitute an independent main clause, it is nevertheless a fully-fledged text sentence in the orthographical-rhetorical sense in which we are employing the term here (cf. Downing & Locke 2006: 274).

Despite this text-oriented perspective which we are adopting, it is indeed customary for writers of academic English to produce text sentences which are either simple or complex sentences according to the definitions given above. That is to say, sentence fragments occur only rarely in academic English. The example given above is admittedly from an important academic work, but it is a work written with a very broad, educated readership in mind, and the style is popularizing and directly interactive throughout. In such writing, it is not uncommon to see, for instance, question-answer pairs, and the reader addressed directly in the second person. By contrast, however, the small corpus of English studied by Tavecchio (2010), which is compiled solely on the basis of articles from academic journals, contains not a single sentence which consists simply of a subordinate clause or which is built around such a clause.

What other things are worth keeping in mind about the basic form of the sentence in academic prose? An important consideration here is the relation between the writer and the reader: these people are not generally known to each other, and that has a profound influence on the shape of sentences. Because of this unfamiliarity with the reader, the writer will not be able to use his/her personality to achieve success in communication; rather, s/he will have to rely on the coherence of the text. This means that many of the devices used by speakers to enliven their speech are unsuitable for written texts. In speech, there is an interplay of statements, questions, orders and exclamations. English academic writing, by contrast, consists almost exclusively of statements: after all, there is no identifiable reader from whom to elicit an answer or to whom to issue an order.[2]

2 The extent to which questions are used in academic writing in fact may differ from one language to another. French academic writing, for instance, commonly uses question-answer pairs.

That does not mean that questions, orders and exclamations have no place in academic prose, but it does mean that their use is somewhat restricted. Questions, in the form of interrogative clauses, are often used to introduce sections of argument. If, for instance, you have set out in your text a number of alternative proposals for solving a problem, and wish now to evaluate them, you may start by formulating a question such as the following:

What, now, can we do about deciding which proposal might prove most effective?

The effect you create is as if you are indeed asking the question yourself, and then going on to provide an answer. But there is also an element of involving the reader in a dialogue. Two warnings are in order, however. First, you should not overdo the use of questions: too many questions can come across as involving a lack of focus in your writing, and may also suggest that you have mainly questions but few answers. Second, you should avoid rhetorical questions, which are in fact statements formulated as questions. The somewhat sober style of academic writing prescribes that you formulate a statement as a statement.

Orders, in the form of imperative clauses, are mainly used to introduce examples and to invite the reader to act. A number of specific expressions are quite common:

Consider the following examples.
See Butler (2003) for a fuller account.
Note that we have not included passives in our analysis.
Compare the analysis offered by Smits et al. (2007).

Finally, note that whereas questions and imperatives do have specific functions in academic text, exclamations are best avoided. This is because they bring too much emotion into play. Even if you are writing about an issue which you feel strongly about, and you wish to voice your opinion, you should try to use lexical means to do so, in a reasonably downtoned fashion and without the use of an exclamation mark, which is used more often in German academic text than it is in English. In the following two examples, the statement in the form of a declarative clause is thus to be preferred over the exclamative clause.

?What a dangerous conclusion to draw!
→ This is clearly a dangerous conclusion to draw.

One final feature of the sentence in written academic English which is worth noting at this early stage is its varied length, with quite long sentences being not uncommon. If you are used to writing quite long sentences in German, then there is no need to adopt a markedly different strategy when writing English. On the other hand, you may still be very much concerned in your writing to produce lexically and grammatically correct sentences, and an exaggerated concern with grammatical correctness can easily lead to a preponderance of rather short sentences with more or less equal length. If you have produced two separate sentences that stand next to each other and are closely connected in terms of meaning, it may well be appropriate to link them together into one more complex sentence.

1.2 Information packaging

The basic building blocks of sentences are clauses. They are built in English following a set of grammatical rules, which you can see as basic moulds for giving shape to your individual messages. But despite the limited number of moulds there is a considerable amount of variation in the ways the moulds can be filled, and this variation has everything to do with communicative intention. The key to producing an effective clause, as the basis for an effective sentence, is thus to package the information appropriately. There are two central decisions that you have to take as a writer when deciding on the structure of a clause:

- *How should you formulate the central message so that the information presented follows most naturally from the previous context and prepares the reader best for what is still to come?*
  This is a decision which relates to the syntactic choices available for shaping the main clause. The choice of grammatical construction relates to the status of information at the given point in the development of the text; for instance, the choice of a clause with an active or passive verb form.

- *How should you formulate each message so that the reader immediately identifies the most important element in the message?*
  This decision follows from the insight that each single message contains a piece of information which the writer takes to be new for the reader, and which s/he wishes to signal as the most important element in the message. When you speak, you have intonation, voice, gesture etc. at your disposal to make clear to the reader what your main point is, but in writing these options are not available. As a counterpart to intonation and gesture, the written language offers a variety of syntactic options, which have a more or less fixed distribution of given and new information, so that the main

element can be easily recognized. On top of that there is a certain flexibility in the ordering of information in the English clause, which you can use to good effect.

To get an idea of the kind of decision that is involved with information packaging, let us look briefly at two examples. First consider the following sequence from a brochure for the *Rijksmuseum* in Amsterdam. The text consists of running prose but we have numbered each sentence for ease of reference. Note also that each sentence in the paragraph is an example of a simple sentence, as defined in 1.1 above; the only subordinate clause is the restrictive relative clause in the first sentence, which is embedded in the phrase *a collection which has justifiably attained world renown.*

1. The Rijksmuseum houses a collection which has justifiably attained world renown.
2. It contains the largest art collection in the Netherlands.
3. The Painting Section represents the most important collection of Dutch painting from the 15th up to and including the 19th century (...).
4. A separate room is devoted to Italian, Spanish and other artists.
5. The Print Room contains approximately one million prints and drawings.
6. Alternating exhibitions of this rich and varied collection are continually being held.

This paragraph has been constructed using a fusion of spatial and analytical elaboration (see Module I, Chapter 3.3). The first two sentences introduce the renowned art collection to be found in the museum, and sentences 3, 4 and 5, which constitute the elaboration, give details about different sections and rooms in the museum, seeking to justify the claim to world renown. The climax, sentence 6, rounds things off with another statement about the collection as a whole.

What is worthy of note here is that each of the main clauses that comprise the elaborational sentences starts with an expression referring to a particular part of the museum: *The Painting Section, A separate room,* and *The Print Room.* The author has thus adopted a very specific organizational pattern by presenting the Rijksmuseum itself at the beginning of the first and second sentences, and following this up with references to specific parts of the museum. This promotes thematic continuity, in that a clear perspective emerges from the writer's choice of how each sentence starts (see chapter 2.1 for more discussion on this). But note that this is not straightforward: the writer has had to make use of a varied lexico-grammatical repertoire to achieve his/her communicative aim. First we have the use of the verb *house,* which takes a location as its subject. Then in sentences 2 and 5 we see a construction with the verb *contain*, which similarly has a locative subject. In sentence 4 the author chooses a specific passive construction using the verb *devote*, which allows the room to be subject, rather than for instance a formulation such as this

> 4'. Italian, Spanish and other artists are exhibited in a separate room.

which not only breaks the thematic continuity but might even give the unintended impression that Italian, Spanish and other artists are less important. We thus see that by organizing the beginning of each sentence in a certain way, the author has achieved a clear, coherent perspective for the reader, but in order to do so s/he has had to make specific lexico-grammatical choices.

Here is a different kind of example. Read the whole paragraph, but concentrate on the sentence in bold:

> There are various names we might give to this discourse – for instance, the individualist discourse of the self, or the Cartesian discourse of the subject. It has a long history, it has at times been 'common sense' for most people, it is the basis of theories and philosophies and can be traced through text and talk in many domains of social life, and its 'scale' is considerable – it generates a vast range of representations. **On a rather less general, but still very general, level, we might identify in the domain of politics a discourse of liberalism, and within the economic domain a 'Taylorist' discourse of management**. By contrast, in Fairclough (2000b) I discussed the political discourse of the 'third way', i.e. the discourse of 'New Labour', which is a discourse attached to a particular position within the political field at a particular point in time (the discourse is certainly less than a decade old). (Fairclough 2003: 125)

In this paragraph the author is talking about different domains and different kinds of discourse. In the sentence in question, printed in bold, he chooses to give more emphasis to two kinds of discourse rather than to two domains. This is because he proceeds in the next sentence to introduce a third kind of discourse, which he wishes to say something more about. And in order to steer the reader towards paying attention to this third type of discourse, what he does is make a very marked word order choice, postponing the grammatical object until the end of the clause and inserting the adjunct phrases *in the domain of politics* and *within the economic domain* between the verb and the object.

These two examples illustrate the idea that the effective writer is one who can effectively construct clauses. But to do so, the writer must first of all have a sense of how individual messages are related to each other within the context of his/her communicative aims at the level of the paragraph, and on top of that s/he needs to be able to draw on a wide lexico-grammatical repertoire.[3]

1.3 Sentencing

The organizing of information into different kinds of sentential units we will call the process of 'sentencing'. For the sentence builder, sentencing involves a number of important decisions:

- *What are the most important ideas that you want to present in support of the communicative aim of the paragraph?*
  This is a decision that helps determine how many sentences you are going to have and what is going to be the communicative core of each sentence.
- *How much information do you want to put in each sentence?*
  This is a crucial decision, relating to the length and complexity of the sentences you produce. In a general sense you may be constrained by the genre: sentences in tabloid newspapers tend to be quite short, while fine novelists have no problem producing elegant sentences of 50 words and more. However, academic texts contain both short and long sentences, so in individual cases it will be important to decide whether you want supporting ideas to be presented together with the ideas they support, or whether you want to present them on their own. If you are building a long and complex sentence, you also have to think about the rhythm of the sentence, which can have an effect on readability.
- *What is the most appropriate way of combining the various clauses in the sentence?*
  If you are formulating a complex sentence, then you not only need to know what is the central idea, the communicative core, but also you need to know how the supporting ideas relate to the central idea. One thing you have to decide on is the position of each idea in the sentence. And depending on the meaning relationship, you will then have a number of options available for combining the elements, using not only different kinds of subordinate clause – for instance adverbial clauses and relative clauses – but also different forms of punctuation – for instance commas, colons and semicolons.

Let us look at some examples of how sentencing decisions can affect the actual shape of sentences. In your paragraph writing plan it may well be that a

[3] You can read much more about this from a lexical perspective in Module III.

small piece of information carries a lot of weight, and in a case like that you can give the information the prominence it deserves by giving it a sentence of its own. In the following example from a literary text, the author goes even further:

> Eighteen months of no work and clinical depression next before a commission to pen a script for a medium-budget British film. I wrote a script that was my best work so far. The producers loved the script, the money people came on board smooth as pie, a star attached their name, the film was a go go.
>
> **Then.**
>
> The producer, who'd just had a big hit by accident, tried to get clever. He didn't want a tough director to stand up to him so he hired a woman who had only ever directed a twenty-nine minute short for BBC Wales who he thought could be pushed around, but who turned out to be both stubborn and stupid. She shot whole scenes – and this was a comedy remember – focused solely on a tin of peas. (Sayle 2000: 26)

The interesting sentence here is *Then*. Note first of all that it is a sentence fragment, as defined in 1.1 above. But on top of that it has also been given paragraph status here, in order to create a certain effect. The prior context contains references to positive events while the following paragraph only reports negative events. By giving *Then* the status of not only sentence but also paragraph, the writer creates a very sharp transition between two larger segments of text and announces in a rather dramatic way to the reader that things are about to change for the worse. The effect would have been totally lost if the second paragraph had begun as follows:

> Then the producer, who'd just had a big hit by accident, tried to get clever.

In this case the writer indeed would still be signalling a new series of events by starting the new paragraph with *Then*, but the reader's attention would not be directed separately to the change. Rather, the idea of a change comes more from the content of the main clause, *Then the producer tried to get clever*, because of the negative connotations of *get clever*. In this alternative version, there is thus much less of an announcement to the reader that s/he should brace him/herself for a major change in the script writer's fortunes.

Now this is not the kind of strongly rhetorically based segmentation that you will be wanting to undertake in the context of writing term papers, but it does emphasize the power of the orthographical unit for pursuing a rhetorical purpose. Less powerful than the first example, but more fitting in the context of academic writing, is the following example. It is a complete paragraph, and we have numbered each sentence separately:

> **Sprat's heart was in the right place** [1]. Everyone would agree that it is desirable for language to be clear [2]. The problem is saying clearly what constitutes this clarity, and this is what Sprat is unable to do [3]. **We can hardly blame him [4]**. No one has ever been able to define the linguistic basis of such notions as clarity, simplicity and elegance [5]. We can usually recognize such qualities when we see or hear them; but *define* them [6]? A century later, grammarians tried again, thinking that the solution lay in a small set of grammatical rules [7]. **That didn't work either [8]**. (Crystal 2006: 64–5)

Sentences 1, 4 and 8 in this paragraph are all really short, with seven, five and four words respectively. Crystal's aim in this paragraph is to argue how difficult it is to get a fix on what the essence is of clear language, but at the same time to show a degree of sympathy with Thomas Sprat, who in the late 1660s was one of the first to complain about decay in the English language and who called for a return to clarity and conciseness. After a short topic sentence, Crystal argues that what Sprat was trying to do may indeed have failed, but it failed because of the sheer difficulty of the task. This point is highlighted by the decision to express the ideas in sentences 4 and 8 by means of two very short and hence quite powerful sentences. These sentences lose some of their powerful effect if they are combined with other elements, as in the following reworked version:

> Sprat's heart was in the right place [1]. Everyone would agree that it is desirable for language to be clear [2]. However, the problem is saying clearly what constitutes this clarity, something which Sprat is unable to do [3]. In fact, no one has ever been able to define the linguistic basis of such notions as clarity, simplicity and elegance, **so we can hardly blame him** [4]. We can usually recognize such qualities when we see or hear them; but it is just very difficult to define them [5]. A century later, grammarians tried again, thinking that the solution lay in a small set of grammatical rules, **but that didn't work either** [6].

In this version we have reduced the number of sentences from eight to six and specified the relations between individual ideas more explicitly than in the original. The nature of the overall argument remains intact, but the insistence on the difficulty of defining clarity is less marked.

The sentence, then, can be quite short and simple, and as such represent a powerful rhetorical instrument for the writer. But it can be long and complex as well. The longer sentences in the example taken from Crystal above are in fact not overly long, being in the region of 18 or 20 words, and this might well be a deliberate choice given the broad audience which the text is aimed at. But sentences in academic prose are quite often considerably longer (cf. Burrough 2002). If you want to make a particular point, but wish to back it up with secondary information which you consider important for your reader but not important enough to present in its own right as a sentence, then you may wish to compose a rather complex and potentially long sentence. In principle, relatively important information – information which you wish to assert – is formulated in main clauses, while relatively unimportant information – often information which can be presupposed – can best be formulated using subordinate clauses ('Nebensätze'). There is nothing against complex sentences; they can become almost mini paragraphs. Here is a rather elegant example of a smoothly flowing sentence with 47 words (the second sentence in the segment):

> We can take another example, also literary but from the eighteenth century. No doubt the English Romantic Movement owed something to Germany and Johann Gottfried von Herder, but I think it owed still more to English rural traditions, which knew nothing about literary fashion and the Enlightenment but perhaps still remembered the Secret Commonwealth of Elves, Faunes and Fairies. (Priestley 1973: 112)

Let us look at this second sentence in a little more detail. Priestley's aim here is to provide an example of the force of popular tradition in English life. The core message in terms of the argument is the coordinated main clause *but I think it owed still more to English rural traditions*. This is separated from the preceding main clause by a comma, which makes it stand out more on its own (see Chapter 4.2.3). The preceding main clause comprises an admission on the part of the writer about an important element in explaining the Romantic Movement, but serves only to pave the way for what the writer finds really important. Priestley could have introduced the sentence using a subordinate clause, as in:

> Although there is no doubt that the English Romantic Movement owed something to Germany and Johann Gottfried von Herder, I think it owed still more to English rural traditions, …

However, the choice of a main clause gives the admission slightly more weight. Even though it is not the main point of the argument, the writer still wants the reader to take the idea on board as valuable in its own right; one could say that the writer still wishes to assert it.

The sentence then rounds off with a non-restrictive relative clause construction (*which knew nothing … fairies*). The aim of this sequence, in fact two coordinated clauses, is to justify the claim in the coordinated main clause. Note that the coordinated clause introduced by *but* is in this case not separated from the preceding clause by a comma. The effect of this is to present the two pieces of information as one unit, despite the contrast.

The result of these constructional decisions by the author is a relatively long but well-balanced sentence which has its own clear rhetorical structure: 'admission – claim – justification'. For the reader it represents one complex rhetorical step, and the author has made it clear how he sees the hierarchical relationship between the three parts.

This example from Priestley illustrates a number of aspects of the three big sentencing questions which we introduced above. First of all, the writer has decided that one of the three ideas is more important than the other two. Secondly, he has decided that the other two ideas are not 'big' enough to warrant their own sentence, at least in the context of formal argued text. The rhythm of the sentence reveals a three-step approach, with a preparatory statement, the central claim, and a further elaboration – an often used pattern in argued text. Thirdly, the writer has made specific choices in terms of clause combining. The first idea is presented as a main clause, suggesting some prominence, but it is couched in a *no doubt ... but* construction, which at the same time suggests it is rhetorically relatively backgrounded. The second idea, the main point to be made, is given prominence by following *but* (cf. Spooren 1989). Finally, the elaboration is presented as a non-restrictive relative clause, which is an elegant alternative to *since it knew nothing about literary fashion*.

Summarizing, what we see from these few examples of different sentence shapes is that the sentence is indeed a rhetorical unit, and in order to build effective sentences which really work within the context of the paragraph, you will in the first instance need to have developed a clear idea of how much weight you wish to give to each idea. This is another reason why the text planning we discussed in Module I, Chapter 1.3 is so important. But once you have developed a detailed sense of your argument, you have to segment your text in such a way that the relative weight of individual ideas becomes clear for the reader, and you have to decide how to express the meaning relationships between these different ideas. This means that you will need a quite comprehensive toolkit to do the job, and in Chapter 3 we will seek to offer you precisely that.

1.4 Overview

This chapter has been introductory in nature. We have made a number of basic points which will be elaborated in the following chapters of this module.

- Sentences are best seen as orthographical-rhetorical units.
- Written academic English makes use of grammatically complete sentences.

- Written academic English is not frightened of long sentences.
- In order to write effectively you will need to think consciously about how much information you want to put into each sentence.
- If you wish to write grammatically complex sentences with more than one unit of information, then you have to know what the most important unit of information is and you have to think about how to express the relationship between the various components.
- In order to write effectively you need to consider the status of information within the individual message, and make lexico-grammatical choices accordingly. The greater your lexico-grammatical repertoire, the more ideas you will be able to express in a given context.

Chapter 2

Information packaging

The main points in this chapter are these:

- The vast majority of English clauses are organized according to a rigid grammatical mould, but there is a wide range of different constructions which fit in this mould. By mastering these constructions you can develop a rich and varied syntactic repertoire in your writing.
- English has a liking for clauses which begin with the grammatical subject, but it also allows a wide range of adverbial expressions to appear before the grammatical subject. These expressions provide a framework for interpreting the clause in the given context.
- English has a variety of grammatical constructions for conveying messages that both fit into the context and allow the most important information to be readily identifiable for the reader at the end of the clause.

This chapter focuses on information packaging. We start off in 2.1 by describing the basic grammatical patterns, or moulds, which English has for constructing clauses. Then, in 2.2, we consider how the appropriateness of a clause in a given context is to a significant extent determined by the order in which the information is presented. For you as a writer, this produces a field of tension: formulating an effective message means that the different pieces of information have to appear in a certain order and have to follow a fixed grammatical pattern. If you could only really use one pattern, and it was rigid, and if you only had a limited vocabulary, particularly in terms of verb choice, then you would have a considerable formulation task on your hands. So what means does English offer you for achieving your goal of an effective formulation? One part of the answer is indeed 'an extensive knowledge of collocations (*make an assumption*) and lexico-grammatical constructions (*Smith is wrong in his assumption that …*)', and we deal with just such lexico-grammatical aspects in detail in Module III. But the other main part of the answer is 'a broad repertoire of very general grammatical constructions'.

Accordingly, the aim of the rest of the chapter, from 2.3 through to 2.6, is to present an array of special clausal constructions, detailing what kinds of contextualized meanings these constructions allow you to express, and what communicative effect they have.[4] You should seek to develop mastery in using these constructions. But remember that mastery lies not in being able simply to produce the forms correctly; rather, it lies in knowing how to use the forms to express your specific communicative intentions.

2.1 Basic grammatical moulds

In the vast majority of written text, but also in the majority of spoken utterances, the basic grammatical unit is the clause ('Teilsatz'). The clause has developed as a basic grammatical mould with an enormous potential for encoding what the language user wants to say, particularly when seen in combination with the lexical potential of the language. The standard grammatical mould for the bare English clause is subject-verb-object, or SVO, as illustrated in this example:

[Sarah Smith]	discusses	[the new interest in spelling].
S	V	O

Alternatively, with copula verbs, the structure is subject – verb – complement, or SVC, as in (2):[5]

[Attention to detail]	is	[a significant feature of Ian McEwan's style].
S	V	C

English has a strong preference for sentences beginning with the subject of the main clause. These patterns can of course be extended by means of adverbials which can appear in certain positions. For our present purposes, the two most important of these positions are at the beginning and end of the clause, exemplified below:

[In this week's number],	[Sarah Smith]	discusses	[the new interest in spelling].
A	S	V	O

[Sarah Smith]	discusses	[the new interest in spelling]	[in this week's number].
S	V	O	A

4 Much of the material presented in 2.3 through 2.5 is a reworking of relevant sections of Chapter 8 of Hannay & Mackenzie (2002).

5 There are more grammatical patterns for declarative clauses, depending on the transitive status of the verb, but these are all extensions of the SVO and SVC structures. See e.g. Quirk et al. (1985: 720f.) for an overview.

This gives us (A) – S – V – O – (A) as an extended basic mould for constructing clauses. We will look later on at how this mould can be used to great effect, but first we should point out that you can also make effective use of two additional, though much less frequent, moulds that English has developed for specific purposes. One of these is the mould for questions, which looks like this:

How	did	[the novel]	gain	[so much power]?
P	Vfin	S	Vnon-fin	O

In this clause mould, P – V – S – V – O/C, Vfin stands for finite verb, Vnon-fin for non-finite verb, and P is a label we have adopted for the special slot for question words at the beginning of the clause. This mould is also used to produce the subject-verb inversion structure:

[Not until 2002]	did	[Dryden's experiment]	come	[to public light].
P	Vfin	S	Vnon-fin	C

If you wish to stress a restrictive adverb phrase such as *never* or *in no case*, which normally comes after the verb, you can place it at the beginning of the clause. You then need to reverse the usual word order in such a way that it resembles that of a question.

Hardly had the government announced the budget than the rumours about new tax increases started appearing.
Not only may the language difference prove a barrier when appointing the management, but it may also be a problem in dealing with the customers.
But in no case has a European population been found to be descended entirely from a single group.
Only if we consult linguists will we be able to analyse the great variety of South African English ...
His characters were tame; **never did they act** impulsively.

The other special mould is P – Vfin – Vnon-fin – S, which is characterized by the subject appearing at the end of the clause. The first example below only has a finite verb, while the second has both a finite and a non-finite verb form.

[To this category]	belong	[a number of rather serious crimes].
P	Vfin	S

For the past five years, the national agency has been working to develop this historic site. [**Working alongside**] **have** **been** [**a number of countryside groups**].

[Working alongside]	have	been	[a number of countryside groups].
P	Vfin	Vnon-fin	S

Clauses which are patterned like this have a specific textual function, and we will return to this point in 2.5.5 below.

Basically, then, what we are saying here is that when constructing a clause in order to convey a message, your job is to find the best way of mapping what you want to say onto the moulds that the English grammatical system provides, but one of the moulds – the basic one – is very dominant.

Now, there are in fact many different ways that A – S – V – O/C – A, the basic clause mould with its simple extensions, can be used to express more or less one and the same content. Here are twelve ways of saying that 'John recently gave me a present':

A John recently gave me a present.
B Recently John gave me a present.
C John gave me a present recently.
D John recently gave a present to me.
E A present John gave me recently.
F I was recently given a present by John.
G A present I was recently given by John.
H There was a present that John recently gave me.[6]
I It was recently that John gave me a present.
J It was to me that John recently gave a present.
K What John did recently was give me a present.
L What John recently gave me was a present.

These sentences are all grammatically correct, but there is not one single linguistic context in which all of them would be appropriate. Indeed, the context plays a major role in determining what is appropriate and what not. For instance, sentence D, assuming the primary accent on the last constituent, *to me*, suggests a context in which it is assumed that John has given a present but it is disputed to whom he gave it. In sentence J the same situation is valid but there is a greater likelihood that the speaker is suggesting that it was not to some specific other person that John recently gave a present, but to her. Finally, with sentence K we can assume that it is already known that John recently did something, but not what, and this sentence specifies what that action was, namely *give me a present*.

---

6 How existential clauses like this might fit into the basic syntactic mould is not a straightforward matter. Here we assume that the grammatical subject – *there* – fits into the subject slot in the mould, while the notional subject – *a present that John recently gave me* – behaves like a complement and hence fits into the O/C slot. For more discussion see Hannay & Martínez Caro (2008: 56).

We can easily test the context sensitivity of these different formulations by seeing what questions they do and do not answer. For instance, a question like *What did John recently give you?* might well lead to L as an appropriate response, but F, H and J would not produce a coherent exchange. Or consider a question like *When did John give you a present?* Here it would be possible to respond using C and I, but it would be difficult to imagine a coherent interpretation for responses like D, G, H, J, K and L.

What does this little exercise reveal? First, you should note that the basic mould is flexible enough to allow you to formulate a message which expresses a very specific content in a given context. But at the same time you will have seen that the distribution of information across the sentences differs considerably from one sentence to the other. To be specific, the first constituent in each of the twelve sentences expresses eight different pieces of information:

A-C-D	John
B	Recently
E-G	A present
F	I
H	There
I-J	It
K	What John did recently
L	What John recently gave me

Moreover, the grammatical subject varied almost as much, expressing six different pieces of information:

A-B-C-D-E	John
F-G	I
H	There
I-J	It
K	What John did recently
L	What John recently gave me

Finally, there were five different final constituents:

A-B-I-J-K-L	a present
C-E	recently
D	to me
F-G	by John
H	me

Indeed, the choice of initial constituent and final constituent is of great relevance in shaping the message, and in the next section we will look at the ordering of information more closely.

2.2 The order of information in the clause

Why are the beginning and the end of the clause so important in terms of the context? There is in fact an interesting analogy to be found with the organization of information at a higher level in the text. In Module I we emphasized that when organizing your text you need to order information according to the function it fulfils. The text and the paragraph can both be said to exhibit a tripartite structure, with a beginning, a middle, and an end. It is the job of the initial unit both to look back and to lay the foundation for what is to come. It is the job of the final unit to state the essence of what you wish to communicate at that level, and often also to provide a point of reference for what is to come next. What we see is that this works very much in the same way at the clause level. Let us look more closely at these two positions in the clause.

2.2.1 The front of the clause

Writing is a planned activity which often takes a long time, so that writers have the opportunity to work out complex thoughts in considerable detail. The potential complexity of the outcome can put a considerable burden on the reader when processing the text. A good writer keeps this burden to a minimum. One way to do this is to make the information given at the start of each message as accessible as possible for the reader. Accessible information may be

- given in the previous context;
- readily inferrable from the previous context or on the basis of world knowledge;
- made accessible at the time of mention by means of a grounding, or anchoring, device.

The examples below exemplify each type of information in turn:

> University teachers love to hear their own voice. **They** see lecturing as performing on a stage.
>
> This paper will discuss an experiment that was conducted in 1991 to discover a cause for the sudden incidence of a rare disease in Africa. **The results** are of major significance for the understanding of the disease.
>
> In this day and age it is difficult to believe that these diseases are still killers. But between them, they cause the deaths of over 1.5 million children and paralyse another 100,000 every year. **Maria Sapateiro, a young mother from Mozambique**, suffered her own agonies as she watched five of her children die.

In the first example, the use of pronominal reference is a signal that the writer assumes that the reader can readily retrieve the intended referent from the immediate context. The expression *They* refers back to *university teachers* and at the same time forms the starting point for what is to come: it is what the rest of the clause is about. In the second example the writer makes use of the definite article in the subject phrase *The results*, again suggesting that the reader can identify the intended referent. In this case, however, the reader has to infer what results are meant by making a link with *an experiment* and using his/her general knowledge concerning experiments, namely that they produce results. In a way, one could say that *The results* here is simply shorthand for *The results of the experiment*, but it is the essence of the inferential relation that allows the writer to be compact and efficient in choosing *The results*: there is no need for the writer to add a sentence such as *The experiment had results*. Finally, in the third example, the expression *a young mother from Mozambique* functions as what is called a grounding device. This expression gives the reader information about the referent which allows him/her to situate that referent with regard to his/her contextual or general knowledge; in this particular case, the text is about the humanitarian disasters in Africa, but the writer wishes to home in on the plight of a particular person, to add a human interest element. Again, the formulation here is compact and efficient because it saves mentioning this background information in a separate sentence such as *Maria Sapateiro is a young mother from Mozambique*. An additional sentence like this would slow down the dynamics of the text and might even lead the reader to imagine asking 'So what?' (for more about this particular technique, see Chapter 3.4.2 in this module).

As the starting point for the development of the message we will call the first constituent the 'theme' (cf. Halliday & Matthiessen 2004). The theme is not only literally the starting point of the clause but it also defines the framework for both the organization of the clause and the comprehension of it. The theme constitutes a prime angle or perspective on what you want to communicate. Having a theme which consists of accessible information has a clear advantage for the reader. If you start with accessible information, then you present information which is already active for the reader, or which is activated and grounded on the spot. And this means quite simply that the reader has a good basis for integrating the new information that is to come into his/her discourse memory. Understanding a text is all about making sense of what is offered as new information in each successive clause, and it makes the task of understanding the value of each clause much more manageable if you know what piece of given information the new incoming information relates to.

In 2.3 and 2.4 we will present a number of grammatical constructions in which a particular kind of information occupies the theme position.

2.2.2 The end of the clause

In written English the most important information – that which would receive primary stress when spoken aloud – tends to occur towards the end of the clause, and preferably in final position. This is known as the principle of End Focus (Quirk et al. 1985: 1357). Here is a segment which illustrates the principle. The expressions in bold express the new information in their respective information units, and hence contain the element with primary stress.

> **The gossip of change**
> Consider, for a digressive page or two, **some personal examples of this gossip of change**. My father always called the knaves **jacks**; but my mother, who had been **a domestic servant in a well-to-do household**, never called them **other than knaves**. Moreover, she consistently referred **to court cards**, whereas my father said **face cards** (much to her amusement). They both pronounced the word *advertisement* with the accent **on the third syllable**, and stressed *controversy* **on the second**. My father pronounced *launch* and *staunch* to rhyme with **Southern British English ranch**, having acquired the habit, I always supposed, **from the naval personnel he met during the course of his work in a shipyard**; if taxed or teased about it, he would reply that he was speaking **the King's English** – the King in question being **George** V. (Nash 1986: 7)

Each of the phrases in capital letters contains the most important information in its clause, and each appears in clause-final position. If you try and rewrite each clause so that the important information comes at the beginning rather than the end, you will see that it is not only very difficult, but also that the result will be a totally incoherent text.

> **Some personal examples of this gossip of change** consider, for a digressive page or two. **Jacks** my father always called the knaves; but other than **knaves** my mother, who had been a domestic servant in a well-to-do household, never called them. Moreover, **to court cards** she consistently referred, whereas **face cards** (much to her amusement) my father said. Pronounced the word **advertisement** with the accent on the third syllable they both did, and ***controversy*** on the second stressed. **Southern British English ranch** my father pronounced to rhyme with *Launch* and *staunch*, **from the naval personnel he met during the course of his work in a shipyard** having acquired the habit, I always supposed; if taxed or teased about it, **the King's English – George V** the King in question being – he would reply that he was speaking.

Just as the themes of a coherent paragraph are connected in a certain way, so there is often a relationship between the final focal elements of sentences. Consider the following fragment:

> The availability of two different perspectives – stemming from two different ways of defining discourse – is partially responsible for the tremendous scope of discourse analysis. If we focus on **structure**, our task is to identify and analyze **constituents**, determine procedures for assigning to utterances **a constituent status**, discover regularities underlying **combinations of constituents** (perhaps even formulating rules for producing **those regularities**), and make principled decisions about whether or not particular arrangements are **well formed**. If we focus on **function**, on the other hand, our task is to identify and analyze actions performed by people **for certain purposes**, interpret **social, cultural, and personal meanings**, and justify our interpretations of those meanings **for the participants involved**. (Schiffrin 1994: 42)

The first sentence in this fragment announces the existence of two perspectives which together carry some responsibility for the scope of discourse analysis. The reader already expects, and gets, two things in the remaining segment: details about both structure and function, as well as details which will underpin the claim about the broad scope of the discipline. Notice how the segment is itself then split in two, structured by means of the parallel sentence-initial expressions *If we focus on structure* and *If we focus on function*. But notice, too, that the clause-final constituents, which form parts of lists, also refer to information which is relevant to first structure, then function. For structure we have the following string of focal constituents: *constituents – a constituent status – combinations of constituents – those regularities – well formed*. For function we have the following: *for certain purposes – social, cultural, and personal meanings – for the participants involved*. The first string involves elements related to form while the second string involves elements related to the interactional side of language, thus clearly reflecting the structure – function distinction.

We should note at this point that the End Focus principle does not hold rigorously in written English. Consider the following example:

> Critics had suggested that the death of three commission members might affect the outcome of the vote on the death penalty. However, it soon became clear **that the new members would not vote any differently on this issue**.

The natural interpretation of this sentence will involve seeing *any differently* as the new information and *on this issue* as contextually given, referring as it does to *on the death penalty* in the previous sentence. The point to note here is that *on this issue* contains the pronominal element *this*, which together with other contextual cues helps the reader determine that focus does not fall on the final constituent. An alternative formulation which upholds End Focus might be the following:

> However, it soon became clear that **on this issue the new members would not vote any differently**.

Note, however, that placing *on this issue* at the beginning of the embedded *that*-clause gives it a framing function. The effect in this case would be to suggest a certain contrast: on this issue, at least, the new members would not vote differently, irrespective of how they might feel about other issues. The two versions are thus clearly rather different, and a strict adherence to End Focus may on occasion be sacrificed to ensure a certain communicative effect.[7] Nevertheless, the principle of End Focus remains very strong in written English, and in 2.5 below we will present a number of constructions whose distinctive feature is the information that appears in clause-final position.

2.2.3 Fitting the sentence into the running text

The two special positions in the clause – beginning and end – are not only relevant as far as the internal dynamics of the message are concerned. They are also relevant with respect to the linguistic context in which the clause occurs. A clause which starts with accessible information and ends with the informational highpoint, information which in the eyes of the writer is the most newsworthy for the reader, has a good chance of fitting well into the context. The other way round, with the informational highpoint at the start and the given or accessible information at the end, runs the risk of being difficult to process. Here is an example of an ineffective segment of text which is difficult to process because the clause in bold print exhibits bad textual fit:

> Regular agriculture is a monoculture agriculture, where the farmers become specialized in the product they grow or keep. ??**Exhaustion of the soil is caused by the monoculture**: the ground is not fertile enough to grow the same product on it every year.

The first sentence describes regular agriculture as a monoculture agriculture and then defines this notion. The second sentence begins with a clause which actually says something about this monoculture, namely that it causes exhaustion of the soil, which is then explained in the clause following the

7 For an overview of other issues concerning the position of focused constituents in English, see Quirk et al. (1985: 1357f.).

colon. Because the portion in bold picks up on the monoculture introduced in the first sentence and itself introduces the notion of exhaustion, which is explained in what follows, it would be more effective to reorder the information in the clause in bold using an active rather than a passive form of the verb, thus producing the following:

> Regular agriculture is a monoculture agriculture, where the farmers become specialized in the product they grow or keep. → **The monoculture causes exhaustion of the soil**: the ground is not fertile enough to grow the same product on it every year.

The advantage of this version compared to the original text is that the reader no longer has to wait until the end of the clause to find out how s/he has to incorporate the notion of exhaustion of the soil into the picture which s/he is building up. The effective and ineffective systems are represented in Figures 1 and 2 respectively. The longer lines in Figure 2 signify a heavier processing task for the reader.

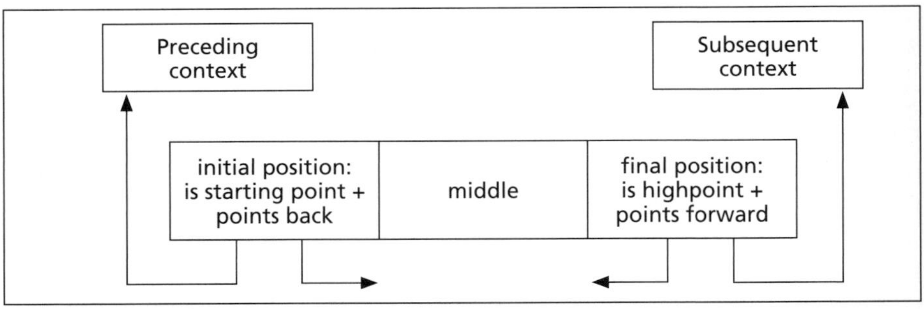

Figure 1: The effective system of information ordering (adapted from Hannay & Mackenzie 2002: 115)

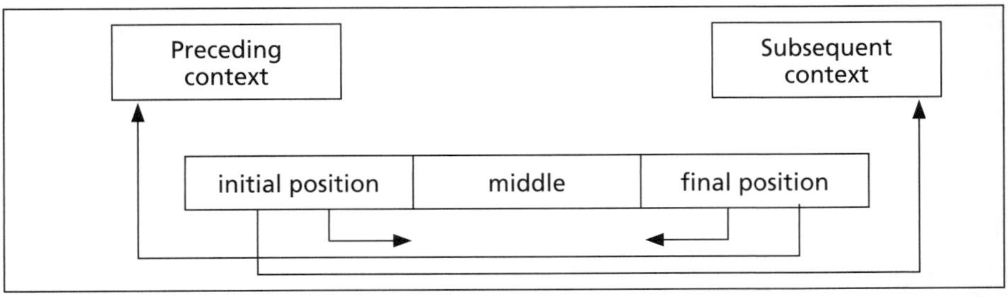

Figure 2: The ineffective system of information ordering (Hannay & Mackenzie 2002: 115)

In practice, we see that writers organize their paragraphs according to different patterns. The case of monoculture agriculture is one where the new information in one clause is picked up to become the starting point of a later clause, but there are other patterns. Consider again the paragraph we discussed in Chapter 1, noting the different expressions functioning as grammatical subject:

> **The Rijksmuseum** houses a collection which has justifiably attained world renown. **It** contains the largest art collection in the Netherlands. **The Painting Section** represents the most important collection of Dutch painting from the 15th up to and including the 19th century (...). **A separate room** is devoted to Italian, Spanish and other artists. **The Print Room** contains approximately one million prints and drawings. **Alternating exhibitions of this rich and varied collection** are continually being held.

In the rest of this chapter we present a series of grammatical constructions which allow you to express a variety of different contextualized meanings. Practice in using these constructions will broaden your grammatical repertoire and increase your ability to express yourself efficiently and effectively. Most constructions, though not all, make use of the basic grammatical mould.

We distinguish between constructions whose main characteristic is that certain information appears at the beginning of the clause (2.3 and 2.4) and others where the special feature is that unexpected information appears at the end (2.5).

2.3 Organizing the starting point

2.3.1 Clauses with passive verb forms

Possibly the best-known grammatical device for switching the order in which elements of the clause appear is the passive. In actual running text, various general reasons may be adduced for preferring the passive form of the verb to the active and vice versa. For instance, the choice may be determined by the text type, by a desire to avoid mentioning the agent, or by your own personal style. But on any one particular occasion the choice of active or passive may also be determined by specific factors in the context. If you opt for the passive rather than the active, then – excluding points of style – there are three basic differences:

- What would have been the subject of the active verb may disappear, because the information is not important in the given context; in practice, this is very often the case.
- You change the subject; the state of affairs described in the clause is now seen from a different point of view.

- The information changes position; you now have a different starting point.

It is mainly the third point that is relevant here. If you have formulated a clause but realize that the textual fit is not good, the simplest solution to your problems may well be to change the form of the verb from active to passive or vice versa. We already saw this with the example about monoculture agriculture in the previous section. Now consider the following active-passive pair:

A O'Connor discusses the general tendency for government revenues to rise more slowly than government expenditures.

B The general tendency for government revenues to rise more slowly than government expenditures is discussed by O'Connor.

The active form in the A sentence would fit well in the A context below, but the passive would not. By contrast, the passive form in the B sentence yields a good fit in the B context:

A O'Connor's (1973) framework is a useful starting point from which to construct an understanding of the uneven revenue imperative confronted by state and local governments after the mid-1960s. **O'Connor discusses the general tendency for government revenues to rise more slowly than government expenditures**. This tendency is based on two theses: ...

B In monopoly capitalism theory it has generally been held that governments will tend to earn a lot less in income from various taxes and other levies than what they need to balance necessary large-scale expenditure. **This general tendency for government revenues to rise more slowly than government expenditures is discussed by O'Connor (1973)**. O'Connor presents two theses to explain the tendency: ...

In the past it was customary for style guides to promote the active voice above the passive voice, suggesting that the active makes the text more lively, or more interesting. In academic writing there is a certain limit on this in the sense that the matters which academic texts deal with often concern abstract concepts rather than human actors; consequently, given the preference for the theme in English to be the grammatical subject, there will be a certain tendency for subjects to be abstract, and that may well lead to a tendency to have passive rather than active verbs, as noted by Robinson (2000: 444). That said, you can often use lexical means to avoid the passive while still retaining the order of information which you need for good textual fit. Here are some examples:

A Freedom and justice are highly valued by Europeans, and they are the foundation stones of the European Union.
B Freedom and justice are very important to Europeans, and they are the foundation stones of the European Union.

A At its birth, the EU was made up of distinct national economies.
B At its birth, the EU consisted of distinct national economies.

A Refugees are given residence permits, accommodation, access to social welfare and medical treatment.
B Refugees receive residence permits, accommodation, access to social welfare and medical treatment.

The most important point to stress here is that the marshalling of information by means of the active/passive choice use is mainly a question of appropriate lexical choice and textual coherence, rather than a matter of style. If you find yourself producing a clause with a passive verb form, and you adjudge what you produce to be idiomatic, and on top of that you feel that your choice of grammatical subject produces a sentence that exhibits good textual fit, then the chances are that you will have made an effective choice.

2.3.2 Fronting

English does indeed have a preference for having the subject as the first element of the clause, and it is definitely less amenable than German to the initial placement of major constituents which are not the grammatical subject, such as direct objects, indirect objects and subject complements (e.g. ***So hoch*** *war der Kurs des Euro schon lange nicht mehr*). But in fact, under specific circumstances English does allow other major constituents to appear before the subject. The most common of these circumstances is the contrastive context which underlies examples like the following:

> The government has issued a number of health warnings; **these** the public should take very seriously indeed. It has also published a set of leaflets about being careful when going on holiday; these relate to far less frightening matters.

If the writer had not chosen to front the object, 'these', in the second clause, then the contrast with the fourth clause would be less pronounced:[8]

> The government has issued a number of health warnings; the public should take these very seriously indeed. It has also published a set of leaflets about being careful when going on holiday; these relate to far less frightening matters.

8 There is an element in this device of what is called parallelism. For more on the coherence-promoting value of parallel structures, see Module IV, Chapter 2.5.

In addition to wanting to contrast two specific pieces of information, you may wish to pick out a specific piece of information for emphasis, without it being the most important, focal information in the clause. Again, fronting may be a useful device for this purpose, particularly if you want to pick up on information which has just been mentioned in the previous sentence. Here is an example:

> Various pressure groups organized campaigns to make it clear to everyone concerned that the environment would not benefit and the local communities would not benefit. **But arguments like these** the government were simply not willing to listen to. For them, economic arguments were all that counted.

The suggestion here is that the government may well have been prepared to listen to certain arguments, but definitely not these ones. There is thus a kind of implicit contrast between one particular kind of argument and all other possible kinds.

Actually, English is not as rigid as it might seem when it comes to fronting. For instance, under certain circumstances verbs and verb phrases can be fronted:

> Caxton was being a wise businessman. He wanted his book to sell. **And sell it did.** (Crystal 2006: 16)
> His critics hardly wanted him to continue, **but continue he did**.
> Most people thought that Blair could not lose the debate, **but lose it he did**.

What happens here is that the process described by the verb is taken as the starting point and then the event in question is either strongly confirmed or rejected. The fronting places much more rhetorical weight on the verb than would be the case if it was not fronted, and suggests a degree of surprise with respect to what one might expect to happen. Compare the following alternatives to the Caxton example:

> Caxton was being a wise businessman. He wanted his book to sell. **And it sold/ And it did sell.**

Fronting like this is admittedly relatively rare in English, also in academic writing (Biber et al. 1999); nevertheless, it may prove a valuable device if you are developing an argument where you want to compare an expected event with what actually happened.

2.3.3 *It*-clefts

If you want to put emphasis on a particular piece of information, but are constrained by the fact that English does not like the most important, focal information at the beginning of the clause, then under certain circumstances you can use a special construction called an *it*-cleft. Here are some examples:

It was only in October last year that the council decided to establish a new fund.
It was not until the 1960s that hanging was banned in Britain.
It is precisely in cases like this that one needs to be particularly careful.

German has this construction as well, and the meaning of the construction is basically the same in the two languages, but it is relatively more frequent in English, and is also structurally somewhat more versatile in English than in German. The *it*-cleft construction is appropriate when you want to identify one piece of information as the only relevant candidate from a range of options. In the first example the writer wishes to emphasize that of all the different kinds of cases where it might be important to be careful, there is one kind of case that sticks out, and wishes to identify the kind involved; this understanding is supported by the word *precisely*, which, like *gerade* or *genau* in German, serves to narrow down the reader's attention to the following item.[9]

The reason why the cleft construction is employed less frequently in German than in English is because it is often possible to produce the intended effect in German simply by making use of the clause-initial position. Here are some examples of clefts in English with equivalent formulations in German:

It is only since 5 October that the town has been allowed to bear the official title of *Hansestadt*.
Erst seit dem 5. Oktober darf die Stadt wieder den offiziellen Titel 'Hansestadt' führen.

It was precisely because of this development that it was decided to repeat the experiment.
Gerade aufgrund dieser Entwicklung wurde entschieden, das Experiment zu wiederholen.

It was only under these specific, formally agreed conditions that the parties were willing to continue negotiations.
Nur unter diesen besonderen, förmlich beschlossenen Bedingungen waren die Parteien bereit, die Verhandlungen weiterzuführen.

Note also that in the case of the first and third examples, a useful alternative would be an inversion construction:

---

9 For a wider ranging discussion of how *it*-clefts function in discourse, see Gómez-González (2007).

Only since 5 October has the town been allowed to bear the official title of *Hansestadt*.
Only under these specific, formally agreed conditions were the parties willing to continue negotiations.

The use of inversion of subject and auxiliary verb, which happens with clause-initial non-subject constituents modified by *only, hardly* and *never* (see section 2.1), awards the initial constituent a kind of natural relief. Just as with the *it*-cleft, it is immediately clear on reading this opening to the clause that the initial constituent should be stressed.

It-clefts have a fixed pattern:

It + BE + one focused constituent + that + clause

Notice that although the focused element does not occur strictly clause-initially, it is nevertheless the first content element of the construction, and thus is placed before all other content information. At the same time the construction fits into the basic S-V-C mould. Here are a few comments on the individual elements of the *it*-cleft.

- the word *it* tends very much to appear in initial position, but for purposes of emphasis (see 2.3.2 above) the focused constituent may also occur initially:

  Just then it was that the world realized that another crisis had arisen.

- BE stands for some form of the verb *be*. The tense of *be* may either agree with that of the following verb, or occur in the present tense. The latter option allows you as the writer to indicate that it is you who are emphasizing the following focused constituent. Unlike German, the verb *be* agrees with the preceding *it*, and not with the following focused constituent: it is therefore necessarily singular.

  It **was** others who made his life difficult back then.
  Es **waren** andere, die ihm das Leben damals schwer gemacht haben.

The constituents which are most commonly singled out for clefting (called the 'cleft element') are subject noun phrases and prepositional phrases (Gómez-González 2007: 128). However, it should be noted that fairly lengthy and complex constituents can also be focused in English clefts, making the construction more flexible than in German, as illustrated by the following example:

It is particularly when their husbands are on active duty that army wives are most concerned.
Besonders wenn ihre Männer im Einsatz sind, sind Soldatenehefrauen sehr besorgt.

- The normal element that appears after the focused element is *that*; where the focused constituent is a noun phrase, however, *wh*-forms such as *who(m)* or *which* are also possible:

  It is precisely these problems which the authors neglected.

  This final clause can be seen as a relative clause, but it is still customary to talk of a cleft construction.[10]

The cleft construction has various discourse functions. For instance, because of its central feature as a device which focuses the attention on one single piece of information, it is a particularly powerful construction to use when you wish to narrow down a domain of inquiry to one point. Consider a text such as the following:

[...] The Third World faces an enormous number of problems for which no solution appears to offer itself. There are ancient conflicts and rivalries that keep breaking through the surface; there is disease and limited medical facilities to deal with it; there is financial mismanagement, inexperience and corruption; and there is poverty, dire poverty. **It is the problem of poverty that** needs the most urgent attention. [...]

The second sentence lists a number of problems. The cleft construction that follows in the clause that forms the third sentence selects one of these (*It is the problem of poverty that needs the most urgent attention*), leading the reader to expect that this will be the topic of the text that is to come.

This selective, contrastive function of the cleft construction means that it is also frequently employed where the writer wishes to redirect the reader's attention. Then we find a combination of the cleft construction with *not... but*, or *not... Rather*, as in the following example, which displays two parallel instances:

While bilingualism and biculturalism may superficially appear to have a detrimental effect on personality, bilingualism is not likely to be the cause. That is, **it is not language that causes personality problems**. Rather, **it is often the social, economic and political conditions surrounding bilinguals that generate**

10 See, however, Huddleston & Pullum (2002: 1416) for a discussion of the difference between the relative clause in cleft constructions and in other constructions containing a relative clause.

> **such problems**. Where the bicultural community is stigmatized, seen as socially inferior, economically underprivileged, and where there is symbolic or physical violence towards the minority language community, personality problems within children may arise.
> (http://www.bwrdd-yr-iaith.org.uk/cynnwys.php?pID=faq&faqID=83&langID=2&search=x; Website of the Welsh Language Board, accessed 22 March 2008)

There is another use of the *it*-cleft which is rather different from the ones we have discussed so far. The prototypical use of the construction is in a context where the cleft constituent is the new, focal information in the clause and the rest of the clause represents given information. But this does not have to be the case. Consider the following example:

> The French also began asserting that Pointe Riche and Cape Ray were identical, and that the west coast of Newfoundland was therefore part of the original French Shore. In short, the geographical limits of the French Shore became a matter of considerable diplomatic debate in the 1760s, a debate that the British were determined not to lose. **It was this that** prompted the first-ever visit to Newfoundland's west coast by a serving governor in 1764 [...]. **It was also this that** motivated the British authorities into commissioning James Cook's cartographic survey work in Newfoundland during the 1760s, including on the west coast. (Janzen, http://www2.swgc.mun.ca/nfld_history/nfld_history_war.htm, accessed 22 March 2008)

The writer has decided to use clefts here rather than straightforward declarative clauses (*This prompted the first ever visit* ... and *This also motivated the British authorities*). The effect of the cleft construction is to highlight the importance of the British desire to win the debate by separating it from the rest of the information in the sentence. The paragraph can thus be divided into two halves: the first half contains a description of a rather static state of affairs and the second half focuses on the action which the British undertook in an attempt to win the debate.

SUMMARY OF THE *IT*-CLEFT

1. The *it*-cleft serves to focus on one constituent in a clause, by identifying it as the one and only piece of information which fits with regard to what is expressed by the rest of the clause.
2. Its use is more flexible and more frequent in English than in German.
3. It has a selective-contrastive function that makes it appropriate for introducing a particular detailed point for further development in the sentences that follow.
4. It is also used to pick up on a referent from the immediately preceding discourse as a topic of particular interest and say something more about it.

2.3.4 Pseudo-clefts

Whereas the *it*-cleft places the emphasized information at the beginning of the clause, the pseudo-cleft construction places this information at the end of the clause. Compare these two formulations, the second of which is a pseudo-cleft:

It is Steiner's bold use of metaphor that is most striking.
What is most striking is Steiner's use of metaphor.

Even without there being an explicit context here, the first example suggests a prior context in which something else was seen as most striking, or in which the issue of what was most striking had been discussed; in other words, this sentence appears to be an explicit reaction to something in the context, which is what one expects when new information is placed so early in the sentence. In the second example, by contrast, there is no presupposition concerning something specific that has already been mentioned; however, with the pseudo-cleft there is a suggestion that there is something in the context which might naturally give rise to a judgment about what is most striking, and there may even have been a specific question in the form of *What is most striking?*

The basic formula for the pseudo-cleft construction is as follows:

[*Wh-*...] + BE + one focused constituent

Let us consider some examples of pseudo-clefts:

Why it is now time to act is because there are only twenty years of coal resources left.
What the government has failed to consider is the effect on old-age pensioners.

These examples show that pseudo-clefts cleave a single clause into two clauses: the latter, for example, is the pseudo-cleft version of *The government has failed to consider the effect on old-age pensioners.* While the focused information appears after *is*, the rest of the clause is placed in an initial clause of its own which starts with a so-called *wh*-word, i.e. *what, where, when, why, how.* The effect is comparable to that of a question-answer sequence compressed into one sentence:

Q: What has the government failed to consider?
A: The effect on old-age pensioners.

Some comments are in order about each of the positions in the formula given above.

- If the *wh*-clause refers to a human being, it is not possible to begin with *who(m)*. The equivalent construction in German can begin with *wer*, although this is admittedly rare in academic German. In English, you have to use a longer expression such as *the one who, the person who*, possibly even replacing *person* by some more specific expression, as in:

  [The politician who had the greatest appeal] [was] [the former president].
  S V C

- Even where a simple *wh*-word is possible, there is a tendency to use longer expressions. Instead of *what*, for example, you could try using *the thing that*, or, to avoid the rather empty word *thing*, other possibilities such as *matter, concern, aspect*, etc. The corresponding long expressions are as follows:

what:	the thing that
why:	the reason that/why
how:	the way that/in which
where:	the place that/where
when:	the time/minute/day etc. that

  Here are some examples:

  The matter that the government has failed to consider is the effect on old-age pensioners.
  The reason that it is now time to act is because there are only twenty years of coal resources left.

  One advantage of using the 'long expression' is that you can expand the noun phrase with adjectives, etc.:

  The most important way in which the economy can be revitalized is by massive investment in the industries of the future.

- The position BE is filled by some form of the verb *be*, possibly further specified by a modal verb, adverbs, etc., as in:

  The time to tackle the problem of rising unemployment may well be now.

  Where you need a form of *be* that agrees with its subject, you have two options available. One possibility is to have *be* agree with the preceding *wh*-clause: if the clause begins with a *wh*-word, *be* will be necessarily singular; if the clause begins with a long expression, *be* will agree with that expression:

> The places that Goethe visited were all the important cities in the Italy of his time.

The other possibility is to let *be* agree with the following expression. This arises when the focused constituent is plural, as in this example:

> What is needed are more leaders prepared to put their country's interest ahead of personal gain.

Even though *What is needed* is the subject, the plurality of the focused constituent enforces plural agreement on *be*.

- The focused constituent, being in final position, can be of unlimited length, and often is indeed quite long. Here is a typical example, with a relatively short *wh*-clause and a lengthy focused constituent:

  > What is of particular interest is the possibility that there might be significant correlations between intelligence and self-perceptions of social competence, a matter that must be examined in future work.

In the previous section we saw that the cleft construction served to select one of a number of relevant candidates for consideration, leading the reader to expect the following text to give more information about the focused constituent. The pseudo-cleft, by contrast, has above all an announcing function: in the *wh*-clause, it picks up on a question that your reader will probably be asking himself and promises an answer to that question. This is why it is so popular at the beginning of lectures. When the lecturer starts speaking, the audience will be wondering what s/he is going to talk about. This situation then yields such announcements as this:

> What I am going to talk about today is how to improve your sales performance.

In writing, you can use the pseudo-cleft construction to arouse your readers' interest in what you will go on to say. After a general introductory statement, possibly at the beginning of a paragraph, you can use a pseudo-cleft to direct your reader to the matter that you wish to develop at greater length. Consider the following sequence:

> The management of personal finances is as important now as it ever was. What remains a constant factor is that every family should be prepared for any disasters that might befall it.

The use of the pseudo-cleft here strongly suggests to the reader that the following text will go into various ways in which a family can prepare itself for misfortune. This construction is thus particularly useful at turning points in the body of your text: where you have been dealing with some topic for a few paragraphs and want to move on to some new subject.

SUMMARY OF THE PSEUDO-CLEFT

1. The pseudo-cleft is recognizable by the initial *wh*-word, which, however, is often replaced by a 'long expression'.
2. It serves to announce the element expressed by the focused constituent.
3. It is particularly useful at turning points in your argument.

2.3.5 The *th-wh* construction

We now turn to a construction which bears some relation to the pseudo-cleft, the *th-wh* construction. An interesting feature of the pseudo-cleft construction is that the order of the information can in fact be reversed, as can be seen in these two examples:

> Sir Winston Churchill is the person who for most Britons remains synonymous with resistance to the foe.

This construction is also actually known as a reversed pseudo-cleft, but it does not have the same function as an ordinary pseudo-cleft. Rather than introducing Sir Winston Churchill into the discourse for further discussion, this merely provides a statement about him: Churchill is here given information, and is likely, in any text containing the other sentence, to have been mentioned before. Conversely, *the person who … the foe* is now new information.

This distribution (Given Subject + *be* + New *wh*-clause) is also found in a construction which is much used in English, and for which there is no structural equivalent in German. We call this the *th-wh* construction, for reasons that will become apparent from an examination of its format:

> *Th-* BE [*Wh-*...]

Here are some examples:

> If universal rules can be discovered, then we can learn about the thinking process. **This is why linguistics is so important**.
> But there are so many views to take into account. **This is where the scientist comes into his own**: a true scientist is totally dispassionate.

As with pseudo-clefts, the *th-wh* construction affords you the possibility of using a 'long expression' instead of the *wh*-word:

If universal rules can be discovered, then we can learn about the thinking process. **This is the reason that linguistics is so important**.
But there are so many views to take into account. **This is the point where the scientist comes into his own**: a true scientist is totally dispassionate.

Note that the *th-wh* construction cannot be reversed, at least in the intended context:

If universal rules can be discovered, then we can learn about the thinking process. *Why linguistics is so important is this.
But there are so many views to take into account. *Where the scientist comes into his own is this.

In both of the contextualized examples above, the word *this* refers back to the content of the previous sentence. But the reversed versions could only be acceptable if *this* referred forward, in which case they would be seen as pseudo-clefts, as in this example:

Why linguistics is so important is this: it helps us understand our thought processes.

Using the *th-wh* construction is a means of having accessible information in initial position which at the same time is the grammatical subject. In particular, it serves to provide a link with the preceding text, while emphasizing that the link is specific to the matter at hand. There is an implicit rejection of any other possibilities. In German, this is achieved by placing any one of a number of conjunctive adverbials in initial position, rather than the grammatical subject:

URLs tell us a lot about the owner of the site. For instance, a lot of site addresses end in com. **That is how** we can see that it must be a commercial site.
So kann man erkennen, dass es sich um eine kommerzielle Internetseite handelt.

The implication of the last sentence is '... and there is no other way'. Had the sentence been formulated as *In that way we can see that it must be a commercial site*, the reader would have been free to conclude that there are also other ways of attaining that aim.

It is important that you understand the context in which the *th-wh* construction is appropriate. Imagine a passage listing all the various objections that have been voiced in Britain to the European Union (centralist bureaucracy; nit-picking regulations; fishing reserves opened to foreigners; threats to national institutions; etc.). If you want to make a specific link between these objections and British unwillingness to enter into closer ties with Europe, then the *th-wh* construction is your only possibility. If you had an idea in mind using something like *deshalb ...*, then it would not be appropriate to use *therefore* in English:

!!Therefore there is great unwillingness in Great Britain to participate more fully in the European Union.
Deshalb herrscht in Großbritannien ein großer Unwille, sich in der Europäischen Union stärker zu engagieren.

This would suggest that your main communicative intention is simply to assert that on the basis of the complex situation you have described one can draw a particular conclusion, namely that there is unwillingness. By contrast, using the *th-wh* construction suggests that there is a particular situation which obtains (in fact, the unwillingness may have already been hinted at in the preceding context) and there is one specific set of reasons why this situation obtains, namely the reasons you have just given.

SUMMARY OF THE *TH-WH* CONSTRUCTION

1. The *th-wh* construction is used to forge a link between a sentence and preceding text where you wish to make it clear that the link is the only relevant one.
2. Unlike pseudo-clefts, it is not reversible.
3. English uses a grammatical subject to express the link with the previous sentence, where German would normally use an adverbial expression.

2.3.6 Non-agent subjects

The desire to have accessible themes and at the same time have initial subjects has meant that quite a number of frequently used verbs in English have taken on a rather special use. Verbs which in their most frequent use have human subjects functioning as the agent in a process have developed an additional use with a non-human, non-actor as subject. Thus alongside the standard use of the verb *discuss* with a person as subject, this verb is also used with subjects like *book, film, television programme, article* etc.

The producer discussed his new series with a group of footballers' wives.
Bosworth's new book discusses the origins of obesity in both Europe and Asia.

We can distinguish a number of subcategories, according to the underlying semantic relationship between the subject and the verb: (a) location and instrument, (b) cause, (c) time, place and events, and (d) text location.

a) Location and instrument as subject

The most telling examples of the location of an event functioning as subject are undoubtedly *sleep* and *dine*.

> Many tents today can sleep eight without any difficulty.
> This table does not look particularly big but in fact it dines six.

Of course, tents cannot sleep and tables cannot dine. Rather, the first sentence will be interpreted as meaning that it is a property of many tents that eight people can sleep in them; and the idea in the second sentence is that it is a property of the table that six people can dine at it. Such formulations are quite common in advertising language because they promote the product. This is particularly clear in the following example, where it appears as if the object referred to by the grammatical subject is capable of doing things on its own.

> This drill bores holes in any wall.

By contrast, the formulations in the sentences below are admittedly more logical, but they are less punchy, and also less idiomatic.

> In many tents today eight people can sleep without any difficulty.
> This table does not look particularly big but in fact six people can dine at it.
> With this drill one can bore holes in any wall.

Here are some more examples of how the choice of a locative or instrumental subject can make the clause more idiomatic:

> But with these arrangements the problem can be solved.
> → But these arrangements can solve the problem.
> In London the highest temperature of the day was recorded.
> → London recorded the highest temperature of the day.

b) Cause as subject

Highly frequent verbs like *make, bring,* and *give* are also used with a non-animate subject. Usually the subject will refer to some kind of event which is causally related to the event described in the sentence at hand. In the examples below, the second sentence in each pair is stylistically more compact than the first.

> With this new agreement the top tennis players have become the best earners in the sports world.
> → **This new agreement** makes the top tennis players the best earners in the sports world.

Due to these recent developments the railways have come to a standstill.
→ **These recent developments** have brought the railways to a standstill.

From this one might get the impression that Amis has become obsessed with London.
→ **This** might give the impression that Amis has become obsessed with London.

Because there is a greater tendency in English for the clause-initial position to be occupied by the subject, we advise you to make good use of the causal subject formulations, which are rather more idiomatic.

c) Time, place, and events as subject
Using the verbs *see, witness* and *mark,* it is possible to present places, events and expressions of time as the subject:

In 1966 Wembley witnessed one of the greatest travesties of justice the sporting world has ever seen.
The introduction of the language laboratory marked the start of a continual revolution.
These early years saw the beginning of Britain's cotton industry.

d) Text location as subject
Finally, a small group of verbs that are commonly used in academic writing allow a locative subject which refers to a text or part of a text. Here are some examples, together with German equivalents, most of which make use of initial prepositional phrases as equivalents for the English subjects:

This study examines the impact of marital stress on young children's development.
In dieser Studie werden die Auswirkungen von Eheproblemen auf die Entwicklung von jungen Kindern untersucht.

The present article provides an answer to all of these questions.
In diesem Artikel werden alle diese Fragen beantwortet.

The first section reviews the literature and the second section presents a new hypothesis.
Im ersten Teil wird die relevante Literatur besprochen, und im zweiten Teil wird eine neue Hypothese präsentiert.

Figure 3 illustrates the correlation.
Abbildung 3 zeigt die Korrelation.

None of the leading newspapers have reviewed his new novel.
Keine der führenden Zeitungen hat seinen neuen Roman besprochen.

Research has clearly shown that ...
Studien haben klar festgestellt, dass ...

The text clearly states that ...
In diesem Text wird deutlich behauptet, dass ...

To a certain extent, German has developed this possibility too, as can be seen from some of the equivalents given here, but the construction is more widespread in English, again probably because of the preference in English for having the first position of the clause filled by the grammatical subject.

2.4 Establishing a special kind of starting point: framing

As we noted in 2.2, various kinds of information can be placed before the subject of the clause. This information will typically be expressed either as a non-clausal adverbial or as an adverbial or participial clause. As a result, we find that in academic writing, about 40% of sentences do not start with the subject of the main clause but with one of those other elements (Tavecchio 2010: Ch. 5). Interestingly, advanced learner writing does not differ significantly in this respect, but there is evidence in learner writing of less variation, both syntactically and semantically (cf. Hannay & Martínez Caro 2008). We saw in section 2.3.2 that under very special circumstances major constituents such as objects can come before the subject, but in fact it is much more common for adverbial elements to do so. In this section we deal briefly with the different kinds of adverbial elements which you can place before the subject of the clause in order to frame your message.

Framing is an important method for organizing your clauses because it allows you, in a very compact form, to present the content of what you want to say from a particular point of view. This can help the reader to construct a coherent interpretation of the text and to understand your authorial view on the content. By having a command of the full range of expression types you will be able to enhance the continuity and variety of your written prose.

For the time being we will restrict ourselves to frames consisting of a single phrasal constituent. Frames consisting of clauses, as well as framing patterns consisting of two or more constituents, are discussed in Chapter 3 within the context of complex sentences.

A standard distinction is made between circumstantial, conjunctive and stance adverbials. Circumstantial adverbials give information about various circumstances relating to the action or state described by the verb; conjunctive adverbials provide a link between the content of the previous sentence and the clause they introduce; stance adverbials express a particular viewpoint about the content of the upcoming clause. Many of these expressions will typically be found at the beginning of the clause for framing purposes.[11]

2.4.1 Circumstantial adverbials

Adjuncts express circumstances such as time, place, purpose, reason and manner. Time and place adjuncts often occur in initial position, where they provide a spatio-temporal framework for the information which follows, and are particularly useful when you want to organize whole stretches of text from a temporal or spatial point of view. Here is an example from a local history book:

> **For a very long period** the Howards had dominated the political life of the town, and **until 1832** one of the Howards was an M.P. and the other member was often a relative. There were always aristocratic connections and sons of peers first made their way into the House of Commons at considerable cost. **From 1796 to 1902** William Huskisson was M.P. for Morpeth with the Hon. George Howard. Huskisson was later killed on 15 September 1830 at the ceremonial opening of the Liverpool to Manchester Railway. **After 1832** the political scene was more peaceful with William Ord, followed by Sir George Grey. **Then** came a great shock. **In 1868** the vote was extended, so that many working men, including miners, were enfranchised. (Rowland 1989: 5)

By placing the expressions of time at the beginning of the sentence rather than in their unmarked position towards the end, there is a single dominant frame expressed which makes the sentences belong together more. Interestingly, the one time adverbial which is not fronted – *on 15 September 1830* – relates to a date which is backgrounded to the overall history of who dominated Morpeth. Consider what would happen if you placed all the other time expressions at the end of the clause rather than at the beginning:

> The Howards had dominated the political life of the town **for a very long period**, and one of the Howards was an M.P. **until 1832** and the other member was often a relative. There were always aristocratic connections and sons of peers first made their way into the House of Commons at considerable cost. William Huskisson was M.P. for Morpeth with the Hon. George Howard **from 1796 to 1902**. Huskisson was later killed on 15 September 1830 at the ceremonial opening of the Liverpool to Manchester Railway. The political scene was more peaceful **after 1832** with

11 For excellent grammatical overviews of these different types of adverbial expression, see Modules 8 and 20 of Downing & Locke (2006) and Chapter 10 of Biber et al. (1999).

William Ord, followed by Sir George Grey. A great shock **then** came. The vote was extended **in 1868**, so that many working men, including miners, were enfranchised.

This now comes over as a rather disjointed paragraph without any clear organizational principle.

2.4.2 Conjunctive adverbials

Conjunctive adverbials provide information which links two independent clauses. There are five basic types:

Contrastive:	*however, nevertheless, on the contrary, rather, what is more*
Additive:	*moreover, furthermore, in addition*
Summative:	*all in all, in conclusion*
Causal:	*consequently, therefore, because of this, for this reason*
Temporal:	*first, first of all, finally*

Conjunctive adverbials can in fact appear in different positions in the clause, but initial position is quite common for the simple reason that these adverbials basically connect two independent clauses, and a position between the two clauses in question is the logical position.[12] You should note that with the exception of *therefore*, all conjunctive adverbials are typically separated from the rest of the sentence by means of a comma (see also Chapter 4.2.4 for more details on punctuation at the beginning of the sentence).

2.4.3 Stance adverbials

Stance adverbials can be split into three categories: epistemic, attitude and style adverbials.[13] Epistemic adverbials express the writer's comment on some aspect of the truth of the proposition expressed by the relevant clause:

Obviously, any rise in the sea level may have terrible consequences for coastal towns.
In fact, what the critics were trying to point out was that the performance was essentially under par.
According to Smith (1999), the proportion of serious road accidents caused during the first five minutes of a journey was more than 30% of the total number.
Many people hold the view that all language is actually metaphorical, because it developed by people using familiar words in unfamiliar contexts. **On this view**

12 In Chapter 3.4.1 we discuss the rhetorical and organizational value of placing conjunctive adverbials like *however* in the second position in the clause.

13 One comes across different labels in the various grammatical descriptions of these phenomena. Here we follow Biber et al. (1999: 854ff).

('in dieser Sichtweise'), language is not a game, and metaphor is not just another literary device.
In grammatical terms ('grammatisch gesehen'), this sentence is clearly correct, but it is hardly idiomatic.

Attitude adverbials express the writer's opinion about the content of the clause:

Pandemonium broke out when one of the delegates walked out. **Wisely**, the world governing body decided to delay the vote until the next meeting.
Quite rightly, all parties concerned backed the decision.
Interestingly, the only grammatical category not represented is the adverb.
As one might expect, the teaching unions reacted to the news by issuing a strike warning.
Clearly, what we are dealing with here is a rather bad case of sophistry.

The use of simple adverbs as attitudinal adverbials is characteristic of English, and English has rather more of them than German (cf. Hannay 1989). Their value in writing is that they form a very compact and elegant way of expressing an opinion on what you are talking about, without pushing yourself into the foreground. The attitudinal adverb is also a neat alternative to the attitudinal clause. Compare the following:

It is interesting to note that the only grammatical category not represented is the adverb.
('es fällt auf, dass; bemerkenswert ist, dass')

It is quite right that all parties concerned backed the decision.
('völlig zu Recht haben ...')

It is clear that what we are dealing with here is a rather bad case of sophistry.
('es ist offensichtlich, dass')

Notice that with the attitudinal adverbial formulation, the content of the main clause is actually being asserted. However, depending on the adjective phrase used, the embedded clause in this latter construction may be seen as containing presupposed information, as is the case here with *it is right that ...*

Finally, style adverbials form a rather special class. They express the writer's view regarding the actual formulation of the sentence which follows (cf. Module III, Chapter 4.2.2, on paraphrase).

Put more simply, form is just as important as function. ('einfacher ausgedrückt')
In short, the UN made a mistake. ('kurz gesagt')
Technically speaking, this is a simile and not a metaphor. ('strenggenommen')

In the first example one might imagine a prior context in which the writer has set out a rather detailed argument which s/he now wishes to paraphrase; in other words, the value of the formulation which follows is that it is in simple language. Likewise, the value of the main clause in the second example is that it is brief. And in the last example the writer is making clear that s/he is using technical language. These are all cases of the writer being explicit about how s/he has chosen to formulate his/her ideas, and they can have a clear rhetorical function in the build-up of an argument.

2.5 Organizing the end point

If you employ the constructions we presented in 2.3, then – with the notable exception of *it*-clefts, which are designed to have the focal information appear early in the utterance – you will find that the new, focal information tends to appear naturally at the end of the clause. But in addition, there are various operations that you can perform on the basic clause which are solely designed to place information at the end, in the prominent focus position. What is characteristic of these constructions is that the grammatical status of the final constituent would normally be associated with a much earlier position in the clause.

2.5.1 Extraposition

The first construction worth mentioning in terms of final position is extraposition, both of the subject and the object. Extraposition occurs when the subject or object is presented at the end of the clause and the dummy element *it* is placed in the position which the constituent in question would normally occupy.

> It came as no surprise **that smoking was eventually banned in all public places**.
> The tobacco industry considered it a disgrace **that they had not been properly consulted**.

With some verbs, subject extraposition is in fact obligatory in English:

> It so happens **that the Government did an immediate volte-face**.
> *That the Government did an immediate volte-face so happens.

> It appears **that the Government is going to have to back down on the matter of cuts to the National Health Service**.
> *That the Government is going to have to back down on the matter of cuts to the National Health Service appears.

However, this is only the case with a small number of verbs. It should be noted that despite the fact that extraposition is optional in the vast majority of cases, it is also in essence the unmarked form. This is because the elements extraposed are themselves clauses and as such are structurally complex and quite often rather long. Combined with the fact that they very often express new information, this means that sentences with extraposed subject and object clauses are comparatively easy to process. The marked form occurs when they appear in their pattern position:

> **That smoking was eventually banned in all public places** came as no surprise.
> The tobacco industry considered the fact **that they had not been properly consulted** a disgrace.

These sentences will occur in a context where the *that*-clauses express given information and where the expressions *no surprise* and *a disgrace* are clearly in focus.

2.5.2 Discontinuous structures

Normally when you construct a clause, you will produce each constituent in turn. For instance, you would not normally produce the verb until you have finished with the subject. Sometimes you will wish to modify a subject or an object constituent, and may end up producing a sentence like this:

> ?A number of major differences between the two best-selling stomach tablets have been found.

But the result here is top-heavy, with the verb phrase coming as an insignificant-sounding appendage to a lengthy subject. A solution can be found to this case of what we call frontal overload (see 2.6.1 below) in adopting a discontinuous structure, i.e. one in which part of the subject, namely the postmodifier, is placed after the verb phrase:

> → A number of major differences have been found between the two best-selling stomach tablets.

The phrase *between the two best-selling stomach tablets* still grammatically postmodifies the semantic head of the subject (*differences*), but is separated from the rest of the subject by the verb phrase: the subject is, in other words, discontinuous. Here are some more examples:

> The suggestion was made that the solution might be found in a replication of the experiment.

An assessment was undertaken of the effect of advertising material on underage drinkers.
The question then arose of what contribution the public should pay.

Relative clauses, too, may be separated from their antecedent and placed at the end of the clause:

Five subjects were found who were willing to submit themselves to electric shock treatment.

You can also opt for a discontinuous structure when dealing with a long object, particularly where it is followed by a complement. In the following example, the object is so long that the subsequent complement is difficult to link back to the main verb *send*:

?The king sent three men who had dared to question his sole right to decide the fate of the country into exile.

The problem can be solved by again separating the relative clause and creating a discontinuous object:

→ The king sent three men into exile who had dared to question his sole right to decide the fate of the country.

The advantage in all these cases is that the new information is placed at the end of the clause. Processing is also eased because the elements concerned are quite long.

2.5.3 Dative shift

One of the most well known alternations in English is between the order indirect object – direct object and direct object – prepositional phrase:

A People who commit suicide often leave their loved ones a short note.
B People who commit suicide often leave a short note for their loved ones.

The difference between these two formulations is that as a rule the A version will be interpreted with *a short note* as focus, whereas in the B version *for their loved ones* will be seen as the most important information. This is quite a straightforward application of the principle of End Focus. Note that a third option is this:

C People who commit suicide often leave for their loved ones a short note.

This has the same order of information as version A but instead of an indirect object following the verb we have a prepositional phrase. The difference between the two formulations lies in the greater formality of version C (version A is stylistically neutral) and also in the extra tension created in version C because there is a sense that the object has been purposely delayed. What we have here is in fact an example of a different device, namely object postponement, and we will now proceed to treat this separately.

2.5.4 Object postponement

One of the most well-known basic rules of English grammar relates to the position of adverbial expressions in the middle of the sentence. Whereas initial and final position are both acceptable, and are related to specific functions, medial position between the verb and the direct object is regarded as at least dispreferred:

Later the victims described their ordeal.
The victims **later** described their ordeal.
The victims described their ordeal **later**.
?The victims described **later** their ordeal.

Smith and his co-workers examined the results **in an elaborate manner**.
In an elaborate manner Smith and his co-workers examined the results.
?Smith and his co-workers examined **in an elaborate manner** the results.

For a number of specific cases the producer accepted the author's criticism.
The producer accepted the author's criticism **for a number of specific cases**.
?The producer accepted **for a number of specific cases** the author's criticism.

But in fact this position in the middle of the clause between the transitive verb and its direct object is often an elegant option for adverbial expressions. Because the object does not appear in its expected position immediately following the verb, we talk of object postponement. First, compare the following two sentences:

?It would appear that it is necessary to specify the conditions under which smoking may be allowed in public spaces **more precisely**.
→ It would appear that it is necessary to specify **more precisely** the conditions under which smoking may be allowed in public spaces.

The formulation in the first sentence is a case of object postponement, and is to be preferred to the second sentence: it is clear that *more precisely* modifies *specify* and not *be allowed*, but in the first sentence, the considerable distance between *specify* and *more precisely* makes processing more difficult. The rhetorical effect of this device is considerable. After a transitive verb, the reader will be expecting the object constituent to appear next, but in this formulation, something else happens. The outcome is twofold: first, the adverbial itself achieves a degree of prominence similar to what it would have in clause-initial position but without acquiring the associated framing function; second, the direct object is made more prominent because its appearance has been delayed, as a result of which the information acquires something of a presentative status (see 2.5.5 below).

Object postponement is of course restricted to those cases where the information presented by the object is the most important, focal information in the clause. Usually it is applied where the object constituent is long, but it is also possible with relatively short object constituents which are clearly weighty in communicative terms.

Let us look at a few examples which illustrate the functioning of object postponement in context. In the following example, the writer is commencing a new paragraph and postpones the object to make sure it appears in final position, since it in fact constitutes the main subject matter of what is to come.

> [New paragraph] In court, such litigants strive to introduce into the trial the **details of their social lives**. Their accounts of their troubles emphasize the social networks in which they are situated, often to the exclusion of the contractual, financial, and property issues that are typically of greater interest to the court. Even an event such as an automobile accident involving strangers may be described in terms of the social history of the parties. (Conley & O'Barr 1990: 58)

The presentative effect of postponement allows the topic of the paragraph to be more clearly announced.

Let us return to an earlier example:

> On a rather less general, but still very general, level, we might identify in the domain of politics **a discourse of liberalism**, and within the economic domain **a 'Taylorist' discourse of management.** By contrast, in Fairclough (2000b) I discussed the political discourse of the 'third way', i.e. the discourse of 'New Labour', which is a discourse attached to a particular position within the political field at a particular point in time (the discourse is certainly less than a decade old). (Fairclough 2003: 125)

Here the author is contrasting the political with the economic domain and a discourse of liberalism with a discourse of management. But the contrast that is relevant for the argument is the latter, since the author continues by introducing a third kind of discourse, the discourse of New Labour. The use of the postponement strategy places the discourses on centre stage rather than the domains, ready to be picked up in the following sentence.

A similar point can be made about this example, which we looked at briefly in 2.2.2:

> The availability of two different perspectives – stemming from two different ways of defining discourse – is partially responsible for the tremendous scope of discourse analysis. If we focus on structure, our task is to identify and analyze constituents, determine procedures for assigning to utterances **a constituent status**, discover regularities underlying combinations of constituents (perhaps even formulating rules for producing those regularities), and make principled decisions about whether or not particular arrangements are well formed. If we focus on function, on the other hand, our task is to identify and analyze actions performed by people for certain purposes, interpret social, cultural, and personal meanings, and justify our interpretations of those meanings for the participants involved. (Schiffrin 1994: 42)

In the second sentence of this segment the author presents a list of three tasks, and the object of the verb in each case involves something relating to constituents. If there had been no postponement in the second of the three parts of the list, there would not have been such a single emphasis on constituents throughout the list, and this emphasis makes sense given the writer's focus on structural aspects of language.

2.5.5 Presentatives

In 2.1 we briefly mentioned the presentative construction as making use of a highly specialized grammatical mould, P – Vfin – Vnon-fin – S.[14] Here are some examples:

[Underlying this argument]	are		[a number of important assumptions].
P	Vfin		S
[Working alongside the agency]	have	been	[a number of countryside groups].
P	Vfin	Vnon-fin	S

Implicit in the theory is the presupposition that all gun owners are potentially violent.

Of particular interest is the possibility that there might be significant correlations between intelligence and self-perceptions of social competence, a matter that must be examined in future work.

---

14 In some grammars this construction is treated under the heading of 'inversion' (e.g. Biber et al. 1999: 911). Here we restrict inversion to the type exemplified by *But in no case has an answer been found*, where the normal order of subject and finite verb form is reversed (cf. 2.1 above). We use the label 'presentative' because this focuses on the communicative function of the construction; for us, the grammatically significant feature of the construction is thus the clause-final position of the subject.

Note that the initial position is occupied by a constituent that one would otherwise expect to find towards the end of a sentence, such as a non-finite verb phrase, as in *underlying this argument,* an adjective phrase, as in *implicit in this theory,* or a prepositional phrase, as in *of particular interest.*

It is important to note that this construction can usually only be used in English under two interlinked conditions. Firstly, the initial element may not consist of one word only. For instance, the adjective phrase must contain a modification:

No less interesting is the claim that ...
Implicit throughout the book is the expectation that ...
*Interesting is the claim that ...
*Implicit is the expectation that ...

Whereas in German we find sentences that begin with a bare adjective followed by *sein* or some other copula, this is not usually possible in English. In the following example, you could express the message conveyed by the German sentence by means of a pseudo-cleft, or otherwise you could add an element linking the notion of importance to the previous context.

A Wichtig ist die Einsicht, dass diese Städte zumindest die Voraussetzungen für eine Fußgängerzone besitzen.
B *Important is the insight that these towns at least fulfil the requirements for a pedestrian precinct.
C → **What is important is** the insight that these towns at least fulfil the requirements for a pedestrian precinct.
D → **Important in this regard** is the insight that these towns at least fulfil the requirements for a pedestrian precinct.

The second requirement is that the initial constituent must contain some link to the immediately preceding context. In the following example, *also necessary* picks up on *will require* in the previous sentence:

Achieving this goal will require a much greater understanding of the perspectives and culture of the various ethnic, racial, social, age and sexual orientation groups that currently make up the national population. **Also necessary is a better understanding of the effects of different intervention strategies among different populations**.

Not surprisingly, expressions such as *also, equally, no less,* and comparative constructions (*Far more likely* ...) are frequently found in such initial elements of presentative constructions. Among the common patterns found in academic writing are the following:

Of equal/major/particular/prime (etc.) importance is/are ...
Of greatest/major/particular/primary (etc.) concern is/are
Of greatest/lesser/particular/special interest is/are ...
Just as surprising is ...

The examples we have seen so far all contain the verb *be*, but other verbs are also possible after a prepositional phrase:

To the class of irregular plurals belong a range of nouns, some Anglo-Saxon in origin, others from as far afield as Arabic.
Into this group fall a small category of exceptions to the general rule.

Another possibility is to use a verb in the passive:

Among other outstanding contributions to twentieth-century physics should be mentioned Einstein's unsurpassed work on relativity theory.

The function of the presentative construction is to introduce a focused subject into the discourse. The construction should thus only be used where you wish to produce that kind of expectation. This means of course that the presentative construction has much the same function as the pseudo-cleft, but it differs from the pseudo-cleft in that its initial element is so firmly anchored in the preceding text.

The presentative construction is particularly well suited to introducing a focused subject in the form of a list, as in this example:

This book deals with a number of matters. **Among them are the pronunciation of Standard English, the major regional accents, the American, Australian and Indian varieties, and an introduction to phonological theory**.

Again, the reader's expectation will be that this text will continue with an elaboration of each of the 'matters' listed in the clause that forms the second sentence.

SUMMARY OF THE PRESENTATIVE

1. The presentative has its own special grammatical mould, with the subject at the end.
2. It serves to introduce the focused subject into the discourse.
3. The initial element is more or less explicitly linked to information in the preceding context.

2.6 What goes wrong in clause construction

When building clauses, learners who are quite advanced and who have mastered the basic clause patterns of English still get into problems. Either they have not fully mastered one of the less common patterns, or otherwise they have failed to arrange the given and new elements in the clause in a way which fits in with the clause-building principles which we have identified in this chapter.

In this section we detail a number of problems that we have identified in advanced learners' writing in English.

2.6.1 Frontal overload

One of the major weaknesses in texts written by advanced learners with regard to information distribution is the production of clauses with what we call frontal overload. Here are two examples:

> ?For MCA, at a cut off of 11 U/ml a sensitivity of 30% and a specificity of 87% is reached.
>
> ?In the diverted ethics discussion, aside from the potential dangers of special problem areas (nuclear energy, genetic engineering, information technology) the possibilities for a 'rational' guidance of technology and a responsible self-limitation are being debated. (Ventola 1995: 100)

These clauses are grammatically correct, but they do not flow well. First there are two framing elements (and in the second case there is additional parenthetical information into the bargain) and these are followed by a focal subject; the clauses are then rounded off with passive verb forms which do not carry any significant communicative weight. These clauses are clearly top-heavy in terms of information distribution: there is too much at the beginning and nothing of any communicative significance at the end. For ease of processing, however, the best thing is to have the thematic information separate from the focal information, and a good way of doing this is to formulate clauses in such a way that the verb acts as a kind of balancing point between the two. The first example above could be rewritten as follows:

> → For MCA, a cut off of 11 U/ml produces a sensitivity of 30% and a specificity of 87%.

This reformulation makes use of a non-agentive subject (see 2.3.6) and an active transitive verb rather than a passive verb: what was a prepositional phrase in the first version has kept its thematic position in the sentence but it has changed its grammatical status, and the original subject has now become the object.

The second example might be rewritten as follows:

→ In the diverted ethics discussion, aside from the potential dangers of special problem areas (nuclear energy, genetic engineering, information technology), a debate is being conducted about the possibilities for a 'rational' guidance of technology and a responsible self-limitation.

Here we still have quite a lengthy first part to the clause, but this is balanced by making sure that the new information concerning the subject of the debate occurs after the main verb and not before it. The key to the reformulation here is that the notion of debating is no longer expressed in the verb but in the grammatical subject. Moreover, the subject has been kept short by making use of a discontinuous structure which allows the postmodifier *about the possibilities* … to occur in clause-final position.

Here are some more examples which show how applying some of the techniques we have presented in this chapter can solve the problem of frontal overload. The first sentence has a case of overload and the second sentence has relieved that overload, either by placing the focal information in clause-final position or by reducing the number of framing elements:

?Even so, the document was widely held to be fair and reasonable. Mr Perez de Cuellar urged the Argentines to accept, but **to his final communication with Buenos Aires no reply** was given.
→ Even so, the document was widely held to be fair and reasonable. Mr Perez de Cuellar urged the Argentines to accept, but his final communication with Buenos Aires received no reply. [change of subject; focus to the end]

?First of all, there is the recession in the sectors of the economy in which the mafia has always had great influence: construction and shipbuilding. **In the South, which has a tradition of high unemployment, in order to get a job one** had to go to the mafia rather than to the government.
→ First of all, there is the recession in the sectors of the economy in which the mafia has always had great influence: construction and shipbuilding. In the South, which has a tradition of high unemployment, getting a job meant having to go to the mafia rather than to the government. [change of subject]

?Usually, Americans take it as a matter of course that **by Western civilization the American way of life** is meant.
→ Usually, Americans take it as a matter of course that what is meant by Western civilization is the American way of life. [change of subject using pseudo-cleft; focus to the end]

In short, if you concentrate on making sure that the most important information in each clause actually comes at the end, then you have a good chance of producing a well-balanced clause in terms of information distribution, and this is just as important as producing clauses which are grammatically correct.

2.6.2 Bad textual fit

In 2.2.3 we stressed the importance of creating a good textual fit for promoting coherence, and gave some examples of bad textual fit arising from an inappropriate grammatical choice on the part of the writer. Here is another example. This time the choice of an active verb form has resulted not only in frontal overload – witness the long focal subject – but also in bad textual fit, since *this*, the last word of the main clause of the last sentence, refers back to the content of the previous sentence but is far removed from it.

> As a result of Turkey's growing tourist industry, relations between citizens changed. However, a much more important reason for the change in relations is that many Turks now have western partners. **?The need to establish contacts with Europeans, especially today when it is more difficult to obtain a work permit for a European country, caused this**.

The straightforward way to rectify the lack of fit here is to make the main verb passive instead of active:

> → This was caused by the need to establish contacts with Europeans, especially today when it is more difficult to obtain a work permit for a European country.

Here are some examples where a different choice of active or passive would improve the textual fit and remove frontal overload. In each pair of examples, the second version is to be preferred.

> ?Another threat is caused by expanding industries, which serve the economy well, but much damage and pollution are involved with these developments so that unprecedented numbers of several kinds of animals are facing extinction.
> → Another threat is caused by expanding industries, which serve the economy well, but which cause so much damage and pollution that unprecedented numbers of several kinds of animals are facing extinction.

> ?Instead of bombing wrecks to burn the pollutants, the way oil spills were dealt with 25 years ago, sprays to disperse the oil, booms to contain it and suction and pumping devices are now used.
> → Unlike 25 years ago, when pollutants were burnt by bombing the wrecks, oil spills are now removed by means of sprays to disperse the oil, booms to contain it, and with the help of suction and pumping devices.

2.6.3 Unclear focus signalling

Written English really likes to have the most important information at the end of the clause. Although it is by no means always the case that this information appears clause-finally, placing information in final position is nevertheless quite a clear signal to the reader that you intend this information to be interpreted as focal. It is thus of paramount importance that you do not give your reader confusing signals about what you regard as the most important piece of information in the clause. Let us consider a case where the writer has been less than successful:

> ?Noise pollution will be experienced personally by everyone; in other words it is subjective.

The expressions *personally* and *by everyone* both naturally attract some attention: they have an intrinsic prominence that will lead them to be pronounced with a certain emphasis. On top of that, *by everyone* appears in final position in the clause. One would therefore expect, irrespective of the context, that the writer considers *by everyone* to be the information in focus in this sentence. However, from the clause following the semicolon we see that this was not in fact the writer's intention. The key phrase here is *in other words*, which is used by writers to reformulate important points using often more straightforward language, for instance to make a strong rhetorical point or to explain a new or difficult concept. The point is that such a reformulation always reveals what the writer's most important point was in the previous utterance, and we see here that it relates to the notion of subjectivity, which strongly suggests that it is the expression *personally* which is intended to carry the information focus in the previous clause. For that reason, a more effective order would be as follows:

> → Noise pollution will be experienced by everyone personally; in other words it is subjective.

The same problem is present in the following example:

> ?Schiphol will have grown into one of the most important airports of Europe by the year 2015; in other words it will have become a mainport.

The impression is given in the first clause here that *by the year 2015* is important information. This stems perhaps from the choice of the expression in final position, and also from the extra words in the formulation, *by the year 2015* instead of simply *by 2015*. The result is a kind of intrinsic salience, but from the rest of the segment it becomes clear that what the writer intends to be the focal information in that clause is in fact *one of the most important airports of Europe*. A better formulation would be something like this:

→ By the year 2015 Schiphol will have grown into one of the most important airports of Europe; in other words it will have become a mainport.

Here is another example which points up another aspect of the value of end focus:

?Many students have to accept a job that they do not like after a period of applying and being rejected, and most of the time this job is beneath their standards.

In this case, the best position for the temporal phrase *after a period of applying and being rejected* is again at the beginning of the sentence, where it can function as a frame for the whole sentence:

→ After a period of applying and being rejected, many students have to accept a job that they do not like, and most of the time this job is beneath their standards.

There are two clear advantages to this. First, the distance between the two mentions of *job* is smaller, and second, there is a clearer emphasis on the two focus elements (*a job they do not like* and *beneath their standards*), which are related to each other in that they both represent negative features of the jobs concerned.

Finally, here is an interesting case where it is not the order of information at clause level that is important but the order at phrase level:

?The only slight increase might be explained by the fact that our sample did not comprise institutionalized women.

What the writer is seeking to point out here is that the fact that the increase was only small might have a certain explanation; he is not singling out one kind of increase from others as being the only one that was slight. In other words, the phrase *only slight* might be seen as ambiguous, and it is not immediately clear that *slight* is intended to be stressed. Compare German *die einzige geringe Zunahme* and *die nur geringe Zunahme*. Because the word *only* in English does not give the reader sufficient information concerning where the focus of information is to be found in the noun phrase, word order has to be called in to help. The readability of the sentence can be significantly improved by incorporating the important information in a relative clause:

→ The fact that the increase was only slight might be explained by the composition of our sample, which did not comprise institutionalized women.

The new formulation has *only slight* at the end of the noun phrase rather than in a premodifying position, and here it will be naturally read as being in focus within the information unit constituted by the noun phrase.

2.7 Overview

This chapter has been about the clause as a grammatical mould for building sentences. We have seen that English has a rigid grammatical frame, but that you can use this basic frame to develop a broad syntactic repertoire in your writing. To do this, it is essential to think in terms of the information structure which underlies each message you want to convey. On the one hand, you can make special use of initial and final position while retaining the basic frame; on the other hand, you can develop your repertoire by using a range of special constructions which allow information to occur in a particular position in the sentence.

We round off with some basic advice regarding how to organize information in the clause, with a view to broadening your grammatical repertoire.

- Make lexical and grammatical choices that ensure that the initial constituent consists of accessible information and the final constituent expresses the most important information.
- Make appropriate use of adverbial expressions at the beginning of the sentence to establish a framework for the utterance.
- Seek idiomatic formulations which allow the subject to appear in clause-initial position (active/passive, clefts, reverse pseudo-cleft, non-agent subjects).
- Make appropriate use of grammatical strategies which place non-subject constituents in initial position (fronting, inversion for emphasis, presentatives).
- Do not overload the front of the clause by making the subject too long or by choosing a subject which is in focus.

Chapter 3

Complex sentences

The main points in this chapter are these:

- Sentences can have different degrees of complexity. The structures available allow you to combine information which is central to your argument and information which plays a more supporting role.
- By combining two or more pieces of information in a complex sentence, you ask the reader to interpret them as one unit within the paragraph.
- English has a wide range of structures for expressing information which plays a supporting, backgrounded role.
- Backgrounded information can be added before, after, and in the middle of the main clause. It serves different functions in these different positions.

At the beginning of Chapter 1 we listed the different kinds of decisions that you have to make in the process of sentence construction. These decisions involve determining what pieces of information to combine in a sentence, how to choose an appropriate form for the information you want to combine, and how best to position the various pieces of information with respect to the communicative core.

We are going to take a number of steps in this chapter to give you insight into how complex sentences are organized and what grammatical devices you need in order to help you gain control over the process of complex sentence construction. We start off in 3.1 with an overview of the different ways in which the simple clause can be expanded and combined with other clauses to make a more intricate grammatical structure. This gives us different kinds of sentence which have different basic shapes. Then in 3.2 we detail the most important characteristics of the structures which English employs for clause combining. We concentrate on subordinate clauses of different kinds, but also consider other structures. After that, in 3.3, we consider the motivations that lead writers to make relatively complex sentences. The next step is to go into more detail about clause combining at the beginning, in the middle, and at the end of the sentence respectively (3.4–3.6). In each case we look at stretches of text from student papers and show how they could be improved by well-judged clause combining. We then round off with a chapter on coordinating and listing and a brief consideration of the relative value in academic English of sentences of different length (3.7).

3.1 Different kinds of sentence

3.1.1 Sentence complexity

From a formal point of view, there are different ways of taking a simple clause and expanding it into a grammatically more complex structure. First of all, clauses can be embedded within a higher clause, as in these examples:

Simple, single clause
The author of this report has had access to secret documents.

Subject clause
Whoever wrote this report has had access to secret documents.

Object clause
The author of this report must have seen **what the secret services have in their archives.**

Restrictive relative clause
The author of this report has had access to documents **which the government has not yet released**.

Restrictive participial clause
Anyone **reading this report** will wonder about the author's sources.

In all these cases, the clause in bold can be seen as a constituent of a higher clause, and hence the information which the embedded clause contains can also be seen as part of the information unit which the higher clause comprises. This means that in terms of constituency we can analyse these sentences in more or less the same way as we would analyse simple sentences.

A different method of constructing more complex structures involves taking two or more independent clauses and combining them. This can be done in two basic ways. First, the clauses can be either simply juxtaposed and linked them by some means of punctuation, or otherwise they can be coordinated using one of the coordinating conjunctions, *and, but, for* and *so*. Here are two straightforward examples:

juxtaposition
The author of this report has had access to secret documents**;** he will have to provide an account of his sources.

coordination
The author of this report has had access to secret documents**, and** will have to provide an account of his sources.

Traditionally, these sentences are called compound sentences, and the relationship between the two clauses is said to be paratactic; that is to say, the information in each of the combined units is presented as having equal status. Another form of paratactic combining involves non-restrictive apposition, as in this example:

Some men, **especially middle-class men**, came to value domesticity more highly. (sn="4456")[15]

Arguably, not all appositions are clausal structures, but they are an important means of linking supporting information to the communicative core in a compact fashion, and for this reason we include them in our treatment of clause combining.

The second method of combining clauses is to use a form of grammatical subordination. In contrast to compound sentences, where there is always a sense in which the two component parts are quite equal in value, the combining of an independent main clause with a subordinate clause follows as a rule from the consideration that one piece of information is in some way less important than another, hence the labels 'main' and 'subordinate'. The relationship between the elements is not paratactic but hypotactic. The combination of main and subordinate goes to make what is traditionally called a complex sentence. Here are some complex sentences involving different kinds of subordinate clause:

Although many people speak two languages fluently, there are few who can speak four or five equally well.
The main difference lies in the use of adjectives, **as becomes clear from Table 2**.
This new collection of poems, **many of which were written in prison**, breathes despair on a frightening scale.

15 Examples given in this chapter with an (sn) coding come from the corpus compiled by Tavecchio (2010).

In this section we will concentrate mainly on hypotactic combining, but we will also look briefly at various forms of paratactic combining. In the context of this book the term complex sentence should be understood as relating to sentences that have either paratactic combining or hypotactic combining, or indeed both. The clause that is combined we will call simply the 'combined clause', while the clause that it is combined with is the 'host clause'. In the examples above, the combined clause is in bold and the host clause is in normal type.

3.1.2 Sentence shapes

Elements that combine with a main clause do so at particular points. We distinguish three basic positions. First, a subordinate clause may be placed before the host clause, in which case it has a framing function (see the discussion of framing in Chapter 2). Secondly, the combined element may interrupt the host clause at various points, where it may have a variety of specifying and commenting functions. Finally, the combined element may follow the host clause, where it elaborates or comments on the information in the main clause.

We can illustrate the different positions of subordinate clauses and the effect of their positioning by considering different combinations of two simple clauses:

> **Although it is in fact a rather vague concept**, 'public opinion' has long been recognized by politicians and governments as highly significant in the political process.
> 'Public opinion', **although it is in fact a rather vague concept**, has long been recognized by politicians and governments as highly significant in the political process.
> 'Public opinion' has, **although it is in fact a vague concept**, long been recognized by politicians and governments as highly significant in the political process.
> 'Public opinion' has long been recognized by politicians and governments as highly significant in the political process, **although it is in fact a rather vague concept**.

The core feature of information with a framing function lies in the fact that information which occurs initially is not being presented as new but rather just provides a context for understanding the information that follows; as such, the writer seems to accept that the concept in question is vague and is suggesting that the reader take this information for granted. This is not the case with elaboration. In the example above, the final subordinate *although* clause appears as more of an afterthought, and the suggestion is present that the writer in fact has a rather critical stance with regard to the value of the concept.

The fundamental effect of interruptive clauses is that the information in the two resulting parts of the host clause is given extra emphasis. Because the combining clause is inserted before the focus, the most important information in the host clause, it still functions to an extent as a relevant context for understanding that information, but it has the additional function of highlighting a particular element in the host clause. When it occurs immediately after the subject, the subject itself is highlighted: something is going to be said about public opinion, but the writer has an opinion about it which s/he wants to be taken into account. But what follows the interruption gains extra importance as well, because the interruption has increased the expectation that something really interesting is going to come. When the interruption occurs after the finite verb, there is a suggestion that what is going to be said of the subject is indeed true; in this case the following information is highlighted too, in that more emphasis comes to be laid on the word *long*, thus emphasizing the contrast between public opinion being a vague concept on the one hand and having a long tradition on the other.

On the basis of the position where the combined element is placed relative to the main clause we can also define a number of basic sentence shapes, which we will call 'framed', 'interrupted', and 'elaborated'. In practice, many sentences are a mixture of these types, but you will also come across sentences which are powerfully framed or powerfully elaborated. Here are two examples:

> **The framed sentence**
> **When he walks with Waldo Crossley in the grounds of Methwold's riverside estate, congratulating his son on the skills with which he has learned to spear leaves and other detritus, flattering him on the way he looks in the Methwold livery, and being rewarded for Waldo's tearjerkingly wide, happy, brainless smile – or when he keeps vigil by Ormus Carma's bedside, seeing in the comatose singer the shadow of his own dead Hawthorne – then** Standish's back is straighter than ever, his jaw firmer, his eye less moist. (Rushdie 1999: 319)
>
> **The elaborated sentence**
> The river is, as ever, flowing south, New Orleansward; **the paddle-steamer is headed north, gaining slow upstream momentum (standard procedure for sightseeing boats, in order to abbreviate the anticlimactic return leg of their tour), and as it begins to make headway, a deckhand ambles aft in process of casting off the vessel's docklines, with the effect that he ap-**

> **pears to be walking in place, with respect to the shore and her angle of view, while the boat moves under him**. (Barth 1996: 80).

We have on purpose chosen rather extreme examples from literary texts, where such complex structures are characteristic of certain writers,[16] in order to emphasize the feel of these two sentence shapes.

The interrupting pattern does not frequently occur in a very excessive form. This is fortunate, since a sentence with clauses that kept being interrupted would undoubtedly be difficult to process. One style guide, for instance, calls our interrupted sentence type 'convoluted sentences' (Kane 1988: 135). However, literary text does provide us again with interesting examples:

> Dear-present-reader Alice suddenly remembers one such occasion, **somewhere or other,** when for a giddy moment it appeared to her that she herself, **aisle-walking**, was standing still, while Train A, Train B, and Boston's South Street Station platform (**it now comes back to her**) all seemed in various motion. (Barth 1996: 80)

Academic text is a lot more restrained in its use of the three combining techniques of framing, interrupting and elaborating. However, as we noted in Chapter 1, it is quite common to come across a mixed pattern which makes use of both framing and elaboration. Here is a typical example:

> In other words, whereas some categories may have strict and fixed boundaries, in other cases boundaries between categories may be fuzzy or variable, their members sometimes only related through 'family resemblances'. (Keizer 2007: 204)

This is a nicely balanced sentence. It starts with a quite complex three-step framing consisting of a prepositional phrase followed by an adverbial clause of contrast followed by another prepositional phrase, and then after the main clause there is an elaboration involving a non-finite clause which gives further detail concerning the nature of fuzzy categories. Let us indeed now have a look at the different grammatical forms that one comes across in such complex sentences.

3.2 Clause combining: the basic forms

In this section we will go through the different kinds of subordinate structure which English has to offer. To a certain extent these structures can of course also be found in German, but English has a number of additional devices

16 *Finnegans Wake*, by James Joyce, contains sentences which go on for a whole page.

which German does not have, and becoming a powerful and confident writer in English involves having a command of a wide range of subordination techniques. To complete this overview of the forms that combining elements take, we take a brief look at non-clausal forms found in paratactic combining.

3.2.1 Adverbial clauses

Adverbial clauses are introduced by a conjunction, such as *when, because, so that, since* and *although*. These words signal the grammatical relation of subordination and at the same time suggest a particular kind of meaning relation between the content of the host clause and the combined clause. Here are some examples of adverbial clauses with a finite verb form; in each case the conjunction is in bold italics and the subordinate clause in bold:

> ***When*** **people live with each other for a long time**, they often start behaving like each other.
>
> The most vehement criticism of New Labour under Tony Blair was the coldness of their relation with the unions, ***because*** **it gave the impression that the Labour Party did not care any more for the man and woman on the street**.
>
> ***Provided*** **one goes through all the procedures step by step**, there is no risk of getting it wrong.

The most common types of adverbial clause are those of time, place, reason, purpose, result, manner, contrast, condition and concession. The most common conjunctions associated with each meaning relation are given below:

time:	after, before, when, until, as soon as, while
place:	where, wherever
reason:	because, as, since
purpose:	in order that
result:	so that
manner:	as, as if, as though
contrast:	whereas, while
condition:	if, unless, on condition that, in the event that, provided (that), providing, supposing (that)
concession:	although, even though, despite the fact that

There are no significant differences between English and German with regard to the kinds of adverbial clause available. However, there is evidence that advanced learners underuse certain semantic relations in comparison with native speakers (Hinkel 2002: 138; Springer, in prep.). Moreover, English has more options when it comes to using shortened forms of adverbial clause (see 3.2.3 and 3.2.4 below).

3.2.2 Non-restrictive relative clauses

In English there is a basic distinction between restrictive and non-restrictive relative clauses. Whereas restrictive relatives provide information which is essential for identifying the entity referred to by the noun phrase, non-restrictives provide extra information about this entity, which is already assumed to be identifiable for the reader. Consider the following two examples:

> RESTRICTIVE: The only data **that are relevant here** are those given in the third column of Table 2.
> NON-RESTRICTIVE: This information, **which was clearly from a reliable source**, quickly became a distinct embarrassment to the authorities.

In the first example, omitting the relative clause would actually change the meaning of the sentence: suddenly the data in the third column would be the only data, but the point is that they are the only relevant data, which suggests that there are other data that are not relevant at that point in the discourse. By contrast, omitting the relative clause in the second example would not change the meaning of the host clause: it would still be clear what information is meant. However, saying that information is omissible does not mean that it is not necessary for the clarity of the discourse. In this example, the information in the relative clause has an effect on the interpretation of the sentence as a whole: the extra detail allows the reader to conclude that the nature of the information was indeed such that the authorities should be embarrassed. In communicative terms, it is therefore not really omissible at all.

The restrictive vs non-restrictive distinction is an important one because the two constructions have distinct formal features in English. First of all, restrictive relative clauses are not separated from the host clause by commas, unlike in German; this means in effect that they are embedded and thus do not fall under clause combining. By contrast, non-restrictive clauses are always separated from the rest of the sentence by some form of punctuation; as such they are combined with a host clause, and are of interest to us here.

A second difference concerns the relative pronoun. While restrictive relatives can be introduced by *that, who, which, where* etc., non-restrictives do not allow *that*:

> This regional airline, *that/which started flying in 1998, quickly grew into a major international operation.

A third difference is that non-restrictive relatives are much more versatile than restrictive relatives in their referential capacity. In most cases the relative pronoun refers to an entity or entities mentioned in the host clause. In this example *who* refers to 'the medical men':

> An important part in the Industrial Revolution was played by the medical men, **who brought down the death rate and enlarged the number of potential industrial workers**.

Sometimes, however, the link may be with another element:

> The colour of the liquid was dark green, **which is definitely not what it should have been**.
> The Cabinet would have preferred to bring the matter out into the open, **which one member actually succeeded in doing, albeit only by means of a complex leak**.
> The Belgian government has again resolved an important internal conflict, **which means that there will be no elections this year**.

Here, *which* refers in turn to 'dark green', 'bringing the matter out into the open', and the complete content of the host clause. These are examples of what are called sentential relative clauses.

Note that while English uses the relative pronoun *which* for both types of relative clause, German normally introduces the sentential relative by the pronoun *was*. However, when a causal meaning is involved, German might use a form such as *wodurch*, as can be seen in the following English example with its German translation.

> Sociologists have sentimental and economic ties with the first group, **which makes it harder for them to maintain scientific detachment.**
> Soziologen sind gefühlsmäßig und ökonomisch an die erste Gruppe gebunden, wodurch es ihnen schwerer fällt, wissenschaftliche Distanz zu bewahren.

The versatility of the relative clause in English also becomes apparent from the relative linkage itself. Consider these examples, with their German translations:

> In what is to become a series of biannual reports, the European Commission highlights a number of issues facing Europe, **perhaps the most important of which are education and training**.
> In einer frisch begonnenen Reihe von halbjährlichen Berichten hebt die Europäische Kommission eine Anzahl von Problemen hervor, die sich Europa stellen, wohl allen voran Bildung und Ausbildung.

> Many metaphors in literary texts need not be understood in a literary way, **which is why a general discourse theory of metaphor is an absolute requirement**.

In literarischen Texten brauchen viele Metaphern nicht wörtlich verstanden zu werden. Deshalb ist eine Diskurstheorie der Metapher ein absolutes Erfordernis.

The renovation work will not be completed before 2006, **by which time there could be a new party in power**.
Die Renovierungen werden nicht vor 2006 abgeschlossen sein. Bis dahin könnte eine neue Regierung an der Macht sein.

English makes considerable use of complex relatives such as *by which time, at which point* and *in which case*. These do not have a precise formal equivalent in German, which often needs to resort to two sentences or to a different construction to capture the nature of the link. Note also that English has a preference for expressions like *the most important of which* and *some of which* rather than *of which the most important* and *of which some*. All in all, non-restrictive relative clauses provide a very flexible means of clause combining.

3.2.3 Non-finite clauses

One of the most important differences between English and German in terms of their reservoir of constructions is that English makes much more use than German does of clauses with non-finite verb forms. There are three basic types, one with a past participle, one with a present participle, and one with an infinitive. These are illustrated in turn:

Overwhelmed by numbers, Ledyard surrendered to Bromfield. (= Ledyard was overwhelmed by numbers and therefore surrendered to Bromfield.)
Many pollutants were totally absent before World War II, **having made their environmental debut in the war years**.
To appease his back bench, the Prime Minister chose to cause havoc in Brussels.

Participial clauses sometimes function as adverbial clauses with conjunctions, but the only conjunctions allowed are *when, before, after, while, since* (in the temporal sense), *if, unless, although* and *as if*. Moreover, they tend to occur before, and not after, the host clause. The main advantage of the non-finite clause is that it is compact. Compare the non-finite and finite forms in the following examples:

When considered from this angle, the difficulties appear insurmountable.
When the difficulties are considered from this angle, they appear insurmountable.
If travelling alone, tourists are advised to contact the embassy.
If tourists are travelling alone, they are advised to contact the embassy.
As though recognizing this omission, Ruskin attacks the selfishness and vanity of the bad painters …

Non-finite clauses with the *-ing* form can also be introduced by a group of words called conjunctive prepositions; these are prepositions that function like conjunctions, although they cannot introduce clauses with finite verbs. Here are some examples:

> Teaching materials are often ideologically based, **without of course appearing to be so**.
> **Despite occurring in almost all our texts at least once**, the construction is not very common.
> The government, **instead of announcing an immediate inquiry**, went on the defensive, which of course was the start of the rot.

Non-finite *-ing* clauses are particularly frequent in all kinds of formal writing. Moreover, since German does not have a ready equivalent, it is an important clause type to master in English. We will therefore look mainly at *-ing* clauses here.

More often than not, the meaning relation which *-ing* clauses have with their host clauses is not a predictable one; rather, it has to be inferred from the context. In the next example, for instance, the *-ing* clause could be paraphrased by an adverbial clause of time:

> **Tramping about the fields**, the investigation team located the outlet points of various drainage tiles.

Often the relationship is a causal one; this always holds for *-ing* clauses with the verb *being* which precede the host clause:

> **Being a committed European**, Mr Heath would not like to see Maastricht end up in the rubbish bin.

In many cases, however, the relation is not one which can be captured by an adverbial clause. For instance, in the two examples below the information in the *-ing* clause clarifies and explains the statement in the host clause:

> Most politicians were taken unawares by the crisis, **failing to understand that Britain is immediately affected by events in Europe**.
> In the eighteenth century the means of calling a minister of the church were rationalized, **vacant parishes being advertised in a nation-wide periodical**.

Usually, *-ing* clauses do not have a specified subject. The normal interpretation will be that the understood subject is the same as that of the host clause. However, sometimes that is not the case:

> This heats the air, **causing it to rise**.
> During World War II, this theory was converted into practice, **giving rise to nuclear weapons and reactors**.

In the first example the interpretation is that the air rises as a result of its being heated. The understood subject of *causing* is thus the content of the host clause as a whole. The second example is similar: it is not the theory that gives rise to nuclear weapons but the conversion of the theory into practice. Often a relative clause is possible in such cases as an alternative to the *-ing* clause:

> This heats the air, **which causes it to rise**.
> During World War II, this theory was converted into practice, **which gave rise to nuclear weapons and reactors**.

In other cases, the lack of a specified subject is more problematic:

> **When presenting strange examples**, it is customary to mark them with one or two question marks.
> **Taking this into account**, a language can be redefined as the infinite set of grammatical sentences in that language.

Technically speaking, the *-ing* clauses here are examples of what is called a dangling modifier. These are often frowned on from a stylistic point of view, and can easily cause hilarity or confusion:

> !!**While on holiday in Barbados**, a group of young lieutenants mounted a coup against the President.

On first reading this suggests that the lieutenants mounted a coup while they were on holiday, which of course would be rather unlikely. Clarity only comes once a full adverbial clause is formulated:

> **While he was on holiday in Barbados**, a group of young lieutenants mounted a coup against the President.

However, as long as they do not cause confusion, these dangling modifiers do not really present a stylistic problem. In fact, they are not uncommon in academic prose, occurring for instance when the understood subject is *one*, as in:

> **When studying the data** it is important to take the age of the different subjects into account

and also when the understood subject is the writer, as in:

> **Before developing this idea further**, it may be useful to summarize the argument so far.

Finally, to finish off this treatment of *-ing* clauses, you should note that they also occur with a specified subject:

Nitrogen can enter the soil through nitrogen fixation, a process carried out by various bacteria and algae, **some of them living free in the soil**.
The Commission finally managed to come up with a solution, **without the issue being brought to a vote**.
This being the case, it makes sign language one of the most varied forms of communication on Earth.

These clauses also occur with the conjunctive preposition *with*, in which case the interpretation will tend to be one of circumstance and reason:

With the hopes for a settlement fading, the price of oil soared again.

All in all, the participial clause with *-ing* is a very flexible device which can be combined with another clause at the beginning, in the middle, and at the end. It also expresses a wide range of semantic relationships.

3.2.4 Verbless clauses

It is worth mentioning three types of verbless clause which occur occasionally in formal written English but do not exist as such in German. The first type is a verbless clause introduced by *with*:

With marihuana already semi-legal in a number of member countries, some people in Brussels think it should be legalized all over the Community.
With mugging on the increase again, many people are afraid to go out on their own in the dark.

This clause type often has a causal interpretation and can be paraphrased using *given the fact that* or *in light of the fact that*, or even simply *because*. The typical position for *with* clauses is sentence-initial, before the host clause.

There is also a very short verbless clause type which may consist of nothing more than a noun phrase or predicative adjective. In non-narrative text, this type also tends to occur sentence-initially, and is often regarded as somewhat literary.

A devout Christian, Mr Blair takes a similar stand to the Conservative party on the issue of family values.
Aware of the dangers, the European Commission quickly backed down.
Linguists are now in a position to go beyond pen-and-paper analysis. **More empirical and less speculative**, their research finally bears comparison with that of hard-pure sciences such as physics and chemistry.
Born 100 years ago, he was the oldest of five children, each about a year apart.

Finally, adverbial clauses can occur in a reduced form including the conjunction, but without a verbal element. The conjunctions that occur in this construction are *(al)though, if, as if,* as *though, even if, unless, as soon as, once, when(ever), where(ver)* and *whether.*

Although a common factor, revenge is not the exclusive motivation for school shootings.
Many linguists have sought to assess how closely, **if at all**, the guidelines for letter writing offered in textbooks are related to real life commercial practice.
These issues need to be looked at not only in German law but also, **where relevant**, in European law.

All these clause types are useful additions to your grammatical repertoire because they are concise and can provide variation from the conventional adverbial clause (for more general remarks on the value of conciseness and variation, see Module IV, Chapter 2.4 and 2.5).

3.2.5 Appositions

Non-restrictive appositions are usually short and compact insertions that are typically used to identify or further specify the referent concerned. However, they are also used to provide examples, to say the same thing in another way, or to characterize the referent in one way or another (cf. Hannay & Keizer 2005). Here are some examples:

Naming
Two more former students at St Andrews, **John Atholl and Richard Guthrie**, were received as bachelors on 3 May 1442, when Athilmer guaranteed payment of the one-florin fee of one of them. (Lyall 1985: 60)

Reformulating
The element *of* is analysed as a separate element linking the nominal determiner **(NomPostD)** and the head noun. (Keizer 2007: 175)

Characterizing
But later, Lloyd George, **a sympathetic friend**, made him Minister of Munitions and then Secretary of War. (Priestley 1973: 106)

Exemplifying
In these experiments we had subjects view videotapes of an actor carrying out a goal-directed event (**e.g. setting up a slide projector**) and then later tested recall or visual recognition [...]. (Brewer & Lichtenstein 1982: 474)

Appositions also occur after colons, in a different kind of construction. These will be dealt with in Chapter 4.

3.2.6 Other structures

Traditional grammatical descriptions of complex sentences in English mention the categories of subordinate clause that we have distinguished above. But a close look at written texts will reveal that complex sentences consist of an even wider range of structures which in some way are combined or have a parenthetical relationship. These are often sentence fragments, but can also be full independent clauses which follow or interrupt the host clause.

> The accident, **from minor electrocution to major explosion**, revealed the ultimate frailty of the networks of modernity. (sn="4602")
> Very poor performance on balance tasks **(some of the children tested could not succeed on any of the three balance tasks)** meant that boys were not involved in football, either in small knock-about games or more formal ones. (sn="5504")

As you become more confident in your writing, you may wish to make use of such devices in order to introduce more variation into your writing. Fragments have the advantage of being concise (cf. Module IV, Chapter 2.4), while full independent clauses are a totally legitimate means of expression for adding your own comment at various points in the sentence.

3.2.7 Shapes again

Now we have given an overview of the structures one finds in complex sentences, let us round this section off with two examples of sentences with a lot of combining, one predominantly framed sentence and one predominantly elaborated sentence. The aim is to illustrate the use of clause combining in practice and to point up the complexity that can arise. The first example was already given earlier as an example of a framed sentence:

> When he walks with Waldo Crossley in the grounds of Methwold's riverside estate, congratulating his son on the skills with which he has learned to spear leaves and other detritus, flattering him on the way he looks in the Methwold livery, and brewing rewarded for Waldo's tearjerkingly wide, happy, breathless smile – or when he keeps vigil by Ormus Carma's bedside, seeing in the comatose singer the shadow of his own dead Hawthorne – then Standish's back is straighter than ever, his jaw firmer, his eye less moist. (Rushdie 1999: 319)

The tabularized version of the sentence reveals that there are six separate subordinate clauses preceding the main clause, which themselves are combined into a complex structure.

The sentence, per combined element	Status of combined element
When he walks with Waldo Crossley in the grounds of Methwold's riverside estate,	finite adverbial clause, framing
congratulating his son on the skills with which he has learned to spear leaves and other detritus,	non-finite clause, elaborating the frame
flattering him on the way he looks in the Methwold livery,	non-finite clause, juxtaposed with previous clause, elaborating the frame
and being rewarded for Waldo's tear-jerkingly wide, happy, brainless smile –	non-finite clause, coordinated with previous clause, elaborating the frame
or when he keeps vigil by Ormus Carma's bedside,	finite adverbial clause, coordinated with initial frame clause
seeing in the comatose singer the shadow of his own dead Hawthorne –	non-finite clause, elaborating coordinated frame
THEN STANDISH'S BACK IS STRAIGHTER THAN EVER,	MAIN CLAUSE
his jaw firmer,	juxtaposed verbless clause
his eye less moist.	juxtaposed verbless clause

This is clearly a top-heavy sentence, and would be less likely to occur in an academic text.

Now consider an example of an elaborated sentence, followed by a combination analysis.

> I had no idea that his real name was Shetty – just as our family's had been until it got Englished years ago – but nobody called him that any more, because, as he himself liked to say 'milkman by fame, I am Milkman by name'; [...] (Rushdie 1999: 65)

The sentence, per combined element	Status of combined element
I HAD NO IDEA THAT HIS REAL NAME WAS SHETTY	MAIN CLAUSE
– just as our family's had been until it got Englished years ago –	adverbial clause of comparison, elaborating main clause
but nobody called him that any more	coordinated clause

because	conjunction introducing adverbial clause of reason, elaborating coordinated clause
as he himself liked to say	adverbial clause of comparison, interruption of reason clause
'milkman by fame, I am Milkman by name'	the rest of the adverbial clause of reason, elaborating the coordinated clause (and consisting itself of a quotation which has a verbless clause as a frame for the host clause)

In fact, this is just the first part of a sentence that has three paratactic units combined using semicolons, but let us concentrate on this first unit. The main clause is followed by an adverbial clause of comparison which is separated from the main clause by a dash. Then there is a coordinated main clause introduced by *but*, followed by an adverbial clause of reason which is itself interrupted by means of another comparative clause – *as he himself liked to say* – which serves as a kind of frame for the quotation to follow.

These are sentences from literary texts, and, as we noted above, academic texts will not by any means typically consist of such complex structures. However, the basic patterns we have seen do indeed occur in academic texts as well. Consider the following example of an elaborational sentence:

> The answer came in the late 1960s and early 1970s, with the emergence of cognitive science, a new discipline concentrating on the workings of the mind which at last offered a coherent framework into which the scattered evidence from philosophy, linguistics, anthropology and psychology could be brought together to build a unified picture of the way in which people perceive and categorize the world around them. (Keizer 2007: 204)

This sentence has a quite simple structure in terms of clause combining: first there is a main clause, followed by a fragment consisting of a prepositional phrase, with that itself being followed by a very lengthy non-restrictive apposition.

To round off this section we would like to make one simple point: by having a wide repertoire of clause combining forms and techniques at your disposal, you can create great variation in your writing.

3.3 Foregrounding and backgrounding

Up to now we have concentrated on the linguistic options that English has for combining clauses into complex sentences. Now we need to look at how the writer can use these options to help the reader understand the complexity of his/her argument. The core concepts here are foregrounding and backgrounding. These are means of signalling the status of individual pieces of information in relation to each other and in relation to the paragraph theme.

When you read a text, you interpret every message in the light of the previous one and in this way seek to build up a coherent interpretation of the whole text. But this does not mean that each new piece of information has the same status as the previous one. On the contrary, some pieces of information are clearly more important than others. This notion of 'more important' needs to be seen in terms of the writer's discourse goals: a piece of information is important if it is central to achieving those goals. To understand how sentence construction is dependent on these aims, consider the following string of four sentences:

A Soon after the election a number of scandals occurred.
B The government started to show signs of nervousness.
C In mid-term a number of safe by-election seats were snapped up by the Opposition.
D The prime minister had his work cut out to keep the cabinet together.

If you are writing about how disastrous a certain term of government was, you may well wish to recount a series of events, noting in addition what the immediate consequences were for the government concerned. In that case sentences A and C are more important than B and D. But if you are concentrating on the effects of a series of events on the government's morale, then B and D will be relatively more important, with A and C playing a supporting role.

If you wish to signal this kind of perspective, you must ensure as a writer that important information is sufficiently foregrounded and that less important information is sufficiently backgrounded. One of the most straightforward ways of backgrounding information is by clause combining. Accordingly, if you want to produce an event-oriented text based on the four sentences above you could write something like this:

> Soon after the election a number of scandals occurred, as a result of which the government started to show signs of nervousness. Then in mid-term a number of safe by-election seats were snapped up by the Opposition, and the prime minister had his work cut out to keep the cabinet together.

And if you want an effect-oriented text, you might put it like this:

> When soon after the election a number of scandals occurred, the government started to show signs of nervousness. And when in mid-term a number of safe by-election seats were snapped up by the Opposition, the prime minister had his work cut out to keep the cabinet together.

We saw in 3.2 that there are many different ways of combining clauses in English, but what emerges from the example above is that when to combine is just as important as how to combine. If you can make good use of the devices available for foregrounding and backgrounding, then you will succeed in giving clear signals to your reader to help him/her assess what you find important and less important, and hence to help him/her understand your message.

Clause combining not only reveals something about the relative importance of information; it also tells the reader in a very simple way that certain pieces of information belong together. When you are building up a paragraph, you should therefore try and shape each sentence as a distinct segment of the paragraph's rhetorical structure. Consider this paragraph from an essay on the liberal Dutch drugs policy; it suffers from having too many sentences. The sentences are numbered for convenience.

1. There are several schemes in operation supporting this idea.
2. Coffee shops in Amsterdam sell cannabis openly.
3. This is done to prevent underground drug movements.
4. Drug victims are given guidance and help to kick the habit.
5. Special drug centres have been set up to give assistance.
6. So far the Dutch policy has yielded positive results.

The six sentences of this paragraph are more or less equal in length and in fact quite short. But first of all not each sentence is equally important, and secondly the point of the paragraph is clearly not to present a string of statements each directly related to the topic sentence. Rather, sentences 2 and 3 clearly belong together, and sentences 4 and 5 probably do too. By reorganizing the information into four distinct segments, you can give the reader a clear signal that certain messages belong together. This improves readability.

> There are several schemes in operation supporting this idea. For instance, coffee shops in Amsterdam sell cannabis openly, thus preventing underground drug movements. In addition, special drug centres have been set up for drug victims, who receive guidance and help to kick the habit. So far this policy has yielded positive results.

This version has a number of advantages:

1. the information that belongs together is presented in one segment;
2. the main information in the body of the paragraph is foregrounded and the supporting information is backgrounded;
3. there is variation in sentence length;
4. the variation in sentence length is functional: the remaining short sentences stand out as having a clear rhetorical function.

To summarize this section, you can use clause combining for two major purposes. The first is to allow the reader to clearly distinguish more important from less important information. The second is to help the reader to determine which pieces of information belong together; consequently you can make each sentence a clear step in the development of your argument.

With this in mind, we now move on to look in more detail at the functions performed by combined elements when they occur in framed sentences (3.4), interrupted sentences (3.5), and elaborated sentences (3.6).

3.4 Complex framing

In Chapter 2 we talked about the framing function of adverbials in initial position, but we only considered adverbs and phrasal expressions. In 3.2 above we saw that subordinate clauses are also frequently used in a framing function at the beginning of the sentence, but when we look more closely we see that this notion of framing is itself more complex. What we see is that the initial framing element is sometimes followed by another adverbial expression which appears to be somehow involved in the framing operation. This second expression is technically speaking interruptive, but we will consider the two elements together here as constituting complex framing. Complex framing is interesting because there are a small number of fixed patterns, and the patterns which are relatively common in the English of native speaker writers tend to be underused by learner writers.[17]

In this section we will present three distinct patterns of complex framing which occur in written English. After presenting the patterns we will look briefly at some data from student essays to see how writers might make more effective use of the patterns.

---

17 See Smits (2002) for details on overuse and underuse of patterns by inexperienced writers. See also Gómez-González (2001) and Hannay (2007).

3.4.1 The basic patterns

The first type of framing involves a stepwise scene setting for the content of the main clause:

> **On the St Petersburg waterfront, if you don't pay off the right people**, you may find that the cane operator will drop your cargo in the water. (NEC 138–127)[18]
>
> **All being well, at the beginning of next month** Suzanne will start a series of injections to stimulate her ovaries to produce the eggs needed to make embryos. (NEC 124–423)
>
> **In fact, according to Tim Newburn, a criminologist at the Policy Studies Institute and co-author of a government-commissioned report**, Persistent Young Offenders, such a group is very hard indeed to identify. (NEC 162–398)

The first adverbial element has scope over the rest of the sentence, while the second adverbial element provides an independent frame for what comes. Thus in the first example above, the initial element, *On the St Petersburg waterfront*, sets the spatial framework for the whole sentence: everything that is still to come is all about a situation which obtains on the St Petersburg waterfront. The second element, *if you don't pay off the right people*, subsequently provides a conditional framework for the situation described by the main clause. We call this the **stepwise pattern** because each adverbial element in its turn provides a framework for everything that follows, and the second element does not in any way modify the first.

The second type of complex framing is markedly different from the first. Here, the second element clearly does modify the initial element, and in a rather specific way. We will call this the **focusing pattern**, and here are some examples:

> In the matter of trout fishing, **of course**, things are much more predictable. (NEC 53–185)
>
> By the early 1970s, **however**, this attitude was changing and Sir Robert Mark, who took over as Metropolitan Police Commissioner, promised to do away with corruption within the force. (NEC 119–329)

It should be noted that the vast majority of frames belonging to this focusing pattern have as their second element an adverbial such as *however, of course, though,* or *for example.*

---

18 The NEC-coded examples in this section come from the corpus compiled by Smits (2002).

In the trout fishing example, the second element, *of course*, modifies the first, *in the matter of trout fishing*, and the two elements together provide a complex frame for the statement to follow. The precise function of the second, modifying element is to draw particular attention to the initial framing element. With regard to the first example, for instance, we see that the most important piece of information is that as regards trout fishing 'things are much more predictable'; moreover, this is presented as being obviously the case, and this obviousness is to be understood precisely as relating to trout fishing. In other words, the writer uses *of course* not so much to tell us that s/he considers it obvious that things are much more predictable, but rather that this obviousness comes from it being trout fishing that one is talking about.

We now turn to the third major type, which we will call the **grounding pattern**. This is similar to the focusing type in that the second element modifies the first, but it does so in a rather different way. Look at these examples:

> Later, **with England converted to Christianity**, the daughters of the great Anglo-Saxon noblemen were sent abroad to France to be educated in the Christian and classical mode. (NEC 3–21)
>
> On Christmas Eve, **when it had become clear that the paper was not going to be scared away**, Yeo authorized a statement, published two days later, accepting responsibility for the child. (NEC 179–513)

Here, the second element grounds, or anchors, the first in that it provides a more accessible frame for the sentence to be built on. Often this is done by describing an event which allows the reader to gain a greater understanding of the relevance of the particular setting for understanding the message to come. The two framing expressions can usually be paraphrased as a kind of orientational proposition, so that the first example above might be interpreted as "Later England was converted to Christianity, and in that situation the following happened". Both subordinate clauses and prepositional phrases are common structures in this grounding slot.

It is not only adverbials that occur in this position following the first framing adverbial. We also see relative clauses and appositions being used to provide a grounding for the initial element. Here is an example:

> There are indeed many differences between the way grammar is used in writing English and the way it is used in speaking it. This is only natural. When we are writing, we usually have time to make notes, plan ahead, pause, reflect, change our mind, start again, revise, proofread, and generally polish the language until we have reached a level that satisfies us. The reader sees only the finished product.

> But in everyday conversation (**which is the kind of spoken language we engage in most of the time**) there is no time for such things to happen. (Crystal 1988: 22)

The second paragraph in this text introduces a new topic – conversation – which is in contrast to the topic of the previous paragraph – written language. But the contrast is more specific than what the reader might expect on the basis of the first sentence of the first paragraph, where a simple distinction is made between writing and speaking. The fact that the new paragraph is not about speaking in general but more specifically about everyday conversation has therefore to be explained to the reader, and this is what the relative clause does. By legitimizing the choice of topic, the relative clause also has the effect of legitimizing the whole sentence, and therefore contributes to the coherence of the text.

These three framing patterns – stepwise, focusing, and grounding – account for the vast majority of complex frames found in written English, and academic texts contain more of them than for instance news texts and literary fiction (Smits 2002). A particularly interesting feature relates to the stepwise and focusing types: if the order of the elements in the focusing pattern is reversed, then what we get is a stepwise pattern. The difference between the two types has to do with how they function in context.

To see what is involved, consider this well constructed example of a complex focusing frame from the German section of the International Corpus of Learner English (ICLE):

> About 1700 years before Christ Hammurabi introduced the first laws in Mesopatamia. These laws treated criminals with retaliating measures in the style of "An eye for an eye, a tooth for a tooth." This idea of frightening people off from crime by corporal punishment lasted for ages. In modern times, **however**, corporal punishment was abolished in most western countries. (ICLE-GE-BAS-0030.1)[19]

The writer wants to contrast modern legal views of corporal punishment with more traditional views. The fact that there is a contrast between time periods is highlighted by placing the contrastive element *however* after the second time expression, rather than immediately at the beginning of the sentence, where the effect would simply be to suggest that there is a contrast between the content of the previous sentence and the content of the one

---

19 Examples in this and later sections with an ICLE coding come from the International Corpus of Learner English. The coding specifies the first language of the writer (GE) and his/her university (BAS), plus an individual essay code. For more information on the corpus, see Granger et al. (2003).

just starting. If this writer had placed *however* at the front of the sentence, the powerful contrast between *About 1700 years before Christ* and *modern times* would be considerably weakened. It would also have been less clear that the temporal contrast is an organizing principle for this segment of text.

3.4.2 Missed opportunities

Learner writers do not appear to employ complex framing less than native speakers, but they do appear to significantly underuse the focusing and grounding patterns (cf. Smits 2002, Hannay & Martínez Caro 2008). One reason for this may be that at the early stages of university writing, students are still concentrating on producing correct sentences rather than effective sentences which have an optimum fit in the context; moreover, they are still getting used to the academic register. An immediate consequence of this may be that they pay less attention to the hierarchical relationship between individual pieces of information in a given context. This may produce a rather monotonous style. By way of illustration, take a look at this segment taken from the ICLE corpus:

> But before one can speak of any conservatism, one must at least have some notion of the past, of how sexuality was the last decades. In the 1960s the sexual revolution took place and phenomena such as partner swapping, group sex and communes became a common feature. The seventies allowed everything and sex was a must; it did not matter in fact with whom. (ICLE-DN-NIJ-0003.7)

The writer opens the paragraph with a topic sentence suggesting a temporal development, and indeed the next two sentences suggest that the idea is to describe each decade from the 1960s onwards. In such a context, what is important for the 1960s is that there were partner swaps and group sex. The context for understanding this is given in the first main clause. Notice, however, that the writer has taken the background fact about the sexual revolution and the main point about the nature of sexuality and combined them using the coordinating conjunction, suggesting that the two pieces of information have equal value. A more appropriate form of combining would be a grounding frame, as in this reworked version:

> In the 1960s, **when the sexual revolution took place**, phenomena such as partner swapping, group sex and communes became a common feature.

A similar example can be found in the second sentence of the following paragraph:

> A good example of this can be found at the English Departments of Dutch Universities. At these departments all students are lectured to in English and it appears that they have a better knowledge of the language than students of, for instance, Business Communication English (a study for which English is also very important) who are lectured to in Dutch. So apparently English lectures do help. (ICLE-DN-NIJ-0002.7)

In the second sentence the writer again uses coordination to combine two main clauses where the first clause in fact provides the background information for the second. A complex frame of the grounding type would reflect the status of the information more clearly and would also serve to add pace to the text, as in:

> At these departments**, where all students are lectured to in English**, it appears that they have a better knowledge of the language than students of, for instance, Business Communication English (a study for which English is also very important) who are lectured to in Dutch.

Now consider a rather different case. In the sentence in bold, the newly introduced referent appears as subject:

> When a criminal had killed someone he was killed too. As the saying goes; an eye for an eye, a tooth for a tooth. Nowadays this doesn't happen anymore. Most countries abolished capital punishment and if they didn't they practically don't issue it anymore. There are also countries though where this is different. **The United States is an example of that.** In the US there are several states that still have capital punishment, and criminals were killed recently. (ICLE-DB-KVH-0052.2)

After its introduction, the United States are only mentioned briefly, and the text slows down as a result of relatively unimportant information being given sentence status. However, expressing exemplification more briefly allows everything to be formulated in one sentence and to fit into the preceding context. This can be achieved by employing a complex framing construction, this time of the focusing kind:

> There are also countries though where this is different. In The United States, **for example**, there are several states that still have capital punishment, and criminals were killed recently.

These examples show that using complex framing patterns can be effective when it comes to making clear the difference between foregrounded and backgrounded information. They are compact and they can prevent the pace of the text from slowing down.

3.5 Interruption techniques

Interrupting a clause is a very different kind of activity than giving information before the main clause for framing purposes. After all, you have already started communicating a relatively important piece of information at the moment you decide to interrupt the flow and provide the reader with additional information. In fact, interrupting is quite a complex business: there can be all manner of communicative aims; there are various points in the clause where it can be useful to interrupt; the interruptions can take different forms and differ in length; and the interruption will undoubtedly have an effect on how the resulting sentence is read and interpreted. In this section we will first have a look one by one at these various aspects of interruption, and then we will consider some examples from student writing which might benefit from using interruption techniques.

3.5.1 Aspects of interruption

The purpose
Writers choose to interrupt the flow of information for a variety of purposes. Common among these are explanation, specification, comment, as well as the focusing and grounding functions which we saw with complex frames in the previous section. Some of these functions are exemplified below:

> *Grounding*
> In one of the finest and earliest examples of prose written in America, William Bradford, **the Mayflower's historian and the first Governor of the Massachusetts colony**, described their situation ['...']. (McCrum et al. 1986: 116)
>
> *Focusing*
> It would be a mistake, **however**, to assume from this a simple process of linear progression, reaching its culmination in the great struggles of 1793–1815. (sn="4170")
>
> *Further specification*
> Some men, **especially middle-class men**, came to value domesticity more highly. (sn="4456")
>
> *Motivating*
> One of the most interesting voices, **because one could argue that it encapsulates the entire modus operandi of *Possession***, is the voice of a child apparently communicated with in a séance [...]. (Todd 1996: 53)
>
> *Commenting*
> Such gerrymandering, **if that is how we are to understand it**, is in all likelihood rife in local government.

The position

Interruption can be in various places. One common position is after the subject, where the functions of the interrupting element are similar to those of the second element in complex framing, as in the following examples:

> But his influence, **through the strong Scottish contingent in Cologne**, would continue there for some time to come. (Lyall 1985: 61).
>
> Its early masters, **it is true**, were largely drawn from Paris and Cologne, but the majority of the students came from the Netherlands, and even the first teachers were frequently Netherlanders returning from the foreign universities where they had made their names. (Lyall 1985: 59)

The position of the interruption in this last case is important from a rhetorical point of view. What the writer is doing here is contrasting the masters and students in terms of where they came from. By placing *it is true* where he does, he sets up the contrast: the first clause is about the masters, and whatever is true is true about them, while the second clause is about the students.

Here are some examples where the interruption follows the finite verb:

> The standard false belief task may be more independent of intersubjective experience, being more of a cognitive-developmental progression than emotional appraisal which requires, **instead**, more appropriate sociocultural scaffolding. (sn="5567")
>
> In putting this hypothesis to the test we are, **however**, faced with two problems. (Keizer 2007: 49)
>
> Typical infants do, **in fact**, appreciate such acts by 11–12 months of age (Sroufe & Wunsch, 1972), but even the children with autism who had higher developmental ages were not reported to laugh at such acts. (sn="5832")
>
> Neither man is ever given a surname, so we are reduced to speculation about their identities. We can, **however**, be sure which of the pair had been assaulted by Stoddart: the man in question was a bachelor *formatus* in theology, but the magistrand of 1452 could not possibly have obtained that status within four years of completing his Arts course. It was almost certainly, **therefore**, the anonymous master who was received at the end of February who fell foul of Robert Stoddart a couple of months later. (Lyall 1985: 63)

In this last example the interruptions again serve a clear function in the argument. The first sentence tells us that we cannot be certain about their identities. By placing *however* in the second sentence after the modal verb, the writer tells the reader to put emphasis on the word *can*, which underlines the contrast with the first sentence. The same technique is then repeated with *therefore* in the third sentence: by placing it after *certainly*, a strong contrast is made between something that could not possibly be the case and something that almost certainly is the case. At the paragraph level, we see that both interruptions serve to emphasize what the writer feels confident about asserting.

Another position worth mentioning is the one following a coordinating conjunction, a subordinating conjunction, or a relative pronoun. In this position the interruption tends to place emphasis on the grammatical marker itself.

> However, if, **as suggested**, we let go of this requirement, close appositions show an even closer resemblance to normal noun phrases. (Keizer 2007: 42)
>
> Acuña-Fariña (1996), who, **as we have seen**, adopts Burton Roberts's analysis for constructions of the type *The poet Burns*, proposes a different analysis for possessive constructions. (Keizer 2007: 46)
>
> We feel fairly certain that the four lower ranks will be present in other discourses; the fifth may also be, in which case, **once we have studied comparative data**, we will use the more general label *interaction*. (Sinclair & Coulthard 1992: 4)
>
> It is hardly surprising that, **due to the role of naming and the importance of words and their meaning in the experiments conducted**, linguistics has been one of the major areas to contribute to and be influenced by the new developments in cognitive psychology. (Keizer 2007: 205)

Note with regard to this last example that subordinate clauses can also occur at the beginning of an embedded clause following the subordinator *that*, where they can best be seen as a frame for a new segment of the sentence rather than an interruption, witness the lack of an initial comma. German writers tend not to make much use of this option in their English. Common combinations include *that because, that before, that by + -ing, that even if, that if, that once, that since, that (al)though, that when(ever)* and *that while*:

> He argues **that because** thieving is his true calling in life, it isn't a sin for him to steal wallets.
>
> We shall see, in fact, **that before** the poem is over even Amans will smile and become England's poet.
>
> Like Joke Dame, Frith maintains **that by** listen**ing** to the voice we are listening to the physical sound of the body.
>
> The hooligans knew **that even** if they were caught, they would be charged only with a minor infraction such as disturbing the peace.
>
> Finally, note **that while** instance methods can use this keyword, class methods cannot.

Finally, here is a sentence with three interruptions in places we have specified above. Despite the interruptions this sentence still runs quite smoothly, but three is about the limit:

> It is important, **however**, to realize that, **as pointed out by Rosch in her later work (Rosch 1978, 1981)**, prototype effects are, **indeed**, effects and do not themselves constitute a theory of the way categories are processed or learned (e.g. Rosch 1978: 28); […]. (Keizer 2007: 205)

The form

Interruptions are often short, chiefly in the form of conjunctive and stance adverbials, but they also can be rather longer, even for instance taking the form of a full independent clause:

> Throughout the century, **indeed**, a steady trickle of Cistercians and of Dominicans came to Cologne from Scotland; the Dominicans, **certainly**, were attracted by the convent and *studium* of their order […]. (Lyall 1985: 56)
>
> Most existing theories, **we have seen**, analyse close appositions as consisting of two (co-referential) NPs. (Keizer 2007: 39)
>
> He also reported that Elizabeth defended her use of the Litany – **and the wording of her justification is significant** – by pointing out that the English Litany 'was set forth in the kying my Father hys dayes'. (sn="4230")

Subordinate clauses are found too, for instance in the position following the subject. Relative clauses, as we have already noted, are used here to identify the subject as a relevant topic in the given context, but other subordinate clauses serve to give circumstantial information, to hint at noteworthy information which is still to come, or to comment on it in advance:

> None of those involved in the official investigation, **even though they understood what was expected of them**, were willing to openly attack the Government's decision.
>
> Charles Darwin, **visiting Sydney in the winter of 1835 on the homeward voyage of the Beagle**, noticed that even the children of Standard English-speaking colonial officials were affected by the convict talk: […]. (McCrum et al. 1986: 293)
>
> The reading public, **if it didn't know already**, quickly came to realize that the manly initials concealed a writer who was in fact a woman, significantly one who was regarded among professional initiates as a late twentieth-century English intellectual with a dense and voraciously allusive style that had elicited comparisons with George Eliot. (Todd 1996: 26)

This last example is worth looking at in more detail. First we are given the subject, *the reading public*, which we will also readily interpret as the topic of the sentence. Then the interruption comes, which means a delay in hearing what is so interesting about the reading public, but we are given a clue: the expression *if it didn't know already* suggests that there is something the author believes they probably knew already. This is an authorial comment on the reading public and at the same time an advance announcement to the reader that what is to come is indeed noteworthy information. This expectation is immediately fulfilled with the expression *quickly came to realize that* ... We thus see that interruptions indeed break a sentence up, but if done skilfully, they draw the reader's attention to particular units of information within the sentence.

It is also possible to provide a double interruption of the subject:

> The executive editor of Byatt's American publisher (**by then Random House**), **Susan Kamil**, is quoted as saying: 'It wasn't just that the book was well reviewed. It was celebrated. [...]' (Todd 1996: 32)
>
> Parini's view, **in other words, for all its allusive and at times off-the-wall cultural shorthand**, is about as good a piece of advertising copy for *Possession* as could be imagined [...] (Todd 1996: 42)

However, you should be careful not to overload the front of the sentence. This can lead to imbalance and draw attention away from the new information at the end of the main clause.

The effect

The basic effect of interruption is that, in addition to highlighting the intervention itself, it at the same time invites the reader to pay extra attention both to what goes before and what comes after.

> It would be a mistake, **however**, to assume from this a simple process of linear progression, reaching its culmination in the great struggles of 1793–1815. (sn="4170")

In this example the positioning of *however* puts extra emphasis on the idea of something being a mistake, and at the same time it increases the tension: the reader wants to know what the mistake actually is.

An additional effect is that it can impose the voice of the author on the content of the text (see Module I, Chapter 2.2). When writing about for instance literary subjects, or in texts of whatever kind where you are evaluating what others have said, then timely interruption can give you the chance to say what you think without coming into the foreground, without dominating the text. It is therefore an important rhetorical technique to master.

However, you should be careful where to interrupt, because the result may not achieve the intended effect. Consider the following example from a student essay:

> Since women become less fertile after the age of thirty, they will look for other ways of conceiving a baby when they, **after a certain period of trying**, are still not pregnant.

The problem here is that the interruption separates and therefore highlights a grammatical subject which should not receive any emphasis at all. A better position would be immediately following the subordinate conjunction, where the adverbials functions as a framing device for the content of the subordinate clause that follows:

> Since women become less fertile after the age of thirty, they will look for other ways of conceiving a baby when, **after a certain period of trying**, they are still not pregnant.

Here is another case of a misplaced interruption from a student essay:

> Nevertheless, the number of students has increased, **as a result of a traditional education**, steadily over the past ten years.

In this case the interruption comes after the verb but splits the verb from the modifier *steadily*, but in the context both *has increased* and *steadily* are new information. When the interruption splits the clause in two like this it is important that the given information should be split from the new information. A better position would therefore be after the finite verb:

> Nevertheless, the number of students has, **as a result of a traditional education**, increased steadily over the past ten years.

One thing to be careful about is the precise position of interruptions with regard to noun phrases. Although the following example comes from a published text, one might argue that the flow of the sentence is unrhythmically interrupted:

> It is symptomatic of this critical neglect that notes, **written in Foxe's handwriting and found among his papers**, about Elizabeth's tribulations during her sister's reign have been almost completely unexamined. (sn="4201")

One way to restore the rhythm in this sentence might be to complete the noun phrase before inserting the extra information. Because there is then a certain distance between *notes* and *written*, the readability of the sentence could be improved by formulating the interruption as a relative clause, thus incorporating a plural verb form which will help the reader see the link with the plural *notes*:

> It is symptomatic of this critical neglect that notes about Elizabeth's tribulations during her sister's reign, **which were written in Foxe's handwriting and found among his papers**, have been almost completely unexamined.

3.5.2 Missed opportunities

One of the functions of interruptive elements is to provide background information on entities which play an important role in the ongoing discourse. Learner writers sometimes present such background information as a separate orthographic sentence, thus affording it more rhetorical weight than it deserves (see Chapter 1.1. of this module). This is the case in the following segment (the offending sentence is in bold):

> But within Labour there are also supporters of the ruling. Tony Blair himself is reviewing the all-women policy. He has never been a real protagonist of it, and now he has a good reason to abandon it. He will not enter the election with an illegal selection procedure of his candidates. **Another supporter of the ruling is Mr. Geach, a former member of Labour.** He said that the ruling will certainly sent a message to the Labour Party, which has a sexist policy in place [announcement of quote from Geach at this point, not included in corpus]. Roy Hattersley, a former deputy leader, called the all-women policy a silly policy. He called on Tony Blair to abandon it. All these different reactions to the tribunal's ruling show that Labour hasn't decided how to react. (ICLE-DN-GRO-0002.1)

In this case there is no great need to make a special point of the introduction of Geach into the discourse: he is mentioned very briefly as an example and does not return in the next couple of paragraphs. If the writer had used an apposition, s/he could have appropriately downgraded Geach's status. Here are two alternative reformulations:

> Another supporter of the ruling, Mr Jim Geach, **a former Labour MP**, said that the ruling will certainly send a message to the Labour Party, which has a sexist policy in place.
>
> Another supporter of the ruling, **former Labour MP Jim Geach**, said that the ruling will certainly send a message to the Labour Party, which has a sexist policy in place.

It is conceivable that the writer shied away from the first alternative so as not to have to use a double apposition, but a double apposition does not really disturb the flow of the sentence here, and the restrictive apposition within the non-restrictive apposition is also not too heavy.

Now consider the following example, which is slightly different but again includes a copula construction which introduces a new discourse referent in a rather prominent fashion:

> I think that the Food and Drug Administration, a institution that creates regulation concerning their field of expertise, will have a tough job on campaigning against the cigarette companies. The FDA is now trying to make smoking look like it is sort of the same thing as drugs <R>. **A new regulation is an ID rule**. This rule says that without a driver's license or an other legal identification card that states that one is 21 or older the youth cannot buy cigarettes. More new regulations are on the way and are all based on trying to reduce the smoking habits among young teenage kids. (ICLE-DN-GRO-0004.1)

There are a number of possible alternatives here which allow the writer to say what s/he wants in one sentence and move the discourse along. The first option below involves a focalization with *for example*, which foregrounds *the ID rule*, while the second uses an apposition to put *the ID rule* into the background.

> The ID rule**, for example**, is a new regulation that says that without a driver's license or another legal identification card that states that one is 21 or older the youth cannot buy cigarettes.
>
> One new regulation, **the ID rule**, says that without a driver's license or another legal identification card that states that one is 21 or older the youth cannot buy cigarettes.

To summarize, we have seen in this section that interruption is a technique which is very good to master because it allows a clear distinction between foregrounded and backgrounded information, it is usually compact, it introduces detail and nuance, and it affords space to the voice of the author. Moreover, it provides variation and it can make a sentence more interesting to read. The danger is that if you do not interrupt at the right point in the clause, you can produce an unrhythmical sentence.

3.6 Elaborational techniques

3.6.1 Elaboration

With framing we saw that subordinate clauses and other structures are used to provide an orientation for what is to come, a framework for a better understanding of the main information in the sentence. With interruption we saw a range of different functions, including clarification, specification, grounding and commentary. We now turn to elaborated sentences. The main formal feature of an elaboration is that it follows the information which it modifies, and as with the other two positional types of combining, it is the position of the information which is key to understanding its function. What is striking about elaboration is that the information is often quite important, rather than being backgrounded as with interruptions. This is because it follows on from the main information and can only be interpreted in the light of that information.

This was the case with a lot of examples of *-ing* clauses and relative clauses in 3.2 above. Here are some more examples:

> The United Nations also called for sanctions, **insisting on an embargo on arms sales to Yugoslavia**.
> During World War II this theory was converted into practice, **which gave rise to nuclear weapons and reactors**.
> Many pollutants were totally absent before World War II, **having made their environmental debut in the war years**.

The function of this new information is to elaborate on the message expressed by the previous clause: the information can be seen as a response to the imaginary request 'tell me more'. For instance, in the first example the non-finite clause gives more detail concerning the nature of the proposed sanctions; and in the second example the relative clause relates to a major consequence of the event described in the first clause. Another common function of elaborating clauses is to clarify (some aspect of) the information in the preceding clause; as such, the new information is an answer to the question 'How come?'. The non-finite clause in the third example explains why many pollutants were not available before World War II.

When attached to an element at the end of the clause, non-restrictive relatives often present new information which is about the next event in a sequence. Again, in terms of importance this information may not at all be subordinate to the information in the main clause.

> First the letters are read by a team of trained assistants, **who then produce summaries for discussion in the editorial meeting**.

In these cases the relative clause can be a stylistically attractive alternative to clauses introduced by *and*.

But the most frequent function of relative clauses in final position is to clarify or explain information concerning the point made in the previous clause. As such they can be a rather elegant alternative to adverbial clauses with *because* and *since*. Here are some examples:

> Why do these countries not select a local language for official use? The problem is how to choose between the many indigenous languages, **each of which represents an ethnic background to which the adherents are fiercely loyal**. In Nigeria, for example, …

> And even if one language did have a clear majority, its selection would be opposed by the combined weight of the other speakers, **who would otherwise find themselves seriously disadvantaged, socially and educationally**. (Crystal 1988: 3)

In the first example, the relative clause helps the reader to understand the nature of the problem: in what sense is it a problem to choose between the languages? The text then goes on to describe the loyal attitudes to the indigenous languages of Nigeria. If the relative clause were missing, there would be a significant gap in the argumentation. The same holds for the second example: here the reader is provided with information about the other speakers, but the function of this information is to explain why the selection of one language would be opposed by so many people.

Note finally that, as we pointed out in 3.2.2, English has a number of complex relative pronouns such as *in which case* and *at which point* which increase the flexibility of elaborational clause combining, as in the following example:

> In what is to become a series of biannual reports, the European Commission highlights a number of issues facing Europe, **perhaps the most important of which are education and training**.

Another elaboration technique involves using complex noun phrases, where the head noun acts as a kind of 'retrospective label', summarizing the ideas that have gone before (cf. Francis 1994; see also Module III, Chapter 2). In the following examples, the phrase *scruffy and undernourished* is picked up by *condition*, and two entire sentences are neatly encapsulated in the nouns *factor* and *point*.

> The animal appeared scruffy and undernourished, **a condition often seen in gorillas from Visoke's northern slopes**. ('was häufig bei Gorillas an den Nordhängen des Visoke zu beobachten ist')
> Mountains and forests made Ulster inaccessible from the central plain, **a factor which remained important until the seventeenth century**. ('was bis ins siebzehnte Jahrhundert von Bedeutung war')
> Monitoring compliance is generally critical in a clinical trial, **a point taken up in detail in Section 3.3**.

The same strategy may be used to make a clear reference in cases where a simple relative pronoun may have double reference. In the following sentence, for example, it is not clear whether *which* refers to *debate* or to *problem*:

Another interesting fact was the debate on the Berlin problem, **which allowed people to realise how difficult things were**.

This can be clarified for the reader by repeating the relevant head noun:

→ Another interesting fact was the debate on the Berlin problem, **a debate which allowed people to realise how difficult things were.**

Finally, we would like to note a rather significant grammatical difference between the subordinate clauses that occur in framed sentences and those that occur in elaborated sentences. The use of elaborational structures to build new information onto an initial main point allows syntactic variation that one would normally expect to be restricted to independent clauses. Some of the word order options that we discussed in Chapter 2 of this module are available in elaborational clauses as well. Here are some examples:

Inversion constructions
The Americans should not be blamed, **since only at a late stage did they really become actively involved**.
*Since only at a late stage did they really become actively involved, the Americans should not be blamed.

Presentative constructions
We must beware of taking too limited a view of the Balkan conflict, **because also involved are the fears of the Greeks and the aspirations of certain Islamic groups**.
*Because also involved are the fears of the Greeks and the aspirations of certain Islamic groups, we must beware of taking too limited a view of the Balkan conflict.

Question forms
Clearly this needs to be looked at again, **since is it not obvious that one of the parties at least is lying?**
*Since is it not obvious that one of the parties at least is lying, clearly this needs to be looked at again.

Fronted objects
Some commentators have urged the general secretary of the United Nations to take a more radical position in this matter, **although really aggressive talk he tends to steer away from**.
??Although really aggressive talk he tends to steer away from, some commentators have urged the general secretary of the United Nations to take a more radical position in this matter.

If you use any of these features, you are actually telling the reader that you are paying special attention to particular pieces of information, which suggests that the message as a whole is also quite important for you. The word order effects thus correlate with this non-backgrounded status. By contrast, such effects never occur in subordinate clauses with a framing or interruptive function.

3.6.2 Missed opportunities

We noted in 2.3.2 that the learner writer's tendency to focus on producing grammatically correct structures often leads to a failure to distinguish adequately between relatively important and relatively unimportant information. Here are some more data from learner writing which point up the value of assessing the status of information before deciding on the best sentence construction option. This time it is not the framing that can be improved by linking sentences together, but rather it is a matter of showing relatively unimportant information by tagging it onto the previous sentence as a form of elaboration.

Here are two examples from student work where relatively unimportant information has been given sentence status:

> The surprisingly small increase might be explained by the fact that our sample did not comprise institutionalized women. In fact, in nursing homes elderly women with urinary incontinence are rather apparent. **Estimates of the prevalence in nursing homes exceed 50%.**
>
> Much of this art is not even inventoried. Dealers labour under much the same uncatalogued overload. **Dealers do not know what they have half the time**. But the professional criminal knows what he is taking, knows the value, and knows how to get rid of it beforehand.

The bold sentence in the first example provides more detail on the claim in the previous sentence without there really being too much newsworthy information: the expression *nursing homes* is repeated, and *exceed 50%* simply specifies *are rather apparent*. The reworked version improves the idiomaticity of the second sentence and incorporates the third sentence by using an *-ing* clause with the conjunctive preposition *with*:

> Indeed, many elderly women in nursing homes suffer from urinary incontinence, **with estimates exceeding 50%.**

In the second example we have a similar situation. The lack of knowledge of the dealers is set off against the highly organized knowledge of art thieves. The second and third sentences are both about dealers, but all the third sentence does is further specify the difficulties mentioned in the second sentence.

From the paragraph point of view, the sentence in bold only has this supporting role, and so the information can best be incorporated into the second sentence as an elaboration on the main clause, as in this rewritten version:

> Dealers labour under much the same uncatalogued overload, **not knowing what they have half the time.**

3.7 Coordinating and listing

So far in this chapter we have concentrated on techniques for combining units of information using grammatical subordination. In this section we pay attention to coordination, which involves combining units which have equal informational status. A special form of coordination is the process of listing, which for present purposes we view as involving a string of at least three coordinated clauses or phrases which are usually separated from the rest of the sentence which introduces them by a colon.

Coordinating and listing are very simple techniques for packing a lot of information into a relatively small space, thus promoting efficient communication. The basic idea is that if pieces of information are similar in status and belong together, then they should be put together; and if they share common elements, then these probably do not need repeating in full. Take a look at this sequence of three sentences:

> Good teachers try to get the best out of their pupils. Good teachers are more interested in questions than answers. Good teachers are never satisfied with a curriculum imposed from outside.

If you wish to make a strong rhetorical point, you may want to give each of these statements its own sentence, as in the above example. Here the writer is inviting the reader to pay additional attention to each statement by repeating the subject, *good teachers*. But if you do not wish to promote such a strong rhetorical line, you can also tie the statements together by making a sequence of three coordinated clauses in one sentence, as follows:

> Good teachers try to get the best out of their pupils, good teachers are more interested in questions than answers, and good teachers are never satisfied with a curriculum imposed from outside.

This version feels more like one rhetorical move consisting of three coordinated steps. However, the rhetorical force is not dissimilar to the first three-sentence sequence, with emphasis still very clearly being put on *good teachers*. It is also possible to go one step further and combine the three original sentences in such a way that you make three statements about one topic:

> Good teachers try to get the best out of their pupils, are more interested in questions than answers, and are never satisfied with a curriculum imposed from outside.

In this last case, more than in the first example, the writer appears to want to simply state three qualities of good teachers.

The same works for the coordination and listing of phrases:

> This model basically consists of four steps: interpreting the question, retrieving the attitude, rendering a judgment, and reporting an answer.

Here the writer deems it unnecessary to state who performs the various actions of interpreting, retrieving etc. The list is well organized because the steps are presented in a clear order and have an identical structure.

Coordinated clauses and phrases are a common feature of all kinds of writing. The production process may also appear relatively straightforward, but in fact you need to exercise a degree of care. Specifically, you need to:

- make clear what is coordinated with what;
- make all the coordinated or listed items structurally uniform; and
- make all the coordinated or listed items semantically uniform.

We will now look at each of these construction principles in turn.

A first requirement when producing coordinated structures, whether they are clauses or phrases, is that you ensure that your reader can immediately identify the element earlier in the sentence that functions as the host, as it were, of the coordinated elements. Here is an example where due care has not been taken. The host expression is in bold type:

> It would be interesting **to look at** the attitudes towards war of youngsters growing up in the shadow of combat and their position in the battle.

On first reading, the expression *their position in the battle* might well be seen as being coordinated with the phrase *the shadow of combat*; after all, the two phrases are similar in structure and, moreover, *battle* and *combat* are semantically related. However, such an interpretation would obviously not make much sense, since one cannot imagine youngsters 'growing up in their position in the battle'. In fact, *their position in the battle* is coordinated with the much longer phrase *the attitudes towards war … combat*. In other words, both phrases are the object of the host verb *to look at*. In cases like this, particularly where there is a considerable distance between the coordinated phrase and its host, what you have to do is repeat at least part of the host element. Here it might not be enough to repeat just the preposition *at*, given the length of the first phrase, and a better option might be to repeat the whole verb, or alternatively go for a synonym, as in the following reformulation:

> It would be interesting to look at the attitudes towards war of youngsters growing up in the shadow of combat and **to consider** their position in the battle.

Here is a similar example:

> A good writer is aware of his options for varying the word order of a sentence and the consequences of those choices.

Here it looks at first glance as if *the consequences of those choices* is coordinated with *the word order of a sentence*. Again, it is only on second reading that it becomes clear that the phrase *the consequences of those choices* really belongs with *his options for varying word order*. Here it is not enough to repeat the preposition *of*, as there are intervening phrases with the same structure, so a fuller repetition is again called for:

> A good writer is aware of his options for varying the word order of a sentence and **is also aware of** the consequences of those choices.

Our final issue relating to the identification of the host element concerns coordination involving the verb *to be*. Consider this example:

> The legal system should offer more than legal justice. It should be competent as well as fair and define the public interest as being aimed at the achievement of justice, with law being a dynamic instrument of social ordering and social change.

We have a double coordination problem in the second sentence. First of all there are two coordinations, with *competent* and *fair* being coordinated by *as well as*, and then the first and second clauses being coordinated as well. It may therefore be advisable to insert a comma after *fair*, so as to keep the two parts of the sentence separate. The next problem then relates to the coordinating of *be competent as well as fair* with *define the public interest*. Although these are both verbal structures sharing the same subject, they do not really have the same structure, since it is in fact the content element *competent* that is being coordinated with *define*, that is to say an adjective with a verb. In cases like this, the problem can be repaired by again repeating *should*, the host element. To make a rhetorically more forceful point, the writer might also consider repeating the grammatical subject *it*:

> The legal system should offer more than legal justice. It should be competent as well as fair, **and it should define** the public interest as being aimed at the achievement of justice, with law being a dynamic instrument of social ordering and social change.

Our basic advice is never to omit forms of the verb *to be* if the structures following it are different. Finally, here is a very clear-cut case:

> This research agenda is based on, and an elaboration of, Cornelissen et al. (2008).

Whereas the first expression with *is* involves the verbal unit *be based on*, the second part of the coordination involves the copula with a nominal complement; in other words we have two rather different structures. Omitting the form of *to be* in cases like this will lead to disjointed text. Here the problem can be resolved by simple repetition of the host or by using a more specific verb like *form* or *constitute*:

> This research agenda is based on, and is//forms//constitutes an elaboration of, Cornelissen et al. (2008).

It seems, then, that writers may sometimes be slightly overzealous when coordinating. It is as if they are in fact applying what they see as a stylistic rule, that one should be as compact as possible and should always omit information which is not strictly necessary. However, the examples we have presented here show that with coordination, an element of repetition may often be advisable.

The examples with *be* lead us rather directly to the second basic requirement, relating to repetition of structure. It is essential that the items in coordinated structures, and in particular in lists, should all be syntactically uniform. Here is a simple case where the writer has not paid due attention to this feature:

> Just like Queen Beatrix, Queen Elizabeth II is a politically neutral monarch, although she does perform some political tasks, for instance by signing new laws. Other activities on the daily schedule of the queen are presenting decorations, opening new institutions, attending charity festivities and the inspection of the guards of honour.

The first three members of the list in the second sentence have *-ing* forms but the last one has a nominalization. This can easily be repaired by writing *inspecting the guards of honour*:

> Other activities on the daily schedule of the queen are presenting decorations, opening new institutions, attending charity festivities and inspecting the guards of honour.

Here is a more complex case:

> The most important amphetamines are mentioned in the Opium Act and have been thoroughly investigated with regard to their effects in several kinds of sports: keeping

> awake as such is of importance in endurance sports; putting off feelings of tiredness for a while; they give a comfortable feeling; they influence one's perception of time.

The items in this list following the colon have a clausal structure, but it is by no means a uniform structure. The first item, *keeping awake as such is of importance in endurance sports,* is an independent clause with an *ing*-form as subject. The second one, *putting off feelings of tiredness for a while,* in fact turns out to be just a phrase, but because it starts off with a participial form of the verb, just like the first item, the reader may well expect that it will again form the subject of a finite verb in an independent clause, in other words that it will be structured in the same way as the first item. Finally, the third and fourth items are again independent clauses, but they have a different grammatical subject from the first item and present information from a totally different perspective. When dealing with the coordination and listing of clausal structures, we strongly advise that you select one construction type, for instance imperatives, participial constructions, nominalizations or independent clauses with similar subjects, as a means of providing syntactic uniformity. In this case, the relevant section could thus be rewritten as follows:

> they allow one to remain alert longer, which is important in endurance sports; they give sportsmen a comfortable feeling; and they influence one's perception of time.

This version is much clearer than the original version, but in addition, the parallel structure created by three independent clauses of similar length with identical subjects promotes a neat rhythm and creates a rhetorical effect which is totally absent from the original version.

Finally, let us turn to the third requirement, that of semantic uniformity. In the following example we have a problem, because the first noun in the coordinated pair is concrete and the second is abstract.

> An important reason for the continuation of Apartheid is that 'the West' still does a lot of trading with South Africa, in spite of the boycott. This often concerns weapons or other dirty business.

The use of the word *other* in the coordinated phrase suggests that it should be possible to say that weapons are business, but they are not. One way of making the pair semantically uniform would be to change *weapons* into *arms dealing,* which like *business* is a process rather than a concrete object:

> An important reason for the continuation of Apartheid is that 'the West' still does a lot of trading with South Africa, in spite of the boycott. This often concerns **arms dealing** or other dirty business.

Here is a slightly different case:

> Aside from the fact that there is no proof or guarantee whatsoever that NRA will be a benefit to the economy, the opposition feels that the plans are far too great a burden on the environment and daily life.

Here, two concepts – *the environment* and *daily life* – have been given equal status, but they do not really belong happily together: put crudely, the environment is a set of objects while daily life involves a set of events or processes. Nevertheless, it is quite possible to envisage both of them suffering from new government plans. In order to emphasize that each may suffer separately, the writer here could simply repeat the preposition *on*:

> Aside from the fact that there is no proof or guarantee whatsoever that NRA will be a benefit to the economy, the opposition feels that the plans are far too great a burden on the environment and **on daily life**.

The effect is to give each phrase a more individual status. We are now no longer talking about 'the environment and daily life' as a coordinated concept, as it were, but rather about two different burdens: a burden on the environment and a burden on daily life.

In this next example the writer can look for a different kind of solution:

> The shortcomings of the British health service are now being tackled by a number of authorities: the Ministry of Health and Social Services, hospital administrations, the nurses' union and the doctors themselves.

The problem here is that neither doctors nor the nurses' union are really authorities, at least not in the sense being applied here. However, rather than reorganize the list, the writer might consider choosing a different superordinate expression to introduce the list. Something like *a number of stakeholders* might do the trick:

> The shortcomings of the British health service are now being tackled by **a number of stakeholders**: the Ministry of Health and Social Services, hospital administrations, the nurses' union and the doctors themselves.

Now consider this more complex case of a list that has gone wrong due to a lack of semantic uniformity:

> Before the capacity of the airport can be increased, it has to deal with the problems of the neighbourhood: devaluation of houses, serious mental problems, sleeping problems, high blood pressure and other health problems.

The list here includes economic and health terms. There is a lack of semantic uniformity in that *devaluation* stands on its own, and on top of that a strong impression is created that it is mainly about health problems. To gain more uniformity in this list, it might be an option to divide the problems into two parts:

> Before the capacity of the airport can be increased, it has to deal with the problems of the neighbourhood: **economic problems such as house devaluation and health problems such as lack of sleep, high blood pressure, and even serious mental problems.**

In this reformulation, the elements have also been reordered so as to have the most serious health issues at the end.

All in all, it appears that managing coordinated structures in complex sentences is not as straightforward as one might imagine: the reader needs to know what is being combined with what, and readability is also served by lists of items which both syntactically and semantically have a uniform composition.

3.8 Problems with sentence length

In our introduction to sentence construction in Chapter 1 we noted that sentences in English academic writing vary in length but can often be quite long. So far in this chapter we have talked about the shape of the sentence but we have not paid much attention to size. By deciding to combine clauses into a complex sentence, you are sending a signal to your reader that you want various pieces of information to be seen as related to each other in one communicative unit. In this respect it is important to see the sentence as the basic building block of the paragraph.

When you decide how big, or how long, to make your sentence, there are two things that you have to take into account. First, you should not put so much information into one sentence that the reader becomes confused about what the main points are. Second, you should not put so little information into one sentence that your reader is forced to wonder why the information should be so important in the given context – we already saw this in the 'missed opportunities' sections above relating to framing, interrupting and elaborating. This does not mean that you should avoid very short and very long sentences at all costs. On the contrary, both short and long sentences have their own specific purposes. But they do need to be shaped with care. In this section we look at a number of specific problems.

3.8.1 Long sentences

In earlier sections of this chapter we presented examples of sentences which are quite long and complex. Often, good sentence rhythm is created by having a tripartite structure of framing – main clause – elaboration. If you construct long sentences, we advise you to (a) restrict framing to no more than two elements before the main clause, (b) avoid long pieces of parenthetical information, and (c) avoid too many interruptions.

Here is an example of a sentence taken from a student essay that contains too many points of detail presented in a syntactic mould that is too complex.

> New drugs and a vaccine alone are not enough to fight malaria. **They have to be combined with improved health-care facilities, for example spraying campaigns, neighbourhood clean-ups to eliminate breeding places for the mosquito and better environmental management including biological controls, such as the use of fish that eat the mosquito in its egg and larval stages.** Only then can malaria be fought successfully.

The new information in the offending sentence here consists of a list of three measures: health-care facilities, clean-ups and environmental management. However, the way that these are presented hampers readability. First, two elements of the list have examples attached to them, the last one being quite long; in addition, the second member of the list is itself syntactically complex; finally, the third list member is exemplified in two distinct stages. By the time the sentence is over, the reader may well have difficulty in determining what is being referred to with the phrase *only then* at the beginning of the next sentence.

Here is an edited version in which the first two members of the list are presented together in one sentence and the longest member of the list has been given a sentence of its own.

> They have to be combined with improved health-care facilities, for example spraying campaigns, and neighbourhood clean-ups to eliminate breeding places for the mosquito. Moreover, there is a need for better environmental management, including biological controls, such as the use of fish that eat the mosquito in its egg and larval stages. Only when such measures have been taken can malaria be fought successfully.

Now consider an example of excessive framing from a student essay. Indeed, the framing elements make up 90% of the words in this long sentence, which suggests that the information needs to be spelled out in a separate sentence first.

> If one considers the consequences of the amount of money that has already been retrenched and if one takes into account a report, recently drawn up by the Department of Trade and Industry, about the need in British industrial life for academics, which says that there is already a shortage of fifteen hundred academics

> qualified in subjects of decisive importance for the new technology, such as computer science and electronics, and which says that in two years this shortage will probably have risen to five thousand, then one may conclude that the universities are indeed facing a crisis.

The effect of the excessive framing is that the reader is left waiting for the main clause, for the point of the sentence, but it takes a long time to come. In fact, at a certain stage the reader may forget that the sentence started with the conjunction *if*. Here is an alternative version with minimal alterations:

> According to a recent report, there is a shortage of fifteen hundred academics in British industry. The report, drawn up by the Department of Trade and Industry, stresses the need for academics trained in subjects of decisive importance for the new technology, such as computer science and electronics, and says that in two years the shortage will probably have risen to five thousand. If in addition to this one considers the cuts which the universities have already had to suffer, then one may conclude that they are indeed facing a crisis.

In this version, the necessary background detail is first presented in two sentences, and only in the third sentence is the reader confronted with the conclusion.

3.8.2 Short sentences

When building up a paragraph, you have to decide whether a particular message is so important that it should be given separate sentence status. There are indeed many situations where it is important to let simple statements stand out. For instance, short simple sentences are often effective as topic sentences because it is of great importance that the starting point of a paragraph is clear and involves one main point rather than several. Short, powerful sentences are also good summarizers at the end of a detailed explanation, where they can have an 'in other words' effect. And short sentences can also be used to great effect at the end of a paragraph as a punchy way of rounding off an argument (see the discussion of 'climax sentences' in Module I, Chapter 3.4). In fact, a short sentence will always be effective if it is clear what rhetorical force is involved in putting a small amount of information into the relatively powerful mould of the sentence.

In the following example, contrast the brevity and simplicity of the basic point made in the opening topic sentence with the length and detail of the ensuing sentences, which elaborate on the first point. Again we have chosen a literary text here, since literary text often weaves quite a number of pieces of information into one complex sentence and at the same time makes use of short sentences for making fundamental statements:

> But he could scarcely have chosen a lovelier. Jane Mack's daughter was about 21 then and a beauty, with a St. Croix suntan to set off her honey-blonde hair and a smashing backless, nearly frontless gown to set off the suntan. Already she was a confirmed overdrinker (it was Singer who, that same evening, amiably corrected my misapprehension that the Yiddish term *shicker* described a Jewish man who, like himself, consorted with *shiksas*) and finally bitten by the theatrical bug. But the booze hadn't marked her yet, and given her looks, her youth, and her small connection with the Industry – which was still dominated by Hollywood in those days – Jeannine's aspirations didn't seem bizarre, at least at a party. (Barth 1979: 82)

By contrast, learner writers sometimes produce short simple sentences that do not have a clear rhetorical function. If you find yourself writing a short sentence, for instance one consisting of a short main clause that has little modification and is less than ten words long, then you should indeed do a quick check: is the content of the sentence important enough, given your paragraph aims, to stand on its own?

Let us look at a number of cases where the value of a separate sentence is highly debatable. First, consider this fragment from a student paper:

> The influences of the different continental dialects on Anglo-Norman as described by Pope run parallel to certain developments in the history of England. In 1066 William the Conqueror came to England, and his followers came especially from Normandy, Brittany and Maine. In 1154 Henry II of Plantagenet, Duke of Normandy and Aquitaine and Earl of Anjou, became king of England. **His vassals replaced the reigning nobility**. They came from all parts of the empire of the Plantagenets, which contained the whole of Western France.

The writer of this paragraph sets out to show that one can trace the influence of dialects on Anglo-Norman by identifying the origin of groups of people who came from France to England. The problem here is the penultimate sentence. Given the aim of the paragraph, the origin of the vassals is more important than the fact that they replaced the reigning nobility. This suggests a reworking of the last two sentences along the following lines:

> His vassals, who replaced the reigning nobility, came from all parts of the empire of the Plantagenets, which contained the whole of Western France.

Here is another example. The problem sentence is the second one, in bold:

> America has the highest level of productivity of the big OECD economies. **Data on absolute productivity are always a year out of date**. A study using OECD

> figures, however, shows that in the mid-1980's America produced almost twice as much for every man-hour worked, across the entire economy, as Japan. One reason for this is Japan's notoriously inefficient services.

This text is about American productivity, and the nature of the data is a background matter. The hierarchical status of the information can be better captured in a concessive clause:

> **Although data on absolute productivity are always a year out of date**, a study using OECD figures shows that in the mid-1980s ...

Finally, consider again the text on Dutch drugs policy which we discussed in 3.3 above. The sentences given in bold are the sole supporting information for the statements in the previous sentence. The supporting information is itself not elaborated upon and is hence a prime candidate for backgrounding.

> There are several schemes in operation supporting this idea. Coffee shops in Amsterdam sell cannabis openly. **This is done to prevent underground drug movements**. Drug victims are given guidance and help to kick the habit. **Special drug centres have been set up to give assistance**. So far the Dutch policy has yielded positive results.

By opting for four sentences instead of six, and by backgrounding the supporting information, you can make it much clearer for the reader that the text involves (a) an opening statement, (b) two illustrations of the 'several schemes' in operations, and (c) a commentary on the success of the schemes. This way, the introduction is short and sharp, and the writer's comment is too. The longer sentences are used to provide the detail.

> There are several schemes in operation supporting this idea. For instance, coffee shops in Amsterdam sell cannabis openly, thus preventing underground drug movements. In addition, special drug centres have been set up for drug victims, who receive guidance and help to kick the habit. So far this policy has yielded positive results.

3.9 Review

This chapter has focused on the construction of complex sentences. We have looked at the function of clause combining, the grammatical forms used for combining, the sentence shapes that emerge as a result of combining, and the problems that arise when writers combine too much and do not combine enough. Here are the main points of the chapter, arranged according to area of attention.

Function

- One of the writer's most important tasks is to foreground important information and consider if there is less important information that can usefully be backgrounded, for instance by presenting it in the form of a subordinate clause.
- By combining two pieces in the first place, you ask the reader to interpret them as one segment within the paragraph. Clause combining thus allows the reader to view the paragraph as consisting of a relatively small number of steps in an argument rather than a string of individual statements.
- By selecting a particular linking device you can signal the meaning relation between the two messages you have combined.
- By placing the dependent clause in a particular position you can strengthen or weaken the backgrounding effect.

Form

- English makes use of different types of finite clause, non-finite clause and verbless clause for clause combining purposes. English uses more non-finite and verbless structures than German.
- One of the most valuable forms of combining to master is the non-finite *-ing* clause. This clause type can occur in all positions in the sentence and can be used to express a variety of meaning relationships.
- Another valuable form of clause combining is the non-restrictive relative clause, which is quite versatile in English both in terms of form and function.

Shape

- There are three basic positions for combining – beginning, middle and end – and consequently three basic shapes that complex sentences assume. We have called these 'framed sentences', 'interrupted sentences', and 'elaborated sentences'. In practice, sentences often demonstrate a mix of these three basic shapes.
- The position of the combined clause in the sentence correlates with its function.

Advice

- You should not be frightened about producing long sentences in English.
- It is important to vary sentence length, but it is even more important to make sure that long sentences do not contain too many points and that short sentences succeed in containing enough rhetorical power.

Chapter 4

Punctuation

The main points in this chapter are these:

- The placement of commas affects the meaning of the sentence.
- Different punctuation marks express different meaning relationships between parts of sentences.
- Appropriate use of punctuation allows you to foreground and background individual pieces of information in the sentence.
- Appropriate use of punctuation can significantly increase the readability of a sentence.
- Punctuation in English is different from punctuation in German in important respects.

As a foreign language student you might well think that punctuation is a relatively unimportant aspect of writing. Yes, you may concede, there are indeed a small number of rules that have to be learned, but otherwise punctuation may be something which you feel does not really require much attention. You may even see confirmation in the frequent comment that the main aim of punctuation is to make the text easier to read, or to help the reader uncover the rhythm of the sentence (see for instance Kane 1988: 275f), and hence you may conclude that the best way to punctuate a text is to follow your own intuition. The aim of this chapter is to show that this is a very dangerous approach to take. Choices that you make with regard to punctuation are just as important as the grammatical and lexical choices you make when it comes to writing effective English. What is more, the comma placement rules for English are markedly different than those for German.

Much of this chapter is devoted to the comma, as this is the most common and the most problematic punctuation device (4.1–4.2). We then go on to consider the colon (4.3), the semicolon (4.4), and brackets and dashes (4.5).

We finish off with a look at comma splicing (4.6), which is a major problem for many advanced learners, and for which the colon and semicolon often provide an elegant solution.[20]

4.1 Commas 1: the principle of semantic unity

If you put a comma, or any other punctuation mark for that matter, in a particular place in a sentence, then what you are basically doing is separating one part of the sentence from the other. The implication is that you are asking your reader to pay separate attention to each segment. Punctuating a text is thus all about helping your reader understand what it is you want to say, what it is that you find important. In that light, 'making a text easier to read' can be understood as 'clearly encoding your communicative intention'. Consider the following sentence:

A woman without her man is nothing.

This sentence can be punctuated in various ways. The two versions have essentially opposite meanings: in the first, a man is key to a woman's well-being; in the second it is precisely the other way around. And this is all down to the use of punctuation.

A woman, without her man, is nothing.
A woman: without her, man is nothing.

Punctuation jokes like this abound on the internet. They are indeed mildly humorous, but at the same time they actually point up an essential function of punctuation: the various punctuation marks separate the sentence into groups of words which in some sense belong together, just as the full stop divides the paragraph into rhetorically meaningful sentential units. Moreover, punctuation marks can reveal different meaning relations and different strengths in the relationship between the units they separate, as we will see in the various sections of this chapter.

---

20 We have chosen to concentrate on those areas of punctuation which are central to the construction of effective sentences, by restricting ourselves to the use of punctuation marks to separate words at the level of the phrase, as well as phrases and clauses at the level of the sentence. Punctuation marks are also used in two major ways which we do not discuss here. First, they can express relations between parts of words, by means of the hyphen and the apostrophe. Second, they are used to indicate speech, omissions in the text, and various illocutionary characteristics, such as questions and exclamations. An overview of these other uses can often be found in punctuation guides (e.g. Gethin 1965), writing guides (for example Kane 1988), or more technical works for authors (e.g. *The Chicago manual of style* (2003) or *New Hart's rules* (2005)).

In order to employ the comma in English correctly and effectively, it is important to get to grips with one basic principle, which following Hannay & Mackenzie (2002: 176) we will call the principle of semantic unity, or PSU. The PSU states that, within the orthographic sentence, constituents which in terms of meaning belong together should not be separated by a single comma or other punctuation mark. In other words, comma placement in English is mainly governed by an assessment of semantic and pragmatic relations, rather than by rules which relate strictly to grammatical structure. This does not mean to say that rules cannot easily be expressed in grammatical terms. On the contrary, the basic rules of punctuation can indeed be formulated in this way, but there is always an underlying semantic or pragmatic motivation. And it is an understanding of this meaning-oriented aspect of punctuation in English which not only allows you to get to grips with where punctuation is necessary, but also informs your decisions about punctuation when you have the option of using a comma or not.

Let us start with the most fundamental rule that follows from the PSU:

Never use a single comma to separate the subject from the verb, or the verb from the object.

The semantic motivation for this is that the subject and the object express the participants most closely involved in the state of affairs described by the verb. If the participants are not expressed, the state of affairs may appear incomplete. For instance, consider these sentences involving a subject phrase which is isolated from the rest of the clause:

* Many writers, have commented on the value of punctuation.
* The final chapter, will deal with recent developments in French cinema.

In each case, the subject noun phrase cannot do without the verb phrase and vice versa. They need each other for the sentence to make sense, and that is essentially because neither of the segments on their own expresses a single complete state of affairs. Accordingly, these sentences need to be comma-free:

→ Many writers have commented on the value of punctuation.
→ The final chapter will deal with recent developments in French cinema.

The same holds where the direct object is separated from the rest of the clause:

* Millions of years ago monsters inhabited, the earth.
* We would not wish to belabour, the point.

Here the direct object is separated from the verb by a single comma, but *inhabit* and *belabour* are transitive verbs which cannot really be used without their object. The reason is that these sentences do not express a complete state of affairs. If we add the object and do not separate it from the rest of the clause, then we get a complete state of affairs expressed in one information unit:

→ Millions of years ago monsters inhabited the earth.
→ We would not wish to belabour the point.

Now, it must be said that learners rarely make comma mistakes like those presented above. However, problems do arise when we consider an important implication of the basic rule. If subject and object phrases need to be integrated into the clause in terms of punctuation, then the same applies to subject and object constituents which themselves consist of embedded clauses, as in the following examples:

What one should not forget in this context is the role of punctuation within the grammar.
Smith (2008) has suggested that plagiarism is nothing more than a stage in the process of learning to write.

Following the PSU, it would be wrong to place a comma after *context* and after *suggested*. The strictness of the basic rule means that even if the subject clause is very long, or itself ends in a verb, then nevertheless a comma is out of place (cf. Nunberg et al. 2002: 1745).

Whether or not the experiments carried out by Johnson can be successfully replicated remains to be seen.
What this new edition still fails to do is reflect the confusion of the period.

The same goes for object and complement clauses, which must not be isolated from the rest of the clause:

* The second consideration is, that the event occurred prior to the girl's sixteenth birthday.
→ The second consideration is that the event occurred prior to the girl's sixteenth birthday.
* Section 3 states clearly, that editors must not publish information about research which is regarded as ethically unsound.
→ Section 3 states clearly that editors must not publish information about research which is regarded as ethically unsound.

You need to be particularly careful here because many verbs which occur frequently in argued texts can take a *that*-clause as object: *say, report, know, suggest, claim, declare,* to mention just a few. Again, none of these verbs should be separated from an embedded *that*-clause by means of a comma.

We should note at this point, however, that there is one small exception to this basic rule. Because the need to ensure readability is paramount in good writing, a comma is occasionally useful to separate adjoining verb phrases, as in this example given by Nunberg et al. (2002: 1730):

> Most of those who can, work at home.

The comma is advisable here to prevent the reader from interpreting *can work* as constituting a verb phrase.

We can now take the PSU one step further, and consider the use of commas in relative clauses.

> RESTRICTIVE: Arts centres **which are not concerned about attracting the wider public** should have their subsidies taken away.
> NON-RESTRICTIVE: Arts centres**, which are not concerned about attracting the wider public,** should have their subsidies taken away.

Whereas the first example is a statement about a specific group of arts centres, namely those which are not concerned about attracting the public, the second example assumes that all arts centres have this lack of concern and claims that they should all have their subsidies taken away. Here the difference in meaning between the restrictive type – with no commas – and the non-restrictive type – with commas – becomes particularly apparent, and it is obvious that the commas play a crucial role in the interpretation of the sentence. Note that relative clauses are thus either separated from the surrounding clause by two punctuation marks or they are not separated at all. The following example is thus incorrect:

> * The assumptions which underlie the modernity school, can be seen in the work of Cohen and Till (1977).

Like relative clauses, appositions, too, can be either restrictive or non-restrictive. Here is an example of each type, from academic texts:

> RESTRICTIVE: The arrival of Heimerich van de Velde (de Campo) from Paris in 1422 introduced to Cologne the neo-Albertist teachings of **the Paris master Johannes de Novo Domo**. (Lyall 1985: 56)
> NON-RESTRICTIVE: The main part of the narrative consists of the privately printed memoirs of **her feckless husband, Archibald McCandless**. (Todd 1996: 146)

Commas serve their standard separating function with non-restrictive appositions and are not used with restrictive appositions, as the examples show. Here is another set:

> RESTRICTIVE: Rivers **such as the Thames** have had to contend with a rise in commercial water traffic.
> NON-RESTRICTIVE: Some rivers**, such as the Thames,** have had to contend with a rise in commercial water traffic.

In the first example, the lack of commas indicates that the writer sees *rivers such as the Thames* as one semantic unit, and this leads more easily to the interpretation that we are talking about a particular kind of river, for instance rivers that flow through large cities. In the second example, on the other hand, the commas which separate *such as the Thames* from the rest of the sentence invite the interpretation that the Thames is just one example of a river that has had to contend with increasing traffic. However, the mention of the Thames is not directly relevant to defining what particular kind of river may be meant; in fact, it may be all kinds of relatively large rivers. The difference in meaning between the two examples is subtle, but it may also be important, and the commas play a crucial role. Importantly, the difference can again be understood in terms of the PSU.

The use of punctuation with regard to a whole host of other structures can also be understood following the major distinction between restrictive and non-restrictive elements. Parenthetical information, for instance, is by definition non-restrictive. Hence, whenever information is inserted parenthetically into a sentence, commas are necessary. Here are some of the examples which we gave in our discussion of interruption techniques in Chapter 3.5:

> Some men, **especially middle-class men**, came to value domesticity more highly. (sn="4456")
> Most existing theories, **we have seen**, analyse close appositions as consisting of two (co-referential) NPs. (Keizer 2007: 39)
> It is important, **however**, to realize that, **as pointed out by Rosch in her later work (Rosch 1978, 1981)**, prototype effects are, **indeed**, effects and do not themselves constitute a theory of the way categories are processed or learned (e.g. Rosch 1978: 28); [...]. (Keizer 2007: 205)

By contrast, various constructions have semantic features similar to restrictive appositions and restrictive relative clauses. Consider the following:

> The financing of the Olympic village will involve much greater tax increases **than the city council imagines**.

The chances of winning the election were so small **that the Liberal Party decided to pull out.**
The fact **that African countries now do so well in major international sports events** does not mean that the IOC is now ready to award the Olympic Games to an African city.

In each of these cases, one piece of information in the sentence serves to define what is meant by another part of the sentence. In the first example, omission of *than the city council imagines* would lead the reader to ask 'greater than what?', forcing him/her to scan the previous context for an answer that might not be there. Similarly, if *that the Liberal Party decided to pull out* was not mentioned, then it would be difficult to know what *so small* meant. And if the *that*-clause were omitted from the third example, the reader would be left wondering what fact is being referred to. In other words, we are dealing here with fixed constructions: *more* [adjective] *than*, *so* [adjective] *that*, and *the fact that*. Here too, then, the PSU applies: because a particular piece of information is necessary for understanding what is meant, it must not be isolated from the rest of the sentence by means of punctuation.

Our final point in this section is of a different order, and relates to the difference between English and German. The PSU allows us to characterise the main difference between the use of the comma in the two languages. The basic rules for comma placement in German with regard to clauses are based on the grammatical status of constituents, whereas we have seen that the English rules are essentially semantic and pragmatic. Here are a number of cases where German prefers a comma but where the grammatically equivalent English structures do not allow punctuation:

Was wichtig ist, ist, dass wir die Kontinuität garantieren.
What is important is that we guarantee continuity.

Schmid behauptet, dass damit ein Zusammenhang zwischen A und C bewiesen sei.
Schmid claims that this proves that there is a relation between A and C.

Das einzige Problem, das aufgetaucht ist, ist der Internetzugang.
The only problem that has emerged is Internet access.

Besonders interessant war die Tatsache, dass die Lösung innerhalb von zwei Wochen implementiert werden konnte.
Particularly interesting was the fact that the solution could be implemented within two weeks.

Wir werden alles unternehmen, um das Problem zu lösen.
We will do everything to solve the problem.

Der Gedanke, den Westen ökonomisch einzuholen, ist in Russland wieder aufgetaucht.
The thought of catching up the West economically has emerged in Russia again.

Sie waren dafür, den Einsatz von Pestiziden drastisch zu reduzieren.
They were in favour of drastically reducing the use of pesticides.

In German, embedded and combined clauses, regardless of whether the verb has a finite form or is an infinitive, are in principle separated from the surrounding clauses by means of commas. This holds for subject and object clauses, complement clauses, adverbial clauses, and relative clauses. What we see in English is that embedded clauses are never separated by punctuation, and that with relative clauses it depends on semantic features whether punctuation is necessary or not.

4.2 Commas 2: optional use

So far we have described the obligatory use or non-use of commas by referring to specific grammatical constructions. In this section we will concentrate on those areas where you have the option of using a comma or not. In the main, the choice depends on precisely what it is you want to say. An understanding of the PSU will help you make a well-motivated decision about whether you need a comma or not.

4.2.1 Separating members of a sequence

The most straightforward function of the comma is to separate items in a sequence. The sequence will often involve adjectives, verbs, or nouns:

Editing involves **reading, understanding and adjusting** someone else's text.
The primary colours are **blue, red and yellow**.
The concepts which typically cause confusion are **conjuncts, disjuncts and subjuncts**.

One problem with this function concerns the use of what is known as the Oxford comma. The final element of a sequence, which is typically introduced by *and* or *or*, is usually not separated from the preceding element of the sequence by a comma. A comma may in fact appear redundant, because the connective is doing its work for it. But the Oxford comma comes in precisely before the connective, where it is not expected:

Editing involves reading, understanding**,** and adjusting someone else's text.

Some writers talk about this punctuation option in terms of feel, or style (see for instance Truss 2003: 85). But a more attractive way to look at it is purely in terms of interpretive effect: the difference between using a comma and not using one is a matter of how much separate attention you want your reader to give to the last element in the list. Remember that the central feature of commas is quite simply that they separate. The effect is that readers will seek to assign an interpretation to blocks of text delineated by punctuation marks as relatively independent units of information. With the Oxford comma, this effect might be described as 'and last but not least'; it is as if you want to make sure that the reader attaches just as much importance to the last member of the sequence as to the first.

4.2.2 Separating adverbial clauses

We have seen that with relative clauses and appositions the use of commas in English is related to the semantic distinction between the restrictive and non-restrictive versions of these constructions. The same distinction is relevant for the punctuation of adverbial clauses (cf. Quirk et al. 1985: 1075f.). Consider the following stretch of text:

> The government at the time declared that environmental concerns had forced it to close down the mines. However, it soon became clear that the decision was taken because the gas industry had bribed senior ministers.

This text contains two assertions. In the first sentence we learn that a certain decision was taken with regard to the closure of mines; the second sentence gives us the reason for the decision. Now imagine that in the second sentence a comma were to be placed before *because*:

> ?? However, it soon became clear that the decision was taken, because the gas industry had bribed senior ministers.

What the comma asks the reader to do here is stop and process the main clause as a separate information unit. The reader will most likely try and interpret this by assigning focus status to the element *that the decision was taken*, and will realise that this does not make for a coherent interpretation, since it may already be concluded from the previous sentence that the decision has been taken. This second sentence actually only makes sense if it is the *because*-clause that is in focus and not the extraposed *that*-clause. It is as if the writer is asserting the same thing twice. If we understand the PSU as relating not only to semantic but also pragmatic aspects of meaning, then again it can help with understanding why a comma is not appropriate in such circumstances.

From the example above we can derive a basic rule:

> If an adverbial clause which elaborates on a preceding clause is the focus of the message conveyed by the previous clause, then the two clauses should not be separated by a comma.

Statistically speaking, adverbial clauses with an elaborational function do not usually have a preceding comma (cf. Chafe 1984). However, certain kinds of adverbial clause almost always have the status of a separate elaboration when they occur after the clause they modify. This is the case with clauses beginning with *while* (in the contrastive sense), *whereas* or *although*; consequently, these are as a rule preceded by a comma.

> Rugby Union is played over the whole of Britain, whereas Rugby League is mainly restricted to Yorkshire and Lancashire.
> Tennis is generally seen as an English sport, although French historians might dispute this.

This is also true for two other clause types: *for*-clauses and sentential relative clauses:

> Unleaded petrol was widely available in Germany before it had even been installed in Britain, which is not surprising given the German obsession with the motor car.

What is characteristic of these clause types is that they cannot be added on to other clauses and still form a single information unit together with them.

To round off this section, let us consider how the use of commas over a longer stretch of text helps the reader to work out the author's intended meaning. Here is a string of two sentences from the introduction to Dryden's translation of Plutarch's *Ten famous lives*:

> The birthplace of Plutarch, we have suggested, was important, for as he walked around Chaeronea he was bound to reflect on the glory and freedom of classical Greece. The date of his birth (approximately 46 A.D.) is also important, because by that time Greece had not only long since ceased to be free but was a province belonging to the Roman Empire. (Plutarch 1962: *xv*.)

The main point in the first sentence is that the birthplace of Plutarch was important. There are two signals that help us understand this. First, the comma after *important* tells us to pause at that point and interpret the sentence so far. Given that the birthplace of Plutarch is an active element in the discourse at this point, and that the author is telling us that he has made the point he is about to make before, we can readily interpret *important* as the focal information in the main clause. Second, the next clause is introduced by the conjunction *for*. As we noted above, a *for*-clause always provides additional information about something which has just been stated independently, in the form of a justification of a preceding statement. In this respect, *for* in English works like *denn* in German.

Something similar happens in the second sentence, except that this time the crucial signal is simply the comma. The writer wants to tell us that Plutarch's date of birth is also important, not only the place. But this second sentence contains the sequence *is also important because*, and an inviting interpretation of these words is that another reason is going to be given for something being important. From a purely formal, punctuational point of view, if there were no comma after *important*, then that would indeed be an obvious interpretation, but because of the comma the reader is forced to interpret *The date of his birth is also important* as a separate information unit, with its own focus. The comma thus helps the reader determine the author's communicative intention and offers a crucial contribution to the coherence of the text.

4.2.3 Separating coordinated clauses

Coordination is one of the most common forms of clause combining, usually with the conjunctions *and* and *but*. As with coordination in phrase sequences (cf. 4.2.1), writers can choose whether or not to separate coordinated clauses by means of a comma. Let us first of all look at *and*:

> Yet there will be few who have had a positive experience of military service: young recruits have difficulty adapting to the life of a soldier when coming from a normal civil environment**, and** problems also arise when soldiers have finished their service and have to adjust to normal life again.

The decision to place a comma or not before *and* is not arbitrary. To start with, if the two clauses are quite long, then the tendency to insert a comma becomes greater, since each clause will require a considerable amount of processing effort. In the example above, for instance, the clauses linked by *and* are themselves rather complex. The comma invites the reader to stop and process the sentence up to that point and by so doing forces him/her to pay separate attention to the two arguments given to support the claim in the first part of the sentence.

Then there are a number of factors relating to how similar the two clauses are in form and meaning. For instance, if the grammatical subject of the two clauses is the same, then the clauses are in all likelihood 'about' the same thing, whereas if there are different subjects, the clauses may be seen as more independent. Similarly, if the verb in the two clauses is in the same tense, then the states of affairs involved will be seen as more closely related to each other than if the tenses are different. Tied up with this is the kind of verb involved, and hence the kind of state of affairs. If both verbs describe an event, then again the clauses will be seen as having an important common characteristic, and no punctuation may be called for. However, if the first verb describes an event, and the second verb is a comment verb, then the two clauses will be seen as relatively separate in terms of content, and a comma becomes an option. All these separateness factors can be traced in the following example, which benefits from a comma being placed before *and*:

> Together these two enterprises **have utterly transformed** the face of bookselling Britain**, and it is worth noting** the main changes that have occurred, not least because they have been linked with related activities in the publishing world. (Todd 1996: 124)

But even if the two coordinated clauses have structural similarities, a comma may be a valuable signal. Consider this example, where the tense is the same in both clauses and the subjects have the same referent:

> What is more, during the last ten to fifteen years **a more rigorously intellectual interest in literary theory has emerged** within the Anglo-American critical tradition**, and it has prompted** attempts to characterize a response to Herbert's poetry in terms of the process of reading itself. (Todd 1986: 1)

Following the introductory *what is more*, one might expect that the author, by coordinating two independent clauses, is presenting two arguments, one in each clause. In fact, it is a complex state of affairs that is presented: first we are told that a certain interest has emerged, and then we are informed about a consequence of this emerging interest. Indeed, even in formal writing *and* can express a wide variety of meaning relationships. Consequently, a comma here is clearly better than coordination without punctuation because it invites the reader to pause and interpret each clause separately.

Additionally, you may often find that a comma is useful before *and* in order to aid understanding of the grammatical structure of the sentence. Consider the following example:

> Football is still dogged by vandalism on the terraces and fraud in the boardroom, and it will continue to suffer as long as governments refuse to take sterner measures.

The comma after *boardroom* is valuable here because it makes clear to the reader that the first instance of *and* serves to link *vandalism* and *fraud,* while the second *and* links the two main clauses together. In other words, the two cases of *and* have different grammatical functions and do not belong to the same level.

Finally, here is an example not of clause coordination but of phrase coordination:

> The production of fiction as a commodity affects the ways both aspiring and established novelists do business with their agents and publishers, and the ways in which they they aim to attract their readers. (Todd 1996: 128)

Here again the use of the comma helps the reader work out which cases of *and* belong together.

The situation with *but* is rather different. Because a *but*-clause involves contrast, the content of this clause may more easily be seen as separate from the clause with which it is combined, and contrast makes the message content of a clause inherently more separate than an *and*-clause, which on the face of it suggests additional information without a change of direction. In other respects the factors determining comma placement with *and* are also relevant in the case of *but*. Thus in the following example, a comma makes sense because the first clause involves an event with a verb in the past tense, whereas the *but*-clause offers comment on this event with a verb in the present tense:

> Most groups taking part in the television debate on euthanasia agreed that something has to be done about the loophole in the new law**, but** that does not mean that they reject the law outright.

Now compare the above example with the following one:

> The social factors relating to euthanasia need to be taken into account **but** must not be allowed to dominate the whole debate.

Here the understood subject of the *but*-clause is the same as the subject of the initial clause, in addition to which the verbs are both in the present tense and are both of the same modal type. Consequently, a comma is not really necessary.

4.2.4 Separating initial constituents

In 4.2.2 we saw that where adverbial clauses follow the clause they modify, a comma is a definite option for the writer. Another point in the sentence where the writer has the option of placing a comma is after an initial adverbial element. Let us look at the beginning of the sentence in more detail.

In Chapters 2.3 and 3.4 we discussed the different framing functions performed by adverbial elements in initial position. We distinguished between three different kinds of adverbial: circumstantial, conjunctive and stance. Conjunctive adverbials provide a link between the content of the previous sentence and the sentence to come, while stance adverbials express a particular viewpoint about the content of the upcoming sentence. In both cases, the adverbial is not part of the propositional content of the clause which they modify. As a consequence of this inherent separateness, conjunctive and stance adverbials are as a rule followed by a comma when they occur at the beginning of the sentence:

Nevertheless, no decision was taken to employ military force.
Surprisingly, no decision was taken to employ military force.
Significantly, no decision was taken to employ military force.

A notable exception amongst conjunctive adverbials is *therefore,* which is hardly ever separated by a comma, wherever it occurs in the sentence. Common stance adverbials such as *unfortunately, clearly* and *obviously* also often occur initially without a comma.

Circumstantial adverbials, which give information about various circumstances relating to the action or state described by the verb, are a rather different story. The general guideline for punctuating initial circumstantials in British English is this:

> The shorter the initial element, the less the need for a comma; the longer the initial element, the greater the need for a comma.

In the first example below there is no great need for a comma, whereas in the second a comma is almost unavoidable for processing purposes:

In Paris the decision to block off the Channel Tunnel came as a great shock.
Despite the fact that English teachers are concerned with both academic and non-academic education, it is the Scots who value a professional training for teachers most highly.

In most cases, a comma is advisable if the initial element is itself a subordinate clause, although length is often a more important factor than grammatical status.

Short expressions of time and place often occur in a framing function at the beginning of the sentence, as in the following examples:

> **In 1868** the vote was extended, so that many working men, including miners, were enfranchised. (Rowland 1989: 5)
> **In the course of this paper** we will distinguish between the underlying events described in a narrative and the linguistic presentation of the events in the narrative. (Brewer & Lichtenstein 1982: 473)

Such expressions will typically not be separated from the rest of the sentence by commas. However, if they refer not only to the following clause or sentence but to a whole stretch of text consisting of several sentences, then these initial expressions take on a text-organizing role and are consequently less tied to the sentence in which they occur. In such situations, a comma becomes more of an option, because it forces the reader to pay more attention to the circumstantial element in its own right. Here is a text segment with two initial circumstantial adverbials in the first two sentences:

> **But from the very beginning,** people saw problems with this approach. **Even in the eighteenth century,** critics such as Joseph Priestley were arguing that it was impossible to reduce all the variation in a language to a single set of simple rules. It was pointed out that no language was perfectly neat and regular. There were always variations in usage which reflected variations in society, or individual patterns of emphasis. There would always be exceptions to the rules. (Crystal 1988: 26)

Here the whole paragraph is clearly within the scope of the two temporal adverbials. The use of the comma in both cases has the effect of strengthening the writer's point about language variation having been an issue for a long, long time.

Finally, another exception to the general guideline on short initial adverbials relates more to the syntactic relations in the sentence than to discourse-semantic aspects, and is similar to the exception to the subject-verb rule presented in 4.1 above. Consider the following sentences (in each case the subject is in bold):

> ? After dark **men and women** strolled around the square.
> ? In order to develop **it** is necessary that architects are given a certain amount of freedom in their work.

In each case it is possible that readers will start interpreting what is actually the subject of the sentence as belonging to the initial element, until they realize that this is not the case. In other words, at first glance it looks as if the first sentence is about dark men and women, and in the second, *it* may initially be interpreted as the object of *develop*. To avoid this kind of interpretation, and hence to ease the reading process by making it clear how the sentence should be parsed, it is advisable to put a comma between the initial element and the subject. Ultimately, this kind of structure-clarifying comma can also be understood from the point of view of the Principle of Semantic Unity: the comma separates elements which might appear as if they form a semantic unit, but they do not.

4.3 Colons

4.3.1 The basic functions

Whereas we described the work of the comma in terms of what it separates, the best way to approach the colon is in terms of what it brings together. The colon is used to express a concrete relation between the information to the left and to the right: in various ways, what follows the colon specifies what goes before it. Here are some examples:

> In 1993, the death rate of motor vehicle occupants was 13.5 per 100,000 population, but it varied dramatically from one county to another: 10 percent of all counties had death rates of less than 10.5 per 100,000, whereas another 10 percent had rates of 41.2 per 100,000 or higher.
>
> Although few regard the agreement as a perfect solution, a large majority hold the view that no better alternative is at hand: it is a choice between the possibility of peace and the certainty of a further escalation of the conflict.
>
> The report makes recommendations in three vital areas: security, building maintenance, and warden salaries.

In the first example the information to the right of the colon provides detail concerning the variation mentioned to the left, thus explaining the use of the expression *dramatically*. In the second example, the information to the right provides a substantiation of the majority's claim that there was another choice available: if this option had not been taken, there would have been greater conflict. And in the third example, the information to the right names the three areas mentioned to the left. This latter use – to introduce a specification in the form of a typically exhaustive list – is particularly common.

A particular use related to the basic specifying function of the colon is to introduce examples and quotes, particularly if they are long and separate from the running text. Instances of colons introducing examples abound in the present text itself, but here is an example of a quote being introduced:

> I take comfort from a comment by Elizabeth Traugott that I noticed again recently: "In my work on the English language, I have constantly been plagued by the problem of word order" (1969: 5). (Denison 1987: 139)

The colon is a very direct and abrupt signal. It tells the reader that there is something he/she clearly needs to know in order to fully understand what is meant by the information given so far, and announces that that information is going to be given in the rest of the sentence. It thus creates a degree of suspense and expectancy, and can be an effective resource for keeping the reader's attention.

The climactic effect of the colon distinguishes it from a full stop. The first two examples above – though not the third, which does not have a clause to the right of the colon – could have been written with a full stop rather than a colon, but that would suggest that the message was in fact complete at that point. Moreover, in each case the reader would have to work hard to understand the relationship between the two resulting sentences, and on top of that the tension created by the colon would be completely lost.

In effect, the colon can do three things: in terms of constructing sentences as basic building blocks of the paragraph, it brings together two independent units of information into one sentential unit; in discourse-semantic terms it suggests a particular kind of meaning relationship between the two elements; and in rhetorical terms it presents this relationship in a crisp and sometimes even climactic fashion. The colon can thus be seen as an important device for clause combining.

4.3.2 Advice

As the colon is a rhetorically powerful device, you are best advised to use it sparingly. It is also easy to use the colon inappropriately. In this section we detail a number of problem areas and give advice on how to use colons effectively.

- *Structure to the left of the colon*

You should make sure that the structure to the left of the colon is a grammatically complete independent clause. This means that the colon should not split the verb from the object (which would be against the Principle of Semantic Unity):

> ?? The period in which this happened has generally been called: the industrial revolution.
> ?? This means: no one shall insult me with impunity. (nonprof55)[21]

[21] Examples coded using the label (nonprof) come from a collection of term papers written by students at the University of Siegen.

In the first example, the solution is simply to omit the colon, thus restoring grammatical completeness to the clause; in the second example, the colon can be replaced by *that*, with the same effect.

The temptation to use a colon may be particularly strong with lists:

> ?? The risks of amphetamine use are: restlessness, dizziness, headaches, palpitations, hypertensive and disrupted regulation of the body temperature, as well as confusion and hallucinations.

Indeed, when the list is separated from the rest of the text and is, for instance, presented using a series of bullet points, this structure is not uncommon in English. Nevertheless, we advise for formal argued texts that you adhere to the basic principle in a case like this as well, namely that the structure to the left should be an independent clause. If you wish to retain the colon, one easy option is to include the phrase *the following* or *as follows* before the colon; otherwise, you can simply omit the colon.

We also advise against using the colon following framing expressions at the beginning of the sentence. Academic English is rhetorically rather restrained in this respect, and prefers a comma:

> ?? And secondly: more students means more money.
> ?? More importantly: it has happened many times that when an immigrant was not granted asylum, he or she started a new procedure in another country.

The same goes for expressions used to introduce quotations. You should avoid using a colon in a situation like this:

> ?? As he tells us early in the novel: "I think that to understand any one thing entirely, no matter how minute it is, requires the understanding of every other thing in the world" (Barth 1956: 13). (Bertens 1987: 251)

Again, a comma is all you need:

> → As he tells us early in the novel, "I think that [...]"

- *Structure to the right of the colon*

The information to the right of a colon does not need to consist of an independent clause. In cases where it does, you may find that the writer has capitalized the first letter of the first word of the clause following the colon, as follows:

> The experiment was flawed: **Design** mistakes were made and cooperation between the participating companies was not as close as had been promised.

Note that this is American English rather than British English practice.

- *Scope*

Given that the colon is a signal to the reader that the tension of the first part of the sentence is about to be relieved in the second part, any failure to provide that specification in full before the next full stop will lead to a readability problem. If you write a sentence using a colon structure, then the reader will tend to interpret a full stop as the end of your rhetorical move, and be prepared for the next sentence to contain a new move. If it then turns out that you have not finished what you started, your reader will have to reinterpret the relation between the two sentences involved. Consider this text from the *Encyclopaedia Britannica* (1947, Vol. 18, p. 118), which has gone terribly wrong:

> ?? The appliances connected with installations for the utilization of natural sources of energy may be classified into three groups: (1) Prime movers, by means of which the natural form of energy is transformed into mechanical energy. To this group belong all such appliances as water turbines, steam turbines, steam engines and boilers, gas producers, gas engines, oil engines, etc. (2) Machinery of any kind which is driven by energy made available by the prime mover. To this group belong all machine tools, textile machinery, cranes – in fact every kind of machine which acquires any considerable quantity of energy to drive it. (3) The appliances by means of which the energy made available by the prime mover is transmitted to the machine designed to utilize it.

Here the writer has clearly wanted to comment on the first two members of the list by giving examples of appliances, and the complexity of the information has forced him/her to formulate a string of independent sentences. As a result, the scope of the colon is in fact five sentences rather than just one. It is clear that the colon structure cannot be used here to any great effect; rather, it can best be replaced by a full stop, with the remaining text being reformulated to produce full sentences. One possibility is as follows:

> → The appliances connected with installations for the utilization of natural sources of energy may be classified into three groups. The first group are prime movers, by means of which the natural form of energy is transformed into mechanical energy; to this group belong all such appliances as water turbines, steam turbines, steam engines and boilers, gas producers, gas engines, oil engines, etc. The second group involves machinery of any kind which is driven by energy made available by the prime mover. To this group belong all machine tools, textile machinery, cranes – in fact every kind of machine which acquires any considerable quantity of energy to drive it. Finally there are appliances by means of which the energy made available by the prime mover is transmitted to the machine designed to utilize it.

The essential thing to note here is that you need to complete the specification of the information to the left of the colon within the same sentence.

- *One per sentence*

The colon is a device which splits the sentence into two distinct parts. The tension rises in the first part and is relieved in the second. Accordingly, you should never use more than one colon in the same sentence. Consider the following sentence:

> ?? Burma is a good example: at present it has market features that would prompt most firms to pass it by: a per capita income of $250 a year, an immature, socialist economy, a foreign exchange deficit, and domestic turmoil.

The problem here is that too much suspense has been packed into one sentence. The information after the first colon provides evidence for the claim made before the colon, while the information after the second colon is a listed specification of market features. The colon structure is rhetorically so powerful that in this case two pieces of information seem to be vying for the dominant position and it is no longer clear what the author's real main point is. There are a number of possible solutions. If the text continues to talk about Burma, then it may be useful to put a full stop after *example* and retain the second colon. But if there is no strong motivation for awarding a short clause like *Burma is a good example* sentence status, then more editorial changes might be called for. For instance, if it has not been mentioned before then *Burma* could be given presentative status in the main clause, with the colon linkage being replaced by a non-restrictive relative clause, and the second colon being retained:

> → A good example is Burma, which at present has market features that would prompt most firms to pass it by: a per capita income of $250 a year, an immature, socialist economy, a foreign exchange deficit, and domestic turmoil.

Note that whatever solution you might choose in the editing stage, you need to consider not only what you want to present as the dominant idea in the sentence, but also what fits best into the surrounding context.

4.4 Semicolons

The semicolon has often been described as a heavy comma, with a position in between the comma and the full stop. Astonishingly, it has enjoyed considerable attention in the media in recent years. While many users of American English find the semicolon too vague and hence of little use in texts where clarity is of the essence, many users of British English find it elegant and applaud the same inherent vagueness (cf. Henley 2008). It is also thought that the semicolon may be on the decline, as a result of an increasing Internet-predilection for short sentences in English (cf. Butterworth 2005). But despite these doubts, the semicolon still has a strong role to play in argued texts in English.

4.4.1 The basic uses

We distinguish three basic functions for the semicolon. The first involves the combining of two independent clauses in one sentence. The requirement is that the ideas presented in the two clauses are somehow related. Here is a paragraph from a museum brochure:

> St Petersburg is often seen as the city of Peter and Catherine the Great, a place full of palaces with art from the 17th and 18th centuries. But the city also took part in the European art movements of the 19th and early 20th centuries. This was certainly the case with the 'new styles' that conquered Europe around 1900. Jugendstil, the Vienna Secession and Art Nouveau found an echo in the city on the Neva. The new art of France was particularly appreciated. **The people of St Petersburg bought the striking French works and had their houses remodelled in the new style; Russian artists created their own version of it**. The last Tsar and Tsarina, Nicholas and Alexandra, were keen followers of the new fashion. In an unusual exhibition, the Hermitage Amsterdam is presenting great examples of French and Russian Art Nouveau. At the centre of the display is the spectacular glass of Emile Gallé and the Daum brothers.
> (From the brochure accompanying the Art Nouveau exhibition, Hermitage Amsterdam, October 2007.)

Half way through this paragraph, the writer makes the point that Art Nouveau was particularly appreciated in St Petersburg. Three statements are then made to support this statement. The first two statements are presented in independent clauses but are combined together, while the third piece of evidence, concerning the support of the Tsar and Tsarina, is presented in a separate sentence. The effect is twofold: first, we are invited to see what is common to the first two pieces of evidence, namely that artists and architects actually translated their appreciation into a visible new fashion; and second, the Tsar and Tsarina are presented as followers of this fashion and given the separate sentence status that befits their social status. By contrast, if the writer had not used a semicolon combination and had presented the evidence in three separate sentences, the reader would have to interpret the three statements following the initial claim about the appreciation of Art Nouveau, and decide what the relationship was between each sentence. What we have here is a rather thoughtful piece of sentence construction, designed to facilitate the reader's appreciation of the argument structure of the paragraph by grouping together ideas that belong together.

Here are two more examples which illustrate the kind of meaning relation involved with semicolon combining:

> The opposition parties have very weak arguments; in fact, one might even say that they have no policy at all.
>
> The New Republic by no means meant a prosperous period for the Dutch nation; it was rather a period of stagnation.

In the first example, both clauses contain essentially the same claim, the second one reinforcing the first and going one step further in intensity. In the second example, the second clause provides a sharp contrast to the first. Indeed, the semicolon is one of the most effective ways of presenting contrast, particularly when the two clauses are of similar length and structure:

> For many people the scheme has obvious merits; for the government it has none.

The second function of the semicolon is related to lists. Semicolons are particularly useful for separating members of a list if the elements concerned are themselves long or complex, or if they contain commas doing other jobs. In this way we see that the hierarchical relation between comma and semicolon can be employed to break the sentence up into identifiable units at two different levels, thus aiding readability. The sequence colon-semicolon is particularly common in this list function, as the following example shows:

> The 'buck' of doping is passed to several departments: the associations, because they set limits which are too high; the coaches and doctors, who regard the performance as more important than the player's health; the labs, which, in a kind of witch hunt, convict the athlete for every molecule of a forbidden substance; commerce, which forces the financial interest of winning; and finally the politicians, who stand by with folded arms.

The third function of the semicolon again follows from the traditional idea that it is a heavy form of the comma. Consider this sentence:

> It was agreed that no member of the team would take with him more than one item of luxury; and that each member should be responsible for a certain part of the equipment.

A comma would be a totally acceptable alternative here; the effect of a semicolon rather than a comma here is to lend more weight to the second part of the sentence. This use of the semicolon is most likely to be found in writers who are seeking to add an air of elegance to their texts (see Module IV, Chapter 2).

4.4.2 The difference between colon and semicolon as combining devices

One of the more difficult problems with punctuation in English is getting to grips with the difference between the colon and semicolon. There are indeed cases where both are equally appropriate and the difference in meaning is difficult to detect, but there remains an essential rhetorical difference between these two punctuation marks (cf. Dale 1992). What the two marks have in common is that when they are used to bring clauses together, the second part of the sentence almost invariably elaborates in some way on the first part. However, you should really only use the colon if there is a clear specifying relation between the two parts. Here is an example from a German student's *Hausarbeit* where the semicolon might arguably be replaced by a colon:

> ?? There is no neutral language; the so-called "PC warriors" argue that all words come with values attached, and that these are variable depending on who is speaking, in what context and within which structure of power.

Here it appears that the writer wishes to provide a justification for the claim that language cannot be neutral; as such, a colon is more appropriate than a semicolon.

By contrast, the same writer uses the colon very powerfully in the following case:

> It is difficult to find out what it first meant and how it was typically used: linguistic corpus study has long had a bias to 'mainstream' sources and to written language. (nonprof37)

Here, the use of the colon suggests that the writer is going to explain why a particular meaning is difficult to detect.

Sometimes, however, both colon and semicolon are possible:

(a) A small majority decided that no further steps should be taken; the feeling was that the people concerned had already suffered enough.
(b) A small majority decided that no further steps should be taken: the feeling was that the people concerned had already suffered enough.

The difference between these two sentences is that the second clause in (a) will be interpreted as a further elaboration on the first clause, while the second clause in (b) will be seen as an explanation for the content of the first clause.

4.5 Dashes and brackets

We noted in section 4.1 above (cf. also Chapter 3.5) that inserted information is typically separated from the rest of the sentence by two commas. In fact, there are two other ways of doing this, the choice depending on how prominently you wish to present the inserted information. The first option involves brackets, while the second involves dashes. There is a considerable difference between the dash on the one hand and brackets on the other. Whereas brackets are used for information which is considered really backgrounded, dashes are used to mark off information which the writer wishes to give special prominence. Dashes are also considered quite informal.

4.5.1 Brackets

At any point in a text, there may be different kinds of information which you might wish to offer your reader as parenthetical, background information. This is information which you wish to include in the text but which you at the same time want to keep out of the main line of argument. We will restrict ourselves here to a few examples. In academic text it is customary to explain the use of technical terms, and this is often done by referring to how others use them, as in the following example:

> Lakoff and Johnson (1980: 130) mention the iconic motivation **(in the sense of Haiman 1983, 1985a, 1985b)** for this alternation; [...] (Thompson 1990: 239)

The author apparently does not feel the need to explain in any detail how she understands the term 'iconic motivation'; perhaps she assumes that the term will be understood by most readers. However, she does wish to show that she is adopting a term used by another author, and so adds a reference to acknowledge that fact.

In the following example, terminology is again the issue:

> Givon (1984a) provides figures from a small text count from a written narrative to support his claim of topicality **(which I will refer to as topicworthiness)**: [...]. (Thompson 1990: 240)

Examples also constitute typically backgrounded information. In the following example, two sets of brackets are used in the same sentence to provide examples.

> Some texts have a fairly pure discourse force **(e.g. popular westerns or mystery stories)**, whereas other texts are deliberately designed to have several forces **(e.g., fables are designed to entertain and to persuade)**. (Brewer & Lichtenstein 1982: 477)

The writer may have thought about using commas, but this alternative would in two respects have had a rather different effect. First, the examples themselves would have been given more status, which in itself would be quite fitting in the context since the use of the expressions *some texts* and *other texts* may well have the reader wondering about possible examples. Second, the use of commas would have split the sentence into four 'punctuation units', each about the same length, as a result of which the basic rhetorical design of the sentence – which is one of contrast – would be less dominant. By using brackets instead of commas the sentence is more clearly split into two halves, and the use of brackets for the examples actually enhances the sentence's parallel structure (see Module IV, Chapter 2 for more on parallel structures as a rhetorical device).

Now consider an example of a rather different kind:

> Berlyne attempted to use constructs from motivational and physiological psychology to produce a general theory of pleasure. He postulated that enjoyment is produced by moderate increases in arousal **('arousal boost')** or by a temporary sharp rise in general arousal followed by reduction of the arousal **('arousal jag')**, and if both processes operate together enjoyment is produced by both the rise and the subsequent drop in arousal **('arousal-boost-jag')**. We attempt to use this general approach to account for the fact that certain narratives are enjoyed and others are not. (Brewer & Lichtenstein 1982: 480)

Here the authors are summarizing work by Berlyne in their own words, but realise that it may be useful to mention the specific terms that Berlyne uses for certain concepts. Because it is the concepts and not the terms that the authors are interested in at this point, they give the terms separately in brackets.

4.5.2 Dashes

Dashes are used in similar situations to brackets and commas for marking off interruptions. However, the status of the information which is marked off by dashes is usually significantly different from what is marked off by brackets. A common use of dashes is in a position immediately following the grammatical subject, where they separate appositions with a specifying function. Here is an example:

> If language as a structure does hang together in a certain way, then the identification of one structural feature – the feature defining the linguistic type – would imply the presence of certain other structural features: "Type is for me a collection of grammatical characteristics, which are close to each other, such that if

one of them is in a given language we expect that the second will be present also, as well as the third, and so on" (Skalička 1941: 4, cited in Greenberg 1974a: 46.) (Croft 1990: 43)

The value of dashes rather than commas or brackets can be paraphrased as 'namely' or 'that is to say' (cf. Module III, Chapter 4.2.2); there is something about the information contained in the preceding noun phrase that makes it not quite complete in the given context, perhaps something that the writer needs to remind the reader of. This is the case in the following example:

> Not surprisingly, these differing definitions of typology – typological classification, typology proper and the functional-typological approach – have led to some confusion about what typology is, or is supposed to be. (Croft 1990: 3)
>
> The two "morals" – of "true nobility" and of "maistrye" – coexist, even though the teller's final "prayer" has firmly returned us to the world of the "wo that is in marriage". (Gray 1987: 20)

When used sentence-finally the dash has a similar function to the colon, although from a stylistic point of view it is more informal, a little less sober. Here are two examples in consecutive sentences. The first dash performs the straightforward specifying function of the colon, while the second might be replaced by either a colon or a semicolon.

> She has also made a name, one powerfully enhanced by several of the short stories in Sugar, for a rare talent – the sensitive, intelligent but not precious description of the visual arts. There were stories of sibling rivalry – many interviewers were to note that Byatt had specified that she wanted to discuss her own work, not that of her younger sister Margaret Drabble. (Todd 1996: 26)

In the following example the dash is used to mark off a comment which the author wants to make about his own statement, in the form of a reformulation.

> The metaphor simply does not work out – or, to use the metaphoric description used earlier, it is *maimed*. (Nash 1987: 42)

This use of the dash is illustrative of its considerable interactional flavour. The dash is the mark of a writer who is very much present in the text, closely monitoring it, aware of the reader's needs, and ready to jump in with a comment, a correction, or a reformulation.

Finally, consider this sentence in which commas, brackets and dashes are used to aid the reading process by clarifying the hierarchical and structural relationships between the various pieces of information inserted between the subject and the verb.

> Martin Amis, who *in propria persona* was 35 at the time of the novel's publication (although of course younger in the year – 1981 – in which the novel is actually set) [sic] is introduced gradually into the novel. (Todd 1996: 192)

The non-restrictive clause is marked off with commas;[22] within this punctuation unit there is then a bracketed unit containing an aside by the author, and within that there is an appositional unit marked off by a pair of dashes which specifies the year mentioned. Although the sentence is quite complex, and also quite top-heavy, the use of different sets of punctuation marks serves as a useful reading aid, and is clearly much better than a version which only makes use of commas:

> Martin Amis, who *in propria persona* was 35 at the time of the novel's publication, although of course younger in the year, 1981, in which the novel is actually set, is introduced gradually into the novel.

All in all, brackets and dashes are useful complements to the comma, semicolon and colon when it comes to packing into one single sentence lots of different pieces of information which entertain different semantic and rhetorical relationships with each other.

4.6 Commas revisited: dealing with comma splices

Many inexperienced writers use the comma as a device to link in one sentence two statements that belong closely together in terms of meaning but which are formulated as if they were grammatically independent. The result is a comma splice, which in written English should be avoided at all costs. Here are two typical examples of comma splicing:

> ?? I believe that when Shakespeare finished the writing for his comedy he was really happy with it, for him, it had everything a good comedy should have: disguise, sexual associations, and, last but not least, a happy ending.
> ?? The public are often not aware of this, however, they are unconsciously influenced by the newspaper's opinion.

The first example consists of a claim followed by a piece of evidence, which is then specified in a list. Even though the writer apparently feels that the claim and the evidence belong together, the best thing to do here is probably split the sentence up into two after *happy with it*, because the second part is itself complex and contains a colon structure:

22 Actually the second, closing comma is missing. The author may have been so concerned with the last piece of backgrounded information that he forgot to put a comma after the final bracket to mark off the non-restrictive relative clause.

→ I believe that when Shakespeare finished the writing for his comedy he was really happy with it. For him, it had everything a good comedy should have: disguise, sexual associations, and, last but not least, a happy ending.

The second example is difficult to understand at first reading. The question is whether the conjunctive adverbial *however* modifies the first clause or the second. The answer can only be found by reading the previous sentence again, after which it becomes clear that it is the content of the first clause that is in contrast with some previous statement. The second clause can then be interpreted as a kind of clarification of the first one. Two small changes – moving *however* to the front of the sentence and altering the comma to a semicolon – would be sufficient to make the writer's intended meaning much clearer:

→ However, the public are often not aware of this; they are unconsciously influenced by the newspaper's opinion.

One possible reason for comma splices being quite frequent in student English is that writers sometimes have an incomplete understanding of how to use words like *however, thus,* and *therefore*. These conjunctive adverbs signal a meaning relation between two information units, and one may therefore be tempted to use them for forging a grammatical relation as well. But this is not the case: words like *however* and *therefore* are adverbs, and as such do nothing more than modify (part of) the sentence in which they occur. If you would like to link two clauses grammatically and semantically at the same time, you are better off using a conjunction, for instance *because, since, when* or *although*. Here is an example:

?? However, youngsters never have a full sense of security, there is always a threat from other gangs or groups.
→ However, youngsters never have a full sense of security, since there is always a threat from other gangs or groups.

If you find yourself producing comma splices and want to edit them out, you will see that an easy solution is to replace the offending comma by a full stop, as we saw with the first example in this section. Often, however, this is not the best editorial solution, since the two pieces of information will tend to be closely related, which is often the reason why writers combine the independent clauses in the first place. A useful procedure is to first assess the meaning relation between the two clauses. A very typical relation is that of clarification or explanation, and you will often find that a colon or a subordinate clause introduced by *since* or *because* provides an effective solution. Here are some examples, again with improved versions:

?? In the first place part-timers have to put up with the problem of low pay, they earn about 60% of the hourly wages of full-time workers.
→ In the first place part-timers have to put up with the problem of low pay: they earn about 60% of the hourly wages of full-time workers.
?? Rushdie turns the fictional upside down, however, he creates fiction out of fiction.
→ Rushdie turns the fictional upside down, however, by creating fiction out of fiction.
?? Firstly, tourism in the east of Germany is lying still, therefore the big new hotels do not get the customers they need.
→ Firstly, tourism in the east of Germany is at a standstill, as a result of which the big new hotels do not get the customers they need.

4.7 Overview

Our main aim in this chapter has been to show that it is worth taking punctuation seriously. For one thing, punctuation works differently in English than in German. However, equally important is the fact that effective use of punctuation contributes to a coherent text. Writers use punctuation to divide the content of complex sentences up into separate information units which they want their readers to pay separate attention to. Moreover, they use different punctuation marks to express different meaning relationships between information units.

Here are 15 basic guidelines for using punctuation marks. First of all, in the following cases you should not insert a comma:

1. Never put a comma between the subject and the verb, even if the subject is itself a clause;
2. Never put a comma between the verb and the object, even if the object is itself a clause;
3. Never put a comma before and after defining information.

By contrast, in the following cases you should insert a comma:

4. Always put a comma between a long initial constituent and the following subject;
5. Always put a comma between an initial constituent and the following subject if the initial constituent is not part of the proposition;
6. Always use commas to separate any kind of interruption from the rest of the sentence;
7. Always use commas to separate an additional message from the preceding message.

The main areas where you can choose to have a comma or not, depending on whether you want the reader to pay separate attention to the relevant information, are the following:

8. A comma is an option before *and* and *or* when introducing the last element in a list of phrases;
9. A comma is an option before *and* and *but* when these conjunctions link clauses;
10. A comma is an option before an adverbial clause when it is combined with a previous clause;
11. A comma is an option following an initial circumstantial element when it has scope over a string of sentences.

With regard to other punctuation marks you should note the following basic uses:

12. Use a colon
    a) to specify in the second part of the sentence what has not been specified in the first part,
    b) to introduce quotes, and
    c) to introduce a list of items.
13. Use a semicolon
    a) to link two independent clauses of similar length and structure into one sentential unit,
    b) to mark off long or complex members of a list, following a colon, and
    c) to separate information that would normally be marked off with a comma if you want to give that information extra weight.
14. Use brackets
    a) in general, to provide background detail,
    b) more specifically, to explain in compact format your use of technical terms, and
    c) to give examples.
15. Use dashes
    a) to punctuate an interruption which you want your reader to pay special attention to, and
    b) as an alternative to a colon at the end of the sentence when writing in a commenting style.

Bibliography

a) Sources of examples

Barth, John 1979. *Letters*. New York: Putnam.

Barth, John 1996. *On with the story*. Boston, New York, Toronto, London: Little, Brown and Company.

Bertens, Hans 1987. The attack on epistemology in recent American fiction. In Bunt et al. (eds), 249–259.

Brewer, William F. & Edward H. Lichtenstein 1982. Stories are to entertain: A structural-affect theory of stories. *Journal of Pragmatics* 6: 473–486.

Bunt, Gerrit H.V., Erik S. Kooper, J. Lachlan Mackenzie & David R.M. Wilkinson (eds) 1987. *One hundred years of English studies in Dutch universities*. Amsterdam: Rodopi.

Conley, John M. & William M. O'Barr 1990. *Rules versus relationships: The ethnography of legal discourse*. Chicago: University of Chicago Press.

Croft, William 1990. *Typology and universals*. Cambridge: Cambridge University Press.

Crystal, David 1988. *The English language*. Harmondsworth: Penguin.

Crystal, David 2006. *The fight for English: How language pundits ate, shot and left*. Oxford: Oxford University Press.

Denison, David 1987. On word order in Old English. In Bunt et al. (eds), 139–155.

Fairclough, Norman 2003. *Analysing discourse: Textual analysis for social research*. London & New York: Routledge.

Gray, Douglas 1987. Chaucer and *gentilesse*. In Bunt et al. (eds), 1–27.

Janzen, Olaf U. A Reader's Guide to the History of Newfoundland and Labrador to 1869. http://www2.swgc.mun.ca/nfld_history/nfld_history_war.htm, accessed 22 March 2008.

Keizer, M. Evelien 2007. *The English noun phrase: The nature of linguistic categorization*. Cambridge: Cambridge University Press.

Lyall, Roderick J. 1985. Scottish students and masters at the universities of Cologne and Louvain in the fifteenth century. *Innes Review* 36: 55–73.

McCrum, Robert, William Cran & Robert MacNeil 1986. *The story of English*. London: Faber and Faber/BBC Publications.

Nash, Walter 1986. *English usage: A guide to first principles*. London: Routledge Kegan Paul.

Nash, Walter 1987. Usage, users and the used: Some reflections on contemporary English. In Bunt et al. (eds), 29–46.

Pinker, Steven 1998. *How the mind works*. London: Penguin.

Plutarch 1962. *Ten famous lives*. The Dryden translation, revised by A.H. Clough. London: The Bodley Head.

Priestley, J.B. 1973. *The English*. London: Heinemann.

Rowland, T. Harry 1989. *Bygone Morpeth*. Chichester: Phillimore.

Rushdie, Salman 1999. *The ground beneath her feet*. London: Jonathan Cape.

Sayle, Alexei 2000. *Barcelona Plates*. London: Hodder and Stoughton.

Schiffrin, Deborah 1994. *Approaches to discourse*. Oxford and Cambridge MA: Blackwell.

Sinclair, John & Malcolm Coulthard 1992. Towards an analysis of discourse. In Malcolm Coulthard (ed.), *Advances in spoken discourse analysis*. London: Routledge. 1–34.

Thompson, Sandra A. 1990. Information flow and dative shift in English discourse. In Jerold A. Edmondson, Crawford Feagin & Peter Mühlhausler (eds), *Development and diver-*

sity: language variation across time and space. A festschrift for Charles James N. Bailey. Dallas: Summer Institute of Linguistics, & Arlington: University of Texas. 239–254.

Todd, Richard K. 1986. *The opacity of signs*. Columbia MO: University of Missouri Press.

Todd, Richard K. 1996. *Consuming fictions. The Booker Prize and fiction in Britain today*. London: Bloomsbury.

b) References

Biber, Douglas. Stig Johansson, Geoffrey Leech, Susan Conrad & Edward Finnegan 1999. *Longman grammar of spoken and written English*. Harlow: Pearson.

Burrough-Boenisch, Joy 2002. *Culture and conventions: Writing and reading Dutch scientific English*. LOT dissertation series. Utrecht: LOT.

Butterworth, Trevor 2005. Two countries separated by a semicolon. *Financial Times*, 17 September 2005.

Chafe, Wallace L. 1984. How people use adverbial clauses. *Proceedings of the Xth annual meeting of the Berkeley Linguistics Society*. 437–449.

Chafe, Wallace L. 1987. Cognitive constraints on information flow. In Russell S. Tomlin (ed.), *Coherence and grounding in discourse*. Amsterdam & Philadelphia PA: Benjamins. 21–51.

Chicago manual of style. 2003. 15th edition. Chicago and London: University of Chicago Press.

Council of Europe 2001. *Common European framework of reference for languages*. Cambridge: Cambridge University Press.

Dale, Robert 1992. Exploring the role of punctuation in the signalling of discourse structure. In *Proceedings, Workshop on text representation and domain modelling: ideas from linguistics and AI*. Technical University of Berlin, 110–120.

Daneš, František 1974. Functional sentence perspective and the organization of the text. In František Daneš (ed.), *Papers on Functional Sentence Perspective*. Janua Linguarum, Series Minor 147. The Hague: Mouton. 106–128.

Downing, Angela & Philip Locke 2006. *English grammar: A university course*. Second edition. London: Routledge.

Francis, Gill 1994. Labelling discourse: an aspect of nominal-group lexical cohesion. In Malcolm Coulthard (ed.), *Advances in written text analysis*. London and New York: Routledge.

Gethin, R.H. 1965. *Remedial English 2: punctuation*. Oxford: Oxford University Press.

Gernsbacher, Morton A. 1990. *Language comprehension as structure building*. Hillsdale: Lawrence Erlbaum.

Gómez-González, Maria de los Ángeles 1998. A corpus-based analysis of Extended Multiple Themes in PresE. *International Journal of Corpus Linguistics* 3(1): 81–113.

Gómez-González, Maria de los Ángeles 2007. 'It was you that told me that, wasn't it?': it-clefts revisited in discourse. In Mike Hannay & Gerard Steen (eds), *Structural-functional studies in English grammar*. Amsterdam & Philadelphia PA: Benjamins. 103–139.

Granger, Sylviane, Estelle Dagneaux and Fanny Meunier (eds) 2003. *The International Corpus of Learner English. Handbook and CD-ROM. Version 1.1.* Louvain-la-Neuve: Presses Universitaires de Louvain.

Greenbaum, Sidney & Gerald Nelson. 2002. *An introduction to English grammar*. London: Longman.

Halliday, Michael A.K. & Christian Matthiessen 2004. *An introduction to functional grammar*. 3rd edition. London: Arnold.

Hannay, Mike 1989. Translating structures: The role of contrastive syntax in translation dictionaries. In J. Lachlan Mackenzie & Richard K. Todd (eds), *In other words: Transcultural studies in philology, translation and lexicology presented to Hans Heinrich Meier on the occasion of his sixty-fifth birthday*. Dordrecht: Foris. 211–234.

Hannay, Mike 2007. Patterns of multiple theme and their role in developing English writing skills. In Chris Butler, Raquel Hidalgo & Julia Lavid (eds), *Functional perspectives on grammar and discourse*. Amsterdam & Philadelphia PA: Benjamins. 257–278.

Hannay, Mike & M. Evelien Keizer 2005. A discourse treatment of English non-restrictive nominal appositions in Functional Discourse Grammar. In J. Lachlan Mackenzie & Maria de los Ángeles Gómez-González (eds), *Studies in Functional Discourse Grammar*. Berne etc.: Peter Lang. 159–194.

Hannay Mike & J. Lachlan Mackenzie 2002. *Effective writing in English: a sourcebook*. Second edition. Bussum, Netherlands: Coutinho.

Hannay, Mike & Elena Martínez Caro (2008). Thematic choice in the written English of advanced Spanish and Dutch learners. In Gaëtenelle Gilquin, Szilvia Papp & María Belén Diez (eds), *Linking up contrastive and learner corpus research*. Language and Computer Series. Amsterdam: Rodopi. 227–253.

Henley, Jon 2008. The end of the line? *The Guardian*, 4 April 2008.

Hinkel, Eli 2002. *Second language writers' text: Linguistic and rhetorical features*. Mahwah, NJ: Lawrence Erlbaum.

Kane, Thomas S. 1988. *The new Oxford guide to writing*. Oxford: Oxford University Press.

Kopple, William J. Vande 1986. Given and New information and some aspects of the structure, semantics, and pragmatics of written texts. In Charles R. Cooper & Sidney Greenbaum (eds), *Studying writing: linguistic approaches*. London: Sage. 72–111.

Macwhinney, Brian 1977. Starting points. *Language* 53, 152–168.

Nash, Walter 1986. *English usage: A guide to first principles*. London: Routledge & Kegan Paul.

New Hart's rules: The handbook of style for writers and editors. 2005. Oxford: Oxford University Press.

Nunberg, Geoffrey, Ted Briscoe & Rodney Huddleston 2002. Punctuation. In Rodney Huddleston & Geoffrey K. Pullum, *The Cambridge grammar of the English language*. Cambridge: Cambridge University Press. 1723–1764.

Quirk, Randolph, Sidney Greenbaum, Geoffrey Leech & Jan Svartvik. 1985. *A comprehensive grammar of the English language*. London: Longman.

Robinson, William S. 2000. Sentence focus, cohesion, and the active and passive voices. *Teaching English in the Two-Year College*. 27 (4): 440–445.

Smits, Aletta 2002. *How writers begin their sentences. Complex beginnings in native and learner English*. LOT dissertation series 67. Utrecht: LOT.

Spooren, Wilbert P.M.S. 1989. *Some aspects of the form and interpretation of global contrastive coherence relations*. Ph.D. Dissertation, University of Nijmegen.

Springer, Philip (in prep.). *Advanced learner writing: A corpus-based study of the discourse competence of Dutch writers of English*. PhD dissertation, Vrije Universiteit, Amsterdam.

Tavecchio, Lotte (2010). *Sentence patterns in English and Dutch: A contrastive corpus analysis*. PhD dissertation, Vrije Universiteit, Amsterdam.

Truss, Lynne 2003. *Eats, shoots and leaves*. London: Profile.

Ventola, Eija 1995. Thematic development and translation. In Mohsen Ghadessy (ed.), *Thematic development in English texts*. London: Pinter. 85–104.

Module III

Lexis and Grammar

Introduction

This Module is about the 'nitty-gritty' of prose writing: in Coleridge's words, putting together 'the right words in the right order'. It falls into four chapters.

Chapter 1 provides a general framework for understanding the rest of the chapter, suggesting that writers form sentences on the basis of memorized constructions rather than grammatical rules.

Chapter 2 discusses the typical grammatical patterning found alongside nouns, verbs and adjectives as well as cross-linguistic differences that constitute common sources of error.

Chapter 3 focuses on lexical patterning, showing how words combine with each other to form larger meaning units. Once you have taken to heart our advice on lexical and grammatical patterning in Chapters 1,2 and 3, you will have progressed a long way towards producing error-free word combinations.

Chapter 4 can be likened to a dictionary; it provides a large amount of re-usable language material which has been categorized by topic. Thus, for example, you will find words and phrases you can use in citing or criticizing other authors or in reformulating bits of your own text.

Chapter 1

A constructional view of language

> The main point of this chapter is that writers should view language in terms of constructions rather than words.

Let us start by asking how experienced writers set about the task of combining words. There are two competing models available, which we might term the 'old' or 'slot-filler' model and the 'new' or 'constructional' model.

Most of us have been brought up and inculcated with the slot-filler model, whereby languages consist of relatively fixed sentence patterns, such as SVO (subject-verb-object); each of the functional slots in such a pattern can be filled with a specific type of material: the subject and object slots with nouns and the verb slot with verbs. According to this model, all the language user does is fill sentence slots with words s/he retrieves either from a mental word store or from a printed dictionary.

Unfortunately, this view of language is at least oversimplistic if not completely untrue. Even the simplest of patterns, namely the SV pattern, cannot be realized with just any lexical material, at least not in authentic prose writing. Thus, although we find sentences like 'vessels sail' or 'houses stand' in some old school grammars of English, they are highly unlikely to occur in real-life texts. This is because, in authentic communication, writers tend to make more complex statements about the movement of ships or the location of buildings. 'The ships sail warily into a bay and drop anchor' is an attested example,[1] and so is 'Here the more attractive old houses stand'. These examples illustrate something that we will explain in greater detail in this Module: the frequent co-occurrence of the subject noun 'ship' (or, in old texts, the word 'vessel') and the verb 'sail' does not mean that their combination in a two-word sentence produces natural-sounding English. In other words, a grammatical description of English cannot simply disregard the environment in which the words 'ship' and 'sail' occur. Indeed, this environment should provide the basis for the description, so that we end up with something like:

1 The vast majority of examples cited in this Module are from a corpus of academic English described in Siepmann (2005) and from web-based corpora. As is common lexicographic practice, no references are given for these examples.

*ships/boats/vessels/*etc. *sail* + place adverbial

We can now give a preliminary answer to the question of how experienced writers choose and arrange words, an answer that we will enlarge on in the remainder of this Module. In fact, good writers do not usually arrange 'words' at all, but rather use memorized 'constructions' of the type shown above. Such constructions allow them only a limited amount of freedom in word choice.

This is, by the way, where the major difference between the old and the new model lies. The old model gave the writer a far greater degree of discretion, suggesting, as it did, that sentence structures exist independently of lexical items. In stark contrast, the new model suggests that lexical items and sentence structures enter into idiomatic combinations. It allows us to generalize from genuine samples of text to the extent that such generalization still yields acceptable English, but no further.

Since, as we have seen, authentic and correct English writing depends so crucially on the ability to mobilize an entire arsenal of more or less ready-made constructions, this Module will offer the reader two things. Firstly, it will describe in broad-brush strokes that part of the arsenal which is characteristic of academic writing. Secondly, it will apprise readers of how to fill gaps in the lexico-grammatical lists we provide (see Chapter 4) and in their knowledge of academic constructions.

In an academic context, the importance of lexico-grammatical accuracy cannot be stressed enough. The larger a student's knowledge of academic vocabulary, the better their chances of obtaining high essay scores (Laufer & Nation 1995). Even in undergraduate programs, an essay riddled with linguistic errors may be rejected outright by university faculty both here and abroad (Santos 1988).

Following the traditional slot-filler model, vocabulary learning has for a long time been viewed as the learning of individual words, and this provides a convenient first approach to pinning down the size of the vocabulary learning task ahead of you. Research into word frequency has found that around three-quarters (75 per cent) of the words in any academic text belong to the two thousand most frequent word families in English, as captured in 'A General Service List of English Words' (West 1953). These are the words you should already be familiar with from school. Another 10 per cent of the vocabulary of any academic text will be made up of general academic words, most of which you will still have to learn. The most frequent general academic words have also been identified by researchers (Coxhead 2000; http://

www.vuw.ac.nz/lals/research/awl/), and many of them have been included in the lists of functional vocabulary in Chapter 4 of this Module. There are also exercise books available which will help you gain full mastery of general EAP (English for Academic Purposes) vocabulary, such as Schmitt & Schmitt (2005). Most of the remaining vocabulary which you will need to master consists of the terminology specific to your own specialist discipline, such as *dénouement* in literary studies, *inflation* in economics and *x-ray* in medicine. This gives us a three-tier model of academic word learning (see Table 1).

Table 1: Three-tier model of academic word learning

Type of vocabulary	Examples	Size	Learning aids
Core vocabulary of English	of, the, he, thing, meet, travel	2000 words	Klett Grund- und Aufbauwortschatz and similar learning aids
General academic words	approach, comprise, observe, valid	3000 words	*Writing in English*; Schmitt & Schmitt 2005; Legler & Moore 2001; Hrdina & Hrdina (2006); http://www.nottingham.ac.uk/~alzsh3/acvocab/
Subject-specific terminology	dénouement, inflation, amniocentesis	unlimited	e.g. Rotter & Bendl (1978) and Werlich (1969) for literary studies; Crystal (2003) for linguistics

However, this simplified picture of vocabulary learning should not mislead you into believing common claims to the effect that a knowledge of 2000 to 3000 academic words will take you a long way (cf. for example Hinkel 2004: 99). While it is undeniably true that acquiring a passive vocabulary of that size is a first step to becoming an academic writer, such thinking may lead to the wrong belief that the ability to write depends on word knowledge rather than knowledge of constructions. The number of constructions you will need to master or, more likely, look up is considerably higher than the number of words.

This will become abundantly clear if we look at the number of two-word combinations entered into by academic nouns such as *assumption (Annahme; Voraussetzung). Oxford Collocations Dictionary for Students of English* alone lists the following:

assumption noun

- ADJ. **basic, fundamental, hidden, implicit, tacit, underlying, unspoken | common, conventional, general, shared, widespread** *shared assump-*

tions between teachers and parents | **correct, reasonable, valid** | **erroneous, false, flawed, incorrect, mistaken, questionable, wrong**

- QUANT. **number, series, set** *Your argument is based on a set of questionable assumptions.*
- VERB + ASSUMPTION **make** *She's always making assumptions about how much money people have.* | **base sth on, start from, work on** *We are working on the assumption that the techniques are safe.* | **accept** | **challenge, disprove, question, test**
- ASSUMPTION + VERB **underlie sth, underpin sth** *the assumptions underlying their beliefs*
- PREP. **on the ~ that** *I set the table for eight people, on the assumption that Jo would come.* | **~ about** *assumptions about how women should behave*

This gives us 37 common two-word combinations or 'collocations' (a term we will define later), to which we could add *assumption + rest on, proceed from* or *faulty*. At a conservative estimate, then, a common noun such as *assumption* has at least 40 important collocates. It is safe to assume that there are at least 1000 nouns in academic English that behave in similar ways to *assumption*. This would give us 40 times 1000 two-word collocations, that is 40,000 lexical items, based on those 1000 nouns alone.

But two-word collocations are not the whole story. Beyond two-word collocations, there is a whole world of more complex constructions. To return to the above example, *assumption* often occurs in existential clauses of the type *there is an assumption of* + noun phrase or *there is an assumption that*. It is also often found in binomials such as *methods and assumptions* or *ideas and assumptions*. Lastly, consider typical sentence patterns such as *a(n) + ADJ + assumption + in + NP is that* or *NP is ADJ in its assumption that*, which is similar to saying *NP is ADJ in the sense that*. Some examples:

An implicit assumption in this approach is that subjects of different intellectual levels have similar conceptions of task demands.
An underlying assumption in regression is that the model describes the cost relationship.
Although **(D) is correct in its assumption that** true/false and multiple choice tests are the most conducive to student-based grading …
This measure is flawed in its assumption that more visits mean more access.

The reassuring thing is that there are a large number of synonymous constructions, so that it is usually sufficient for a particular purpose to know one member of a set of constructions. The following constructions, for example, all express the same underlying idea:

It (e.g. a theory/model/group of people) is incorrect in its assumption that ...
It is mistaken in its assumption that ...
It is incorrect in assuming that ...
It is mistaken in assuming that ...
It is wrong in supposing that ...
It is wrong in its contention that ... (etc.)

From what has just been said it is clear that we need to revise our original model of word learning to accommodate constructions. Again, we propose a three-tier model of constructions (see Table 2), and we introduce an additional distinction between functional and content vocabulary:

- **Content Vocabulary**: these are the words and phrases that have to do with the subject of your text. For instance, if you wish to write a text about AIDS, you might want to use all or part of the following content vocabulary: *an AIDS sufferer/patient, to catch/develop AIDS, to have AIDS, to test s.o. for s.th., to test positive for s.th., a killer disease, to spread through sexual contact, to be promiscuous, a drug user, contaminated blood, a haemophiliac, to adopt safe sex practices, ...*
- **Functional Vocabulary**: this is the vocabulary that helps you describe the logical connections between different content words and phrases as well as between sentences and paragraphs. This includes nouns such as *difference, contrast, similarity, example, demonstration* or verbs such as *to increase, to differ, to cause, to stem from,* but most importantly, linking words and phrases such as *however, nevertheless, also, then, surprisingly, it is clear that, the same is true of,* etc. Most functional words combine in very similar ways across the wide diversity of academic texts. Thus, *question + ask/raise* or *difference + substantial/significant* can be found in almost any variety of written text.

Table 2: Three-tier model of academic constructions

Type of vocabulary	Examples	Size	Learning aids
Core constructions of English	**1. functional**: however, on the other hand **2. content**: go to university, study a subject	~ 100,000	Adamson (1995), Chalker (1996)

General academic constructions	**1. functional**: it should be noted that, there is growing recognition that **2. content**: a thorough analysis, challenge an assumption	60,000	*Writing in English*; Kraus (1999), Kraus & Baumgartner (2002); http://www.phrasebank.manchester.ac.uk/
Subject-specific constructions	rise in inflation, strong collocation, non-timber products	unlimited	

It is immediately obvious that content vocabulary is infinite and can only be covered in large, sometimes specialist dictionaries. By contrast, the overall amount of functional vocabulary is limited. It is fairly easy to develop a confident command of a large amount of functional vocabulary and use this again and again in different contexts. Chapter 4 of this Module is mainly devoted to such functional language; it saves you the trouble of making your own lists of function words, so that you only need to collect the content vocabulary of each subject you wish to deal with. Many of the exercises on the accompanying website provide the necessary content vocabulary, thus allowing you to concentrate on acquiring the essential functional vocabulary of English.

Note that even the most general academic content words such as *reaction* enter into different constructions in different disciplines (e.g. *suffer a reaction* in medicine vs. *trigger a reaction* in chemistry; cf. Blumenthal 2007, Hyland & Tse 2007). This is another reason why a word-based view of academic vocabulary may be inappropriate; ultimately, you as an academic writer will have to pay particular attention to a) 'general' functional constructions (*a wide difference, raise a question, it is clear that, there is growing recognition that*) and b) the general and subject-specific constructions that are particularly common in your own discipline.

A stylistically acceptable text should contain a great variety of content vocabulary and – since there are comparatively fewer functional words and phrases – a smaller variety of functional vocabulary. Before writing your rough draft, you should therefore proceed as follows:

1. Collect as much content vocabulary on the subject on which you wish to write as you can find. If possible write the vocabulary down in the form of constructions. Note down the patterns of nouns, adjectives and verbs (patterns will be described in greater detail in the following sections).
2. Learn the words and constructions by heart so that you can use them in your text.
3. Finally, start writing your paper. While writing, look up functional vocabulary in this book or on such websites as http://www.phrasebank.manchester.ac.uk/. This will help you combine your ideas logically.

More generally, since this Module cannot possibly provide you with all the constructions you need, one of the key strategies you must adopt is to read like a writer.

- Read as much academic material as possible, especially from your own field of study.
- Before you start on a term paper, read native-speaker dissertations or articles on the subject you are dealing with. As you read, make a note of typical constructions in a notebook.
- Take special trouble over the style and correctness of the introduction to your paper, as this will convey a favourable impression.
- Buy at least one good bilingual dictionary and one good monolingual dictionary (the *Oxford Phrasebuilder Genie* is a good choice since it includes the *Oxford Advanced Learner's Dictionary* and the *Oxford Collocations Dictionary for Learners of English*).

Chapter 2

Academic lexis and patterning

The main points of this chapter are these:

- The academic writer needs to know where words have their normal places in clauses; in other words, s/he needs to become acquainted with the basic syntactic patterns associated with verbs, nouns and adjectives.
- In the simple English sentence, more depends on the verb and the pattern it generates than is the case in an equivalent German sentence.
- Both English and German academic writing rely heavily on nominalization, but English uses fewer nonce compounds and complex compounds.
- English academic writers use a great variety of objective and evaluative adjectives whose exact meaning has to be mastered.
- Academic English uses a large number of specific prepositions and puts common prepositions to specific uses.

Just as a piece of music consists of an organized system of sounds, so a language falls into patterns which its speakers use again and again. That analogy can be taken a little further. Once you know how the organized system of sounds works, you can compose any number of harmonious tunes. In the same way, once you know the patterns associated with particular words and meanings, you can create a large amount of new language. We have already seen this illustrated in a rather complex way with reference to the noun *assumption*. A much simpler illustration is the most basic English clause pattern, i.e. the sequence of a subject followed by a verb (see Table 3).

Table 3: Subject + verb patterns

Subject	Verb
Opinions	differ.
Meyer	agrees.

As explained in the introduction to this Module, isolated S-V clauses are by no means the most frequent pattern in any variety of English, but they are commonly found alongside the verbs *agree* and *differ* in academic English, usually with slight additions. Thus, *differ* often occurs in constructions which indicate contrast:

> ... while Europe and Japan have made gains. But the European and Japanese patterns differ.

The patterns just illustrated are governed by the verb, but there are also patterns governed by nouns and adjectives as well as other 'constructional' patterns. We will deal with them in turn, starting with noun patterns.

What is important to remember at this stage is that every English sentence you build must keep to the usual patterns employed by native English writers.

2.1 Nouns and noun patterns

Here are some simple sentences:

> We will discuss **some of these problems** later.
> Jane is **a bright young girl**.
> **The hole in the ozone layer** is **a significant threat to humanity**.

As you can see, a simple sentence often consists of a verb (*discuss, be*) and one or two noun phrases, which have been set in bold in the example sentences. A noun phrase has as its central element or 'head' a simple noun (*teacher, class*), pronoun (*him*) or nominalized adjective (*the poor*), either alone or preceded by one or more words called determiners (*a, the, some,* etc.).

The noun may be surrounded by a theoretically unlimited number of words known as modifiers which identify it more specifically. In the above examples, *some of these, bright young* and *significant* are premodifiers (preceding the noun phrase) and *in the ozone layer* and *to humanity* are postmodifiers (following the noun phrase). In academic writing both premodifiers and postmodifiers can be extended considerably:

> **a real but hidden** threat **to the rights and liberties of parents and children**

Noun phrases can be combined, so that one 'governs' the other.

> a child with a speech disorder
> a three-day conference on AIDS

Here the noun phrases surrounding the nouns 'child' and 'conference' govern the noun phrases around 'speech disorder' and 'Aids' respectively.

Table 4 sums up what we have learned about the noun phrase so far.

Table 4: The noun phrase

determiner	**premodifiers (adjectives, participles, other nouns)**	**noun/pronoun**	**postmodifiers (relative clauses, infinitive clauses, prepositional phrases, noun phrases)**
		he	
the		teachers	
the	new salary	scales	for teachers
a	significant	threat	to humanity
a		study	on the effect of terminology on L2 reading compre-hension
	hidden	variables	

When building a noun phrase, one of the most important things to consider is the correct use of prepositions in postmodifiers. It is quite common for an English noun to take a completely different preposition from its German equivalent. Thus, we say *Bedrohung* ***für*** in German, but *threat* ***to*** in English. It is equally vital to distinguish between the *to*-infinitive and the preposition *to*, which is followed by a gerund. Compare:

> *his approach* ***to*** *describ****ing*** *symptoms* vs. *his claim* ***to be*** *a rational creature*

Another common problem is the correct choice of relative pronoun: *who* is usually used for people, *which* or *that* for things. With collective nouns such as *team, committee, family, group* or *population*, the pronoun *which* is associated with a singular verb, while *who* is associated with a plural verb:

> *the group which have used contraceptive measures has a higher rate of pregnancies
>
> → the group which has used contraceptive measures has a higher rate of pregnancies

Table 5 provides a list of the most common nouns in academic English, including patterns and translations.

Table 5: Common nouns and their patterns

English noun	Patterns	German equivalent
alternative	**to** sth; **of** sth/v-*ing* (*the efficient ~ of railroads, Leibniz found the ~ of postulating …*); *the/an alternative would be to*-INF	Alternative
approach	**to** sth/v-*ing*; **towards** sth	Herangehensweise, Methode, Ansatz, Weg
concept	**of** sth (*the concept of competence*)	Begriff
criterion (pl. criteria)	**for** sth; **of** sth (*the ~ of abstractness*); **by/according to** this ~	Kriterium
data	**on/about** sth	Daten
entity	(no specific patterning)	Ding, Gebilde, Wesen, Wesenheit
environment	**around** s.th./s.o.; **for** + sth/v-ing (*an ~ for exploration and experimentation; a stimulating ~ for exploring the lexical resources of the language*); **of** sth (*an ~ of rapid technological change*); **in** a(n) ADJ ~	Umgebung, Umwelt, Milieu
guarantee	**against** sth (*… is no ~ against racism*); **for** sth (*a ~ for the success of any project*); **that**-clause	Garantie
hypothesis	**about/as to/on/regarding** sth; **of** sth (*the ~ of a god; the ~ of independence of traits*); **that**-clause; according to a ~	Hypothese
impact	(of sth) on sth	Auswirkung(en), Einfluss
overlap	**among/between**; **in** sth (*~ in the techniques used*); **of** sth (*this ~ of function*)	Überschneidung, Überlappung, teilweise Entsprechung; Überlagerung
period	**of** (*a few weeks/cooperation*); **during/over/for/in/throughout** a ~; *the poems* ***of*** *this ~; another writer* ***in*** *this ~, Roger Money-Kurle, takes the view that …*	Zeitraum, Periode

perspective	**on** sth; **from** a ... ~	Perspektive, Standpunkt
phase	**of** (adjustment; 48 weeks); **during** a ~	Phase
portion	**of** sth	Teil, Anteil
potential	**for** sth (*the ~ for unauthorized copying*); (of sth) **to**-INF/**for** v-*ing (the ~ to earn money)*	Potenzial, Möglichkeit(en), Fähigkeit(en)
range	**of** (*a wide ~ of workers*); **from** ... **to** (*a ~ from 10 to 100 MHz*); **in** *the ~ of 3.0 – 4.5*	(Mess-, Skalen-, etc.)Bereich; Reihe; Spektrum
relevance	(of sth) **to** sth; (sth is) of ~ to; with ~ to (*pedagogical theories with ~ to basic writing*)	Bedeutung, Relevanz, Wichtigkeit
role	**in** sth/v-ing (*their central ~ in organizing research*); **of** (*the ~ of mentor*); **as** (*Atticus' ~ as the defence lawyer*); **for** (*a new ~ for women*)	Rolle

The ability to build noun phrases is essential to academic writing. One important reason is that noun phrases help writers to condense information which appears in the form of clauses earlier in the same text. Rather than repeating the same clause over and over, you can opt for a shorter, synonymous form of words. The meaning link thus created between the clause and the noun phrase ties your text together, creating what is known as 'lexical cohesion'. Here is an example:

> It is important to note here that Mrs. Forrester, in noticing the boys, distinguishes between Niel and George and the other "little boys". This distinction is based on their family reputations.

Here the information contained in the clause built around the verb *distinguish* is condensed into the noun *distinction*. Such condensation or 'nominalization' meets the requirements of an impersonal academic style (see Module IV, Chapter 1.3) in that the people who initiate the processes described by the noun phrase are not mentioned. The process is thus sometimes portrayed as being a 'timeless' truth (cf. Thompson 1996: 170–171).

There is a wide range of nouns in academic prose which serve this condensing function with some regularity. Corpus evidence suggests a significant underuse of such 'retrospective labels' in texts produced by non-native speakers from various backgrounds (Hinkel 2002: 82). It therefore makes a lot of sense to become acquainted with these items. They can be usefully categorized into three major groups (cf. Francis 1994, Chalker 1996: 94): nouns referring to actions and events, nouns referring to facts and nouns referring to text as text. Such nouns are frequently used to replace sentential relative clauses (see Chapter 3.6.1 of Module II). Table 6 provides a few typical examples.

Table 6: Examples of nouns acting as retrospective labels

Group 1: nouns referring to actions and events		
a course of action/a course	The third possible response to the oncoming tidal wave is that we accommodate dramatically increased numbers of college students without a commensurate increase in educational resources. Obviously, **such a course of action** would only diminish the quality of education dispensed by our institutions of higher education.	Handlungsweise, Vorgehensweise, Vorgehen
a practice	Sometimes, a short report is delivered live by the anchor. **This practice** has become extremely frequent in the short news flashes of non-stop news channels.	Vorgehensweise
Group 2: nouns referring to facts		
an allegation	Pitt claims that the Prime Minister at the time managed to see some of his ideas prior to publication and incorporate them into his own budget. Whatever the truth of **this allegation**, Pitt certainly did not adopt all of Paine's plans.	Behauptung, Unterstellung
Group 3: nouns referring to text as text		
a paragraph	**In this paragraph** the author paints a picture of, and indicates some of the reasons for, the 'isolation, insularity and exceptionalism' of America before World War I.	Absatz

Other, usually bare nouns are employed to tell the reader what to expect in the text which follows. Among the most common 'advance labels' of this type are *argument, reason* and *explanation*. They, too, are thus extremely useful as text-structuring devices. Combined with a suitable verb, they can help you prepare the reader for the next step in your argument in a completely unambiguous manner. Because you have explicitly stated the fact, your reader can be sure, for example, that this next step is an explanation rather than a counterargument:

> They advanced the explanation that all the wisdom of Plato and the other Greeks was due to the inspiration of the Logos.

The same tendency towards condensation as with retrospective labels can be observed when an entity is directly brought into the text as a complex noun phrase rather than as a full clause. The usual progression to be found in such cases follows the ladder of generalization upwards from the more specific to the more general, often according to the following schema:

> N + postmodifier > premodifier + N > simple noun > pronoun (Biber et al. 1999: 586)

This may give rise to sequences like the following:

> One basic distinction psychologists make is between **behavior that is shaped by instrumental judgments about the incentives or punishments associated with engaging in the behavior** and behavior that is value-driven. **Instrumentally motivated behavior** is shaped through the promise of rewards ...

The noun *behavior* in this excerpt first occurs with a long postmodifier (*that is shaped ...*) whose content is then picked up by a fairly short premodifier (*instrumentally motivated*). This progression represents an increasing economy of expression over the course of the text. First mentions are usually more elaborate, while subsequent mentions become increasingly economical.

More often than not the condensed wording is already so firmly established within the academic community that technical terms are directly introduced in this form. Here there is no great effort needed on the part of the writer provided that s/he is familiar with the subject-specific terminology, such as *relative pronoun* in linguistics and *urban growth* in geography:

> In this sentence, the **relative pronoun** is neuter plural.
> The first are policies designed to guide **urban growth** and change at a national scale, i.e. between urban regions.

2.1.1 Complex noun phrases in English and German

It is well recognized that both German and English academic writers rely quite heavily on nominalization. As seen above, one of the reasons for this is the desire for economy of statement and an impersonal, objective style. Related to this is the greater conceptual precision which usually comes with noun phrases (we will discuss some exceptions below). Rather than saying 'the student who is able to write in the foreign language', we talk of 'die Schreibfähigkeit des Zweitsprachenlerners' or 'the second language learner's writing ability/writing skills'.

That said, even a brief look at German and English scholarly publications will reveal at least partially countervailing tendencies in the use of noun phrases. Modern German has a clear predilection for nouns converted from verbs:

das Problem klären → die Klärung des Problems

This trend towards formal nominalization is somewhat less pronounced in English, with the exception of one type of nominal construction that is more or less specific to English: abstract noun + *to be* (+ prep.) + noun phrase (e.g. *the development has been from A to B*; see Module IV, Chapter 1.3.2 for further examples). Thus, although word-for-word nominal equivalents are often available in English (e.g. *Klärung* → *clarification*), the preference goes to verb-based constructions and, though to a considerably lesser extent, to wh-clauses. The preference for verb-based constructions is aptly exemplified by the entry for *Klärung* from *Das große Oxford Wörterbuch Deutsch-Englisch* (see also Table 7 below). Since the entry neglects literal and nominal renderings, we have added two additional examples:

Er war für die Klärung organisatorischer Fragen zuständig. → His job was to resolve organizational problems.
Bis zur endgültigen Klärung hat die Polizei jede Auskunft verweigert. → Until the case is finally solved, the police have refused to give any information.
vor der Klärung der Eigentumsverhältnisse → before ownership is established
Sie fordern eine gerichtliche Klärung. → They want the issue to be settled by the court. (*Das große Oxford Wörterbuch für Schule und Beruf Englisch-Deutsch/Deutsch-Englisch*, Berlin: Cornelsen 2003, s.v. *Klärung*)
Diese Zahl bedarf einer Klärung. → This figure will need to be clarified.
Sie wünschen eine weitere fachliche Klärung dieser Punkte. → They want further technical clarification of these points.

The following example shows how the noun-heavy style typical of many writers of English with a German-speaking background can be turned into a more readable style by recovering nominalized verbs.

?He consequently argues for an approach towards education in which focused attention is paid to the development of an awareness of the constructed nature of culture and a reflection about personal cultural identity.
→ He therefore argues for an approach to education which focuses on developing awareness of the constructed nature of culture and helps students reflect on their cultural identity.

Here three noun phrases have been turned into verbs (*focused attention is paid* → *focus*; *development* → *develop*; *reflection* → *reflect*), giving us a less wordy and more smoothly flowing sentence. Note carefully that we have also placed the subject initially (see Module II, Chapter 2.1) by starting the relative clause with *which* rather than *in which*.

In the next example there is an infelicitous accumulation of *of*-phrases, leading to a high density of nouns:

> ?the meaning constructed in a learner's response is conceptualised as the result of the application of knowledge of subject-matter in engaging in the activities required by the task.
> → the meaning constructed in a learner's response is conceptualised as the result of applying subject-specific knowledge patterns while engaging in the activities required by the task.

The corrected version is more verbal and clarifies the link between the participial clause 'engaging in the activities required by the task' and the rest of the sentence (cf. Module IV, Chapter 2.3 on the various functions of participial clauses).

Another feature of academic German which sets it apart from academic English is the widespread use of nonce compounds (*Augenblickskomposita*), i.e. compounds created only for a particular occasion. Thus, we could coin the German compound *Augenblickskompositahäufung* to describe the frequent use of nonce compounds in a piece of text, but a corresponding English compound like 'nonce compound accumulation' would be rather unpalatable. In English such coinages are usually shorter, and they occur more commonly in newspaper language, especially in headlines.

From what has been said so far, it should be clear that the extremely dense use of more or less complex nominalizations in German academic writing should not normally be transferred to English. While German academic writers may exploit nominalization to display a high level of competence, such an attitude would achieve the opposite effect with an English-speaking audience.

Complex noun phrases are by no means impossible in English, but analytic forms of words (*a solution to the problem*) are somewhat more common than synthetic compounds (*a problem solution*). It is therefore on the whole safer to distribute the information contained in overcomplex noun phrases across several word groups. Thus,

> Augenblickskompositahäufung → accumulation of nonce compounds/dense use of nonce compounds (etc.)

It is also worth noting that, as a rule, noun + noun combinations can be made in English only if adjective + noun compounds with the same meaning are not available. Thus,

?biology research → biological research/research on biology
*culture norms → cultural norms

This rule is, however, subject to a number of exceptions; thus, we find both *language communities* and *linguistic communities*, with little difference in meaning.

A further complicating factor is that long English compounds are usually more ambiguous than shorter ones. Take, for example, the word group *customer data input*. On its own, this may give rise to two different interpretations:

(customer data) input → input of customer data
customer (data input) → input of data by the customer (Smith and Bernhardt 1997: 235)

This does not mean that you should always refrain from using such compounds. Their inherent ambiguity is usually resolved in context, or the subject knowledge shared by reader and writer will allow only one interpretation. If you are uncertain whether your readers have that knowledge or if the compound is too unwieldy, it is usually a good idea to unpack it. Heavy premodification may have the advantage of greater concision and may give an impression of objectivity and learnedness, but this is often bought at the expense of readability (cf. Module IV, Chapter 2.3).

The safest strategy in such cases is a) to determine the implicit logical relationship holding between the modifying noun and the head noun and b) to reformulate this relationship as a phrasal lexeme (*Wortgruppenlexem*), a verb phrase, a prepositional phrase, an entire clause or some form of combination of these, according to the following schema: N1 + N2 + Head Noun → Head Noun + Preposition + N2 + Preposition + N1, for example:

customer data input → input of data about/by the customer (Smith and Bernhardt 1997: 235ff.)

If the compound is already institutionalized in some particular field of study (e.g. *program development tools* in computing), there is no point in unpacking it. If, on the contrary, you are writing about a new, highly specific tool, it is often preferable to use a verb phrase when you first introduce the tool. The second mention of the same tool could then be in compound form, for example:

tools for developing multimedia content → multimedia content development tools

When you are at a loss for an English equivalent of a German compound, you may be tempted to turn to dictionaries. Be warned, however: even when the dictionary renders a German compound as an English compound, it often pays to have a healthy mistrust of the solutions offered there. You should always explore various possibilities and test your translation proposals against Google (see Chapter 3.1). The theoretical range of possibilities extends from translation as a simplex noun to lengthy periphrasis, as illustrated in Table 7 by means of German compounds based for the most part on the noun *Verfahren*.

Table 7: Translation of German compounds

English construction used	**German compound**	**English translation**
1. simplex	Anwendungsverfahren	application
	Reflexionstagung	symposium
PREMODIFICATION		
2. gerund + noun	der Amtsantritt	taking office
3. compound	das Wasserheilverfahren das Fertigungsverfahren	hydrotherapy production process
4. adjective/present participle + noun	das Diagnoseverfahren	diagnostic method
5. (noun + participle) + noun	das Brunnenbauverfahren	well-sinking method
6. s-genitive + noun	die Lehrergehälter	teachers' wages
POSTMODIFICATION		
7. noun + prepositional phrase	das Untersuchungsverfahren das Stabilisierungsverfahren	method of investigation method of stabilization
8. noun + complement clause	das Rücktrittsangebot	offer to resign
MULTIPLE PRE- OR POSTMODIFICATION		
9. multiple pre- or postmodification	das Cross-Verfahren (a method used in civil engineering)	method of moment distribution
PARAPHRASE		
10. paraphrase	das Lesepensum (*für den Fremdsprachenlerner ist das* ***Lesepensum*** *wesentlich geringer*)	(*the foreign language learner will not work through anything like the same amount of reading material*)

	der Reflexionsstand (*der aktuelle **Reflexionsstand** der Hochschuldidaktik im Bereich …*)	(*current thinking among university specialists in …*)
	der Erkenntnisstand (*… den aktuellen wissenschaftlichen **Erkenntnisstand** berücksichtigen.*)	(*… have due regard to the body of scientific knowledge currently available.*)

Sometimes there are several alternative renderings:

> Produktanalyseinstrumentarium → tools for analysis of products/tools for analysing products

Note that the mere existence of word groups such as *examination procedure* or *suggestions for improvement* (= *Verbesserungsvorschläge*) is no guarantee of their appropriateness. The danger for many foreign-born writers is that they may memorize such fixed items as stock solutions to be applied anywhere and everywhere. However, noun-based phrases may not always fit smoothly into the relevant context. For example, a medical specialist may have looked up or memorized the phrase *examination procedure* as a standard equivalent of *Untersuchungsverfahren*. Faced with the following sentence skeleton, however, s/he has to resort to using the noun *method* or *procedure* with an *ing*-construction introduced by the preposition *for*:

> In the adrenal gland, by contrast, CT has become the noninvasive method of choice … patients with suspected tumors or endocrine hyperfunction (= die Hauptuntersuchungsmethode bei Patienten mit Tumoren oder endokriner Überfunktion …)
>
> → In the adrenal gland, by contrast, CT has become the noninvasive **method** of choice **for examining** patients with suspected tumors or endocrine hyperfunction.

In the same way, *Verbesserungsvorschläge* does not always correspond to *suggestions for improvement*; nor does *Beurteilungskriterien* invariably translate as *judgment criteria*. Whenever another noun follows, a participial rendering is advantageous: *suggestions for improving* NP/*criteria for judging* NP.

A further difficulty involved in building complex noun phrases is the sometimes obligatory addition of prepositions and relative clauses, especially *ing*-clauses and *ed*-clauses. German tends to use free-standing prepositional phrases (*die Probleme* **bei der Übersetzung von** …) where English ties the circumstantial element in more closely with the noun. Sometimes the possibilities are varied and numerous, as in the case of *problem*:

problems associated with the translation/connected with the translation/attendant (up)on the translation/(involved) in translating (etc.)

At other times it is safest to use the noun with the preposition which its pattern requires and to follow this up with an *-ing*-clause. Here is a list of common noun + preposition + *-ing* constructions (in decreasing order of frequency):

N + for + *-ing*

reason for believing, **justification** for believing, **strategies** for implementing, **basis** for analysing, **procedure** for applying, **rules** for determining, **system** for predicting, **argument** for saying, **way**(s) of seeing, **context** for interpreting, **procedure** for dealing with, **frame of reference** for thinking about, **framework** for understanding, **language** for describing, **instructions** for making, **machinery** for resolving, **method** for doing

N + of + *-ing*

method of doing, **way** of describing, **danger** of being, **means** of achieving, **cost** of providing, **effect** of making, **advantage** of using, **process** of making, **prospect** of being, **problem** of deciding, **risk** of having, **difficulty** of finding, **task** of determining

N + in + *-ing*

role in shaping, **difficulty** in obtaining, **usefulness** in determining, (play some/a) **part** in determining, **skills** in using

N + to + *-ing*
approach to learning, **commitment** to enabling, **guide** to deciding, **obstacle** to regarding, **key** to understanding, **resistance** to modernizing, **response** to helping, **alternative** to solving, **route** to establishing, **impediment** to developing, **barrier** to obtaining, **contribution** to changing, **prerequisite** to improving

N + with + *-ing*
difficulty with doing, **problem** with implementing, **concern** with incorporating, **preoccupation** with producing

N + from + *-ing*
gain from using, **exemption** from paying

N + from + *-ing* + to + *-ing*
move from (using authentic materials) to using (ready-made published materials), **progression**, **shift**

An alternative formulation using a noun + preposition + noun phrase construction is often possible in theory, but usually dispreferred in practice:

(?)Another important question is the development of a suitable language for the description of these phenomena.
→ Another important problem is the development of a suitable language for describing these phenomena.
(?)The significance of race and ethnicity for an understanding of organizational behaviour.
→ The significance of race and ethnicity for understanding organizational behaviour.

There may also be slight differences in meaning between more nominal and more verbal constructions. Compare:

The Family and Its Role in the Transmission of Culture (heading; the nominal construction suggests that this role is more or less permanent)
The deer tick and its role in transmitting Lyme disease have already been mentioned. (role = one of a number of agents or factors)

2.1.2 Productive nominal patterns

German and English share some very productive patterns for creating noun compounds with which the fledgling writer can hardly go astray. Thus, for example, it is possible to negate a large number of nouns by means of the prefix *non-*: *non-equivalence, non-interference, non-intervention, non-smoker, non-member, non-acceptance* (cf. Wilss 1996: 137). Another common type of word formation follows the formula (N1 + N2) + N3, with the two bracketed nouns usually joined by a hyphen: *part-whole relation, teacher-learner conflict, student-teacher ratio, figure-ground relation, man-machine interaction* (cf. Wilss 1996: 144–145). Of a similar make-up are compounds such as *16-inch slab* or *15-year-old boy*. Note that when you pluralize these adjective + noun compounds the noun preceded by the numeral is not made plural: *15-year-old boys* (also: *15-year-olds*).

2.1.3 Position and length of complex noun phrases

It is advisable to limit subject noun phrases in size so as to adhere to the principles of end weight and end focus (see Module II, Chapter 2.2). In German, front-heavy sentences occur somewhat more frequently; witness the following example, where the subject has been underlined:

Der Beitrag deutscher Einwanderer und ihrer Nachkommen zur Entwicklung und damit zur Geschichte zunächst der britischen Kolonien, dann der Vereinigten Staaten von Amerika, ist ausführlich in der Ausstellung dargestellt.

The subject of the second clause in the following sentence might be considered overlong and should be recast, especially since it contains new information (cf. Module II, Section 2.6.1):

> (?)Topics are important in face-to-face interaction, the development of shared estimation about the people, things, activities, ideas etc. talked about seems to be just as important.
>
> Topics are important in face-to-face interaction; what seems to be just as important is the establishment of shared esteem about the people, things, activities, ideas, etc. discussed.

Module II (mainly Chapters 2.3, 2.5 and 2.6) discusses various strategies for placing complex noun phrases in clause-final rather than subject position (discontinuous structures, pseudo-cleft clauses, shift from passive to active voice, etc.). Module IV, Chapter 1.3 discusses differences between nominal and verbal style (see also Königs 1998: 5, especially footnote 6).

2.1.4 General strategies for noun phrase building

When building up noun phrases in English, ask yourself three main questions.

a) What determiner does the noun phrase take?
b) Does the noun phrase fit in its context?
c) Is the noun phrase easy to understand?

a) What determiner(s) does the noun phrase take?
Unlike their German equivalents, nouns like *information, advice, knowledge, news* or *luggage* are uncountable. This means that, in ordinary everday usage, they have no plural and they are not used with the indefinite article *a* or *an*. If you want to refer to one individual thing, you can often use expressions such as 'a piece of (information)' or 'an item of (news)'. Table 8 shows typical translation equivalences for such nouns.

Table 8: German countable nouns vs. English uncountable nouns

German	English
Sprecher A spricht **ein** sehr flüssiges Deutsch.	Speaker A speaks very fluent German.
... – **ein** guter Rat, den man beherzigen sollte.	... – a good **piece of** advice of which to take note.
je ein Code für die **drei** Informationen	one code for each of the three **pieces of** information

Since there are many more uncountable nouns in English than in German, it is wise to check in your dictionary whether an English noun is countable or uncountable before you use it. The following are some of the most important uncountable nouns in academic English.

> advice, awe, behaviour, consent, courseware, equipment, ethics, etiology, friction, gravity, hardware, health, homework, inflation, information, integrity, intimacy, knowledge, labour, linguistics, logic, machinery, mathematics, minimum, maximum, news, philosophy, phonetics, phonotactics, pollution, pragmatics, prestige, progress, reluctance, research, semantics, software, trade, traffic, vocabulary, wealth, welfare

Although these nouns are generally considered uncountable, they may be made plural in particular academic contexts. Thus, psychologists may talk of 'reducing stress-related behaviours', and physicians may take account of 'gender-specific etiologies'. A noun like *vocabulary* is uncountable in its general use (= German *Vokabular, Vokabeln*), but can be pluralized when it refers to wordlists dealing with a particular author or a particular subject, as in 'specialized vocabularies' (= German *Fachwortschätze*). German *Vokabel* in the sense of an item to be learned is *vocabulary item* or (*vocabulary*) *word* in English.

It is important to note that uncountable abstract nouns take no article when they refer to a general notion; this also applies to premodified abstract noun phrases:

> their main topics may be personalities or **history**
> The first part lists three stages of **human evolution** from the earliest to the most recent: ...
> **listening comprehension** (*a listening comprehension → a listening comprehension exercise/activity)

But when the same noun or noun phrase is postmodified, especially by an *of*-phrase, the definite article is common:

> His book stresses **the history of** styles ...

That said, however, nouns such as *use, growth, rejection* or *modification* often occur without the article even when they are postmodified:

> Use of the tense serves virtually as a legal escape clause, an avoidance of liability for the truth of what is alleged.
> This has been subject to critical evaluation by other authors.
> Demand for many marketed services has (...) remained stable over time ...

Generalizing somewhat, we can say that if the noun is embedded in a common word combination, it is likely to dispense with the article (cf. Siepmann 2001 for further details). Thus, for example, verb + adjective + noun collocations based on the verb-noun collocations *make use of s.th.* or *pay attention to s.th.* invariably dispense with the definite and indefinite articles (with the exception of *make the best use of,* clearly motivated by the use of the superlative); similarly with verb + adjective + noun combinations based on *place/put/lay emphasis on s.th,* which in the vast majority of cases are accompanied by the zero article. Outside these complex combinations, however, the definite and indefinite articles do occur with *use/emphasis* + adjective. The following examples of *use* illustrate this contrast:

> Investors must work towards **making proper use of** these opportunities.
>
> Systems supporting the cluttered desktop metaphor can suffer from figure-ground ambiguity. Fortunately, the figure-ground distinction can be enhanced by **the proper use of** graphic devices such as borders, highlighting, overlapping, graying out, colors, etc.

It is also worth taking a brief look at nouns which occur only in the plural form and therefore require a plural verb. Some of these plural nouns are usually learned at a very early stage in English language teaching; they refer to items of clothing and other objects consisting of two parts: *pyjamas, tights, leggings, scissors, binoculars*. Other nouns of this kind which are common in academic writing include:

> *arms* (= 1. Waffen, 2. Wappen), *clothes, congratulations, contents* (of a bag, pocket, book, letter; cf. *content* [= the ideas contained in a piece of writing or a film]), *customs, earnings, effects* (= Vermögen, Hab und Gut), *funds, goods, looks* (= Aussehen), *odds* (= Chancen, Wahrscheinlichkeit), *papers* (Dokumente, Schriftstücke), *particulars* ([persönliche] Details), *premises, regards, remains* (= Überreste), *savings, spirits* (= Gemütsverfassung), *stalls* (= 1. Chorgestühl [in church]; 2. Parkett [in theatre or cinema]), *surroundings, troops, wages*

Some of these nouns can be used in the singular, albeit with a different meaning.

Some nouns of Latin or Greek origin have irregular plurals. Nouns ending in *-is* often take *-es* in the plural: *crises, theses, hypotheses*. *-um* and *-on* often become *-a*: *media, criteria* (but *museums*). Nouns like *series* and *species* do not change their spelling in the plural.

b) Does the noun phrase fit in its context?

Many nouns and adjectives are used with particular prepositions. There are no hard-and-fast rules to help you choose the correct one in many cases, so you will have to learn by heart which word combines with which preposition. For instance, the noun *visit* is always followed by the preposition *to* ('my visit to Munich was extremely interesting'), as are the nouns *ambassador* ('the British ambassador to Spain') and *rival*. Sometimes, however, if you look at words with a similar meaning such as *typical, characteristic, expressive* and *symbolic*, you find that there are clear recurrent patterns. Many such patterns have been categorized by meaning group in *Collins Cobuild Grammar Patterns* (Francis, Hunston & Manning 1996, 1998). We have listed a few typical cases where students often go astray in Table 9.

Table 9: Divergent regularities in patterning

German	English
ein Beispiel/Zeichen/Anzeichen **für** etw.	a(n) example/sign/indication/measure **of** s.th.
typisch/symptomatisch/charakteristisch **für**	typical/characteristic/expressive/ symbolic/symptomatic/indicative **of**
ein(e) Bedrohung/Gefahr/Nachteil/ Herausforderung/(schwerer) Schlag **für** j-mden/etw.	a threat/danger/drawback/challenge/ blow **to** s.th./s.o.
gefährlich/giftig **für**	dangerous/poisonous **to**

Remember that many nouns are used with a preposition followed by a gerund, such as *way of seeing* (for further examples see above).

Some nouns may only occur in a particular pattern under very specific conditions. Compare the way a student used the pattern *way + to s.th.* (see the starred sentence) with its use in natural-sounding English:

> *Parents can support children at least at the beginning **of their way to autonomy**.
>
> … because Dante's specific sin is *acedia*, he must actively pursue the right way, **the way to heaven and God**.
> Fashioning identity into an instrument of exclusion is, he warns, **the way to civil war and genocide**.
> The Divine Order is both knowable and achievable. Thus, **the way to Heaven** is clearly marked, and each of us has a chance to find it …
> … industrialization began to **steamroll its way** across the face of the planet …
> … as they try to **point the way to salvation,** they make most of the migrants squirm with discomfort.
> its second generation members may **be on their way to** the top group …

The difference between the two sets of examples is extremely subtle. Although the student has correctly understood that English *way* + *to* + N [abstract], like German *Weg* + *zu* + N [abstract], may serve to express the idea of 'progress' or 'development', she has failed to notice that this meaning occurs mainly in fixed expressions with the pattern ***on** the/one's way to* + N, verb + *one's* + *way* + *to/into* (e.g. *find/steer/steamroll one's way to success*) and *point/pave/lead the way to* (note that the case is different with other meanings of *way*, such as *tell/show/ask s.o. the way to* + N[place]). However, what makes this example particularly tricky is that there are also a handful of fixed expressions in which *way* can be used in the pattern *way* + *to* + N [abstract], such as *the way to peace, the way to heaven* and *s.th. is the way to s.th*. Another problem with the student sentence seems to be the clustering of nouns in clause-final position: *at the **beginning** of their **way** to **autonomy***. The sentence might be improved as follows:

Parents can support children on their way to autonomy, at least at the beginning.

c) Is the noun phrase easy to understand?
As discussed above, nominal compounds such as *multimedia content development tools* may be difficult to understand under certain circumstances. If you think such circumstances apply, break the compound down into its component parts and use other word groups instead.

2.2 Adjective patterns

Adjective phrases allow writers to restrict or more specifically identify the meaning contained in a noun. They consist of an adjective as head, optionally preceded by other words (modifiers) and followed by noun phrases or prepositional phrases (preposition + noun phrase), as illustrated in Table 10. When adjective phrases are part of a noun phrase (*highly interesting work*), they are called 'attributive'. When they are not part of a noun phrase, they are called 'predicative' (*his work is highly interesting*).

Table 10: The adjective phrase

modifier(s)	head	modifier(s)
highly	interesting	work
very	disappointed	in his brother
four hundred miles	long	

2.2.1 Major groups of adjectives

Three major groups of adjectives can be found in academic text: attributive objective, attributive evaluative and predicative evaluative adjectives (cf. Soler 2002). Attributive objective adjectives (i.e. objective adjectives that can be placed before a noun) are usually part of subject-specific content vocabulary; thus, we find *nuclear* (*nuclear membranes*) or *monoclonal* (*monoclonal antibody)* in biology, *monosyllabic* and *suprasegmental* in linguistics, *anticyclical* and *recessionary* in economics. Such adjectives clearly serve a classificatory purpose, helping the researcher to forge new terminology and to indicate the position of a particular concept within a taxonomy.

Attributive evaluative adjectives are less subject-specific; examples include *remarkable* (*a remarkable degree of structural plasticity*), *valuable* (*a valuable method*) or *significant* (*significant correlations*). Although there is some overlap between evaluative adjectives in everyday language and in academic writing (e.g. *remarkable, effective, dramatic, intriguing, crucial*), you should be wary of using adjectives such as *wonderful, great, terrible, good,* etc. in research papers unless they occur in typical collocations such as *great number*. There are more neutral-sounding alternatives such as those listed in Table 11. In writers with a German-speaking background, there is also a certain overuse of phrases with a modal meaning such as *it is necessary to* or *it is possible to* (use *have to/ need to/must* or *can* instead), and a tendency to modify adjectives to an unusual extent, e.g. inappropriately writing *very important* rather than *important* or *crucial*.

Many evaluative adjectives can also be used predicatively (i.e. after link verbs such *be, seem, appear,* etc.): *programmed cell death is crucial to the plasticity of the developing nervous system*. If you are unsure whether you can use an adjective attributively or predicatively, turn to your monolingual learner's dictionary or use Google Books (see Chapter 3.2 for more information). Sometimes the information given in dictionaries cannot be trusted, or lags behind real usage. Thus, for example, *Collins Cobuild English Dictionary* (2001) states that *unhappy* in the sense 'not satisfactory or desirable' always precedes a noun. In academic books, however, we also come across predicative uses:

> Husserl also tries to show that different occurrences of the same word with the same meaning may have different referents, e.g. two occurrences of *horse* in sentences saying of different creatures *This is a horse,* but **the example is unhappy** because the predicative use of the noun need not be referential.[2]

[2] From Barry Smith. 1995. *The Cambridge Companion to Husserl*. Cambridge: Cambridge University Press, p. 111; underlining ours.

Table 11: Common evaluative adjectives and typical noun collocates

positive evaluative adjectives	typical noun collocates	negative evaluative adjectives
accurate	account, description, information, judgement, measurement, translation	**inaccurate**
careful, thorough	analysis, assessment, definition, examination, experiment, measurement, inspection, reading, reappraisal, study, work	**sloppy, flawed**
correct	assumption, belief, conclusion, idea, impression, interpretation	**erroneous**
competent	handling, management	**incompetent**
clear	account, appreciation, choice, concept, demonstration, example, thinking	**confusing, unclear; muddled** (+ account, concept, thinking)
remarkable, impressive	accuracy, achievement, book, consistency, ease, judgement, performance, piece (of writing), skill, variety	– (e.g. with insufficient accuracy, a controversial [or: questionable] book, weak judgement)
useful, valuable	aid, clue, contribution, exercise, experience, feedback, information, (re)source, role	**useless; futile** (+ exercise, role)
other positive adjectives: **convincing** (*argument, demonstration, evidence*), **elegant** (*style*), **important**, **innovative** (*approach*), **interesting**, **significant** (*difference*), **masterful** (*assessment*), **masterly** (*synthesis*), **skilful** (*use, way*)		other negative adjectives: **incomplete** (*picture*), **inconclusive** (*evidence, debate*), **inexact** (*understanding*), **lengthy** (*passage, discussion*), **limited** (*value, range*), **misconceived** (*argument*), **misguided** (*belief*), **misleading** (*picture, information*), **narrow** (*focus, scope*), **obscure** (*reference, language*), **puzzling** (*contradiction, explanation*), **questionable** (*assumption, validity*), **specious** (*argument, proposal, logic*), **unconvincing** (*suggestion, interpretation*), **unfortunate** (*error, practice, tendency*), **unsatisfactory** (*nature, state, conclusion*), **unsound** (*ideology, judgement, method*), **untenable** (*position, theory, doctrine*)

Evaluative adjectives are often modified by 'softening' adverbs such as *quite* or *somewhat* (cf. Römer 2005):

He goes on to build up a complicated and **somewhat obscure** case.

It is worth bearing in mind that some adjectives may be interpreted differently in different fields of study. Thus, *complex* may mean 'sophisticated' in some of the humanities and 'messy' or 'confused' in science or medicine (Swales & Feak 1994: 137).

2.2.2 Participial and compound adjectives

Apart from adjectives such as *important* and *masterful*, there are two other types of adjective, which can be formed from the past and present participles of verbs. These are called participial adjectives (*increasing, continued*) and participial compound adjectives (*time-honoured, life-enhancing*). Note that, for greater ease of reading, the latter type should be spelt with a hyphen, although closed compounds are also found (e.g. *bloodborne*).

It is difficult to predict precisely when a participial adjective cannot go before the noun. One clear case is when pre-position would give the participial adjective a different meaning, as with *used* (= old, second-hand). This is a frequent source of error, as shown by the following examples from student papers:

> *the used tense is the present
> *I would like to add a few words concerning the included moral at the end of the story.
> *the mentioned passage

If in doubt, you should therefore place the participial adjective after the noun. The following participial adjectives strongly prefer postposition:

> discussed (the theories ~), mentioned (the matters ~), used (the words ~), analysed (the texts ~), provided (the services ~), concerned (the person ~), involved (the processes ~), studied (the patients ~), obtained (the results ~), conferred (the powers ~), presented (the data ~), covered (the period ~), encountered (the problems ~), reached (the conclusion ~), produced (the output ~)

By contrast, the following participial adjectives are often preposed in academic English:

> implied (the ~ terms), required (the ~ information), prescribed (the ~ form), intended (the ~ word), desired (the ~ record), expected (the ~ number), labelled (the ~ cells), added (the ~ advantage), alleged (the ~ offence), perceived (the ~ threat), printed (the ~ version), agreed (the ~ terms), estimated (the ~ amount), listed (the ~ categories), observed (the ~ spectrum), proposed (the ~ transaction), published (the ~ reports), signed (the ~ documents), projected (the ~ area), shared (the ~ experience)

Some uses of participial adjectives seem to be restricted to specific fields of study. Thus, in biology the phrase 'the introduced material', in the sense of 'the material inserted into some body' is fairly common, but its use in a text on language pedagogy strikes one as decidedly odd:

*the strengthening of the introduced speaking material

Some German and English compound adjectives rely on the same adjectival bases, such as *-free* and *-frei*, *-bewusst* and *-conscious* or *-freundlich* and *-friendly*. Note that the English compound adjectives are always hyphenated, whereas their German counterparts are spelt as one word. Examples:

-bewusst: gesundheits-, ernährungs-, kalorien-, mode-, kosten-, macht-
-conscious: health-, nutrition-/diet-, calorie-, fashion-, cost-, power-

-freundlich: umwelt-, verbraucher-, benutzer-, leser-, patienten-
-friendly: environment-, consumer-, user-, reader-, patient-

This should not be taken to suggest, however, that all compound adjectives translate easily. Even with bases such as *-friendly*, appearances are deceptive: *magenfreundlich* is *kind to the stomach*, *regierungsfreundlich* is *pro-government* and *servicefreundlich* is *easy to service*.

In most cases the ideas expressed by highly specific German compound adjectives can be rendered into English by means of non-compounds:

gegenstandsbezogen → factual
entwicklungsgeschichtlich → evolutionary
konjunkturbedingt → cyclical
praxisbezogen → practical

Sometimes a compound may be available for one combination, but may be lacking for another. Compare:

literaturgeschichtlich = literary-historical
kulturspezifisch = culture-specific
kunstgeschichtlich = art-historical
geistesgeschichtlich = in/of/relating to the history of ideas

As a rule, however, such compounds as *literary-historical* or *optimality-theoretic* are felt to be rather learned and pretentious; they should, if possible, be rephrased by shifting the main burden of meaning onto a noun, along the lines of the above translation proposed for *geistesgeschichtlich*:

gesundheitspolitisch → in/of/relating to **health policy**
gemütsarm → lacking in **feeling**

Writers in some disciplines may use sophisticated compound adjectives as technical terms, where others would fall back on a circumlocution. Thus, in psychology the German compound adjective *kontaktscheu* and *konfliktscheu* may be equivalent to *contact-avoidant* and *conflict-avoidant* (or *conflict-averse*). In literary studies a contact-avoidant person would probably be described as 'shying away from human contact' or 'misanthropic', and a conflict-averse person as 'avoiding or shunning conflict'.

2.2.3 General strategies for building adjective phrases

When building up adjective phrases, use the following strategies:

a) Replace such run-of-the-mill adjectives as *good* with more precise variants such as *accurate* or *elegant.*
b) Ask yourself whether you are using the adjective predicatively or attributively. Can you use it in the intended way?
c) When using participial adjectives, check whether you can place them before or after the noun (e.g. *the cases discussed* rather than (?)*the discussed cases*).

2.3 Prepositions and prepositional phrases

The correct use of prepositions is among the hardest things to master in foreign language learning. Most prepositional usage depends on the natural patterns found with nouns, verbs and adjectives (e.g. *different **from**, come **onto** the market, request **for***), a subject we have already discussed at some length. However, there are also a few cases where very general rules apply that cannot always be described in terms of patterning. The following examples are meant to illustrate some of the main differences between German and English usage, especially with regard to academic/scientific texts (cf. Kraus 1989).

German 'auf' and its English equivalents
German 'auf' corresponds to English 'in' in such locative contexts as:

> in the street/yard/square, in the field(s) (the farmer was working in the field), in the world, in the British Isles/Isle of Wight/the Bahamas

It corresponds to English 'on' in the following locative contexts:

> on the field (the players were on the field), on the pitch (= field), on the table/on the floor, on (the) earth, measuring instruments are provided on the front of the cubicle

It is equivalent to 'at' in other locative contexts:

at the Hanover fair, upon arrival at the construction site, at the conference

'At' is also used with nouns such as 'request' or 'suggestion':

at the customer's request, at the instigation of the manufacturer, at a command from the control room (cf. also by special request, by order of), at my sister's urging

'For' is used to describe the purpose of an activity:

examine s.th. for its structure, check s.th. for defects, analyse s.th. for its chemical composition

'To' is used to designate a value to be attained:

the parts are worked to an accuracy of 0.01 mm (die Teile werden auf eine Genauigkeit von 0,01 mm bearbeitet), lift to a certain height, control the temperature to the desired value, solve an equation correct to 4 decimal places (eine Gleichung auf 4 Stellen hinter dem Komma genau lösen)

'To within' marks a limit:

Atomic clocks are accurate to within billionths of a second. (auf Billionstel einer Sekunde genau)

German 'bei' and its English equivalents (cf. Kraus 1978)

In such German sentences as the following, 'bei' is usually equivalent to either a temporal clause introduced by 'when' or a conditional clause introduced by 'if'. The choice depends on whether the conditional or the temporal sense prevails.

beim Einschalten des Lichts → when the light is switched on/when switching on the light
bei eingeschaltetem Licht → if (or: when) the light is switched on

If the emphasis is on duration, 'bei' corresponds to 'while' and 'as':

It is not possible to remove the cover while the motor is running. (bei laufendem Motor; cf. also with the motor running).

When 'bei' expresses anterior time, (up)on + V-ing or N is the usual equivalent:

Salt solutions exfoliate rocks on evaporating. (Beim Verdunsten bringen Salzlösungen Gestein zum Abschiefern.)
upon removal of the heat source (bei Wegnahme der Wärmequelle)
upon completion of the work (bei Fertigstellung der Arbeit)

A notably common equivalent of 'bei' in academic texts is 'with' (or its synonym 'in the case of'). It is used to single out a particular entity for further discussion.

> However, with some of these nouns, forms with a final -n in the nominative singular (eg der Frieden rather than der Friede) are now more frequent ... (bei einigen dieser Nomina)

English 'in', 'at' and 'on' with times of day
The preposition 'in' is used with the nouns 'day', 'morning', 'afternoon', 'evening' and 'night' when these are used on their own. If they are used with an adjective, an *of*-phrase or a relative clause, the preposition 'on' is used.

> in the morning/afternoon/evening, at night, but: on the night we first met, on the morning of 14 June, on a wonderful morning

English 'on' and 'by' with means of transport
The prepositions 'on' and 'by' are often used with means of transport.

> I met him on the train/bus/plane/ship.
> He came by bus/train/ferry/plane (but: on foot).

Other prepositions
The following examples illustrate other uses of prepositions that German writers of English often get wrong.

> This is an article **by** Peter Nicholson.
> **At** puberty/**at** (the age of) 15 we put aside the ways of childhood, not only the toys and stuffed animals, but also our secret and magical sense of the world.
> He opted to play **by** the rules of patriarchal culture (by + norm, criterion, rule, standard, yardstick, etc.).
> Such an interpretation of our nature is not humane and not sustainable **over** time.

We now move on to consider complex prepositions and prepositional phrases. These can be divided into two major groups:

a) discourse markers which fulfil a common rhetorical function (e.g. *in contrast to, by virtue of, on grounds of, by analogy with, in anticipation of, by reference to, in the absence of, in terms of*)
b) subject-specific prepositional phrases with narrower meanings (e.g. *by ingestion of, in pursuance of*)

The first type of prepositional phrase has received fairly extensive treatment in dictionaries and in our lists of functional vocabulary provided in this Module. Since the second type is subject-specific, it cannot be documented in full here.

There is also a residual group of complex prepositions which falls into neither of the above categories: *in tune with, in collaboration with, in combination with, for ease of, without loss of, by analysis of, at risk from (abuse/neglect/predators/seaborne invasion), by courtesy of, by recourse to, for consideration by, in tandem with.*

There are wide divergences between different professions in the number of special prepositions they use. While literary scholars do not employ any 'unusual' prepositions, legal writers have to familiarize themselves with a wide variety of complex prepositions, most of which are archaic in everyday usage. Examples include *in breach of, in consequence of, in pursuance of, pursuant to, in consideration of, without prejudice to, by appeal to, in compliance with, in contravention of, with effect from, in restraint of (trade), by operation of (law), in satisfaction of, in violation of, in substitution for,* etc. Medical writers also use a number of 'frozen', prefabricated prepositional phrases, such as *during/by treatment with, for treatment of, after administration of, after incubation of, during infusion of, in subjects with (severe enzyme deficiency), after injection of, after adjustment for (sexual risk factors).* Here is a sentence-length example from a medical text:

> Coeliac disease is exacerbated **by ingestion of** wheat, rye, barley, and probably oats. (British National Corpus)

It is interesting to note the extent to which text type and prepositional usage are interdependent. Thus, a phrase such as *by addition of* occurs almost exclusively in chemical texts, whereas *by ingestion of* is peculiar to medical texts.

Many of the 'frozen', grammatically irregular prepositional phrases just cited are derived from phrases put together by application of more general rules. Usually the only difference between the frozen phrase and the expression it comes from is the use of the zero article with the former:

> by the addition of → by addition of, without any prejudice to → without prejudice to

Once the article has been dropped from one phrase, the pattern thus created may serve as a model for an entire class of phrases:

> by N of → by activation/aspiration/auscultation/biopsy/compression/culture/demonstration/elevation/examination/excretion/formation/ingestion/inhalation/insertion/recovery/removal/widening of

> during N with → during anaesthesia/incubation/treatment/therapy/washing with

This underscores the need for close reading of texts in your own discipline. Be sure to make notes on those prepositional phrases that dispense with the article; also note down their typical semantic associations (e.g. *by ingestion of* + food, *with effect from* + date, *after adjustment for* + variables/factors).

2.4 Verbs and verb patterns

This section begins with a brief look at common academic verbs and then moves on to discuss verb patterns.

2.4.1 Common academic verbs

In recent years corpus linguists (Biber et al. 1999, Leech et al. 2001) have been able to produce fairly reliable statistics on common verbs in academic English. According to their studies, there is a central core of around 40 verbs which are absolutely essential to master. Since most of these are part of the basic vocabulary of English, we assume that you have already met them and feel confident in using them:

> affect, allow, appear, arise (from/out of), assume, cause, change, consider, constitute, contain, determine, develop, emerge, find, follow, form, include, increase, indicate, investigate, involve, lack, leave, obtain, occur, produce, prove, provide, reach, reduce, reflect, relate, remain, represent, require, result (in), seem, tend

We nevertheless provide example sentences and translations for some of the more difficult words which are not mentioned in the thematic vocabulary lists to be found in Chapter 4 of this Module (see Table 12).

Table 12: Some essential verbs in academic English

Verb	Example	Translation
constitute	*In this account, subjectivity unfolds from the social norms that constitute everyday existence.*	bilden, darstellen, ausmachen
determine	*Ordering within the group was determined by the constituent class of the final element.*	bestimmen, feststellen, ermitteln
emerge	*A number of themes emerged from our overview of the National Academies' work.*	sich ergeben, sich herausstellen; entstehen
investigate	*In one experiment which investigated the acquisition of color words in 3 year old children, Elsa Bartlett found that ...*	untersuchen, erforschen
involve	*The study of metaphor will inevitably involve a discussion of tropes.*	mit sich bringen; verbunden sein mit; nach sich ziehen; umfassen, beinhalten

lack	*That does not mean that these words lack other meanings – they may well be polysemic.*	fehlen
occur	*The number of times a particular sense of a word occurs in a corpus can be an important influence on the way the entries are organized.*	vorkommen, begegnen
reflect	*Malraux's and Hemingway's early work reflects the painfully dislocated human landscape left by the First World War.*	widerspiegeln
remain	*But certain features have remained consistent over time.*	bleiben
require	*But successful academic writing requires an objective stance on the part of the writer.*	erfordern, verlangen
tend (to be)	*Masochistic activity tends to be ritualized and chronic.*	gewöhnlich sein; gern sein; dazu neigen zu sein

Beyond this bare minimum there is less agreement on which verbs are important. Collections such as Hinkel (2004: 181), for example, contain general (*ascribe, comprise*) as well as subject-specific (*auscultate*) verbs. As with nouns, we would advise you to study the lists provided in Chapter 4 of this Module and the Academic Word List (http://www.vuw.ac.nz/lals/research/awl/; cf. also Schmitt & Schmitt 2005) in order to gain full mastery of academic verbs.

It is worth stressing again at this point that academic writers do not normally use individual words but rather specific constructions. Some verbs tend to occur in only one form in academic writing, such as *associated, observed, inducing, predicts* and *reveals* (cf. Granger 2006). A key verb like *argue* is overused by learners in patterns such as 'some people argue' or 'many people argue' but underused in the following patterns:

It can be argued that
as argued above
Giddens argues that
By arguing this, Marx … (Granger 2006)

This is why we offer you a large variety of natural patterns in Chapter 4 of this Module.

2.4.2 Verb patterns

In the simple English sentence much depends on the verb. If we compare the verb to a planet, we might say that this planet has a certain gravitational pull which allows it to attract, or keep in orbit, satellites that revolve around it. In a similar way the verb exerts a binding force which allows it to tie together other sentence elements. The ways in which verbs and other sentence elements combine are called 'verb patterns'. For instance, in Table 13, the verb 'fit' has the pattern 'subject' + 'verb' + 'with+noun phrase':

Table 13: The verb pattern found with 'fit'

Noun phrase (Function: Subject)	Verb	With + Noun phrase (Function: Prepositional Object)
That	fits	with our data.

The pattern in Table 13 is a fairly simple one. Table 14 shows a more complex one.

Table 14: Complex verb patterns

Subject	Verb	Noun phrase	as	Adjective phrase
We	accept	this belief	as	fundamental.
People	might interpret	unemployment	as	welcome or unwelcome.

There are hundreds of different verb patterns in English, and there is usually a large number of verbs able to take each pattern. For example, the first pattern shown above also admits the verb 'correspond' (*this corresponds with the latest figures*), and the second the verbs 'see', 'characterize', 'write off', 'brand' and 'certify' (for further information, see Francis, Hunston & Manning 1996, 1998).

Verb patterns contain obligatory and optional elements. 'This belief' is an obligatory element; if we leave it out, the sentence becomes ungrammatical: 'We accept as fundamental' does not make sense; the reader is left wondering 'what is accepted as fundamental?'. By contrast, optional elements can be left out without the sentence becoming unacceptable. For instance, in 'We accept this belief as fundamental', 'as fundamental' can be left out. The sentence we then get is: 'We accept this belief'. This is a perfectly natural English sentence (see Table 15).

Table 15: Obligatory vs. optional elements in verb patterns

Obligatory		Obligatory	Optional	
Subject	**Verb**	**Noun phrase**	**as + Adjective phrase**	
We	accept	this belief	as	fundamental.
People	might interpret	unemployment	as	welcome or unwelcome.

An important traditional distinction is that between transitive and intransitive verbs. Transitive verbs are directly followed by a noun phrase functioning as a direct object (see Table 16).

Table 16: Transitive verbs

Verb phrase	Noun phrase (Function: Direct Object)
to utter	a sound
to create	texts

Table 17 shows a few examples of the ways in which transitive verbs tie together a subject and an object.

Table 17: Examples of patterns with transitive verbs

Subject	Verb	Direct Object
He	signed	the contract.
Shakespeare	wrote	*Romeo and Juliet.*

By contrast, intransitive verbs are never followed by a noun or a pronoun as a direct object, but they may be followed by some other constituent (see Table 18).

Table 18: Examples of patterns with intransitive verbs

Subject	Verb	Complement
Snakes	can move	quite fast.
He	looked	as if the sight of her worried him.
They	were behaving	like thirteen-year-olds.

Many English verbs have the same patterns as their German counterparts, but there are probably more verbs in English that have different patterns. An example of this is provided by the German verb *beneiden* and its English equivalent *envy* (see Table 19).

Table 19: *envy* vs. *beneiden*

Subject	Verb	Object	Preposition	Object
Sie	beneideten	ihn	um	sein Vermö-gen.
They	envied	him	–	his fortune.

Finally, let us look at clauses starting with 'there' (existential clauses). This is a very common pattern, and one that is often misused by Germans (see Table 20).

Table 20: Existential clauses

There	Verb	Complement
There	are	three other criteria
There	are	two important results of such work.
There	has been	debate about ...
There	appear	to be problems with ...
There	seems	no reason to doubt that ...
There	remains	plenty of room for jokes ...

As Table 20 shows, the only verbs that enter this pattern with any regularity are *be, exist, appear, seem, follow, occur, remain, come, arise, emerge, grow, grow up, stand* and *lie*, so you would be well advised not to use any other verbs in this construction.

Appear and *seem* often occur in complex verb constructions with *be* (i.e. *there seems/appears to be*).

There-clauses perform a range of functions in academic text, the most general of which is to signal to the reader that a new item of information is going to be introduced. They are thus comparable to presentatives (see Module II), enabling the writer to avoid clauses which mention new or 'weighty' elements in initial position. Thus, consider the following sentence from an abstract:

[This examination reveals several deficiencies. First, health economic studies of newborn hearing screening are not randomized; most studies are not even controlled. The majority of studies therefore focus on incremental rather than average cost-effectiveness ratios (i.e. cost per case identified).] **Second, evidence on long-term outcomes of screening and early interventions is insufficient.**

From a purely grammatical perspective this sentence is fine. It would be perfectly acceptable in a context where the subject noun phrase is a summary of what has been said or where the specific evidence is in contrast with previously mentioned evidence. In the present case, however, the notion of evidence and the notion of insufficiency are both equally new, which is why it is preferable to use a *there*-clause:

Second, there is insufficient evidence on the long-term outcomes of screening and early interventions.

Such sentences are particularly common in abstracts, summaries or conclusions, where they may serve to report research findings. Here are a few examples:

There was/were (no/some/little/considerable/...) evidence/a correlation/an association/an increase/a decrease/a tendency/differences/no extended discussion of ...
The study showed that there was a significant increase in retention.

These examples illustrate typical features of *there*-clauses; the referent introduced by *there* is usually a noun phrase, which is often modified by determiners such as *several, a number of, a few, no* or a cardinal number. *There*-clauses thus allow writers to use nominalizations rather than verbal formulations (a typical feature of academic style; see this Module and Module IV, 1.3.2), and to achieve greater syntactic unity by coordinating several nouns (Rodman 1996: 659–661). Compare:

(?)Measurement and model agree very well for the three ions.
There is excellent agreement between measurement and model for the three ions.

Similarly, *there*-clauses offer a nominal alternative to passive clauses introduced by *it*. Thus, instead of *it is generally agreed that* or *it cannot be doubted that,* we find:

There is general/broad/widespread/overall agreement that enhanced training facilities will help to correct the 'mismatches' which currently exist between supply and demand in the labour market.
There is little/no doubt/question that/there is a (strong/real) possibility [the possibility] that/there is a growing recognition that (= die Einsicht setzt sich durch,

dass)/there is every/no indication that/there is a danger that/there is (no/little/every/good/strong) reason to believe that

The referent introduced by a *there*-clause can be expanded by means of adjectival phrases, prepositional phrases, relative clauses and other devices. Some of the adjectives (or participles) typically found in these patterns may be considered redundant from a German speaker's perspective but make for greater naturalness of style.

The most important, though rather obvious, point to make is that there is a balance **involved**: that our laughter moves close to the desperate or the hysterical as the balance shifts to terror ...
There is still too much choice **available** in the open model.
There is no distinction **possible** between the religious and the secular.
There is a certain amount of hubris **evident** in the annual surveys by the World Bank ...
... there is little reported case law **extant** in this area ...
There are weaknesses **implicit** in traditional 'hard-edged' thinking ...
There are now several extensive grammars **used** in computational systems.
There is no effort **aimed** at the physical security of these machines.

Another highly productive construction that can be used with a wide variety of adjectives is *there is/are (not)* + *something/nothing/anything* + ADJ + *about/in* + N/V-*ing*.

There is **something** new and unusual **about** the electronic environment ...
Although his anger is fierce and relentless, there is nevertheless **something** noble **in** it.

There may be an active or passive infinitive following the notional subject:

... there are a variety of business models **to consider**.
... there is a large volume of results **to be dealt** with ...
... there are benefits **to be gained** by pooling their resources.

Some of the above example sentences illustrate that expanded *there*-clauses may violate the principle of end weight (see Module II) in that old information (*for the three ions, in it*) is placed at the end of the clause. In these cases, as in the following, modern English prefers to have new information in mid-position (*some significant differences between the two discourses*) and old information (*where this is concerned*) in final position (cf. Macheiner 1995 for similar examples):

The basic problem for Marxist and socialist feminists is one of constructing a model of society which incorporates both class and gender relations. There are some significant differences between the two discourses where this is concerned; but in subsequent analysis there are many overlappings.

Constructions of the type *there is* + NP + *to* + NP often correspond to German sentences containing *haben* or *kennen*; the first NP slot in this kind of pattern is usually filled by nouns such as *advantage, appeal, aspect, dimension, element, feature, flavour, logic, pattern, point, quality, ring, side, strand* or *symmetry*. Most of these nouns always have an adjective, a determiner such as *another* or a number before them (cf. Francis, Hunston & Manning 1998: 265).

There is **no hierarchy to** the affective domain.
(Das Gebiet der Affekte kennt keine Hierarchie.)
A weak EXPLICIT vocabulary learning hypothesis holds that there is **some benefit to** vocabulary acquisition from the learner noticing novel vocabulary …

Another frequent use of *there*-clauses is in introducing lists or enumerations. Since this contributes to clarity and economy of expression, German writers of English should have no qualms about repeating the same pattern several times.

To begin, we must recognize that at least **two objectives** exist. **First, there is** peace: the end of widespread and continuing violence. **Second, there is** broad-based recovery that improves the incomes and human development indicators of the majority of people.

A dictionary like the *Longman Dictionary of Contemporary English* can help you avoid mistakes by showing you the key patterns of almost all the verbs in the language. Another very detailed source of verb patterns is *A Valency Dictionary of English* (Herbst et al. 2004), which sets out to provide a scholarly and comprehensive account of the complementation patterns of 511 common English verbs, 274 common nouns and 544 common adjectives. This dictionary aims for depth rather than breadth of coverage, focusing on high-frequency lexical items whose complex patterning calls for lengthy treatment or may create difficulties for advanced learners of English.

Despite the availability of good reference works, you should constantly be on the lookout for patterns you have not met yet. One pattern you may come across in academic texts is the object + infinitive pattern entered by verbs such as *extend* or *alter*; witness the following examples:

The structural options have been extended to include 'loosely coupled systems'.

In German the infinitive is unnecessary in such constructions:

Die strukturellen Optionen sind auf 'lose gekoppelte Systeme' erweitert worden.

Another construction to which dictionary makers have until now given little consideration is *the way* + subordinate clause. This kind of clause is often used in place of *wh*-clauses beginning with *how* (e.g. *it's difficult to understand the way their minds work*). This is a fairly serious oversight to the extent that such clauses are in many cases more idiomatic than a corresponding *how*-clause or an abstract noun; thus, for example, a search for the string 'change the way people + V' yields around 30,000 results on *www.google.co.uk* alone, while the corresponding sequence 'change how people + V' produces in the region of 900 hits.

By way of further illustration, Table 21 shows practically all the verbs that serve to describe the manner in which purposeful scientific processes lead from a starting point to a desired result. Most German writers of English, even those with a good command of English, would be tempted to use the preposition *by* in place of *from* here.

Table 21: Patterns entered by verbs describing scientific processes

Explanation	Examples
from + *N* is used to designate the starting point for some research. It occurs with a limited number of verbs such as *adapt, calculate, compute, deduce, determine, develop, estimate, evaluate, evolve, forge, form, gather, generate, illustrate, infer, measure, modify, obtain,* etc. This kind of construction normally occurs in the passive voice.	Pollution levels are **obtained from** an analysis of atmospheric data. ... the large amount of material **recovered, quantified and analyzed from** the Late Hellenestic Building ... ... the model of cognitive architecture that Peters has **assembled from** empirical psychology and introspection ... ... this corpus was **created from** one containing ... This essay is **adapted from** Chapter 3 of my book. ... the WISD is **calculated from** closing option prices ... ... a table **compiled from** auction catalogues in the Restoration The figures before 1801 are **computed from** the registers of births and deaths. ... the Apolline festival has to be **conjectured from** the Sicyonian Pythia ... That measure is **constructed from** a principal-components analysis ... ... interstitial soil salinity was **determined from** the conductivity ... ... a suitable model could be **developed from** family systems theory

2.5 The interface between verb patterning and sentence-building

Differences between languages in verb-patterning are inextricably linked with differences in clause-building and intersentential linkage; this is the interface between Modules II and III. As we have seen, the structure of any kind of clause is heavily dependent on the verb; the verb is usually the central element of the clause. Returning to our planet analogy, we might say that the verb keeps in orbit a number of natural satellites. These satellites we called the obligatory clause constituents. With a verb like 'write', for example, the obligatory constituent is the subject. To this we may add optional constituents which resemble artificial satellites that we put into orbit.

To take two examples, the sentence *Schliemann wrote* is a perfectly good English clause, with a verb and an obligatory constituent in subject position. The same goes for the verb *reappear*, which helps you form a sentence like *Titles reappeared* (see Table 22).

Table 22: Optional and obligatory elements

Obligatory	**Verb**	**Optional**
Subject		**Prepositional Object**
Schliemann	wrote	to Sayce.
Titles	reappeared.	

Of course, people do not go round saying or writing very short sentences like these all the time; they sometimes add optional and free elements. Of these, only the optional element is connected to the verb; the free element is just that: it is unconnected to the verb and, like the optional element, it may be left out. In English and German such free elements are often adverbials or prepositional phrases expressing circumstances (see Table 23).

Table 23: Free, obligatory and optional elements

Free	**Obligatory**	**Verb**	**Optional**
Adverbial			**Prepositional Object**
After bad reviews	Schliemann	wrote	to Sayce.
Under Napoleon	titles	reappeared.	
During these years	the institution	evolved	in substance, form and purpose.

Once you have understood this system of obligatory, optional and free elements, you can grasp an important difference between German and English: English has a much larger number of verbs which govern two or three (optional or obligatory) sentence constituents than does German. Let us take a few examples, some of which were already mentioned in Module II, Chapter 2.3.6 (see Table 24).

Table 24: Differences in clause patterning

Elements governed by the verb	= Free elements
This article discusses the problems associated with ...	**In diesem Artikel** werden die mit ... verbundenen Probleme erörtert.
Recycling helps to reduce waste.	**Durch Recycling** lässt sich (kann man) Abfall vermeiden.
A closer look at ... suggests Closer examination of ... may reveal (alongside: on inspection, on closer inspection, on closer examination)	**bei genauerem Hinsehen** stellt man fest bei näherem Hinsehen bei genauerer Sichtung bei genauem Hinsehen bei genauem Zusehen bei genauer Betrachtung

The difference we can see here is that English cannot readily integrate into its system of verb patterning those types of adverbials and prepositional phrases which have been set in bold. As we have just noted, one reason for this is that verbs which govern two or three sentence constituents occur with greater frequency in English than they do in German. To come back to our planet analogy, we might say that English verbs have a greater gravitational pull than German verbs. The result is that on average German clauses have a larger number of free elements that fall outside the scope of verb patterns. That is why, in translation, free-standing German adverbials or prepositional phrases (free elements) are often turned into subjects or objects in English; these subjects and objects are then governed by the verb (whereas in German they are free elements that are totally independent of the verb).

To put this yet another way, we might say that we rarely find the subject slot of a German sentence filled by a noun phrase designating circumstances – i.e. place, time, reason, instrument, purpose and so on – whereas the opposite tendency is discernible in English. This is also quite evident in the following examples:

a further difficulty is that ↔ erschwerend kommt hinzu, dass
a more serious problem is that ↔ noch schwerer wiegt, dass
a first problem is that ↔ zunächst einmal ist problematisch, dass
a second reason/argument is that ↔ zweitens gilt, dass

a further argument against (...) is that ↔ gegen (...)/dagegen spricht ferner, dass
one explanation is that ↔ dies erklärt sich zum einen dadurch, dass

It is also this kind of linguistic divergence that accounts for the frequent use, in English, of verbs such as *make* and *help*, which allow circumstances to be placed in subject position:

Its success has helped it to gain new audiences. (**Durch seinen Erfolg** erschloss es sich neue Publikumsschichten.)

To recapitulate: at the broadest level, the question of syntactic difference between German and English resolves itself into a question about the gravitational pull of verbs in the two languages.

Chapter 3

From word to collocation

The main points of this chapter are these:

- English words are rarely fully equivalent to German words; great care is therefore needed in retrieving words from dictionaries.
- Words combine into patterns called 'collocations'; along with grammatical patterns, these are the basic building blocks of any text.
- Collocation, grammatical patterns and semantic associations interact in often complex ways.
- Dictionaries are still a long way from recording all the lexical, semantic and grammatical patterns in the language.
- The academic writer needs to find out about the typical lexical realizations of underlying semantic patterns.

So far we have confined ourselves to the grammatical patterns of English. However, the lexical regularities are at least equally important, as can easily be seen from the following sentences:

> * Beautiful ugly women hate the men they love.
> * When he says that she has done it, he is on the logging-path.
> * The politician has held a speech.

All these three sentences are grammatically perfect in the sense that they can be easily parsed (i.e. analysed into their constituent parts). Noun, verb and adjective patterns are used correctly; even the use of tense is above reproach. Yet these sentences are unacceptable. The first is nonsensical because no-one can be ugly and beautiful at the same time; nor can they love and hate men at the same time. The second translates a German concept (*auf dem Holzweg sein*) word-for-word into English, and the third combines two words which do not go together in English (*hold* + *speech*). This goes to show that mastery of grammar in itself is not enough; you also have to be able to choose the right words and combine them appropriately.

In this chapter we will first consider single words (e.g. *actually*), and then words in combination (e.g. *Ziel + erreichen = aim + achieve; Grenze + fließend = boundary + hazy*).

3.1 Words, words, words

When writing in a foreign language, your knowledge of your mother tongue can be both a hindrance and a help. On the one hand, thinking in your mother tongue may interfere with and slow down your English writing. On the other hand, given that your expressive ability in English will usually lag behind your communicative needs, it may be useful to jot down the occasional German word or phrase when working on your first draft in order to avoid interrupting your train of thought. In your second draft you can then attempt to translate your German jottings into English.

When doing so, you have to remember that few words are exactly alike across languages. In fact, this is only the case with scientific terminology: the words *resistance* and *Spannung*, as used by the physicist, or the words *atom* and *Atom*, as employed in chemistry, can be said to have identical meanings in English and German. Not so with everyday language. Take, for instance, the nouns *house* and *Haus*. Although these words apparently have a similar meaning, there appear, on inspection, to be wide differences between the real-life objects they refer to. In Britain, for example, it is still very common to find long rows of identical terraced houses – a rare sight in German cities. Similar remarks apply to concepts like *Freiheit* and *liberty/freedom*, or *Erziehung/Bildung* and *education*. Here one language offers a choice of two words to render the concept into the other language. However, the German notion of *Bildung* is quite different from *education*. The word *Bildung* evokes ideals of a liberal education, free from down-to-earth considerations of utility, allowing individuals to fully realise their potential. By contrast, *education* is an all-encompassing term whose scope of reference embraces 'child-rearing', 'schooling', 'university learning', 'self-realization', etc.

In most cases, however, the difference between languages is even more complex. A fine example is provided by descriptive verbs, such as the verb of motion *skim*, which literary scholars may use in descriptive passages. Consider the sentence *the hovercraft/the birds skimmed across the water*, where the verb *skim* lays emphasis on the quick, smooth movement from one side of a river or lake to the other, probably close to the water's surface. An idiomatic rendering of this sentence into German would be *die Vögel/das Luftkissenfahrzeug glitt(en) rasant über das Wasser* or *die Vögel bewegten sich im schnellen Gleitflug über das Wasser*. It appears from this that the verb *gleiten* alone, though able to express smooth movement, cannot render the implication of great speed inherent in the English verb. This latter meaning component therefore has to be rendered by an adverbial (*rasant, im schnellen Gleitflug*) in the German translation. In a different kind of context, such as *the ball skimmed over the net*, where the emphasis is on the fact that the ball barely missed the net or only touched it lightly, *gleiten* cannot be used: *der Ball ging/flog noch gerade so über das Netz*. This is because the meaning component 'barely missing something' is not at all present in the German verb *gleiten*.

The way we structure the world also differs from one language to another, a fact which leads to one-to-many relationships between English and German. Thus, speakers of German do not make a distinction between *streets* lined by houses and *roads* connecting towns, preferring to talk of *Straße* in both cases. While an Englishman may describe pieces of furniture used for storing things as *bookcases, cupboards* and *wardrobes*, a German will talk of various types of *Schrank*. In the English-speaking world you may take a *boat* to travel, say, from Southampton to New York, whereas in the German-speaking world a *Boot* would probably not take you that far. In the English-speaking world animals and humans *eat*, in the German-speaking world a distinction is made between *fressen* for animals and *essen* for humans.[3] Such examples could be multiplied indefinitely.

Closely connected with such divergences between German and English words are lexical gaps, which occur most commonly in the case of culture-specific concepts. The noun *coroner*, for example, is difficult to translate into German. There is an endless list of such culture-specific terms: *Berufskolleg, Büttenrede, closed shop*, to name but a few more examples.

Lastly, there are words which look similar or the same in English and German, but have different meanings. These are known as deceptive cognates or false friends. A well-known example is the word *actually*, which translates as *eigentlich* or *in Wirklichkeit* into German, not as *aktuell*.

How can you learn about such differences? There is an abundance of information on well-known differences between German and English, but most of it is scattered across many different publications. It can be found in textbooks on translation such as Friederich (1969), Gallagher (1996) or Königs (2004), in dictionaries of synonyms such as Meldau (1981), in style guides

3 Some of the examples are taken from Friederich (1969) and Gerzymisch-Arbogast (1994).

such as Speight (1998) and Stevens (1999), in academic monographs such as Leisi (2008) and even in general-language bilingual dictionaries. Thus, the latest editions of the *Collins English-German Dictionary* include culture-specific information on a large number of terms. For example, this is what the entry for *Gesamtschule* looks like:

> The **Gesamtschulen**, created during the educational reforms of the 1970s, were intended to replace the traditional three-way division of schools into **Hauptschule**, **Realschule** and **Gymnasium** with a single system. Pupils have the chance to learn a subject at a level appropriate to them: for example, if their lack of ability at mathematics has meant they cannot go to a **Gymnasium**, they may still study, say, languages to a high level at the **Gesamtschule**. In addition, pupils who may not initially have been considered suitable to take their **Abitur** can still have the opportunity to take it.
>
> (© Langenscheidt KG, Berlin und München und HarperCollins Publishers Ltd)

A cursory acquaintance with German educational terminology will help you to identify useful equivalents of German words and expressions which you might not find elsewhere in the dictionary:

> three-way division of schools = dreigliedriges Schulsystem (also: tripartite school system)
> study languages to a high level = Sprachen auf hohem Niveau lernen (etc.)

Although works of reference may frequently provide assistance, you will sometimes have to undertake your own comparisons of German and English, using dictionaries, corpora and the Internet. As a novice writer you will naturally consult such sources dozens of times during the writing process, but as you progress they will play a somewhat less important role, especially if you start to compile subject-specific or text-type-specific vocabulary lists of your own.

Let us go through a few examples. Note that these examples concern only the word level, and that most lexico-grammatical problems cannot be solved at the word level. However, it is probably most expedient to start here.

Many novice writers wrongly assume that English words listed in a German-English dictionary entry can serve as one-for-one equivalents. Unfortunately, this is rarely the case. One reason is that dictionary entries may simply be incorrect. Thus, in a number of German-English dictionaries, *Bildungsangebot* is translated as *educational offer*, and this may have caused the following error:

> *The experience gained in experiments should be examined as to whether the **educational offer** for the five and six-year-olds can be united.

Similarly, the following error is probably due to the fact that bilingual dictionaries record *respectively* as an equivalent of German *beziehungsweise.*

*... although being the first settlers **respectively** people on a continent.

This raises two questions:

a) How can you make sure a dictionary equivalent is correct?
b) If it turns out to be incorrect, how can you find a correct solution?

If the equivalent you have opted for is a single word, check your choice in a monolingual learner's dictionary, such as *Collins Cobuild English Dictionary.* A look at the entry for *respectively* reveals that it has a different meaning from German *beziehungsweise* and enters a different construction.

respectively means in the same order as the items that you have just mentioned.
Their sons, Ben and Jonathan, were three and six respectively.
They finished first and second respectively.

A correct equivalent can be located in *Collins English-German Dictionary*:

- **beziehungsweise** *conj*

a) (= oder aber) or
b) (= im anderen Fall) and ... respectively; **zwei Briefmarken, die 25 beziehungsweise 55 Cent kosten** two stamps costing 25 and 55 cents respectively
c) (= genauer gesagt) or rather, that is to say

What the writer of the above sentence intended to say is captured in subentries a) or c): *or (rather)*. The correct sentence would read thus:

... although being the first settlers, or rather people, on the continent.

If the equivalent you wish to use consists of two words, as in the case of a compound noun, things are more complicated. Usually you will have to work out which word carries the weight of the meaning or which is the base of the compound, and then check its meaning in the English-German section of the bilingual dictionary and in a monolingual dictionary. With *educational offer, offer* is the weightier word. The dictionary entries for *offer* supply us with the following information:

An **offer** is something someone says they will give you or do for you.
The offer of talks with Moscow marks a significant change from the previous Western position.
'I ought to reconsider her offer to move in', he mused.
He had refused several excellent job offers.
N-COUNT (Collins Cobuild English Dictionary 2001)

The OED lists the following main senses; all the other senses are archaic or regional:

> **1. a.** An act of offering something for acceptance or refusal; an expression of intention or willingness to give or do something if desired; a proposal, an invitation.
> ***1964*** *E. BAKER Fine Madness xiv. 165 Oliver's offer had sounded so logical and generous to him that he couldn't believe Shillitoe was refusing.* ***1992*** *Good Food December Dec. (BNC) 68 The Open Christmas is now so well established that food manufacturers take the initiative with offers of help.*
> **b.** *spec.* (in elliptical use, with complement implied): a proposal of marriage. Now somewhat *arch.*
> **c.** The act of offering a price or equivalent for something; a bid. ***under offer***: having had a price offered or bid made.
> ***1986*** *K. MOORE Moving House x. 120 The board by the gate now said 'Under Offer'.* ***1993*** *G. STEDMAN Takeovers (BNC) 86 In a contested bid, the offerer will need to think carefully about what arguments it will put forward in order to persuade the target's shareholders to accept the offer against their board's recommendations.*
> **d.** The condition of being offered; (*Marketing*) the fact of being offered for sale, esp. at a reduced price, as a sales promotion. ***on offer***: available or obtainable; (also) on sale.
> ***1992*** *Today (BNC) Advt., Special pre-Christmas offers ... such as Panasonic Ladyshave half-price.*

We can see from these dictionary entries that the English noun *offer* is countable and refers to a concrete intention to give or do something or a concrete thing which is offered. An 'educational offer' might thus be construed to mean a cheap offer for students, but it could not normally refer to the educational establishments and policies a country or institution puts in place to educate a particular group of people. However, this is precisely what the German word *Bildungsangebot* means:

> *Angebot an Bildungseinrichtungen und -möglichkeiten* (Duden: Das große Wörterbuch der deutschen Sprache)

We now know that *educational offer* is unsuitable as an equivalent of German *Bildungsangebot*. Alternatively, we could have typed the phrase 'educational offer' into Google Books (remember that if you search for an exact phrase, you must put the phrase in inverted commas) or *www.google.co.uk* with the option 'UK only'. This search produces comparatively few results, most of which are from non-native writers of English and should therefore be discarded. With very few exceptions, the remaining results from authentic English texts date back to the early 20th or 19th centuries and illustrate the sense 'promotional item' mentioned above:

> An **educational offer** makes it possible for any employee who is a student in a public class of instruction to be reimbursed for tuition ...[4]

We are now completely sure that *educational offer* cannot be used in the above text. The question then remains how to ferret out a more suitable equivalent. Sometimes a specialist dictionary may help us out, but this is by no means certain. There are two main ways of getting us out of this predicament:

a) consultation of target-language texts and
b) paraphrase on the basis of the German meaning.

The first option requires a Google search for texts containing words like *education, schools, courses, government* and the like; the closest equivalent you may find in this way is 'educational provision'. If you do not want to go to such lengths, you can choose the second option and paraphrase the definition found in the *Duden* ('Angebot an Bildungseinrichtungen und -möglichkeiten'); here it would be wise not to dwell on the translation of *Angebot* because this is precisely the problem you have not been able to solve, but rather to translate *Bildungseinrichtungen und -möglichkeiten* as freely as possible, again checking possible solutions against the Internet:

> educational institutions, (range of) educational activities, (range of) educational and vocational choices, educational policies, education programmes, educational opportunities, learning opportunities (etc.)

You could then recast your original sentence as follows (note that the construction 'examined as to whether' is slightly old-fashioned and may also have to be replaced):

> The experience gained in experiments should be examined as to whether education programs for five and six-year-olds can be unified./... educational activities for five and six-year-olds could be brought together.

Another reason why dictionary equivalents may not work is that their semantic features do not fully overlap. As noted above, the English verb *skim (across)* has as its main meaning components a) movement close to another object or surface and b) great speed. Only one of these meaning components, namely a) is present in the German verb *gleiten (über)*.

Moreover, both words and collocations carry connotations that are immediately associated with them by a competent speaker of the language. The word 'home', for instance, evokes feelings of warmth and belonging, and the sole purpose of the word 'venerable' is probably to put old age in a good

---

4 From Blair, Thomas Stewart 1911. *Public Hygiene*. Boston: R.G. Badger 1911, p. 36.

light. The same goes for *set in,* whose subjects usually refer to unpleasant states of affairs; among the most typical subjects we find *rot, decay, ill-will, infection, numbness, anarchy, disillusion, putrefaction, the rain seems to have set in for the day* (Sinclair 1991).

Sometimes you may have got hold of the correct word, but you may not be aware of its natural patterning, a point we discussed in Chapter 1. Consider the following example:

> *A number of things like organizing **the study** as well as planning **the run of the day**, and **not at last** the discipline whether to **visit** a **university offer** or not, depends on oneself.

In the present case the writer has correctly chosen the word 'study'. This word can indeed translate 'Studium' in such contexts as 'the study of medicine'. However, if you consult the monolingual dictionary or an unabridged bilingual dictionary, you will find that you use the plural 'studies' to refer to university courses. In addition, close inspection of the examples in monolingual learners' dictionaries will reveal that the plural noun is used with a possessive pronoun in this sense. So we get:

> A number of things, such as organizing your studies ...

You may well find these procedures somewhat tedious and time-consuming at first, but we would like to reassure you that they will soon become second nature to you. With a bit of luck, you will begin to like them because they help you to expand your knowledge of English and to make yourself fully understood. As with sports, so with writing: real enjoyment comes only with a certain accomplishment.

One final point we would like to emphasize is that words and phrases may also differ in their stylistic value (cf. Module IV). Although the boundaries between spoken and written English style have become increasingly fluid in recent years, some constants remain. In formal academic writing, it is still unacceptable to use colloquial phrases such as 'a couple of' or 'and so on', and most academics still frown upon the use of such connectors as 'so' rather than 'consequently, as a result, therefore, thus'. You should also beware of using common words with a wide range of meanings instead of more explicit ones. Thus, in the following sentence, the semantically loose word 'right' should be replaced with its more formal equivalent 'correct':

> (?)... the right use of prepositions ...

Table 25 lists a few more such infelicities.

Table 25: Informal/neutral vs. formal expressions

German word or phrase	Informal/neutral equivalent	Formal equivalent
viele, zahlreiche	a lot of (people)	a large number of (+ more specific word: researchers, businessmen, etc.)
bis	till	until
genug	enough	sufficient
vielleicht	maybe	perhaps, may (+ INF)
angemessen, vernünftig	not too bad	reasonable, acceptable
nebenbei bemerkt	by the way	incidentally; it may be noted in passing
im Alter von (zehn Jahren)	when I was (ten)	at the age of (ten)

SUMMARY OF STRATEGIES

1. Use the latest version of a reliable unabridged bilingual dictionary, such as *Collins English-German Dictionary (http://dictionary.reverso.net/)* or *PONS Großwörterbuch Englisch (www.pons.eu)* or, preferably, both.
2. Read the entire German-English entry.
3. Check the meanings, usage patterns and style level of the equivalents you want to opt for against monolingual learners' dictionaries or against the Internet (preferably Google Books or *www.google.co.uk*). Make sure the texts thrown up by your search have been written by native speakers of English.
4. Make a habit of browsing through various types of dictionaries and learn vocabulary by heart from thematically organized vocabulary books. Correct dictionary entries where necessary. Make lists of subject-specific vocabulary, including information on the natural patterning of words.
5. Do not use any words with which you do not feel one hundred per cent secure.

3.2 How words go together

Some words in English and German go together with a great many other words, and there is no difficulty in using them. The adjective *blue* is one such word. Thus, you can talk of *a blue car, a blue pullover, a blue door, a blue book, blue eyes,* and so on. Most words, however, do not combine as freely as *blue*. For instance, the noun *visit* is used only with the verbs *pay* or, more rarely, *make* in English (*the German Chancellor paid a visit to his British counterpart*), but not with *do, take* or *carry out*. Likewise the German noun *Rede* typically occurs with *halten,* but not with *machen* or *abhalten*. When two or more words (e.g. *pay + visit* or *give + good + example*) are habitually used together like this, linguists speak of (a) 'collocation'. In other words, a collocation is a combination of two or more words which occurs repeatedly in text and can be instantly retrieved from memory by a competent native speaker. We also say that one word 'collocates' with another.

Collocations often differ from one language to another, and as a language learner you need to be aware of such differences. To take up the example just mentioned, in German you say *eine Rede halten,* whereas in English the same concept is expressed by *make a speech* or *deliver a speech*. Another good example is the German verb *fahren*. In German you can say *mit dem Zug nach London fahren, Auto fahren* or *Motorrad fahren,* each of which would require a different collocation in English – respectively *go (to London by train)/take (the train to London), drive (a car)* or *ride (a motor bike)*.

As shown in Table 26, there are fifteen common types of collocation, the most important of which have been printed in bold. The examples chosen illustrate that German words do not always enter into the same collocations as English words.

Table 26: Examples of collocational types

	Type of collocation	**Examples**
1 (base: noun phrase)	**N + ADJ**	bad pain
	N + PREP + N	shift in public opinion, men of a certain age
	N + INF	failure to act
	N + GENSUBJ	a resurgence of interest
	N + GENOBJ	loss of control, the insertion of an intra-uterine device, fear of the unknown
2 (base: verb phrase)	**N + V**	thunder roars, lightning flashes
	V + N	to spread gossip, to give a concert
	V + ADV	to fail abysmally, to lose by a considerable margin

	V + INF	try to avoid, look to see, seek to establish, venture to claim
	V + PP	to flush with shame, to squirm with impatience
	V + SUBCOMP/V + OBJCOMP	to fall ill, to keep s.th. warm, to get s.th. in order
3 (base: adjective phrase)	**ADJ + ADV**	madly in love, seriously injured, widely different
	ADJ + PREP + N	white with fear, numb with cold, subject to revision
	ADJ + INF	easy to use, keen to fit in, ready to compromise
4 (base: adverb phrase)	ADV + ADV	well behind, long after, back in order
Other phraseologisms	PHR	somewhere between 100,000 and 200,000 years ago, not wildly original

A fairly clear distinction can be drawn between collocations and idioms. Idioms have a figurative meaning that is not predictable from the meaning of their individual constituents. Thus, the idiom *to have to carry the can* (*die Sache ausbaden müssen; den Kopf hinhalten müssen*) has nothing to do with people moving cans from one place to another. Interestingly, such idioms do not normally pose problems for the foreign-born academic writer. One reason is that they are comparatively rare in academic English, especially in pure sciences such as physics or medicine. However, writers in the humanities in particular may use the occasional idiom to add spice to what might otherwise appear a rather insipid piece of writing:

> For the moment, this little book is simply a guide to **the lie of the land**, and an introduction to a field that so far has borders only where you want to draw them. (*the lie of the land* = fig. die allgemeine Lage; lit. die topographischen Gegebenheiten)
> Due to their illegal status, squatters occupy a **blind spot** in official statistics. (*blind spot* = blinder Fleck)

The second reason lies in the semantic opacity of idioms: idioms make the reader wonder what they mean and thereby stick in the mind.

By contrast, language learners easily overlook two-word or multi-word collocations whose meaning is more or less transparent, such as *be fun* (**make* *fun*), *make a speech* (**hold a speech*) or *it follows (from this) that*. If you want to avoid letting such collocations pass unnoticed, you should, at least occasionally, ask yourself how you would translate into German typical collocations you come across in your reading.

As a complex example of this, let us now consider the German noun *Praktikum* and its English equivalents. *Praktikum* normally collocates with two verbs (*machen* and *absolvieren*), and the syntactic link between the noun and the verb is always very simple, as in the following examples:

Anwar hat ein Praktikum bei der Polizei gemacht.
1967 hat er bei einer Baufirma im heimischen Neckarsulm sein Praktikum absolviert und als Eisenflechter Geld für das Studium an der TH Stuttgart verdient.

The British English equivalents of *Praktikum* are much more difficult to handle. *Placement, industrial placement, job placement, training placement, work placement,* and *work experience placement* collocate with the verbs *give, win, start, take up, go on* and *do*, and they often occur in relatively complex syntactic patterns. Here are a few examples; try to decide in each case how you would have translated the collocations in question:

Within three weeks, he had persuaded Evans Hunt Scott to **give him a placement**; three weeks after that, they gave him a permanent job.
He originally wanted "the glamour of being an art director" and didn't embrace copywriting until **he won a work placement** at Saatchi & Saatchi.
After a few months of training, preparing and applying for jobs, I was able to **start my first placement**.
If they fail to find a job they are required to **take up placements** – mainly in the voluntary sector for 13 weeks – or lose their benefit.
Now aged 16, he's doing an art jewellery course at a further education college in London, and has just been offered a job by the firm where **he's doing his work placement**.
Alexis did a work placement at Time Magazine office in New York before taking up a place at Kingston University to study Journalism.
He went on a placement during his studies with Essex probation, who offered him a job when he qualifiied.
He is currently **on an industrial placement**.
I was offered a job while **I was on my placement** and the company kept it open for me so I could finish my course.
The court heard that the first incident occurred while **Jordan was on a work experience placement** from her school in Chard.
Students who wish to **spend a year in a job placement** in the third year of their studies can do so — an option that boosts chances of finding a job later.

> **Clare spent six months on work placement at Kodak** during her course in business studies at Portsmouth Polytechnic, from which she graduated with a 2:1.
> So luckily my parents supported me through college and then I went to university for two years and then **got a work placement** at the hospital here in town.

One special point of interest is that the noun *placement* frequently occurs in prepositional phrases: ***on*** *a placement,* ***on*** *an industrial placement,* ***on*** *my placement,* ***on*** *a work experience placement,* ***in*** *a job placement,* and ***on*** *work placement. Placement* is generally preceded by an article (e.g. *on* ***a*** *placement*), but in certain cases the article may be omitted (e.g. *on work placement*). In most cases, the preposition *on* is used (e.g. *on a work experience placement*), but *in* is also possible (e.g. *in a job placement*).

Another point to note is that the prepositional phrase containing the noun *placement* is invariably preceded by one of three verbs: *to go, to be,* and *to spend.* As a rule, the verbs *to go* and *to be* are immediately followed by the prepositional phrase containing *placement* (e.g. *to go on a placement, to be on a placement*). The verb *spend,* however, is always followed by an expression of time which indicates the duration of the placement. To give a specific example, we say that someone has spent a year in a job placement or on work placement. This type of construction is impossible in German. If we wish to translate *Clare spent six months on work placement at Kodak,* we have to say *Clare hat ein sechsmonatiges Praktikum bei Kodak absolviert* (although in colloquial German we might also say *Clare war ein halbes Jahr bei Kodak im Praktikum*).

One last point to be made in this connection is that it is not always necessary to render *placement* as *Praktikum.* This becomes apparent when we look at the collocations *to give (someone) a placement,* which does not translate as **ein Praktikum geben,* but rather as *(jemandem) eine Praktikumsstelle/einen Praktikumsplatz anbieten/geben.* Similarly, *to be on a placement* or *to do a placement,* in addition to *ein Praktikum machen* or *im Praktikum sein* corresponds to the German word combination *als Praktikant arbeiten.*

Some authors have falsely claimed that ready-made phrases such as collocations should not be overused. Even famous writers such as Orwell tend to labour under the illusion that language can and must be used creatively (cf. Lewis 2000: 188). Here is what Orwell has to say on the proper use of language:

> 'This invasion of one's mind by ready-made phrases (lay the foundations, acquire a radical transformation) can only be prevented if one is constantly on guard against them, and every such phrase anaesthetises a portion of one's brain.' (quoted from Lewis 2000: 188)

It will be interesting to see whether Orwell practised what he preached. Considering his deep aversion for fixed expressions, it is quite amusing to look at the following excerpt from *Animal Farm*, one of his bestsellers:

> **It was a bitter winter**. The **stormy weather** was followed by **sleet and snow**, and then carried by a **hard frost** which did not **break** (break + frost) **till well into February**. The animals **carried on as best they could** with the rebuilding of the windmill, **well knowing that** the **outside world** was watching them and that the envious human beings would **rejoice and triumph** if the mill were not **finished on time**.

As you can see, Orwell himself cannot do without collocations and other phraseological items (cf. the items in bold); in fact, his text consists almost entirely of prefabricated phrases, some more colloquial and others more literary. Although these items appear to consist of several words, they are in fact single units of meaning which the writer recalls from memory ready-made. There is – or was in the 1940s – hardly any other convenient way of expressing the intended meaning, however 'creative' you may wish to be. Just as you would normally choose to call a 'cow' a 'cow' rather than 'a female bovine which gives milk', so you would normally opt for a collocation like 'stormy weather' rather than 'weather in which there is a lot of wind'. Put another way, both words and collocations are linguistic signs imbued with denotative and connotative meanings. As a rule, only one or two collocations will fill the bill at any particular juncture in a text. Only rather exceptionally will there be a choice among several synonymous alternatives (e.g. *keep to the speed limit, stick to the speed limit, obey the speed limit, observe the speed limit*), but even the use of such alternatives can hardly be considered 'creative'. So much for Orwell's quest for creativity!

What you as a novice writer have to realize, then, is that effective writing is made up of familiar, prefabricated constructions. These prefabs are interspersed with just a sprinkling of more novel, innovative word combinations or grammatical patterns which the language-user creates for a particular occasion. The reason for this is simply that the imitative use of language makes texts both easier to produce and easier to understand. In cognitive science terms, we would say that it relieves the listener's or reader's 'processing load'.

Successful writing thus stands or falls by the writer's ability to retrieve a large number of contextually adequate collocations from memory or, as the case may be, from writing aids such as dictionaries (especially *Oxford Collocations Dictionary for Students of English*), corpora or the Internet. If you want to retrieve particular collocations that you cannot think of, you can use wild cards (*) on Google (remember to use inverted commas):

search: "have * a proposal → results: have received/submitted/put forward/etc. a proposal
search: "complex * of factors → results: complex array/interplay/set/interaction/combination/mix/web/etc. of factors
search: "fill in all the * details → results: fill in all the gory/sordid/missing/fine/etc. details

We can gain an idea of just how much lexis competent native speakers have at their disposal if we multiply the number of common words by the number of collocations they enter into. Take a word like *Angst* in German. How many two-word collocations containing this word can you bring to mind? At the very least, you will probably come up with the following noun-verb collocations: *Angst haben, bekommen, einflößen, einjagen, empfinden, verspüren; Angst befällt, beschleicht, erfasst, ergreift, quält; Angst bereiten; Angst abbauen, schüren, loswerden*. This gives us 15 common noun-verb collocations, and there would be as many noun-adjective collocations. At a conservative estimate, then, a common noun such as *Angst* has at least 30 collocates. It is safe to assume that there are two thousand nouns in German that behave in similar ways to *Angst*. This would give us 30 times two thousand collocations, that is 60,000 collocations, based on those two thousand nouns alone.

3.3 Collocation of semantic-pragmatic features

If word combining were the whole story, then language use would indeed be wholly uncreative. Fortunately, there is also an element of creativity involved in the writing process. This is because underlying the word level is a level of semantic features which writers can exploit to great effect.

Collocation of semantic features may take two forms:

a) the collocation of a word or collocation with a semantic feature (e.g. /something negative/ + *set in*)
b) the collocation of two or more semantic features of words or collocations (e.g. /number/ + /time/ + /journey/, as in *a thirty-hour ride by bus*; cf. Hoey 2005).

Such semantic associations are not immediately obvious from the word itself, but will emerge from a close study of its collocates. As an example of a), we have already considered the verb *set in*, which, unlike its direct German equivalent *einsetzen*, usually collocates with items of an unpleasant nature.

Similar considerations hold for the verb *commit*: people commit a foul, an offence, a fallacy, a crime or suicide. The unfavourable connotation can be seen to reside not simply in the word *commit* itself, but rather in the stretch of text consisting of *commit* and its collocate. Another fine example is provided by co-occurrences of the adverb *beautifully* with participial adjectives such as *carved, draped, drawn, restored,* etc. The verbs on which these participial adjectives are based share a common semantic feature in describing artwork or craftwork. Thus, there is a lexical dependency between a specific semantic feature and a lexeme.

In the case of a collocation such as *apt description,* we have to look at the wider context to realize that it is often used in a humorous or ironic sense. Here are a few published examples:

> Not so long ago Betty Carter released an album entitled *It's Not About The Melody,* an apt description of her idiosyncratic approach to the art of song.
> This last work is called *Complete Omnivore,* which is an apt description of Cragg as an artist.

We must also take account of cases which admit of a great deal of variation. One typical case is the collocation of the contrast marker *not so* with lexical items such as *surely, seem, appear, you/one might think that, it was hoped that* or *one hears that,* all of which contain a semantic trait implying 'uncertainty' or 'error'. *Not so* usually occurs as a non-clausal sentence (cf. Module II). The 'error' part of this pattern may also be found in nominal form; in the following example from an academic text, *you might think* has been converted to the more formal noun *misconception*:

> Another **misconception** about meditation is that the meditator should fall into a trance. Not so. As a famous Chinese Buddhist put it: There is a class of foolish people who sit quietly and try to keep their minds blank (...)

A more complex realization of a long-distance collocational pattern is seen in the following extract:

> But if one considers that in college dictionaries the average number of column-lines allotted to each entry (not each definition) is a bit less than two, one will see why space is at a premium.

In the present case the collocational relationship holds between two types of multi-word sequence which occur in, respectively, the main clause and the sub-clause of a complex sentence: the topic shifter (*if*) *one considers* (+ *wh*-clause/NP) and the suggestor *one will see* (+ *wh*-clause/NP). Again, it is not so much the lexical items themselves which enter into collocation; rather, we are dealing with a recurrent type of semantic-functional relationship, where both the second and the first part of the collocation may be replaced by other lexical items. A few more examples follow:

> If **one considers that** the various paths do not exist except as perceived by some mind, then **one immediately arrives at the conclusion that** the probability of a path should be chosen proportionally to its algorithmic information.

> If **we consider** the nature of Christian persecution as it is currently understood, **we can easily see how** the personal attitudes of the presiding official could have been a significant factor in any particular trial.

Turning to the collocation of semantic features, we find that many word combinations, phrases and even entire clauses can be represented in a semantic 'deep' structure. This is easiest to understand in the context of a literary example; underlying a collocation such as *the scenery passed by* (*die Landschaft rauschte vorbei*) is the semantic schema

> OBSERVER (sitting in VEHICLE) OBSERVES OBJECT (seen from VEHICLE) in MOVEMENT

Table 27 shows a few more instances of this pattern from a concordance.

Table 27: Scenery/landscape + V

d his eyes. Through a curtained window,	scenery was whizzing by at dizzying spee
head and fixate my eyes upon the moving	scenery whizzing by the window. I stare
Scully looked out of the window as the	scenery passed by. She seemed to be dozi
impassive profile, at the brown October	landscape passing behind her outside the
t the window, the rural	scenery: pastures, barns, etc., the othe
om the window, trying not to see the	landscape reeling outside. SARAH (
e stared out the window and watched the	scenery roll by as they headed back into
asn't used to it. The dark forms of the	landscape rolled soothingly past outside
..... Her eyes fluttered open to a dark	landscape rolling past the window. There
r eyes and looked out the window at the	scenery rolling past. "At least the scen
er sat in the back seat and watched the	scenery fly past the window. He had two
and she takes a sudden interest in the	scenery flying by outside her window. I

This underlying schema allows us to create lexical variety (on variety as a stylistic principle, see Module IV, Chapter 2.4). We can express the same or similar ideas using different words describing the act of observing, the object and the nature and speed of the movement (see Table 28).

Table 28: A semantic schema

OBSERVATION	OBJECT	MOVEMENT
watch	the scenery	roll past
see	the landscape	fly past
fixate my eyes on	the houses	flitting by the window

Collocation of semantic features has not yet been fully captured in dictionaries and therefore constitutes one of the major problems for non-native writers. Collocations are often closely associated with specific rhetorical moves, so that putting freely conceived constructions in their place will give your text a tinge of awkwardness. For example, the following sentence from the introduction of a student term paper is intended to signal to the reader that, for reasons of space and time, the author's treatment of his subject may not be exhaustive:

> (?)Because of not having enough time and space, I will concentrate on learning vocabulary with word cards and vocabulary books.

Underlying this sentence is a standard rhetorical move which could be described as follows:

> SPACE (AND/OR TIME) LIMITATIONS induce LIMITATIONS IN TREATMENT OF SUBJECT

Apart from the doubtful acceptability of the negated participial construction in this kind of context, the writer was unaware of the standard lexical realizations of the rhetorical move in question:

> The scope of this paper does not permit/allow (a) (ADJ) discussion/consideration/exploration/indication/sketch (etc.) of ...
> Space (and time) limitations preclude/do not allow (etc.) ...
> For reasons of space, I will focus on ...
> Space only allows ...
> Limits of space and time only allow ...
> We have space enough to mention only a few.

We have therefore devoted Chapter 4 of this Module to lists of such standard rhetorical moves.

3.4 Collocational gaps and incompatibilities

In much the same way that there are lexical gaps, there exist cases where not even one element of a collocation can be rendered by the same word in another language. The German verb-noun collocation *(eine) Qualität + gewinnen* is a particularly interesting instance of such a 'collocational gap' because neither the node *Qualität* nor the collocate *gewinnen* can serve as a basis for translation. The following sentence by a German writer of English shows interference with the German collocation and needs to be completely rephrased:

In the computer age challenges have gained a new quality …

Here a more natural English sentence would be:

The challenges facing us in the computer age are of an entirely different kind.

By way of further illustration, consider the German collocation *sich jemandes Beurteilung entziehen,* as evidenced in the following sentence:

Ob die Rezeption des griechischen sprachlichen Ausdrucks (…) auch eine Rezeption materieller Rechtsvorstellungen implizierte, oder wie und warum es sonst zu ihr gekommen sein mag, **entzieht sich meiner Beurteilung.**

In the case under consideration, the phrase would have to be rendered by 'I am in no position to judge', but there are no adjective-noun collocations containing the noun *judg(e)ment* or verbs such as *escape* which translate the fixed phrase under discussion.

It may also be the case that one language offers a different number of collocations to express some particular idea than does another. This kind of collocational incompatibility may pose problems for writers. We noted above that English has a far larger range of verbs expressing movement, with the result that English collocations are also more numerous in this area. But this is not all. The English noun *resemblance,* for example, collocates with a wide variety of adjectives denoting 'strangeness', with German showing a significantly smaller range of collocations:

Table 29: Collocational incompatibility

English	German
s.o./s.th. bears a (superficial/slight/feeble/vague/certain/passing/fair/… // close/remarkable/*uncanny/eerie/curious/bewildering/unsettling/disturbing/…* // dangerous/depressing/factitious/… // stylistic/family/…) RESEMBLANCE to s.o./s.th.	etw./j-m hat/besitzt [weist … auf] (eine/einige/viel/große/ausgeprägte/weitgehende/gewisse/entfernte/geringe // verblüffende/*merkwürdige/seltsame/bizarre/…* // strukturelle/konzeptionelle) (Struktur-/Wesens-) ÄHNLICHKEIT mit etw./j-m

Another good example is afforded by the collocational constraints placed upon the nouns *Marktlücke* and *gap in the market* or *market gap*, which collocate with rather different adjectives in English and German. Whereas German business journalists readily associate adjectives meaning 'promising' with market gaps (*vielversprechend* + *Marktlücke*), this kind of collocation is hardly ever found in the British or American press. In both languages, however, market gaps are regularly described as being 'profitable'. These observations may, however, be subject to rapid change, for in a globalized marketplace the newspaper language of one country readily impinges on that of another.

Table 30: Collocates of *market gap/gap in the market*

English	German
a genuine // clear/definite // significant // profitable market gap (gap in the market)	eine echte // klare // große/vielversprechende // lohnende Marktlücke

3.5 Making creative use of collocation

A simple way of being creative as a writer is to combine words in accordance with their collocational properties. Let us begin by looking at a small number of adjectives and verbs that go with the noun *example* for purposes of illustration (see Table 31).

Table 31: Collocations based on the noun example

verbs	noun	noun	adjectives
give			good
provide			pertinent
cite	**+ example**	**example +**	apt
afford			well-chosen
adduce			fine

All the verbs on the left-hand side collocate with *example*, so that you can say *I'd like to give an example* or *the author provides an example* and so on. The same goes for the adjectives on the right-hand side, so that possible adjective-noun collocations include *this is a good example* or *a fine example of this is …* You can then move on to blend the verb-noun collocations with the adjective-noun collocations, which will give you more complex collocational patterns such as *the author provides a good example* or *Thomas Mann's* Bekenntnisse des Hochstaplers Felix Krull *affords a fine example of stylistic mastery*. The above table alone provides you with a total of 25 ways of combining the noun *example* with suitable adjectives and verbs. The tables presented in Chapter 4 go well beyond such numbers.

A more complex example is provided by the German adjective-noun collocation *fließend + Grenze*, as in:

Die Grenzen von der Unkenntnis zur Unredlichkeit waren fließend.

Grenze corresponds to English nouns such as *borderline, boundary, boundary line, demarcation, dividing line, line* or *line of demarcation*. *Fließend* may be rendered by a wide range of adjectives, but the resultant adjective-noun combinations do not always have the same meaning or fit into the same syntactic patterns as *Grenze + fließend*. We may use adjectives which express opposite ideas. On the one hand, we have words which express distinctness (e.g. *clear* or *clear-cut*), and on the other hand we have words that express indistinctness (e.g. *hazy, imprecise, obscure, uncertain*). If we use an adjective belonging to the first group and the noun *dividing line*, our translation of the German example sentence might read as follows:

There was no clear dividing line between ignorance and dishonesty.

If we choose an adjective from the second group and the noun *boundary*, we may modify the syntax to produce the following translations:

The boundary between ignorance and dishonesty was an uncertain one.
The boundaries between ignorance and dishonesty were uncertain and vague.
The boundaries between ignorance and dishonesty were rather obscure.
The boundaries between ignorance and dishonesty were often indistinct.

It should be clear from the foregoing that knowing a word such as *example*, *(work) placement* or *boundary* involves a lot more than memorizing its meaning in the abstract or being able to translate it. In addition, you have to be familiar with the collocations that the word enters into and with the constructions that these collocations are normally used in. Acquiring a command of a broad range of collocations, and becoming aware of such interlingual differences as have been discussed in this chapter, is an important first step on the road to native-like writing.

3.6 The interplay of collocation and patterning

Based on what you have learned thus far about patterns and collocations, you should be able to form correct sentences at least 90 per cent of the time. This chapter discusses some of the stumbling blocks which still need to be overcome before your writing reaches perfection at the lexico-grammatical level. These stumbling blocks concern the sometimes extremely subtle interplay of collocation and patterning.

3.6.1 A worked example

Our first example is from an essay by a first-year student of English:

> *In the private field of newcomer students there will also be some changes.

This sentence clearly betrays its German author. The underlying semantic schema is as follows:

> CHANGE occurs in PRIVATE LIFE

The sentence itself conforms to the patterns usually found alongside the German noun *Privatsphäre*:

> In der Privatsphäre der neuen Studenten wird es auch einige Veränderungen geben.

Unfortunately, *Privatsphäre* cannot be translated as *private field*. If you look up *Privatsphäre* in a reliable bilingual dictionary, you will find translations such as *private sphere* or *privacy*. What the dictionaries do not tell you, however, is that the noun *privacy* can be used only in the pattern *in* + NP + *of* + NP(place where privacy reigns), but not in the pattern *in* + NP + *of* + NP(person): *in the privacy of one's home* is acceptable, while **in the privacy of newcomer students* is impossible.

The situation is somewhat more complex with *private sphere*, which can occur in the second pattern, but then has a meaning which opposes it to *public sphere*: *in the private sphere of the family/the household* (etc.).

One collocation which enters the above pattern is *private life/lives*. But the result is still unsatisfactory:

> (?)In the private lives of newcomer students there will also be some changes.

This is because the underlying semantic schema is normally expressed differently in English. Using monolingual dictionaries, we find patterns like the following:

A makes/causes/brings about change in B
B changes/undergoes change/experiences change/is subject to change

The general difference underlying these specific patterns is the English language's preference for subjects over adverbials (see Module II, Chapter 2). Since the cause of change (A) is not mentioned in the sentence in question, we thus end up with something like:

The private lives of new students (or: new students' private lives) will also be subject to change.

3.6.2 Exemplificatory infinitive clauses

Let us now consider another authentic example of doubtful acceptability:

(?)To demonstrate this with a simple example, the sentence 'the weather is hot and cold' is contradictory (...)

What the author of this sentence is doing here amounts to a familiar rhetorical move: 'giving an example' or 'exemplification'. One way of accomplishing this move in both English and German is to use an infinitive clause, which normally precedes the example. Table 32 shows typical constructions and typical collocations found in authentic texts.

Table 32: Exemplificatory infinitive clauses

1. take + example: to take but one example to take an extended example to take two random examples to take only the most distinguished example to take a common example of NP 2. give + example: (just) to give (you) an example to give a few examples to give two examples 3. cite + example: to cite another example to cite one example among many 4. name/mention + example: to name but two examples to mention a not atypical example 5. to pick just one example to use the example above	1. Beispiel + nennen: um nur ein Beispiel zu nennen 2. Beispiel + anführen: um ein paar Beispiele anzuführen 3. Beispiel + geben: um ein Beispiel zu geben 4. Beispiel + bleiben bei: um bei diesem Beispiel zu bleiben: 5. Beispiel + aufführen: um ein kleines Beispiel aufzuführen 6. Beispiel + aufgreifen/einbringen/vorwegnehmen/ergänzen/herausgreifen/wählen/zurückkommen auf: um auf das Beispiel der NP zurückzukommen um nur ein besonders markantes Beispiel herauszugreifen um nur ein Beispiel unter zahlreichen herauszugreifen Beispiel + vorführen/deutlich machen/einbringen/aufnehmen: Um nur ein Beispiel in diesen komplizierten Zusammenhängen zu erwähnen

Table 32 shows that German exemplificatory infinitive clauses can express many more shades of meaning than their English counterparts. English contents itself with five major verb choices (*take, give, cite, name, mention*), while German resorts to a far larger and more varied array of verbs. Consider, as an example, the German exemplificatory infinitive clause *um ein Beispiel vorzuführen*, which carries clear overtones of scientific demonstration. Although the collocation *to demonstrate s.th. with an example* is available in English in such sentences as 'let's demonstrate this with an example', an exemplificatory infinitive clause along the lines of *to demonstrate this with an example* would seem to run counter to the typical patterning of such clauses in English academic prose. The experienced English writer is rather more likely to fall back on one of the standard infinitive clauses introduced by *to-infinitive + take/give/cite*, so that the above student example should be rephrased as follows:

> To take a simple example, the sentence 'the weather is hot and cold' is contradictory.

This shows that, other factors being equal, the non-native writer must check the compatibility of collocations with particular linguistic environments. Collocational equivalents may work perfectly in some contexts, but may not fill the bill in others.

3.6.3 Summary: Strategies for forming word groups

A word group must be constructed at three levels, which should by now be familiar to you and which we have here called 'lexical mechanics', 'syntactic patterning' and 'semantic-pragmatic features'. To make sure that you form a word group correctly, you need to work your way up through these levels in chronological order.

a) Lexical mechanics (word A + word B) → dictionaries of collocations, monolingual learners' dictionaries

This involves asking yourself 'What words does the word I want to use team up with?' *Oxford Collocations Dictionary for Students of English* is currently the best source for getting the mechanics of collocation right. You should be careful, however, when forming three-word or four-word collocations which contain a polysemous collocate (i.e. one which has several meanings) or a fixed expression. Thus, for example, the noun *accountancy* collocates with the adjective *creative*, which in its turn collocates with *highly* and *very*. However, the three-word combination 'very creative accountancy' would sound rather odd. Similarly, *abortion* teams up with *perform*, and *perform* with *manually*. Nevertheless, the collocation *perform an abortion manually* (rather than, say, *induce an abortion by medication*) would run counter to accepted usage. What you 'perform manually' are tasks that could equally well be done by computers or machines, but even the best dictionaries are silent on such field-specific restrictions. Note further that *Oxford Collocations* does not normally allow you to distinguish between the collocations of different forms of the same word. The singular and plural forms of *mix*, for example, have different preferred collocates; *mix* likes to co-occur with *wide* or *curious*, collocates which *mixes* tends to avoid.

When writing a literary study, it is also worthwhile consulting Reum's *Dictionary of English Style* (Reum 1931), Rotter & Bendl (1978) or Werlich (1969).

b) Syntactic patterning → monolingual learners' dictionaries
Here the question you should ask is 'What grammatical patterns does the word or collocation I want to use favour?' The syntactic patterns which words or word groups prefer or avoid have not been fully captured in reference books. According to Klotz (1999: 38), monolingual dictionaries such as *Oxford Advanced Learner's Dictionary* list around 60 per cent of all possible verb patterns, 35 per cent of noun patterns and 25 per cent of adjective patterns. These figures may even be on the high side, since Klotz's investigation is itself based on a potentially incomplete – though vastly superior – reference work, namely *A Valency Dictionary of English* (Herbst et al. 2004).

In view of this situation it is probably safest to stick to the patterns found in the reference works just mentioned. Although *Oxford Advanced Learner's Dictionary* and *Cambridge Advanced Learner's Dictionary*, to take but two examples, are a long way from providing an exhaustive list of the syntactic patterns entered by *placement* (= *Praktikum*, see above), they offer useful examples on which you can model your own sentences:

The third year is spent on placement in selected companies.
The course includes a placement in Year 3. (OALD, s.v. *placement*)
I think we can find a placement for you in the accounts department.
The trainee teachers do a school placement in the summer term. (CALD, s.v. *placement*)

The example sentences also suggest that *placement* commonly occurs as the object of the clause.

By contrast, the examples of *consequence* in the same dictionaries do not tell us that the singular *consequence* usually appears as the subject of a clause, while the plural *consequences* tends to be object (cf. Hoey 2005). We have to turn to yet another learner's dictionary to find this contrast well illustrated:

> consequence /'kɒnsɪkwəns/ noun [C] *** a result or effect of something: *She said exactly what she felt, without fear of the consequences.* ▲ **+ of** *The consequence of such policies will inevitably be higher taxes.* ▲ **serious/disastrous/dire consequences** *Climate change could have disastrous consequences for farmers.* ▲ **economic/social/health consequences** *Consider the long-term health consequences carefully before deciding.*
>
> (*Macmillan English Dictionary*, under *consequence*)

Bilingual dictionaries are usually a bad choice when it comes to patterning. If we look up *Praktikum* in *Collins Großwörterbuch Deutsch-Englisch*, for example, we find neither the correct translation nor any useful patterns.

As with lexical mechanics, dictionaries do not normally distinguish between different forms of the same word.

c) Semantic-pragmatic features or associations
This involves asking two questions:

1. 'What meanings does the word or collocation I want to use typically have?'
2. 'In what sort of text type or context can I use the collocation?'

Thus, the collocations *scholarship + get* and *placement + do* (see b) above) may be regarded as inappropriate in a piece of academic writing simply because the collocates *get* and *do* are rather informal verbs typical of spoken English (read: *scholarship + win/receive; placement + go on*).

Other semantic-pragmatic features attach to the entire collocation, as seen above with the ironic use of *apt description*. These cannot normally be located in dictionaries. When you are unsure about the semantic-pragmatic features of an academic collocation, look at examples of it on *Google Books* (http://books.google.co.uk/; remember to put your search phrase in inverted commas).

Chapter 4

Rhetorical moves and their lexical realizations

The main points of this chapter are these:

- Functional language items can be categorized by topic.
- Such categorization helps the academic writer to retrieve and memorize items.
- The good academic writer uses a variety of different functional items.

This chapter lists and explains general-language vocabulary items which the academic writer can use across all disciplines. We are dealing here with a general functional vocabulary rather than the unlimited and steadily growing mass of content words. As you will see, there is a close link between lexical choices on the one hand, and the types of texts and paragraphs you want to construct on the other. In keeping with the general emphasis of this book, we have focused on constructions rather than words to the extent that this was feasible considering the limited space available in any printed work.

4.1 Stating your topics and objectives

Whenever you start a new topic, this should be clearly signalled to your reader by means of appropriate functional vocabulary. A distinction can be made between 1) introducing topics or excluding topics from consideration (this section) 2) changing the topic (see Section 4.4) and 3) topicalizing specific items (see Section 4.5).

4.1.1 Introducing a topic

The most common way of introducing the main topic of an essay or research paper is by using verbs such as ***consider, discuss, explore, examine, review, treat, focus on, argue, deal with*** or noun + verb collocations such as ***give an overview of*** or ***give an account of*** with a non-human subject such as ***article, paper, book, report, chapter, section, work*** or ***volume***:

This article focuses on two areas: …
This book presents a contemporary account of principles of learning.
This chapter reviews trends in the nation's overall investment in IT research.

Note that native writers prefer constructions which observe the initial subject principle (see Module II, Chapter 2.1), whereas writers with German mother tongue tend to use adverbials:

In dieser Arbeit sollen die verschiedenen Ausprägungen und Funktionen von Frageanhängseln untersucht werden.
(?)In this paper the various forms and functions of question tags will be examined.
→ **This paper will examine** the various forms and functions of question tags.

However, if you decide to use first-person pronouns (i.e. *I* to refer to yourself or *we* for multiple authors), it is fairly natural to resort to adverbials in clause-initial position.

In this chapter I will explore the parallels between language and other complex systems.

It is also quite common to place the topic in subject position and to follow this up with a passive verb. Note, however, that this type of construction may result in overlong subjects (see Module II, Chapter 2.6.1) and is therefore best reserved for cases where a previously mentioned topic is picked up again by means of a pronoun such as *this* or *which* or where the treatment of some particular aspect of a topic is deferred until later.

This **will be discussed** in Chapter 4.
This point **will be discussed** in detail shortly.
… the 'Ten Books of History' turns up numerous examples of royal involvement in the election of bishops, some of which **will be discussed** in this paper.

(?)Finally, questions concerning the connections among various contrasts between two languages and the possibility of subsuming them under higher-level generalizations can be pursued within a contrastive analysis …
→ Finally, contrastive analysis can help answer questions about …

Another common construction involves the use of nouns such as ***purpose, aim, objective, (main) point, topic, theme*** or ***subject***. (Note that, strictly speaking, a distinction has to be made between the *aim* and the *topic* of a paper.)

> **The purpose of this article is to** consider the options available for statutory reform.
> **The purpose of this paper is twofold**: (1) to review our current state of knowledge of semantic prosodies ... and (2) to give a more adequate account of ...
> **The subject of this paper is** the English periphrastic genitive.
> **The first topic we will address is** the so-called relativity hypothesis.
> An early consideration of these principles is, therefore, relevant to a study of building construction and **it is the purpose of this chapter to** introduce the broad principles underlying the behavior of the main components parts of a building under load ...

If you wish to give special emphasis to a particular (sub-)topic, you can use lexemes such as ***attention, concern, emphasis, focus*** and ***focus of attention*** in several different constructions.

> In this paper, **special attention is given to** the shear lines in easterlies.
> **The focus of attention will be on** the kinds of reasons the judges use.
> Although **the most immediate focus is on** text-intrinsic linguistic features, it will not be forgotten that whether the reader chooses to read a text in a literary way, as a literary text as it were, is one crucial determinant of its literariness.
> **My (prime/main/principal) concern is to** elucidate religion (notably the 'world religions') as it functions in complex societies.
> **Our main concern is with** ethics from Aristotle to Cicero.
> **My primary emphasis is on** desire as an organizing category.
> While **the emphasis is firmly on** isotope systematics and a process-based understanding, a small number of case studies are included to illustrate specific points ...

4.1.2 Excluding a topic from consideration

If you wish to exclude topics from consideration, you can simply negate the aforementioned verbs or you can use such constructions as ***restrict/confine oneself to*** + V-*ing*, ***refrain from*** + V-*ing*, ***it is no part of my/our concern to*** + INF, etc.

> **We will not be discussing** this rather exotic type of material any further.
> However, having noted that, **I will not consider** such a ternary relation any further in this paper.
> This topic **will not be explored further** here, save to refer to References 19 and 20.

Here **I shall restrict myself to** considering some of the historical problems.
But it is no part of our concern to dwell on that question.
For similar reasons **I have refrained from** treating historical, literary, and dramatic elements of the dialogue.
Furthermore, among the higher order prosodic constituents, intonational phrases **will be excluded from consideration.**

The following phrases are commonly used to exclude a topic from consideration because of space requirements or similar considerations.

The scope of this paper does not permit/allow (for) (a) (ADJ: complete/exhaustive/etc.) discussion/consideration/exploration/indication/sketch/review (etc.) of this broad and diverse field.
Space (and time) limitations preclude/do not allow (etc.) even an abridged listing here of these dictionaries.
For reasons of space, I will focus on just one type.
Space only allows that I assert them.
Limits of space and time only allow a brief discussion of such issues.
We have space enough to mention only a few.
I can hardly do it justice **in the short space available here**.

If you wish to treat a topic later on in your paper, you can use constructions like the following.

This point **will be discussed further** in Chapter 3.
The impact of inflation **is further considered**, in detail, in Chapter 4.
The subject of how we incorporate the locational aspect of sample data **is deferred until Section 1.4.**
It is best to defer further discussion of tag questions to 3.5ff.
This is an extremely complex area ... and **a proper treatment must be deferred to** Chapter 8.
Consideration of these issues must be left until Chapter 5.
Cyclic alkanes **will be considered separately later** in this chapter.
The idealization of data associated with this tradition leads to the exclusion of too much that is relevant to translation, **a point discussed separately** below.
Cough is not only an important physiologic process, but also an important symptom, **a topic we will address fully** in Chapter 11.
One important role will be conspicuous by its absence: the humorous use of lexical items, **which receives separate treatment** in §22.
... but energy has special twists that **require separate discussion**.

4.2 Reporting, summarizing and paraphrasing

Much of the writing you will do at university will require you to report what someone else has said. Such reports can take three major forms. One is to restate in your own words the essential information contained in the original source, i.e. to write a summary or abstract. Another is to restate all the information in your own words, i.e. to paraphrase it. A third option is to repeat a stretch of text exactly as it originally occurred – in other words, to quote it. We will deal with these three options one by one (see Module I, Chapter 2.2).

4.2.1 Summaries and abstracts

Since summaries are as varied in their linguistic make-up as the primary sources they are based on, we cannot provide any specific language material for summary writing. We would caution readers, though, to avoid the common misconception that summaries must not contain any words and phrases used in the source text. As will become apparent from the examples of paraphrase given below, key terminology, for example, should not normally be paraphrased. In more concrete terms, if you are writing a linguistics research paper, you should not normally try to come up with circumlocutions for terms such as 'morpheme', 'great vowel shift' or 'collocation'.

That said, explanatory summaries or 'abstracts' do exhibit recurrent linguistic features which can be listed systematically and learned by heart. Although conventions vary from one discipline to another, abstracts may mention the author's name and summarize the structure of the text together with its message. Research abstracts in scientific disciplines are often couched in an impersonal style and in short sentences.

Research abstracts can be divided into three parts, stating

1. what the study is about and what its aims are (research questions)
2. how it intends to achieve its aims (methodology) and
3. what was found (results).

It is therefore advisable to start with an introductory sentence or two indicating the subject of the text or study being summarized:

The text is about/deals with …
The author of the text is concerned with …
The author of this report addresses the question why …
The author attacks/supports/… the idea that …
The author suggests that …

This paper discusses/presents/explores ...
The purpose/aim of the present paper is to ...
This paper introduces a new approach to ...

There is a variety of ways in which you can indicate the organizational scheme of the text you are abstracting:

in the first/second/third (etc.) paragraph (of the text [under discussion]/of the excerpt [etc.])
in the first/second/third (etc.) section/part (of his/the book/work /...)

the author **first** cites two examples of ...
next, he points out/suggests/notes, observes/says/argues/claims/reports that
then he discusses/shows/demonstrates/describes/analyses
finally, it is shown how/found that ...

having + V-ed
having explained ..., the author gives two examples of ...

the author **opens the text by + v-ing** (saying/remarking/pointing out ...)
Clinton opens his inaugural address by remarking that
the author **begins by + v-ing**
Gassendi begins by addressing a question ...
the author **goes on to + inf./moves on to + inf./proceeds to + inf.**
the author goes on to point out/examine/explain (etc.) ...
this is followed by + NP
this is followed by a discussion of the problems ...
the author **ends/concludes by + v-ing**
the author concludes by saying ...
to conclude, the author stresses ...

With some argued texts, you can also use noun + verb collocations based on the nouns 'argument', 'premise' and 'thesis' in order to describe the thread of the argument. An argument is what a person produces when he or she makes a statement and gives reasons for believing the statement. The statement itself is called the conclusion of the argument; the stated reasons for believing the argument are called the premises. In other words, a premise can be defined as something that you accept as true and that you use as a basis for developing an idea. Finally, a thesis is an idea that is expressed as a statement and is discussed in a logical way. Here is how these words can be used in connected text:

The **premise** is that ...
Cicero **starts from the premise** that ...
The authors **proceed from the premise** that ...

This collection of ten essays reverses that trend, **working from the premise that** it is necessary for context once more to assume the highground of literary criticism.
Their reasoning **rested on two premises**: that …
The PTP concept **is founded on the premise that** …
This move **was premised on the assumption that** …

The **thesis** of this paper **is that** …
It is the **thesis of this study** that …
His **thesis** is that …
He **argues the thesis** that …
She **advances the thesis** that …
He **supports his thesis** by/with a quotation/an example // by quoting (from) an authority
As evidence for the thesis he makes a conjecture about "animal learning.
Hierocles **presents a lengthy argument for the thesis that** …
Developing the thesis propounded by C. S. Singleton, Hollander argues that …
To begin with, Leibniz **held the Scholastic thesis** that "being" and "one" are equivalent.

In *Summa Theologica*, Thomas Aquinas **gives three arguments against** the permissibility of suicide.
David Simon **provides two arguments for/in favour of** encouraging local broadcast service.
Malebranche **offers two arguments in defence of/in support of** premise (d) above.
He **offers two arguments why** …
He **uses the argument that** …
They **advance/deploy/put forward the argument that** …
Brutus appeals to Antony's intellect **with the argument that** 'pity to the general wrong of/Rome… Hath done this deed on Caesar'.
It is nevertheless quite important for MacDonald's **central argument that** …
His **argument rests on** the idea that …
In his argument for the necessity of disciplinary integration in psychology, James Wertsch pointed to …
If an insult is followed by a war, **the argument goes**, the system was already fated for war through objective factors.

The author comes to/arrives at/reaches/draws the **conclusion** that …

The following samples illustrate a) an explanatory summary of a newspaper text, b) a translation studies abstract and c) a medical abstract. Reusable words and phrases have been underlined.

a) In his article entitled 'Does work make you stupid?', [(the) British journalist] David Nicholson-Lord **deals with** the effects of modern working practices on employees. He **starts from the premise that** the two sides of the brain, the abstract left brain and the intuitive right brain, need to be kept in balance. He

goes on to advance the thesis that changing work practices may lead to an over-use of the left hemisphere because state-of-the-art technology reduces real human contact. The result is that left-brain-'heavy' employees who climb the corporate ladder may not be able to act effectively at the top, where creativity becomes more important. Nicholson-Lord **proceeds to quote** authorities who **suggest** that the best ideas spring to mind when you are relaxed and that office environments do not foster creativity. He **concludes by making a plea for** 'more-people friendly working practices' in order to overcome the imbalance.

b) **The purpose of the present paper is to bring into sharper focus** the highly complex problems associated with translation equivalence. **The author begins by examining** the equivalence concept itself. **Then he discusses** various devices for establishing translation equivalence. **Finally, he attempts** to determine the limits of equivalence. The abundant exemplificatory material, which is intended to assist the reader in following the argument, has been culled from various periods and cultural areas. The numerous **sources laid under contribution** include texts in English, French, German, Italian and Latin. **The author comes to the conclusion that** equivalence between source and target texts is not always feasible and not always desirable although adequacy (in the functionalist sense of the term) is always feasible and always desirable.

c) Background
Phoenix Firefighters have had abnormally high rates of tuberculin skin test (TBST) results on medical surveillance. **The objectives of this study were to** evaluate our firefighters using QuantiFERON-TB (QFT), comparing the results to their TBST results.
Methods
Using QFT results obtained during the study, **we compared** previously positive TBST responders (Cases) to negative responders (Controls). We also compared both groups for QFT results for Mycobacterium avium (MA) exposure.
Results
QFT effectively monitored our working population. 12.9% of the 148 cases, and 3.2% of the 220 controls had a positive QFT result. Another 14.8% of cases and 4.5% of controls had conditionally positive QFT results. There was an unusually high rate of MA response on QFT testing in both groups.
Conclusion
Phoenix Firefighters have higher than expected TBST and QFT results, which cannot be explained by the increased MA rate. The decreased level of QFT positivity in comparison to TBST results may indicate a considerable false positive TBST rate. The QFT offers many advantages as a surveillance method over TBST in exposed worker populations.

4.2.2 Strategies for paraphrasing

Unlike a summary, a paraphrase captures all the information from the original source and puts it into your own words. It is not uncommon for paraphrases to be longer than the original passage, whereas a summary will always be shorter. You may wish to paraphrase another author's work because

- it supports your own views
- it contradicts your own views and you want to argue against it
- the author's position is too well-known or not sufficiently memorable to warrant quoting

Your paraphrases should reflect the original text objectively and fairly. That is, you should avoid using emotive language which reveals your own views on the subject in question. To do so, you can use neutral introductory phrases such as 'Miller notes that' or 'as Miller points out/notes/remarks'. However, there may also be times when you want to express immediate agreement with the author's views. In this case you can use a routine formula such as 'as Miller correctly points out/observes' or 'as Miller rightly notes'.

Here are some useful strategies for paraphrasing academic text:

1. Select a passage of 1–5 sentences that is relevant to your own text.
2. Change individual words, sentence structures and/or the order of ideas in the passage. One way of doing this is to cover up the original text and to rephrase the main ideas or findings cited there.
3. If you find it hard to come up with substitutes to the author's wordings, turn to dictionaries of synonyms or thesauri. Thesauri are now included in most monolingual learners' dictionaries, such as the *Cambridge Advanced Learner's Dictionary* and the *Longman Dictionary of Contemporary English*.
4. Check the meanings, usage patterns and style level of the lexical items you want to opt for against the alphabetical section of your monolingual learner's dictionary. Replacement words you find in a thesaurus may be stylistically inappropriate.
5. Introduce your paraphrase with a suitable reporting pattern (for examples, see below).

Let us consider an example (see Table 33). The major lexical changes which have been made are indicated by arrows.

Table 33: Paraphrasing an original passage

Original	Rough paraphrase	Final paraphrase
There are times when for good practical reasons one has to modify a quotation for the particular readership of the dictionary in question, and sometimes even invent a quotation based on what the corpus evidence has told one about the likely context and syntax of the use of the word (Landau 2001: 208)	According to Landau (2001: 208), it is sometimes necessary to change or make up illustrative examples because dictionary users may find real examples difficult to understand, imprecise or inappropriate. **there are times when … → sometimes** **one has to → it is necessary to** **invent → make up** **quotations → illustrative examples** **readership → users**	Landau (2001: 208) claims that it is sometimes unavoidable to alter illustrative examples or even to make them up on the basis of corpus evidence. This is because dictionary users may find real examples difficult, imprecise or inappropriate. **necessary → unavoidable** **change → alter** **based on → on the basis of** **because → this is because**

Paraphrases are generally introduced by a reporting verb (*Landau claims*), noun (*Landau's claim that*) or phrase (*according to Landau*) which allow writers to mark material that is not their own and to attribute it to its source. Here is a list of the most common reporting verbs; the choice of verb will depend on the stance you are adopting (cf. Module I, Chapter 2.2):

> argue, assume, believe, comment, conclude, describe, discuss, emphasize, find (= feststellen), hint at, hypothesize, imply, indicate, mention, note, outline, point out, observe, quote, report, say, suggest, state

Most reporting nouns are related to the verbs just listed. They are normally followed by *that*-clauses (e.g. *the observation that*), *of*-phrases (*the recognition of*) or infinitive clauses (e.g. *the proposal to-INF*). Commonly used nouns include:

> acknowledgement, allegation, argument, assertion, caution, charge, claim, comment, concession, confirmation, contention, criticism, demand, explanation, implication, information, objection, observation, plea, point, prediction, proposal, proposition, recommendation, remark, report, revelation, specification, statement, suggestion, warning, view

There are also a number of reporting nouns which can be used in reporting well-known content such as proverbs or mottos. They do not have a related verb (cf. Thompson 1994: 75):

> adage, aphorism, cliché, dictum, maxim, motto, proverb, riddle, slogan

You may modify verbs and nouns with appropriate adverbs and adjectives to express your attitude to what you are discussing; German learners often underuse this kind of construction, especially the type where an adjective + noun collocation is followed by a *that*-clause:

Machiavelli **makes a powerful argument that** it is better for a leader to be feared than loved.
The committee **has made a definite recommendation that** ...
It is often a shattering revelation that the recovering substance-abusing family member is still a difficult person to live with even when sober.

Here are some citation patterns which occur with particular frequency:

1. Landau (2001: 208) says/notes/suggests/argues/points out/... that NP + V
2. As Landau (2001: 208) notes/suggests/observes/remarks/..., NP + V
3. For/according to Landau (2001: 208), NP + V
4. In Landau's view/understanding/analysis, NP + V

It is also possible to summarize the work of one or more authors without citing a specific source. Phrases that can be used to introduce such passages include:

It is often said/claimed/argued that ...
It was argued by historians that ...
It has been proposed that ...
Much ink has been spilled (on + NP: his role as a catalyst of the revolution/in + ing-clause: in trying to prove that .../+ -ing-clause: trying to prove that)

The routine formulae just listed are also often used to initiate a new (sub) topic in the current text.

If you wish to draw attention to a resemblance between the views expressed by two researchers, you may opt for one of the following formulations:

Brown writes to similar effect. (= ähnlich äußert sich Brown)
Brown writes to the same effect.
Brown expresses similar views/a similar attitude/a similar concern/... (= ähnliche Überlegungen [etc.] finden sich bei Brown)
A similar view/sentiment/attitude/thought/... is expressed by Brown.
Brown takes/adopts a similar view.

You may also cite a source directly and then proceed to pitch the source's main point in a nutshell using a phrase such as 'briefly put' or 'tersely stated':

For details, see Dowd (1994, 1995). **Briefly put**, the central bank would create a new type of financial instrument.

Similar phrases can be used to summarize or paraphrase information mentioned in an earlier part of your own text. This type of reformulation occurs in four major patterns:

1. as + past participle (+ adverb): as already said, as argued above, as noted, etc.
2. as + I/we + reporting verb: as we mentioned earlier, as I explained above, as we reported
3. place adverbial + I/we + reporting verb: several chapters back, I described ...
4. it + passive reporting verb: it has already been pointed out that, it will be recalled

These patterns usually include time or place adverbs such as *above, earlier, already, in the above discussion, in earlier chapters, elsewhere* or *in the preceding section*. The present perfect tense may occur with adverbs such as *above* or *earlier* (*as we have seen above, as we have discussed earlier*), but it is safer to use the past tense (cf. errors like **as I have pointed out in Chapter 2* [as written in Chapter 3]). The patterns in question usually appear initially, but may also be placed in medial or final position:

The base/superstructure paradigm also has a demoralising effect on women, because it dictates, **as I already noted**, that gender oppression is the result of class oppression in the material base.

You can also use devices such as *in other words, put another way, that is, meaning* (*that*) or *i.e.* (= id est) to introduce reformulatory passages of widely varying length. *In other words* often helps the writer to rephrase the information contained in the previous context in a more succinct manner. It may also sometimes introduce a reinterpretation or a conclusion.

in the year 2020, **in other words** in ten years' time
it might be a temporary depression: **in other words** a suicide wish
Arbitration was slow and worthless. **In other words**, the mechanics of contractual relations had effectively broken down, at least in Ruby Bagwell's opinion ...

That is and ***meaning*** commonly introduce an explanation or a definition of what goes before.

A hypersolid, **that is**, a portion of four-dimensional space, may be separated into two parts by a three-space.
In addition, popular theatre may be construed as a practice within "popular culture," **meaning** the culture of everyday life unbounded by class or social group.

Namely and *viz.* – the latter is slowly falling out of use but still common in legal parlance – serve to specify or identify things or ideas that have been announced in the preceding discourse. They are thus close in function to the colon (:), which is often substituted for them in contemporary usage (cf. Module II, Chapter 4):

> To this generalisation there is one exception, namely Japan.

Namely may also introduce an appositive *that*-clause:

> The great characteristic of equitable estates, **namely that** they will be destroyed if the legal estate gets into the hands of a purchaser for value without notice, still holds good.

If the passage following *that is* amplifies the preceding discourse rather than just explaining it, *that is* is synonymous with *namely*. Cf. the following example:

> Scott (1986) advocates a third usage of the term gender, **that is**, as an analytical category for understanding the 'complex connections among various forms of human interaction'.

The abbreviation ***i.e.*** is preferred over *that is* at the beginning of bracketed elements serving to introduce a list or an amplification of the preceding discourse:

> expenditures for personal property items (**i.e.** drapes, office equipment, furniture and certain carpeting)

If you wish to paraphrase or abbreviate short expressions or terms, you can use a set of reformulators based on adverb + past participle collocations drawing on a small number of verbs: *know, call, refer to, name, describe* and *term*. While they may just indicate an alternative name for a particular object or idea (*also called, otherwise called, variously known as*), they are more commonly used to suggest frequency of use (*usually called, often termed*) as well as diachronic (*anciently known as, now called, traditionally referred to as*), stylistic (*popularly known as*) or geographic (*known as … in the US*) variation. Here are two examples:

> These radiations, **also called** 'super-soft roentgen rays'
> (…) money was obtained from the complaining witness by trick through a procedure **variously known as** the flimflam, faith and trust, or confidence game …

For short, rather than any of the above expressions, is used to introduce an abbreviation or a shortened reformulation of the preceding discourse; it may precede or follow the word or phrase it refers to:

part of a worldwide program identified as the International Geophysical Year, IGY **for short**.

Reformulatory devices such as *henceforth, hereafter* and their variants *hereafter termed, henceforth referred to as* (etc.) serve to introduce a convenient shorthand for a technical term, a book title or a proper name, usually in the form of an initialism which will then be consistently used throughout the subsequent discourse. This device is especially useful in writing reviews.

Giorgio Morandi Pittore, hereafter abbreviated GMP.

An idiomatic feature of English is the use of *or* as a reformulator indicating that two entities are equivalent; in this mode or is usually set off by a comma. Here we may distinguish four main functions:

1. translation: *Satyagraha, or 'Truth Force'* (variant: *Satyagraha, literally 'Truth Force'*)
2. substitution of non-technical language for a specialist term: *light-emitting polymers, or plastics*
3. expression of one unit of measurement in terms of another: *20 shilling, or 240 pence*
4. translation of absolute into relative figures or vice versa: *19 per cent, or 19 cents on the dollar*

The expressions *more precisely, more accurately* and *more exactly* introduce a more precise restatement of a form of words or a finer point upon an idea:

Some children are highly sensitive to sugar – or more precisely, to the change in adrenaline levels caused by an infusion of glucose into the bloodstream.

For further guidance on reporting, summarizing and paraphrase, see Thompson (1994), Wilhoit (1997: 45–56) and Siepmann (2005: 141–218).

4.2.3 Quoting

If you want to use someone else's exact words in your research, you have to enclose them in quotation marks and document them. When and how you should quote is discussed in Module I, Chapter 2.2. This section confines itself to discussing the language patterns which can be used to introduce quotations.

From a linguistic point of view, it does not make sense to distinguish between the two basic types of quotations, viz. a) block quotations and b) shorter, integrated quotations, since both types of quotation may be introduced by the same kind of multi-word marker. It is probably wiser to list the verbs and nouns of saying that commonly introduce a quotation on the one hand, and other ways of announcing a quotation on the other.

The choice of verb or noun depends on the overall tone of the passage you are writing. Common verbs used in quoting include:

argue, assert, assume, believe, claim, comment, conclude, contend, describe, discuss, emphasize, explain, find (= feststellen), maintain, mention, note, outline, point out, observe, report, say, suggest, state

Here is a list of nouns frequently used in quoting:

allegation, argument, assertion, charge, claim, comment, criticism, objection, observation, original, plea, point, remark, statement, suggestion, warning, view, words (pl.)

These verbs and nouns occur in the aforementioned patterns (see 'Reporting, summarizing and paraphrasing'):

1. Landau (2001: 208) says/notes/suggests/argues/points out/… that NP + V
2. As Landau (2001: 208) notes/suggests/observes/remarks/…, NP + V
3. the/his/her/the author's NP (view, comment, etc.) that … (e.g. *Miller's view that*)

Mature writers tend to be quite imaginative in the way they use nouns to introduce quotations. Here is a small sample of the constructions they use:

The paper ended with the optimistic **statement**: '(quote)'
'(quote)' With this NP/with these **words** author/narrator VP …
'(quote)' With these **words** the narrator of Moby-Dick begins the tale of how …
'This epidemic carries off those who are in perfect health,' was a **remark** frequently heard during the 1918 'flu' epidemic.
'(quote)' This **statement** is too sweeping.
'(quote)' This **remark** was made by …
The **original** reads: '(translation)'
'(quote)' Such were the **words** which the great Cyprian, Bishop of Carthage, addressed to …
Comments by the poet … could well apply to the human race as a whole: '(quote)'
It was from this perspective that he wrote his **dictum**: 'if one has claimed: the style of an author is the whole man, how much more should not the whole person contain the whole author', or phrased more poetically, 'if you want to understand, travel in the poet's land'

Note that the verbs *put, phrase* and *have* also crop up in quotation patterns. Unlike the other reporting verbs, however, they are always followed by the pronoun *it*.

Efficient management without effective leadership is, **as one individual has phrased it**, 'like straightening deck chairs on the Titanic'.
That hospitality is what I will now firmly identify as and with culture; or, **as Derrida has it** in a different context: 'Hospitality is culture itself and not simply one ethic amongst others'.

In this construction 'have it' may be slowly falling out of use, but is still notably common in semi-fixed expressions reporting general language events, such as 'as rumour/legend has it', 'as the proverb/adage/cliché/aphorism/slogan has it':

To include all the material (to 'conflate', **as the jargon has it**) risks presenting a repetitive script that Shakespeare never intended.

Modifying reporting nouns with adjectives and reporting verbs with adverbs is a valuable signal to your reader of the specific status given to the quotation: you may agree or disagree with the quoted material, you may find it insightful or succinct or you may be citing a particularly famous quote. Probably the most common way of modifying a quote is to use the verb phrases 'put it', 'phrase it' or 'have it' with an appropriate adverb, as illustrated in some of the following example sentences:

as Miller has so vividly put it
as aptly put by Miller
the recognition that (as he delicately put it)
as Aristophanes disdainfully put it
As a recent US treasury study dryly put it
Efficient management without effective leadership is, **as one individual has phrased it**, 'like straightening deck chairs on the Titanic'.
as Miller famously remarked

Other constructions used especially in introducing block quotations include:

This is what Landau **has to say on** NP: 'quote'
in his own words from the preface: 'quote'
the importance of ... is very clearly expressed **in the words of** X: 'quote'

In academic writing short, integrated quotations often foreground technical terms or interesting uses of language.

to quote Lewin
to use Sinclair's term
to use Iser's terminology
to borrow a well-known formula
to adopt Plath's phrase

in Baker's terminology, a parallel corpus consists of ...
in Sinclair's words
in the Marxist idiom

When the quotation precedes the citation, you can use constructions such as 'wrote/said/noted/argued/warned (etc.)/writes/says (etc.) + NP', 'NP + writes/says/observes/goes on/adds/argues/tells us (etc.)' or 'we are told'.

'I want to know,' **wrote Voltaire**, 'what were the steps by which men passed from barbarism to civilization.'
If we 'look at the West from the point of view of the Indians,' **Worster observes**, 'what could it look like but a failure?'
Some of the "pros" have "comfortable homes, and families, and thousands of dollars in the banks," **we are told.**
"What they did," **the poet tells us**, "all men must do/When the time comes!" (2708–2709).
"The strong man and the waterfall," **says the proverb**, "channel their own path."

If you wish to start a new sentence after the quote, you can use constructions such as 'so wrote', 'to which NP adds' or 'this was said (by ...)'.

This theatrical grangerizing of *Much Ado* culminated in Beerbohm Tree's 1905 production, which supplied 'all the lovely things Shakespeare dispensed with'. **So wrote** Shaw in the *Saturday Review* of 11 February 1905, ...
"How I pity you for having no servant!" – **to which Poussin replied,** "How I pity you for having so many!"

4.3 Expressing opinions and criticizing

Academic writers do not normally confine themselves to reporting or quoting the work of others, but also respond to it either in the light of their own experience or according to a range of more objective criteria. In both cases they use evaluative expressions to say whether they think the work reported is good or bad, interesting or surprising, etc. We listed some evaluative adjective + noun collocations which can be used for this purpose in Table 11. Examples given there include *an accurate account, a misguided interpretation, a sloppy experiment,* etc. Here are a few examples of how such collocations can be used in extended text for expressing opinions.

More recently Arnold (1980) has argued that there is **insufficient evidence** to prove widespread infanticide.
The final criticism that offers **a potentially fruitful line of research** is methodological in nature.

Perhaps **one of the most glaring research weaknesses** is the **scant attention** paid to the effect of liability on the rhetorical choices of apologists when they respond to allegations.

In judging the strengths and weaknesses of previous research, authors often resort to another common construction involving evaluative adjectives: *the* NP (i.e. *author/book*) *is* ADJ (*strong/weak/correct/wrong/instructive/good/excellent/short/heavy*/etc.) *on*. Two examples:

The volume is instructive on the influence of American law and the extensive borrowing from other colonies, especially from Australia.
The book is strong on the main props of the sociologist – statistics and concern – but **I find it weak on** the lay virtues – clear thinking and accuracy.

Another useful evaluative construction is NP *lies in* NP/V-*ing*/*wh*-clause, where the first NP slot is typically filled with nouns of the type *strength/virtue/value/difficulty/problem* (etc.). A few examples:

The uniqueness of the volume lies in the selective presentation of the materials and their organization.
The significance of *The Peasants* lies in the fact that the author consciously chose and crafted an idiom other than standard literary Polish.
The problem lies in how this capital is allocated – at what rates and into what kinds of investments.
Indeed, **the single most exciting aspect of this book lies in** its invitation to the reader to generate further discussion.

As can be seen from most of the above examples, academic writers rarely introduce their opinions explicitly because it is usually clear from the context that a particular statement is a personal view. Hence expressions such as *in my opinion, in my view, to my mind,* etc., which are commonly used in speech, are not often found in academic writing.

Instead, academic writers use an impersonal style and make use of the power of suggestion in order to influence the attitude adopted by the reader. The devices they use for this purpose may therefore be called 'suggestors'; typical examples include *it is important/crucial/essential/interesting/surprising* + to-INF or it is ADJ (*interesting/noteworthy/remarkable/...*) *that* + clause as well as more institutionalized items such as *no-one could deny that* or *it goes without saying that*.

There are also hundreds of sentence adverbs which may help authors show their attitude to the work of others. Most of these can be derived from an equivalent clause:

it is surprising that → surprisingly
it is interesting that → interestingly
it is significant that → significantly

Almost equally productive is the collocational framework ADV + *speaking*, of which the most common example is the fixed phrase *strictly speaking*:

literally speaking, musically speaking, psychologically speaking, properly speaking, relatively speaking, relativistically speaking, religiously speaking, roughly speaking, semantically speaking, technically speaking, textually speaking

It should have become clear by now that academic authors are generally fond of varying suggestors stylistically. By way of further illustration, consider expressions such as *it is a reasonable assumption that,* which can be transposed to a verbal construction: *it is reasonable to assume/suppose that* (= *es ist/steht zu vermuten, dass*). And if you wish to say that something is almost true, you can use any of the following:

it is hardly/scarcely an exaggeration to say/state that; it is no exaggeration to say that; it is not an exaggeration to say that

Table 34 shows some devices intended to suggest that something is obvious; each group metaphorizes 'obviousness' in a different way.

Table 34: Suggestors

Obviousness as	English	German equivalents
"Clarity" (proximity to inference markers [e.g. *it is clear from this that*]; see also "Visibility")	obviously, clearly, plainly, evidently, manifestly, ...; it is obvious/clear/plain/evident/manifest ... that; it seems that/it would seem that	offensichtlich; es liegt auf der Hand, dass
"Absence of doubt"	no one could deny that ...; it is undeniable/incontestable ... that; there is no denying the fact that	es steht außer Zweifel, dass; es ist unbestritten, dass; zweifellos
"Certainty"	one thing is certain: ...; it is certain that; it is safe to say that; it seems safe to assert that; there are good grounds for believing/doubting that	alles/vieles/einiges spricht dafür, dass; man kann mit Recht/Sicherheit/Bestimmtheit behaupten, dass
"Visibility" (proximity to inference markers)	a little consideration will show that; it requires little thought to see that; it will	es dürfte ohne weiteres einsichtig sein, dass; der aufmerksame/kundige/

	be readily seen that; it is easy to see how; the observant/careful/attentive ... reader will notice/note that; it will be seen that	theoretisch geschulte Leser wird feststellen/bemerken, dass; es fällt auf, dass
"Self-evident truth" (see also "Clarity")	it is self-evident that	es versteht sich von selbst, dass
"Stating the obvious"	needless to say; it goes without saying that	(es ist) selbstverständlich
"Common knowledge"	everyone knows that; as is well known; it is well known that	bekanntlich; es ist allgemein bekannt, dass
"Rapidity"	a moment's thought suggests that; a moment's reflection allows us to see that; a moment's reflection is enough for us to realize; a cursory glance suffices to show	es bedarf keiner Erörterung, dass
"Effortlessness"	(very) little thought is required to see that; it will be readily seen that; it will be readily apparent that; it is easy to see how	es bedarf nur geringer gedanklicher Anstrengung um festzustellen, dass
"Inevitability" (proximity to inference markers)	everything suggests that; there is little cause to disagree with the view that; it is no accident/coincidence that	~ alles deutet darauf hin, dass; es spricht wenig dagegen, dass; es ist kein Zufall, dass
"Quasi-conclusion"	it is as if; you would think; one could be forgiven for thinking/assuming (etc.) that	es ist, als ob; man könnte meinen, dass; der Schluss scheint sich aufzudrängen, dass

To make their claims sound less definite, native writers often use verbs such as *seem, appear, suggest, indicate* or *tend* or modals such as *might* (for very weak claims), *may, could* and *should* (which express greater degrees of certainty). This is an important feature of English academic prose; some non-native writers tend to state their ideas with much greater certainty and therefore risk coming across as immodest and arrogant. Let us look at a few examples of how to soften criticism by means of the devices just mentioned:

> If ESL students who complete this textbook are to be ready for full-time undergraduate study, as the preface suggests, **it would seem essential that** they be introduced to more technical prose as well.

> Perhaps more importantly, even if there could be a resolution of the abortion dilemma, **it could be argued that** this resolution should not be adopted.

In the first of the above examples, rather than saying 'the students must be introduced' – which is really what the author thinks – he uses a far less threatening construction involving 'dummy' *it*, the non-committal verb *seem* and the adjective *essential*. The entire construction requires the use of the subjunctive mood in the complement clause, that is, a verb form that expresses wishes rather than certainties.

Similarly, in the second example, the author uses the very common marker *it could be argued that* rather than, say, *I have serious doubts whether*.

You can also use nouns such as *criticism* and *comment* or verbs like *qualify* to introduce an adverse point. We list just a few of the manifold possibilities; note that such constructions as *the caveat is that* or *NP has been subjected to criticism* can be used in two ways: they may help you, firstly, to direct criticism at others and, secondly, to ward off potential criticism of your own position.

> A number of criticisms have been levelled at/have been made of/have been raised against NP.
> There have been a number of criticisms of NP.
> Several criticisms have been launched against NP.
> One of the main criticisms levelled at … is that …
> One major criticism of NP is that …
> The only major criticism which can be made is that …
> There is a major criticism to be made here.
> One note of criticism that could be sounded regards the page layout …
> But there is a further criticism to be made.
> My main criticism of NP is that …/centres on …
> I have two main criticisms of + NP
> The Bible is open to criticism.
> Behaviourism is open to several criticisms.
> Some epidemiological studies, in particular, are vulnerable to criticism.
> NP has been subjected to criticism.
> NP has come in for/generated/provoked (etc.) severe/serious (etc.) criticism
> A similar criticism can be made of NP
> This view is not immune from criticism, especially in so far as …

> NP merits/needs/requires/warrants/calls for some comment/a few words of comment.
> Several passages here are worthy of comment.
> The same comment applies to NP

There are two arguments against this position.
Note that this runs counter to Halliday, who argues that …

The caveat/constraint/difference/difficulty/downside/drawback/exception/problem/proviso (etc.) is that the research was conducted at a time when computer systems were new.
My quarrel/argument/problem/concern (etc.) with this phrase is that it implies that there is no evidence that brain chemistry is related to mental problems.
My quarrel/discomfort/dissatisfaction/disagreement/problem (etc.) with this orthodoxy arises from/stems from its failure to take due account of two works published by Milton in 1658.
The objection to this/the argument against this/the factor militating against this (etc.) is that this heavenly figure initiates the harvest at the command of "another angel".
What this suggests is that Hypotheses 3 and 4 are valid for Conservatives too, with the caveat that the residual gender gap leaves room for the suspicion that …
with the caveat/constraint/difference/exception/restriction/peculiarity/proviso/twist that …
subject to the proviso that …
with the crucial proviso that …
with the principal difference that …

This (assertion/claim/etc.) needs to/must be **qualified** (somewhat). (= German *relativieren*)

It is **open to debate/doubt/question** whether + clause

I would take issue with Engerman and Rosen on one of their points.

The following constructions are often used in commenting on statistics:

the estimations in terms of hours should be **taken (or: viewed) with a certain degree of reservation** …
A number of **adjustments have to be made** to this figure.
In employing data on building permits to represent change in housing units, **an allowance has to be made for** the time lag between the issuance of the permit and completion of the unit for occupancy.
… **a deduction has to be made for** those enumerated at the census but who died before the end of 1972

If you wish to introduce a second adverse point, you can use the following items (= German *erschwerend/komplizierend kommt hinzu, dass* or *noch schwerer wiegt, dass*):

a further/another/a second criticism/problem/difficulty/disadvantage/constraint/complication/complicating factor/troublesome point/worry/caution … is that

to complicate matters further
to further complicate things
to further confound the picture
to make matters worse
the situation is further complicated by the fact that …

4.4 Enumerating ideas and changing the topic

Among the many ways to compose a text or paragraph (cf. Module I, Chapter 3.4), the easiest is probably to enumerate a number of objects, ideas or topics. The textual markers used for this purpose, such as *firstly* or *in addition*, are called 'enumerators'. There is a large number of one-word enumerators and a smaller number of multi-word enumerative markers (see the tables below).

Enumerators indicate that a stretch of text is to be viewed as one item in a total or series, and they help us to show the reader exactly what part of that total or series we are currently writing about. They can do so prospectively, thus performing an additive function, or retrospectively, thus signalling a boundary between two stretches of text. It is usually preferable to use an additive structure, i.e. to list items in clear succession and to place enumerators at the beginning of the sentence. Just as a traffic sign placed at the start of a bend warns drivers to slow down, so a fronted enumerator makes it easier for readers to follow the writer's train of thought.

There are different types of enumerators in English which you can choose from (see Table 35; cf. Arnaudet & Barrett 1990: 52–60). Note that some markers require a different sentence structure from others. Compare:

Smoking has many risks. **First**, you might develop cancer if you smoke for a prolonged period of time.
Smoking is dangerous. **The first kind of risk** (you will run) is (that of developing) cancer.

Markers like *first, second, third* treat all items as being of equal importance. Markers like *less/more importantly* arrange items in descending or ascending order of importance. It is possible to blend these different marker types in one enumeration. A schematic example:

There are various reasons for this. First, … Second, … The chief reason, however, is …

For obvious reasons, you should refrain from such blends as **firstly … second … in the third place*.

Note also that the following enumerators should be used sparingly in modern academic writing: *besides, what is more, lastly, I now pass to.*

Table 35: The vocabulary of enumeration

The vocabulary of enumeration		
First and ***firstly*** are used to refer to the first item in a list; they can be used at the beginning of a sentence or inside it. These markers should not be confused with ***at first***, which is used to describe the order of events in a story or report.	*Vines are grafted, **firstly** in spring, secondly when they are in flower.* *My primary sources in this work fall into three categories. **Firstly,** I will quote from logs taken of sessions on MUDs.*	= erstens; ~ an erster Stelle
First and ***firstly*** are often preceded by collocations composed of a numeral adjective and a pluralized general noun such as ***ways, respects, reasons, questions, problems, points, advantages***, etc. Of similar frequency are adjectives ending in *-fold*: ***twofold, threefold*** etc.	*The current study differs from previous research **in several ways. First,** the majority of previous studies sampled adolescent mothers while the current study sampled pregnant teens.* *The methodology used in this project was **twofold: first**, a printed document was created to instruct students how to access hypertexts on a computer (…)*	
Second(ly), third(ly), fourth(ly), etc. are used to introduce the second, third, fourth item in a list.	*Economics has then as its purpose **firstly** to acquire knowledge for its own sake, and **secondly** to throw light on practical issues.*	= zweitens, drittens, viertens
In addition, additionally, and ***also*** are used to add new information. They are often used in listing several actions, and are usually found at the beginning of sentences or inside them.	*… they favored the representation of luxury in clothing and jewelry, intense coloring, and anecdotal detail. **In addition**, they developed subjects that, though inspired by European engravings, were culturally distinct …* *… the principal cereal of the Chinese is rice, not wheat, and they also eat meat, birds, fish and eggs. They are **in addition**, as is well known, great tea drinkers.* *Nevertheless, alignment to the Act has not been completed yet. **Also,** recent legal conflicts with respect to the mutual recognition of professional qualifications bear witness to frictions in the implementation of the principles of free market access in practice.*	~ außerdem, zusätzlich, darüber hinaus, noch dazu

For one thing is used to give a reason for something. It is usually followed by ***for another (thing)***, which introduces a second reason.	*His lifestyle is unusual to the villagers of Raveloe. Weavers,* ***for one thing****, are uncommon in England.* ***For one thing*** *it has a legitimizing effect, and* ***for another****, it does offer significant options for the more privileged social groups …*	~ erst einmal; zum Einen … zum Anderen
Next is used to introduce the second action in a time sequence or the second item in a list.	***Next,*** *Thoreau refers to the stories he has heard of how Walden came to be …* *… he added another treatise, Remedia amoris, on curing love. The best remedy is hard work;* ***next,*** *hunting; third, absence.*	~ als nächstes, dann
Moreover, furthermore, further and, more rarely, ***what is more*** can also be used to add important information. They are especially useful when you are trying to emphasize or prove something. These connectors typically occur at the beginning of sentences, but may also be used inside them. ***Further*** also occurs in additive constructions such as ***note further that*** or ***it should be further noted that***.	*His letters rival Cicero's in elegance and urbanity, surpass them in vivacity and wit.* ***Moreover****, his Latin was his own, not imitatively Ciceronian; it was a living, forceful, flexible speech …* *The real existence of a slight extension in the fourth dimension would,* ***moreover****, simplify certain scientific theories.* *She* ***furthermore*** *suggests that the Nereids had the ability to immortalize others …* *… they instantly reverse their opinion of him and think him to be the worst man in the world.* ***Further,*** *they all claim that from the beginning they were actually a bit suspicious of his character.* *Paragraphing is quite conservative.* ***What is more,*** *B.'s volume cannot stand alone …* *Within these aggregate figures,* ***it should be further stressed that*** *North Carolina's rural population was far more available for industrial work …*	~ außerdem, darüber hinaus, überdies, ferner, weiterhin
Further can also be used as an adverb with a simple additive meaning. In this sense it is usually placed before the verb.	*The book* ***further*** *shows that Plato anticipated the Christian project of transcending revenge.*	~ außerdem, darüber hinaus
Finally is used to introduce the last item in a list or the last action in a sequence.	*Thirdly, police work may be covert and non-deceptive, an example being passive surveillance operations.*	~ schließlich

Much the same function is sometimes served by constructions of the type ***it remains* (*for* s.o.) to-**INF.	***Finally,*** *there is police work that is covert and deceptive …* ***It remains to add*** *that a number of estate agents use printed contracts which have English translations.* ***It remains for us to define*** *uses of the "personal" in literacy instruction …*	
Last and ***lastly*** serve much the same function as *finally*, but do not occur with the same frequency.	***Last,*** *and most important, globalization has its own defining structure of power …*	~ schließlich, an letzter Stelle
Last but not least is used to introduce the final person or item in a list, in order to say that they are equally important.	*Cicero the orator, Seneca the courtier, Marcus Aurelius the emperor, and* ***last but not least,*** *Sextus the doctor.*	
Numerous markers can be used to add another point or to change the topic: ***I/we now come to, I/we now move to, we now move on/proceed/go on to* + INF *(consider, discuss, etc.), this brings us to, this leads on to, I/we now turn to, I want to turn now to, we may now turn to, (it is) to this (NP) we now turn,*** etc.	***This brings us to*** *another point, the distinction between shares of stock and certificates of stock.* ***We now move on to consider*** *some major issues related to research implementation.* ***We now come to*** *the terminology that Turner developed to interpret these ritual processes and others like them.* *However, simply changing goals may be an inadequate response by itself, since the relationship between goals and performance often demands some consideration of the organization structure.* ***It is to this we now turn.*** *With these general trends in mind,* ***let us now turn to*** *the case of the UC.*	
The same topic shifters can introduce clauses in participial form. They are then typically followed by constructions such as *there is* + NP, *we find/note/see*, etc.	***Moving now to*** *emotions, there is a school of thought in psychology, associated primarily with Paul Ekman (eg 1992, 1993), which holds that …* ***Turning now to*** *'phantasy' I will begin by pointing out that …*	
The same function of topic shift is served by markers which combine verbs such as ***explore, consider, describe*** and ***discuss*** with the adverb *now*.	***Now let us consider*** *a case where deverbalisation is indispensable.* *The analysis was divided into six main steps which* ***are now discussed*** *in turn.*	

	Each category was then further divided into semantic and lexical sets. These will now be ***discussed*** *in more detail.*	
A similar function is performed by ***the moment has now come + to***-INF.	***The moment has now come to*** *show that Nero is not afraid to see blood …*	
Such multi-word topic shifters can also be extended creatively, as shown in the examples.	***I now want to turn an analytic eye to*** *the urge to dismiss the subject.* ***As we turn to consider*** *the relationships between the play's characters,* ***we see*** *the same multiplicity of possible frames of reference …*	
to return to, returning to and ***to come back to*** can be used to resume a topic that you have already discussed.	***Returning to*** *the example of a virtual autograph given before, if the computer specifies a novelty of 0.6 …* ***To return to*** *the mosaic metaphor, diversity is hardly translating into a religious art-form …*	
Some authors combine verbs such as ***deserve, require*** and ***merit*** with nouns such as ***comment, remark, explanation, mention*** (etc.) to add a point or single out a particular topic for detailed consideration.	*Persian clover (Trifolium resupinatum), which has rapidly been gaining ground in bio-dynamic farms for a number of years,* ***deserves a quick mention*** *here.* *Roscher's conjecture (**kakws** for **kalwx**)* ***deserves a mention****.* *Some limitations of our study* ***require comment. First,*** *…* *Two aspects of the combat with Love* ***require further comment*** *here.* *The last Scottish historian whose name* ***calls for mention*** *here is Andrew Lang …* *His other works* ***hardly need mention****.* *The question of who spoke for artisans* ***requires a final comment.***	verdienen, erwähnt zu werden; einer Erklärung bedürfen (usw.)
The order of information in the collocations just discussed is reversed in expressions such as ***mention must be made of, special attention should be given to, (another) comment is necessary on***, etc. Variants such as ***only the barest mention can be made of***	***Some mention should be made of*** *the rules and procedures under which the Constitutional Convention operated from May to September.* ***A brief mention should be made of*** *fiore (The Flower), the authenticity of which has been questioned by many scholars.* ***Mention might also be made of*** *a few other general books.*	

+ NP enable the writer to (de-)emphasize the importance of a particular item in a list.	***Comment is necessary on*** *the mouldings bordering the corner angles of the crosses.*	
Much the same function is served by items containing the verb ***add***.	***It must be added, however, that*** *in one of his epigrams Callimachus returned to more orthodox Greek tastes: …* ***It may be of interest to add that*** *young Walter was not placed in an accountant's office.* *To his remarks* ***it should be added that*** *Onegin and Rudin are never so open with the women in their lives as in the letters they write to them.* *Continuing with the same example,* ***we might add that*** *people in the past were ignorant about a number of crucial properties of smallpox.*	
There are also other ways of listing or coordinating items. These are discussed in greater depth in the section on **comparison and contrast** below. For example, you can sometimes replace 'and' or 'not only … but (also)' by 'as well as', 'besides' or 'in addition to' followed by a gerund, thus achieving greater syntactic compression.	***Besides*** *be**ing** robust, they possess other characteristics. (= They are robust* ***and*** *they possess other characteristics.)* ***In addition to*** *slashing the funds for social, regional and energy policies, the Council in Brussels had rejected calls for 'first steps towards limiting agricultural spending'. (= The Council had slashed the funds …* ***and*** *had rejected calls …)* *The Council in Brussels had slashed the funds set aside for social, regional and energy policies****, as well as*** *reject**ing** demands for initial steps towards putting a limit on agricultural spending. (Gallagher 1996: 239)*	~ nicht nur …, sondern auch …
You can also use the constructions we recommended for abstracts here, with the difference that you must use first-person pronouns.	*In this section,* ***we will first discuss*** *rules in general, and then we will discuss the formal logic accounts of reasoning …* ***I will begin by describing*** *how this paper fits into the existing literature on consumption and saving.* ***Beginning with*** *an outline of how this conviction of Einstein's is based on a certain understanding of experience,* ***I will proceed to discuss*** *how Einstein brings this understanding of experience towards a theory of Cubism.*	

	I will conclude by showing *how the choice of a realist or an anti-realist position concerning a field has important consequences for subsequent research.* ***Let us begin by establishing*** *some appropriate vocabulary for this chapter.*	
another, other, a further and ***an added*** can be combined with noun phrases to introduce an additional item in a list or to change the topic.	***An added*** *advantage is that a map close to the finished product can be checked while still at the site.* *There is* ***a further*** *objection to my position, which might be rehearsed as follows.* ***A further*** *question which arises is whether …*	= ein weiterer Vorteil besteht darin, dass …
Another way of listing items clearly is by using ***the first/second/third/fourth (etc.)/next/last/final*** + NP or ***one/another/still another/yet another***.	***A first point (to note) is that*** *humans are not particularly good at one-trial learning.* ***Yet another possibility is that*** *undesirable characteristics may develop …*	= zunächst einmal ist festzustellen, dass … = es könnte außerdem noch sein, dass …
Not to speak of, to say nothing of, not forgetting and ***not to mention*** are used to emphasize an item in a list (usually the last). They can be used in widely varying constructions, of which we here show only the most important.	*Changes in grade school readers,* ***not to speak of*** *the many changes in the disciplines and programs in higher education, are signs that state power is shifting.* *The person chosen to manage the transfer of this great human responsibility,* ***to say nothing of*** *the literary inheritance, would be carrying a considerable burden.* *Thus while prior to Galta Ramanandis may have denied outright the relevance of caste* ***(not to mention*** *gender) distinction … (+ ADJ/N + N)* *Nooks in the bowels of a steam engine were hot, grimy, and cramped,* ***not to mention*** *dangerous if located near moving parts. (+ ADJ)* *… the discord that must be overcome in the physician/patient relationship,* ***not to mention*** *the physician/nurse relationship, which has deteriorated over the last forty to fifty years. (+ NP)* *Having failed to elicit support for his revolt in an audience with*	~ ganz zu schweigen von, ganz abgesehen von; nicht zu vergessen

	*Cleomenes (**not forgetting** Gorgo) at Sparta, Aristagoras of Miletos tried the same at Athens.*	
Let alone, much less, still less and ***never mind*** are used after a negative statement to emphasize how unlikely a situation is because something much more likely has never happened.	*In the final section of the article we will argue that the Act ultimately failed to confront, **much less** remedy, the crisis in English defamation law.* *These grammars are very limited in their scope compared with Hill or Sledd, **never mind** Sweet or Jespersen.* *Those who seek to enter the House of Commons and to go through the gruelling ordeals that accompany becoming a parliamentary candidate – **never mind** getting elected – are driven by an obsession.*	geschweige denn, ganz zu schweigen von
A similar purpose is served by constructions such as ***this is only part of the picture*** or ***this is not the whole story***.	*But **this is only part of the picture**. **Added to this are** fears that a major price increase would cause riots.*	
More/most important(ly) are used to introduce a point you consider to be more important than the previous one. They can link sentences or parts of sentences.	*Despite large amounts of uninteresting cyberjunk, the WWW can be a valuable research tool. **More importantly,** as schools rush to evolve their computer curricula, the very fact that students can progress from being consumers of web pages to being authors of web pages opens up a world of possibilities.* *This clearly depends on force levels, composition and, **most importantly,** on whatever restrictions may be imposed by arms control agreements.*	~ von noch größerer Bedeutung ist/am Wichtigsten ist …
The most important/significant/crucial/essential **(etc.)** ***// the main/chief/primary/strongest*** (etc.) are combined with a noun phrase to express an ascending order of importance.	*However, **the most crucial** time in our life for achieving the separation from parents is during adolescence.* *The **primary** use of cobalt is in the manufacture of aircraft engines and parts.*	~ der (etc.) wichtigste …, der Haupt-, der stärkste … (etc.)
More and ***most*** can be fairly easily combined with other sentence adverbs such as ***seriously*** and ***significantly*** to achieve a similar effect.	***More extremely,*** *books like* Finnegans Wake *exhaust print topography to a point that only computers can transcend …*	~ in noch extremerer Weise

	More gravely, *when his 25-year-old daughter, Marie-Jo, decided to shoot herself in 1978, …* *A final consequence is of course that translators should be trained to carry out this wider range of mediatory tasks.* ***More pointedly***, *they should be trained to know when not to translate.*	= schlimmer noch:
	No alternative possibility can be discussed, even conceived. ***Still more strikingly***, *even the fact that the world does not agree with us cannot be acknowledged.*	= noch auffälliger ist, dass
	… she was criticised for being an "almost exaggeratedly cultivated and sensitive Chopin player," and one who, ***more tellingly***, *"lacks a powerful, intensive tone".*	~ was noch vielsagender ist
	More worryingly, *data about safety are scarce for particular groups, (…)*	~ schlimmer noch: …, noch beunruhigender ist, dass …
	Even more worryingly, *many herbal medicines can interact with other drugs …*	~ was noch schlimmer ist …
First and foremost means 'most importantly' or 'above all'.	*Musicology has a number of branches, each largely self-contained.* ***First and foremost*** *are acoustics, the study (predominantly biological and physical) of the nature of sound …* *This work,* ***first and foremost***, *is an attempt to apply and extend aspects of lexicographic theory …*	zu allererst (ist … zu nennen)
First of all implies that this is the first thing you want to mention, but not necessarily the most important thing. It is not particularly frequent in academic writing.	*Placement relates to the curriculum in two main ways.* ***First of all***, *it plays a part in the planned development of legal skills.*	zu allererst; in erster Linie
Here too ***more*** and ***most*** can be used with specific sentence adverbs to suggest a descending order of importance or a higher degree of specificity.	***More narrowly***, *myths are attempts to explain, or at least bring nearer to our comprehension, such matters as the beginning of the world.*	

4.5 Topicalizing specific items

Closely related to enumeration is the need to give special emphasis to items worthy of note in a comparison or a list. This can be done with the help of such 'topicalizers' as *with regard to, as regards, as for, as to* and *with respect to,* which help writers to add a related point, to return to a previously mentioned point or to make sharp two-way contrasts between statements. The latter function is notably common in journalism and popular science writing rather than academic prose.

> *Having a look at the listening and speaking skill one can say that the listening skill plays even a more important role …
> → **As for** listening and speaking, it is fair to say that that the skill of listening is more important …

> Butler clearly believes in the autonomy of the conscience as a secular organ of knowledge. Whether the conscience judges principles, actions or persons is not clear, perhaps deliberately since such distinctions are of no practical significance. What Butler is concerned to show is that to dismiss morality is in effect to dismiss our own nature, and therefore absurd. **As to** which morality we are to follow, Butler seems to have in mind the common core of civilized standards.

> The restrictions we make are of two sorts: those on (1) the pragmatic function of the ironist's actions, and those on (2) the context by which readers make sense of these actions. **As for** the pragmatic functions of the ironist's actions, we first need to examine what these actions are.

> Marriages, he says, 'seem to thrive on, proportionately, a little negativity and a lot of positivity'. **As to** divorce, Gottman's research leads him to conclude: 'It is an unpalatable, but inescapable truth that some marriages cannot and should not be saved.'

Adverbs like *by the way* or *by the bye* are not normally used in academic writing. They can usually be replaced with the adverb *incidentally* or one of the aforementioned phrases. If you wish to add a footnote or an aside, you may use phrases such as *it may be noted in passing that* or *NP may be mentioned in passing* or the aforementioned constructions of the type *NP deserves a brief mention* (see 'enumeration').

> **It may be remarked in passing that** Locke's conception of a substratum or property-less subject of properties betrays the same confusion.

4.6 Exemplification

In the previous sections you learned how to arrange language material in a logical and cohesive manner by using enumerative and 'topicalizing' structures. Another thing you will need to do in writing simple paragraphs is to give examples of, or supply evidence for, the phenomena, objects or ideas you are discussing. This is the subject of the present section.

English offers abundant resources for the purpose of exemplification: constructions involving nouns like *example* or *illustration* (*we can clarify this by/with an example*), infinitive clauses (*to take an example*), the direct second-person imperative (*take, for example, ...*) the hortative (*let us consider an example*) and the inclusive (*let me give you an example*). Of these last two, the former is around five times more frequent than the latter, showing a high degree of reader orientation among native English writers.

The direct second-person imperative contributes to economy of expression; urged by journal editors to shorten the length of their original articles, academic writers may, for example, prefer the succinct imperative *take* (*, for example*) to the more elaborate sentence stem *a good example is provided by*. Since writers in German avoid second-person imperatives altogether (with the exception of *siehe*), you may have to make a conscious effort to use exemplificatory imperatives.

Some English patterns, such as the *as* + adverb + participle construction are fairly productive. 'New' adverb-verb collocations can be coined on the model of the corresponding adjective-noun collocations shown in Table 37: *striking* + *example* → *as strikingly exemplified, convenient* + *example* → *as conveniently exemplified, vivid* + *illustration* → *as vividly illustrated,* to name but three among dozens of possibilities. This is another interesting contrast with German, where much less variety is to be found.

The most important exemplifiers are briefly sketched in Table 36. A full listing is given in Table 37.

Table 36: Essential exemplificatory moves

Many English words have been taken over from other languages. **Take, for example,** the noun 'sauna'.	nehmen wir zum Beispiel ...
Many English words have been taken over from other languages. A **fine example** is the noun 'sauna'.	ein gutes Beispiel ist ...

Many English words have been taken over from other languages. The noun 'sauna' **provides** a **pertinent example**.	... liefert ein treffendes Beispiel.
Many English words have been taken over from other languages. **For example,/For instance**, the noun 'sauna' comes from Finnish.	zum Beispiel
Many English words have been taken over from other languages. 'Sauna' and 'admiral' are **such** words.	solche
Many English words, **such as** *sauna* and *admiral*, have been taken over from other languages.	wie z.B.

Table 37: Exemplification

Exemplification		
Examples are often introduced explicitly by means of nouns and verbs. The nouns most commonly used for this purpose are ***example***, ***illustration*** and ***instance***. These occur a) in a number of relatively fixed patterns, and	*see, for example, NP* *take, for example, NP* *take, as an example, NP* *consider, for example, NP* *as examples of NP, consider NP* *as a further (interesting) example, there is the fact that (...)* *as an illustration of this/by way of illustration, consider NP* *An example: (...)* *To take/give a (concrete) example, (...)* *Let us take/cite/consider/offer an example.*	Nehmen wir zum Beispiel ... Nehmen wir ... als Beispiel Betrachten wir ... zum Beispiel Da wäre zum Beispiel ... Dazu ein Beispiel: ...
b) in freer combinations, with verbs like ***clarify, demonstrate, illustrate, illuminate, indicate, make clear, give, provide, afford, see, show, be, suffice***	*We can **clarify** this **by an example**.* *This phenomenon can best be **illuminated by an example.*** *This idea can best be **demonstrated with the help of an example.*** *A few examples of this phenomenon will **make** the dimensions of this problem **clear**.* *The example of NP might **make this clearer**.*	Dies soll an einem Beispiel **erläutert**/erhellt/demonstriert/verdeutlicht werden.

	A pertinent illustration ***is afforded by*** *NP A good example* ***is provided by*** *NP* *Another such example* ***is afforded*** *by NP* *At this point, perhaps, an example* ***should be given.*** ***..., as we see from such examples as ...*** *A simple example of NP* ***is seen in the case of*** *NP* *Flowering plants also respond to their environment****, as shown by the*** *charming* ***example of*** *Linnaeus' flower clock.* *The full extension of this theme* ***is best evidenced*** *(clearly illustrated / nicely exemplified)* ***in*** *the play within the play itself.*	Ein gutes Beispiel liefert ... Hier sollte ein Beispiel gegeben werden. ..., wie man es an Beispielen wie ... sehen kann
We sometimes find other nouns or noun phrases such as ***demonstration*** and ***case in point*** used for the purpose of exemplification. ***Case in point*** usually occurs at the end of the sentence. Sometimes a phrase like '***to round off this picture***' is placed before the sentence which serves to introduce the examples.	*A vivid demonstration of the impact of experience on the developing brain is in studies of 'rich' and 'poor' rats.* *The relation of cities to their population and environment is a case in point.* ***To round off this picture,*** *we must give a concrete example.* ***To get our discussion on a concrete footing,*** *let us consider ...*	Besonders deutlich wird ... in Studien von ... Einschlägig dafür ist ... ... ist ein einschlägiges Beispiel. Um das Bild abzurunden, müssen wir ... Zur Konkretisierung unserer Ausführungen ließe sich ... anführen.
Clauses starting with ***here is/are*** and elliptical clauses are also quite common.	*A frequent example is ...* *Two examples will suffice.* ***Here are*** *some examples: ...* *An example: ...* *Further examples: ...*	... ist ein häufig genanntes Beispiel. Beispiel: ... Es folgen einige Beispiele. Weitere Beispiele: ...
Most of the aforementioned verbs, and some others besides, can be used to say that the author of a text gives an example. The name of the author is often quoted.	*Meyer also* ***cites/gives/ adduces/provides/quotes*** *(some / further / ...) examples of NP, such as NP* *the most notable example* ***cited*** *is Brazil* *as an example, Gray* ***refers to*** *NP* *he* ***cited/instanced*** *NP as an example of NP*	Meyer führt Beispiele an; zitiert, gibt, liefert, bringt Beispiele.

	he mentions NP by way of illustration *in illustration of the absurdity of NP, he* ***appeals to*** *NP*	
There are a number of adjectives that collocate significantly with 'example'.	*a(n) good, fine, splendid, prime, classic, perfect, supreme, excellent, obvious, typical; oft-cited, well-known; useful, pertinent; clear, revealing, telling, noteworthy, striking, stark; simple, elegant, crude; concrete, vivid, thought-provoking, instructive, moving, emotive, extreme; brief, small example*	gut, treffend, glänzend, hervorragend, klassisch, perfekt, herausragend, exzellent, naheliegend, typisch; häufig genannt, bekannt; brauchbar (nützlich), treffend; aufschlussreich, markant; einfach, elegant, wenig elegant; konkret, lebendig, nachdenklich (stimmend), lehrreich, bewegend, emotional gefärbt, extrem; kurz, knapp
'Example' can also be used with the participial adjective 'accompanying'.	*thirty-three categories and accompanying examples*	33 Kategorien mit (passenden) Beispielen
For example and ***for instance*** can occupy front, mid or end position in a sentence.	*For example: ...* *Some English words have been taken over from other languages.* ***For example****, the noun 'sauna' comes from Finnish.* *Some English words have been taken over from other languages. The noun 'sauna'****, for example,*** *comes from Finnish.* *Haydn was not a composer to rest upon his laurels, so the last of the set, in B flat, includes,* ***for instance****, a fantasia for the second movement cast in the unusual key of B major as well as a set of variations and a fugue.*	zum Beispiel
e.g. stands for the Latin expression 'exempli gratia' (i.e. 'for example'). It is often used between brackets to refer to or cite source texts or to introduce brief examples in the form of noun phrases.	*These examples show cases where a two-word collocation is translated as one word* ***(e.g.,*** *health insurance), a two-word collocation is translated as three words (****e.g.,*** *employment equity), and how*	z.B.

	words can be inverted in the translation ***(e.g.****, additional costs).* *Caligula proposed to put his own statue there, and the resulting furore is echoed in the New Testament (****e.g.*** *2 Thess. 2: 4).* *Bouton (****e.g.*** *1988, 1990) has argued against this summation notion, pointing out that in his own experiments the size of the CR seems to be uninfluenced by the associative value of background cues.*	
Thus is sometimes used in a similar way to *e.g.*	*The first part of Granger's investigation focuses on restricted collocations, specifically on amplifiers functioning as modifiers of adjectives (****thus****, bitterly cold, unbearably ugly)*	so z.B., wie
Such comes before a noun and refers back to an adjective in the preceding context.	*Some words represent proper names. Lynch and quisling are* ***such*** *words.* *Another way of providing linkages between individual and often seemingly unrelated stories is by grouping them under the same thematic headings. One* ***such*** *broad heading is of course 'home news', as opposed to 'foreign news'.*	solch, derartig
As when and ***as in*** can also be used to introduce typical examples.	*Verbs can be made from nouns,* ***as when*** *we say we are going to tape a programme or butter some bread.* *Verbs can be made from prepositions****, as in*** *to down tools.*	wie (z.B.) wenn wie (z.B.) bei
And the like and ***or suchlike*** suggest a list of other, similar objects.	*Where entertainment on a more humble level is concerned it seems evident from colour supplements, television documentaries* ***and the like*** *that consumers of these products*	u.ä., und dergleichen, u.a.m.

	particularly wish to be informed about those who chance to seem either substantially more, or less, fortunate than themselves. We then suppose that our community has already compiled knowledge about them in the shape of interpretants, i.e. other more discursive signs, which a more knowledgeable person might know or which might be stored in books ***or suchlike****.*	
Exemplificatory infinitive clauses can occupy front or end position in a sentence, with front position being the usual choice. They are normally based on the verbs ***take, give, cite, name, pick, use*** and ***mention***.	*Thus,* ***to take virtually random examples****, in the parable of the pearl of great price (Matt. 13: 45,46), Clement transposes the signification by extending the …* *… the properties of new chemical elements like Gallium, Scandium, and Germanium,* ***to give but a few prominent examples****.*	um wahllos einige Beispiele herauszugreifen um nur einige herausstechende Beispiele anzuführen
You can form exemplificatory clauses by combining *as* with the past participle of verbs like *illustrate, demonstrate* and *exemplify*. Clauses introduced by these exemplifiers can occupy front or end position, with end position being the usual choice.	*as strikingly exemplified by* *as shown by* *as illustrated by* *as reflected in* *as evidenced by* *as amply demonstrated by* *(etc.)*	
say	*In their view the problem of consciousness goes no deeper than the "problem",* ***say****, of breathing.*	~ sagen wir, …
among which is/are	*Whether they are, in fact, adopted in modern circumstances depends on many issues,* ***among which*** *is the intensity of the crises resulting from unsustainable management of ecological and social systems in coming years.*	~ unter denen/deren ist/sich befindet…

as witness	*... **as witness** the following: ....*	wie ... zeigt
witness	*This rule is not invariable, however; **witness** the following examples: ...*	wie folgende Beispiele zeigen/bezeugen
Notably is used to introduce an outstanding example.	*Prospects for overseas earnings will hinge on the recovery of emerging market economies, **notably** Hong Kong.*	insbesondere

4.7 Comparison and contrast

You have already learned how to elaborate on a particular topic by interlacing a simple paragraph with examples. Another common strategy in academic discourse is to compare people or things, that is, to point out either similarities or differences (contrasts), or both. In this chapter we will look at comparative and contrastive paragraphs. Often only a comparison can provide the kind of context in which a piece of writing becomes fully meaningful or relevant. By viewing the subject of your text from a new angle, you can achieve greater vividness of description and produce a lasting imaginative effect on your reader. The following sample paragraphs provide a fine example of this; comparison and contrast words have been underlined:

> (...) By a rather unpleasant irony, the US was involved in bloodshed as well. Unpleasantly ironic because **while** the Soviets stood by and did nothing in Rumania, the US was violating its pledge under the charter of the Organization of American States not to invade a neighbour. **In most ways**, of course, the downfall of Panama's General Manuel Noriega **had little in common with** Ceausescu's overthrow. The Rumanian was driven out by his own people, the Panamanian by an outside army. **The Rumanian ran and was caught; the Panamanian found sanctuary in the Vatican nunciature in Panama City** and may yet escape punishment. What the two episodes **had in common** was the simple fact that they rid the world of two dictators.
> **As tyrants go**, Ceausescu was surely **crueler, more methodical and more blood-soaked than** Noriega, who often came off as a tin-pot dictator. Yet **the similarities were striking. Like** many of their kind, both described themselves as reformers, Ceausescu as a leader independent of Moscow, Noriega as a Panamanian nationalist ... (*Time*, 8 January 1990, p. 26)

Comparisons can also help to explain complex subject-matter by referring to familiar everyday experience. The following sample paragraphs from a popular scientific work will serve to illustrate what is meant:

The death of cells and the synaptic dance

The connections between cells are constantly changing. In certain parts of the brain with particularly rapidly changing connections, it has been estimated that the average life of any one synaptic connection may be as short as eight hours. Neurones have been filmed, showing a continual, restless flux in their connections with other neurones.

It is just as well, therefore, that our sculptured brains do not lose their shape when some synapses disappear: if they did, we would all be like newborn babies, having to relearn each day the basics of living. In principle, however, the way the brain functions is little different from the way in which human organizations – companies, clubs or universities – work. These social groupings do not – unless they are very badly organized – collapse if a particular individual becomes sick or leaves. If an individual – even a very senior person – does go, the organization continues doing its job. It goes on because what it does is defined largely by the relationships between the employers, and these exist through roles and rules. Hence if the book-keeper runs off with the postroom supervisor, the organization will not grind to a halt. Other employees can be drafted in to help out in these roles. To the outsider, the organization will continue working as if nothing had happened.

So it is in your brain. Today the connections between brain cells will change, yet tomorrow your family and workmates will not notice anything different about you. This is because the billions of connections which make 'you' preserve the patterns which store your experience and memory, even when some of the individual connections in these patterns disappear. (Ian Robertson, *Mind Sculpture*, London: Bantam Press 1999, p. 12)

In this excerpt a meaningful comparison is made between the workings of an organization and the way the brain functions. The connection between the two areas is explicitly signalled by the sentence 'so it is in your brain'.

Note the use of *that of/those of* or the *s*-genitive when two things or persons are compared:

the introduction of the bill of exchange was **more significant than that of** gold coinage for international trade
a vision **strikingly like that of** the New England Transcendentalists

Note further the possibility of modifying the comparative (e.g. ***much*** *quicker*, ***far*** *better*, ***considerably*** *slower*, ***no*** *better than*, ***not any*** *better than*). Such modification is especially useful in writing data commentaries when you do not wish to enumerate long lists of data. It enables you to give readers your interpretation of the data without them having to turn to tables or graphs. Examples:

GNP per capita in the richest countries is **almost sixty times larger than** in the poorest, which also have **almost four times as many** people. The richest countries consume **nearly twenty times more** energy than the poorest.

These rates are **close to three times** the rates experienced by drivers in general at night.

Another interesting use of comparatives is in constructions which give the reason for something.

It is rather startling to recognize how little we really know about these and other fundamental problems, **the more so because** theories of education require a theory of modelling.

Table 38 presents a quick survey of the commonest ways of making comparisons in English; Tables 39 to 47 offer an in-depth treatment.

Table 38: Comparison and Contrast

Comparison and Contrast: The Essentials	
Is the soul **the same as** the body or distinct from it?	das gleiche **wie**
exactly/precisely/(not) quite/much/roughly the same	genau/(nicht) völlig/in etwa gleich
He is **similar** in appearance **to** his brother.	ähnlich **wie**
Her performance was **worse than** that of the native-born American. (*comparative + than*)	schlechter **als**
Her pronunciation was (not) **as** good **as** that of the native-born American.	genauso gut **wie**
(Un)like the native-born American, the Asian employee did not dare to contradict her boss. (*like + noun phrase*)	wie/im Gegensatz zu
As in many other matters, the party has got it wrong. (*as + prepositional phrase*)	wie
Compared with/in comparison with/compared to Clinton, Schroeder is a nobody. Similarly, in another study, suicidal patients endured more pain **as compared to** accident victims who had similar levels of injuries.	im Vergleich zu; verglichen mit
Women who remain single or childless have a higher chance of advancing to higher academic ranks. **By comparison/In comparison**, men in academia marry at a rate similar to that of the general male population.	im Vergleich dazu; vergleichsweise

Clark is not afraid of saying why he's so interested in adolescents. 'Their bodies are prettier'. Elderly bodies, **by contrast/ in contrast**, are 'awful'.	dagegen; im Gegensatz dazu
In contrast to the other celebrated architects of her time, Morgan was vehemently opposed to showiness in interior and façade.	im Gegensatz zu
Contrary to what their name suggests, all species are not red in colour; some are green, yellow or orange.	im Widerspruch zu, widersprechend, entgegen, anders als, im Gegensatz zu
Her behaviour was rather **like**/greatly **resembled** the native-born American's **in that** both of them were ready to fight for their rights.	ähnelte … insofern als
There are (clear) **similarities/differences of** approach **between** Europeans and Americans. Her approach **bore** a **resemblance** to mine. Her behaviour **is/stands in** (marked) **contrast** to the Native American's.	Gemeinsamkeit/Unterschied Ähnlichkeit haben mit im (in deutlichem) Gegensatz stehen zu
Her behaviour **differs/deviates from** that of the native-born American **to the extent that** …	sich unterscheiden/abweichen … insofern als
This only applies to prose. **It is** somewhat **different with** verse and drama.	anders verhält es sich mit
If the Clinton-Gore team can effectively respond to the global agenda – understanding, explaining and carrying out intelligent policies to meet new changes – it will have demonstrated true leadership. **But** that is a big 'if'.	aber
Studying at Stanford is hard work. The rewards, **however**, are worthwhile.	jedoch, indes, aber
Both Bush **and** Cheney are Republicans.	sowohl … als auch

Table 39: Prepositions used for comparison

Prepositions used for comparison		
The two words most commonly used in modern English for pointing out similarities are ***like*** and ***as***. Somewhat weaker in	***Like** most hobbits, Bilbo is content to stay at home.* ***Like** most Greek islands, Leros has changed hands on many occasions.*	wie

meaning is the phrase ***not unlike***. ***Like*** and ***not unlike*** are directly followed by a noun phrase.	*The adrenalin rhythm is* ***like*** *that of body temperature.* *To pass from Raymond Lully to John Duns Scotus is* ***like*** *emerg****ing*** *from Carmen into the Well-Tempered Clavichord.* ***Not unlike*** *his tougher American counterpart Ginsberg, Horovitz writes in a rather pompous style.* *My primary interest in reading James is* ***not unlike*** *Posnock's own, insofar as we both aim to present a more nuanced account of aesthetics and politics as ongoing cultural activities.*	 ganz ähnlich wie
As is placed in front of prepositional phrases starting mainly with 'in' and 'with'.	***As with*** *autism, delusions and hallucinations are characteristically absent.* ***As in*** *many similar experiments (Finn et al., 1997), participants found that …* ***As at*** *Oxford and Cambridge, the collegiate system is still alive at this university.*	(ähnlich) wie
Like collocates with a number of adverbs which normally indicate the degree of similarity: *nothing, remotely, somewhat, a bit, slightly, rather, quite, pretty much, much, very much, just, exactly, perfectly*	*The plays are* ***almost like*** *fairy tales.* *The ad showed a cuddly polar bear* ***just like*** *the one in the Coke spots.* *The department store seems* ***more like*** *the souk.* *It will wake up at scheduled intervals to receive data,* ***much like*** *a modem, at 9.600 bits per second.* *His new wife was* ***nothing like*** *him.* *I have never witnessed anything* ***quite like*** *it.* (usually with negatives) *It is* ***rather like*** *one of those 'Magic Eye' pictures.*	fast wie (→ ähneln) genau wie eher wie ähnlich wie ganz anders als
In slightly more elaborate style, a number of other adverbs are used to pin-	*… an order of monks* ***dangerously like*** *Hindu priests.*	gefährlich/verdächtig (usw.) nahekommen

point the exact nature of the likeness: suspiciously, dangerously, remarkably, uncannily, incongruously (etc.)		
A comparison with ***like, not unlike*** or ***similar to*** allows for the possibility of explicity naming the basis of comparison (the quality in terms of which two things or people are related) by using a sub-clause beginning with *in that, insofar as, in as much as* or *to the extent that.*	*My primary interest in reading James is **not unlike** Posnock's own, **insofar as** we both aim to present a more nuanced account of aesthetics and politics as ongoing cultural activities.*	insofern als

Table 40: Conjuncts used for comparison

Conjuncts used for comparison		
(just/much) as/while/in the same way that/as + CLAUSE + (so) + CLAUSE': this construction is used to say that two people or things are equal in terms of some quality (known as the 'basis of comparison', or 'tertium comparationis', cf. the first example sentence) they possess, or that the situation in the second clause depends in some way on the situation in the first clause and takes place at the same time (cf. the second example). In this kind of construction, the main clause, introduced by ***so, so too, so also, likewise*** or ***in the same manner***, is usually placed after the sub-clause. The word order in the main clause is usually inverted ('inversion') if the writer wishes to avoid using the same form of	***In the same way that** cars need fuel to help them move, we need fuel to keep our bodies going.* ***As** the city grows in size, **so** the number of citizens is likely to grow at an ever increasing rate.* ***Just as** more books are written than ever before, so they are more written about.* ***Much as** humans have hunches, favouring some new ideas over others, **so** does this program.* ***As** food is taken into the gut, **so** there is a controlled sequence by which food is passed towards the anus.* ***As** Liberty and Tyranny have no common meeting place, so protestantism and popery cannot be reconciled.* ***While** the prosecution of the war itself calls for a high degree of mobility*	So wie Autos Kraftstoff zum Antrieb benötigen, so benötigen wir Nahrungsstoffe, um unseren Körper in Gang zu halten. In gleichem Maße wie die Stadt wächst, so wächst auch die Zahl der Bürger immer schneller an. So wie mehr Bücher als je zuvor geschrieben werden, so wird auch mehr über diese geschrieben.

words in the second half of the sentence ('ellipsis').	*of labour and capital, so does the need to adjust to the very different economic situation which emerges after the war.* ***Just as*** *Emilia is the most sympathetic character in Othello,* ***so*** *is Horatio in Hamlet and the Nurse in Romeo and Juliet.*	
The construction just discussed is similar in meaning to a '***the + comparative***' construction.	***The*** *older I get,* ***the more*** *optimistic I get (= As I get older, I get more optimistic.)* ***The more*** *people you know,* ***the less*** *time you have to see them.*	je … desto, je … umso
It is sometimes preferable to use a sub-clause with ***as***, which is not normally followed by ***so*** in this case. A similar meaning can be expressed by linking two clauses introduced by comparatives. One comparative clause is sufficient if the other clause contains a verb expressing gradation.	***As*** *the threat diminishes, the instability increases. (= The smaller the threat becomes, the more instability there is.)* ***As*** *I get older, I get more optimistic.* ***The*** *denser such networks in a community,* ***the more*** *likely that its citizens will cooperate for mutual benefit.* *The pressure of spending seems to grow* ***the more*** *that is spent.*	Mit der Abnahme der Bedrohung wächst die Labilität. je enger …, desto eher … … je mehr
A similar function can be performed by the patterns found opposite. The sometimes concessive nature of these patterns may be reinforced by the use of adversative conjunctions (***nevertheless***) or comparatives (***far more difficult***). Note that ***much as*** can be both fully equative and fully concessive.	***Harsh and disturbing as the Athenians may be*** *at times, they* ***nevertheless*** *have a positive, if rather bleak, project.* ***Trivial as the story is,*** *its idyllic charm is ingratiating.* ***Much as*** *they differ on parts of the picture and other issues, there is a shared belief across this spectrum that history changed course dramatically when Kennedy was assassinated …* ***As much as*** *humans might like to repudiate myth and*	so (sehr) … so

	archetype, it seems unlikely to me that humans can do without them.	
To the extent that is used to show how far something is true.	*That means it is only necessary for us to lean on the United States* ***to the extent that*** *the other Allies lean upon us.*	in dem Maße, wie
both … and	*Both Airbus* ***and*** *Boeing have been working on designs for a doubledecker super-jumbo, capable of carrying 800 people.* *Diaghilev and Stravinsky* ***both*** *preferred Massine's choreography to Nijinsky's.* *Quinn* ***and*** *Gooding,* ***both*** *35, have signed 18-month contracts.*	sowohl … als auch beide
alike	*Common sense and law* ***alike*** *dictated the police should be subject to no sanctions.* *Surgeons are regarded as notoriously arrogant by students and nurses* ***alike****.*	sowohl … als auch; ebenso wie
not only … but also ***not only … also***	*Another major step that must be taken by the federal government, to affect* ***not only*** *telecommunications* ***but also*** *many other aspects of U.S. business …* *Libraries not only collect and preserve material; they* ***also*** *provide access to it.*	nicht nur … sondern auch
together with ***along with*** ***in combination with*** ***in conjunction with*** ***in tandem with***	*A simple form of problem list used in clinical practice is shown,* ***together with*** *a case illustration, in Table 12.* *Doubts about Yeltsin's grip on power,* ***together with*** *concerns about his health, are alarming the West.* *BAC* ***along with*** *several other theatres in London*	mitsamt, nebst, samt, (zusammen) mit; in Zusammenarbeit mit; in Verbindung mit

	operates a pay-what-you-can scheme.	
You can sometimes replace ***and*** or ***not only ... but (also)*** by ***as well as, besides*** or ***in addition to*** followed by a gerund, thus achieving greater syntactic compression.	***Besides*** *being robust, they possess other characteristics. (= They are not only robust, but also possess other characteristics.)* ***In addition to*** *slashing the funds for social, regional and energy policies, the Council in Brussels had rejected calls for 'first steps towards limiting agricultural spending'.* *The Council in Brussels had slashed the funds set aside for social, regional and energy policies,* ***as well as*** *rejecting demands for initial steps towards putting a limit on agricultural spending.*	Sie sind nicht nur widerstandsfähig, sondern besitzen auch andere Eigenschaften. Der Brüsseler Rat hatte die Mittel für die Sozial-, die Regional- und die Energiepolitik erheblich gekürzt und die geforderten "ersten Schritte zur Eindämmung der Agrarausgaben" abgelehnt.
apart from	***Apart from*** *anything else, there must always be two totals given when presenting the size of a person's vocabulary: one reflecting active vocabulary and the other reflecting passive vocabulary.*	~ abgesehen von, außer
neither ... nor	***Neither*** *he* ***nor*** *others involved in the campaign can provide detailed accounts as to how the money was spent.* *While* ***neither*** *as extreme* ***nor*** *as obvious in Britain as in Africa, malnutrition nevertheless remains a problem here.*	weder ... noch
not ... any more than: This pattern involves a negative clause followed by a clause introduced by ***any more than***. Unlike the patterns discussed above, it is used to say that the situation in the first clause is equally untrue or un-	***Not*** *all women are* ***'carers'*** ***any more than*** *all women are 'victims' or 'contractors'.* *According to Freud, one cannot disown these evil impulses* ***any more than*** *one can disown the id from which they originate.*	sowenig ..., sowenig nicht ... ebensowenig wie

desirable as that in the second clause.	*Theiaitetos sleeping is* ***not*** *quite the same as Theiaitetos waking,* ***any more than*** *Alcibiades drunk is Alcibiades sober.*	
other than	*I see no reason,* ***other than*** *fear, why that should make shorter and more occasional loves impossible.* *In paintings* ***other than*** *portraits, he gave too much prominence to physical features …* *The aesthetic is what allows us to imagine ways of life* ***other than*** *those we live.* *… the recent proliferation of corpora devoted to languages* ***other than*** *English.* *It is impossible to think of homosexual narratives as anything* ***other than*** *marginal or supplementary.* *None* ***other than*** *Einstein made that remark.*	außer … andere Lebensweisen als … … anderen Sprachen als … kein geringerer als

Table 41: Discourse devices used for comparison

Discourse devices used for comparison		
so + do/be ***do/be + too***	*The Neo-Impressionists evidenced the same concern, and* ***so did*** *Van Gogh /* ***and*** *Van Gogh* ***did, too.***	ebenso, und auch, und gleiches gilt für
neither/nor + do/be	*Bob McIsaac's crimes are not blamed on circumstances,* ***and neither/and nor*** *is Myrla's prostitution.*	ebenso(wenig)
The pattern ***the same goes for*** is used to say that what has been stated about one person or thing is also true of another one. This pattern has a wide range of variants. Some examples:	*Strictly speaking, what we hear is not a coach in which we might travel, but its noise.* ***The same goes for*** *the coach we see.* *Working women, especially if they have children, may not have time for*	gleiches/entsprechendes/analoges gilt für

1. ***the same is true of/ for/with*** NP 2. ***the same can be said of/for*** + NP 3. ***the same is true where*** + CLAUSE 4. ***Likewise (with)*** + NP	*community activities.* ***Likewise*** *working men.*	
The following patterns are similar to the above, except that they do not express sameness but similarity: • ***similarly for/with/in*** + NP • ***similar considerations hold for*** + NP • ***a similar statement can be made about/of*** + NP • ***something similar happens with/in***	*[1iii] has any number of possible answers, and is therefore an open question;* ***similarly with*** Who attended the meeting?, *and so on.* *The tensions and ambiguities of action, knowledge and meaning lived by Oedipus are thus reflected in the formal structure and language of the play.* ***Something similar happens in*** *a Socratic dialogue.*	

Table 42: Nouns, verbs and adjectives used for comparison

Nouns, verbs and adjectives used for comparison		
There is a fairly wide range of nouns which imply some sort of similarity: ***similarity, resemblance, likeness, points of similarity, points of resemblance, points of contact, parallel, analogy*** They are here shown with the verbs and prepositions that most commonly go with them.	*s.o./s.th. bears a/many a/more than a* ***resemblance*** *to s.o./s.th.* *s.th. has clear* ***resemblances*** *with s.th.* *s.th./s.o. bears/shows/displays a/more than a/some* ***similarity*** *to/with s.th./s.o.* *there is/are a* ***similarity/similarities*** *among/between* *there are* ***similarities of*** *background and approach/****in*** *style*	Ähnlichkeit
	a close/clear/interesting/obvious/striking/direct/exact ***parallel***	Parallele
	s.o./s.th. bears a ***likeness*** *with s.o./s.th.*	Gemeinsamkeit
	s.o./s.th. has an ***affinity*** *with s.o/s.th.*	Affinität

	there are few ***points of similarity/points of resemblance/points of contact*** *between X and Y*	Berührungspunkte
similarity and ***resemblance*** also occur with a great variety of adjectives	*a superficial, slight, vague, certain, clear, striking, strong, close, remarkable; uncanny; stylistic, cultural* ***resemblance, similarity*** *there are certain / many / several* ***similarities*** *between …* *the* ***similarities*** *are striking: …*	Ähnlichkeit, Gemeinsamkeit
The nouns in question can also be used with other verbs in order to say that the author of a text makes some sort of comparison.	*Gallagher sees, notes, finds, detects a* ***similarity/ parallels*** *between / among …* *Peters then offers an* ***analogy*** *between the balanced individual and a balanced society.* *Francis makes / draws an* ***analogy*** *with s.o. / s.th.* *Kleinschmidt suggests a* ***likeness*** *between X and Y* *The* ***analogy*** *I made was with a factory worker.*	
Other predicate structures used for expressing likeness include: ***have … in common, resemble, be/look the same (as), be alike, be similar to, correspond (to/with), be equivalent (to), match, to be s.o.'s equal (in)***	*They* ***have*** *certain / many / several things / features / aspects / qualities / characteristics* ***in common.*** *They vaguely / closely / clearly / greatly* ***resemble*** *each other.* *After the earthquake the city* ***resembled*** *a battlefield.* *He looked* ***just the same as*** *his sister.* *No two electrons are* ***alike****.* *No two men's goals will be* ***the same****.* *Paul is very* ***similar*** *in appearance to his brother.* *A 22% increase in car travel* ***corresponds*** *with an 18% drop in cycle mileage per person.*	gemeinsam haben, gleichen, ähnlich sein, entsprechen, übereinstimmen mit, verwandt sein mit, zusammenhängen Kein Elektron gleicht dem andern.

	*Is thirty pounds **equivalent** to 100 marks?* *This **corresponded** with findings by the French neurobiologist Broca.* *Their strengths in memory and spatial skills **matched**.*	
analogous, common, identical, comparable, parallel, similar, related	*Emotional intelligence and social success are closely/loosely **related**.* *broadly/almost/roughly/not strictly/not remotely/closely **comparable*** *extremely/remarkably/strikingly/uncannily/very/broadly/quite/rather/somewhat/superficially **similar***	analog, gemeinsam, identisch, vergleichbar, ähnlich, verbunden
As with the preposition *like*, ***in that, in as much as, insofar as*** and ***to the extent that*** can be used to introduce sub-clauses which state the basis of the comparison. When there is no sub-clause, the basis of comparison is usually introduced by *in* or *with respect to.*	*The two poets resemble one another **in that** each is inexperienced and youthful.* *Genetic relatives tend to be alike not just **in** facial features, but **in** all sorts of other respects as well. For instance, they will tend to resemble each other **with respect to** genetic tendencies to play.*	insofern als was ... angeht
Another way to express similarity is to negate some of the words and phrases implying contrast which are explained below.	*This is **not unlike** the example mentioned earlier.* *... there is **not much difference** between ...* *... very often it is true that there is **no practical difference** in meaning between two different expressions ...* *Program effects showed **little difference** in achievement between SFA and control students.* *... in Milton's day there was no **great divide** between moderate conformists and moderate puritans ...*	nicht unähnlich kein großer Unterschied

Adjectival phrases can also be used to make comparisons. Examples are ***in agreement with, in accordance with, concordant with, in line with, in keeping with***	*Milosevic's lifestyle is* ***in keeping with*** *his image as a man of the people.* *His interest in the developmental aspects of these difficulties is also very much* ***in line with*** *current thinking.*	in Übereinstimmung mit

Table 43: Sentence connectors used for comparison

Sentence connectors used for comparison		
If you want to reinforce a point you have just made, or add some detail that is closely related to what you have just said, you can use the sentence connectors ***in the same way, likewise, by the same token, equally, correspondingly*** and ***similarly.***	*Such redundant discussions of familiar issues threaten to overwhelm and obscure rather than reinforce the valuable particular contributions which this study makes.* ***Likewise*** *the summaries of past scholarship, sometimes on incidental or peripheral matters, tend to be overexhaustive and to distract attention.* *We live in a time when film-actors are elected to political office, ranging from the mayoral to the presidential, and when sitting presidents, both Democratic and Republican, do not disdain to appear on Saturday Night Live.* ***By the same token****, the nation in which I now write has formally espoused, and hitherto has (however imperfectly) striven to protect, not only its citizens' life, liberty, and pursuit of happiness, but also specifically their freedom of expression.*	Wir leben in einer Zeit, in der Filmschauspieler in politische Ämter – vom Bürgermeister bis hin zum Präsidenten – gewählt werden und in der amtierende demokratische und republikanische Präsidenten es nicht für unter ihrer Würde halten, in der Samstagsnachttalkshow aufzutreten. Unter gleichen Vorzeichen hat die Nation, innerhalb derer ich schreibe, nicht nur für das Leben, die Freiheit und das Glücksstreben seiner Bürger offiziell Partei ergriffen, …
to put this in perspective	*This implies that the failure rate for these controllers is at least once in 64 runs.* ***To put this in perspective,*** *imagine a human*	um das richtig zu verstehen; ~ um das ins rechte Licht zu rücken

	driver who averages one collision every 64 automobile trips!	
to understand what this means	*Coleman and his colleagues concluded that the quality of schooling a student receives accounts for only about 10 per cent of the variance in student achievement.* ***To understand what this means,*** *consider the following example: ...*	~ um sich vor Augen zu führen, was das bedeutet...
to make sense of NP, ...	*In order* ***to make sense of these data,*** *a good understanding of the cognitive behavior is necessary.*	um NP zu verstehen

Table 44: Prepositions used for contrast

Prepositions used for contrast		
You can use a fair number of prepositions to indicate contrast. These are ***unlike, in contrast to (by contrast with), contrary to, rather than, sooner than, instead of, as against*** and ***as opposed to.***	***Unlike*** *babies, we do not eat or drink just because we are hungry or thirsty.* *He predicted that building societies, many of which have issued credit cards in the last two years, would be hardest hit.* ***Unlike*** *banks, they did not enjoy the extra cushion of profits from the processing of plastic transactions for merchants.* ***Unlike*** *adherents of other contemporary religions, except Judaism, Christians regarded their religion as expressing the purpose of God in history.* *Roman society had begun to introduce a day of rest,* ***unlike*** *ancient Greece where there were not even any school holidays.*	im Gegensatz zu
	In contrast to *the other celebrated architects of her time, Morgan was vehemently opposed to*	im Unterschied zu

	showiness in interior and façade. *It is a view which, **by contrast with** that of Morgan and Engels, is now totally abandoned.*	
At variance with is the opposite of *in line with* or *in agreement with.*	*The idea of perfection as an inward condition of the mind and spirit is **at variance with** the mechanical and material civilisation in esteem with us.*	im Gegensatz zu (stehen)
as distinct from	***As distinct from** overt translation, in covert translation, the translator attempts to re-create an equivalent speech event.*	im Gegensatz zu, im Unterschied zu
Versus is used to draw a clear distinction between two or more things or ideas.	*… French gant **vs.** German Handschuh …* *The Man **versus** the State (book title)*	gegen, versus
Contrary to is used to say that something is true even though most people do not believe it to be true. It frequently co-occurs with abstract nouns like ***belief, opinion, view, assumption*** or ***intuition(s)***.	***Contrary to** popular opinion, the slim person's weight is not exactly the same every day.* ***Contrary to** many reports, government incentives for ranching have been maintained.* *They conducted what was effectively an 'industrial policy' (**contrary to** official rhetoric) …* ***Contrary to** received wisdom, this is not so.* ***Contrary to** what their name suggests, all species are not red in colour; some are green, yellow or orange.*	entgegen, im Widerspruch zu, im Gegensatz zu, wider
as opposed to	*Think about what can be accomplished by using a computer **as opposed to** using a textbook.* *Care should be taken to ensure that the content (**as opposed to** language) of the materials is neither too basic nor too advanced for the learners.*	im Gegensatz zu

as (NP-plural) go	*In fact,* ***as parties go****, the whole affair was something of a non-event.* ***As tyrants go****, Ceausescu was surely crueler, more methodical and more blood-soaked than Noriega, who often came off as a tin-pot dictator.*	im Vergleich zu (anderen Partys)
You can also use ***rather than*** or ***sooner than*** to express contrast. These prepositions introduce a thing or state of affairs that is not the case or that you do not want or approve of.	*He is indifferent* ***rather than*** *lazy.* *Some may turn to spending* ***rather than*** *saving.* *I fear it will lead to larger lists, time being spent checking the healthy* ***rather than*** *treating the ill and more bureaucracy.* *Break any of these rules* ***sooner than*** *say anything outright barbarous.* (George Orwell)	und nicht, eher … als …
instead of, in place of, in lieu of	*She mates with several males* ***instead of*** *one.* *The spaghetti and rice could be brown* ***instead of*** *white.* *Ominously too,* ***instead of*** *staying within a mile or so of home like normal dogs, they turn into restless wanderers, propagating the virus far afield.* ***Instead of*** *a decimal system like ours, the Maya worked with a system of numeration based on the number twenty.* *Nitrous oxide emissions built up* ***in place of*** *carbon dioxide.* *It is entirely reasonable for him to use the name 'Porticus Europae'* ***in lieu of*** *'Porticus Vipsania', especially in the context of this poem.*	(an)statt
as against	*For a start, the female body has a greater fatty mass than that of the male (22–25%* ***as against*** *17%) …*	gegenüber im Vergleich zu

	In 1957 the American Association of University Professors counted among its members 4239 English professors and 1160 physicists – ***as against*** *only 742 philosophers.* *How much should neonatal intensive care units have* ***as against****, for example, renal units?*	

Table 45: Discourse devices used for contrast

Discourse devices used for contrast		
Not so with …	*An autobiography seeks to tell all from beginning to end and displays a definite chronological development.* ***Not so with*** *the memoir.*	ganz anders bei …
It is different with …	*This only applies to prose. It is somewhat* ***different with*** *verse and drama.*	anders verhält es sich mit …
(…) – a contrast with	*Such items as NATO or laser would never have periods separating the letters –* ***a contrast with*** *initialisms like BBC, where punctuation is often present.*	im Gegensatz zu
it is a different/another story, it is a different/another kettle of fish, it is another/a different matter	*In 'Being Boring',* ***it is a different story****.* *Robin Smith is* ***quite a different kettle of fish.*** *Action is necessary. Whether our politicians can respond is* ***another matter.***	… liegen die Dinge anders; … ist eine andere Frage/Sache
***one thing* (usually followed by *another [thing]*), *it is one thing + to-inf.* (usually followed by *it is another [thing] + to-inf.*)**	*Planning a house is* ***one thing****, and building it* ***another****.* ***It is one thing to*** *plan a house.* ***It is another to*** *build it.* *… peaceful protest is* ***one thing****, but violent protest crosses the boundaries of acceptability.*	… ist eine Sache … ist etwas ganz anderes

the reverse/opposite is true, quite the reverse/opposite, the reverse is seen (etc.); rather the reverse	*This idea, that longer activity spans would be followed by longer sleeps and vice versa, does not find experimental support.* ***The reverse is seen****: long daytimes tend to be followed by shorter sleeps and vice versa.* *So the 'colonial' view of the self is not supported by the evidence,* ***rather the reverse****, as …*	das Gegenteil ist der Fall/trifft zu eher umgekehrt

Table 46: Nouns, verbs and adjectives used for contrast

Nouns, verbs and adjectives used for contrast		
difference	*there is a subtle/crucial/dramatic/great/major/(statistically) significant/considerable/essential/substantial/fundamental* ***difference between*** *X and Y* *there are great (etc.) differences between X and Y.* *Even so, considerable* ***differences*** *between people and cultures exist.*	Unterschied ein feiner/wesentlicher/dramatischer/großer/bedeutsamer/grundlegender (signifikanter) Unterschied
	there are ***differences of*** *(age/degree/detail/kind/quality/generation and sex/social class)* ***between/among*** *X and Y* *there are differences* ***in*** *(age/quality/****the*** *degree of …/****the*** *kind of …) between X and Y* *there are* ***differences in*** *employment status* ***between*** *men and women* *there are* ***differences between*** *men and women* ***with respect to*** *employment status* *…* ***difference*** *of form implies difference of meaning.*	Altersunterschiede, graduelle Unterschiede, Detailunterschiede (usw.)
	s.th. ***shows*** *a significant* ***difference*** *between X and Y*	

	*We found a significant **difference** in the performance of males and females.*	
contrast	*s.th. is in (marked/striking/strong) **contrast** to, with s.th.* *s.th. stands in (complete/remarkable/sharp/stark) **contrast** to, with s.th.* *s.th. **forms/presents/offers/provides** a (marked/direct/notable/paradoxical/pointed/strong/stark/striking/vivid) **contrast** to s.th.* *they **make** a sorry **contrast** even with the animals* ***there is** (a clear/no clear-cut) **contrast** between X and Y*	Gegensatz etw. steht im Gegensatz zu/in deutlichem/krassem (usw.) Gegensatz zu etw. bildet einen Gegensatz zu etw.
divergence	*the problems posed by stylistic **divergences between** German and English* *a **divergence** in methodology **between** …* *The figures show a **divergence from** previous trends.* *At the center of the **points both of convergence and of divergence** between the two philosophers is the issue …*	Unterschied, Divergenz, Abweichung
A ***disparity*** is a large difference, especially one between measurable things.	*The **disparity between** rural and urban communities still **existed*** ***… there is** (a) **substantial disparity in** the way they are measured …* ***we are still seeing** a **disparity** between their earnings*	Ungleichheit, Disparität
A ***discrepancy*** is a difference, usually a small but significant one, between things that ought to be the same.	*… there is a **discrepancy** in the experimental results.* *Reiss and Wagner (1972) found that a novel stimulus was more effective than a familiar one in*	Diskrepanz

	disrupting the CR, whereas Kremer (1972) found the opposite. *Research suggests a* ***discrepancy between*** *knowledge and understanding of ethical principles.* ***a huge/large/notable/serious discrepancy***	
dissimilarity	*to discover similarities and* ***dissimilarities*** *between …*	Unähnlichkeit, Unterschied(lichkeit)
diversity	*These figures show the* ***diversity*** *of the cases dealt with under section 2* ***a*** *(rich / wide)* ***diversity*** *of opinion(****s****) / approaches / feminist legal theorie****s***	Vielfalt, Mannigfaltigkeit eine (breite) Meinungsvielfalt
unlikeness	*…* ***unlikeness*** *of interests*	Unähnlichkeit
extremes	*… represent* ***the polar extremes*** *… somewhere in between* ***the two extremes***	Extreme, Extremwerte
distinction	*an important / key / fundamental / clear / clear-cut / marked / rigid / sharp / strong* ***distinction*** *He draws / makes a* ***distinction*** *between the laws of production and those of distribution.*	Unterscheidung
Different is the most commonly used adjective which expresses difference.	*The way the brain functions is little* ***different*** *from the way in which human organizations work.* *The dry surface of Venus is completely / entirely / totally / very* ***different*** *from that of Earth.* *quite / rather / somewhat / slightly different* *fundamentally / markedly / radically / significantly / strikingly* ***different*** *temperamentally* ***different***	unterschiedlich, verschieden

differing, countervailing, contrasting	*… **differing** perceptions of resident counselling …* *… **countervailing** tendencies …*	unterschiedlich; gegenläufig; gegensätzlich
***no comparison, not bear/stand comparison with, poles apart, world of difference, yawning gap** (etc.)*	*There is no comparison between the Irish and Danish situations.* *This writer does **not stand/bear** comparison **with** Goethe.* *… there is **a world of difference** between a farmer and a homesteader.* *… they are **poles apart*** *A **yawning gap** divides rich and poor in many countries.*	kein Vergleich dem Vergleich nicht standhalten ein himmelweiter Unterschied … trennen Welten eine riesige Kluft
be dissimilar, be unlike, contrast, conflict, be at odds, differ, diverge, deviate, depart from	*Regions no more than 100 miles apart often record unemployment rates which are **widely dissimilar**.* *The very name 'New Times' implies that what is being described is **unlike** anything that has come before.* *As writers their styles **contrast** quite dramatically/sharply/strongly.* *Our findings **differ markedly/considerably/radically/materially/significantly/greatly/widely/slightly from** those of earlier studies.* *The incidence of the disease **differs** greatly **between** countries.* *This interpretation is **markedly/profoundly/somewhat at odds with** most contemporary Western scholarship.* ***… at odds with** accepted theory/the situational context/the definition/the purposes of the law* *In doing so he **diverges from** common sense.* *One would expect the*	unähnlich sein sich (deutlich) unterscheiden, in (dramatischem) Gegensatz zueinander stehen, abweichen, divergieren

	*silver price trend curve to be the same as that of the currency trend curve. When they **diverge**, however, one is forced to look for a cause.* *How free are they to **diverge** from the syllabus?* *It **deviated from** Judaism chiefly **in** insist**ing** that the Messiah had come.* *One can **deviate** from neutrality to a greater or lesser extent.* *The native American who **deviates** in appearance from the presumed norm.* *Any translation can be shown to **depart** from the original in one way or another.* *The law should **depart** from this in cases where death is caused.*	
distinguish, differentiate (A from B/between A and B)	*Engineering has spread into so many branches that it is difficult to **differentiate** between them.* *The Diastole is a comma inserted between the parts of a compound word, to **distinguish** it from another word consisting of the same letters.*	unterscheiden
the contrary, the reverse, the opposite	*The writer does not foresee nor conjecture: he projects; for the reader of the book, it is quite **the contrary**.*	Gegenteil
Another way to express contrast is to negate some of the words and phrases implying similarity which have been explained above.	*s.th. bears **no/little resemblance** to s.th.* *s.th. has **no similarity** with s.th. (etc.)*	

Table 47: Conjuncts and other sentence connectors used for contrast

Conjuncts and other sentence connectors used for contrast		
But is the most general of contrastive (or concessive) linking words. It helps the writer to deny something that follows from what has been said before. It can co-occur with a large number of other discourse markers, but not with *however*. It is, we may note in passing, a myth that there is something wrong in beginning a sentence with *but*.	*The situation in countries where English is primarily a second language is fluid and varies. In the past these countries have looked to British and American English for language norms.* ***But*** *there are indications that in some countries – such as India, Nigeria and Singapore – local models of English are being sought that are based on their educated varieties.*	aber
But may imply contrast between various syntactic units, e.g. between two clauses or sentences (1,2) or two adjectives (3,4,5). ***But*** may co-occur with a number of other linking words, but not with ***however***.	1. *I knew this represented a departure from traditional notions of research,* ***but*** *it compelled me in a way the other methods did not.* 2. *There is a great deal of activity in this subfield of linguistics,* ***but*** *unfortunately there is no space to discuss it here.* 3. *A fall in the price of a particular kind of tea may cause it to be substituted for an inferior but cheaper variety.* 4. *… the introduction of some difficult* ***but*** *clearly valuable change in teacher attitudes …* 5. *… the lyric* ***but*** *combative genius of Milton …*	
(not only/not merely/not simply/…) – but also	*… for it illuminates* ***not only*** the Argonautica, ***but also*** *its many models.* *The book helps us to understand the implications of formulaic language,* ***but also*** *insists on the individual originality of Homer …*	nicht nur …, sondern auch …

	This is not simply a temporal issue, ***but also*** *one of imagining the world in terms that are intrinsic to the system described.*	
but nevertheless/nonetheless	*Theaitetos dreaming is not the same as Theaitetos waking –* ***but nevertheless*** *the dreams of a wise man are not those of a vicious one.* *… an isolated* ***but nevertheless*** *characteristic response to …*	aber nichtsdestotrotz; allerdings
but rather	*… the practice of surrogate mothering is not a threat to the family,* ***but rather*** *promotes the family as the basic unit of society …*	sondern vielmehr
but yet	*The difference is fundamental, but it is only one of degree. Biology tends to show that the animal and vegetable kingdoms have a common origin.* ***But yet*** *there are fundamental differences between mammals and trees …*	(und) dennoch; allerdings
not … but	*The association is* ***not*** *haphazard or accidental,* ***but*** *causal.*	nicht …, sondern …
However is very similar to *but* when used at the beginning of a sentence. It also signals that the sentence it introduces is a denial of, or contrast with, something which has been said before. It may also introduce an element of concession. ***However*** is more common in the middle of the clause than at its beginning or end. As can be seen from the example sentences, ***however*** can occupy a large	***However****, there were no adverse effects.* *… was,* ***however****, a little publicised event …* *policy has* ***however*** *been dogged by an excessive fear of* *In private,* ***however****, all are making judgements about the …* *… managed to rectify this omission,* ***however****, by playing a hitman …* *… sounded a little attenuated,* ***however****, and the general attack …*	jedoch, indes

number of different positions in a sentence.	*Some bankers, **however**, are beginning to have doubts about …* *The rewards, **however**, are worthwhile.* *Sir Leon stressed, **however**, that …* *The fact remains, **however**, that …* *World War I claimed a heavy toll in lives. However (not: *nevertheless), the number of casualties in World War II was even higher.*	
Nevertheless and ***nonetheless*** are stronger than ***however***. Unlike ***however*** they can only be used to contrast facts about the same thing or idea already mentioned in the previous sentence (cf. the first example given).	*In the time period covered by this collection, few if any **women** were acknowledged as scholars. **Nonetheless women** read, discussed, acted in and wrote about the plays of Shakespeare.* *As Cronquist has pointed out, most evolutionary scientists have been zoologists and have given relatively little thought to the very different problems of plants. **Nevertheless** botanists have long been aware of the difficulties and have offered many explanations for them.* *(+ but) Lamont thus reiterates C.H. George's warning about relating Puritanism to modern abstractions but **nevertheless** concludes the book by arguing that there are certain interconnections between Puritan dilemmas and those of twentieth-century society, citing the works of John Updike to support this claim.* *(+ while) **While** his book is more interested in crime, it seems, than in poverty, it is, **nevertheless**, a welcome contribution to an*	nichtsdestotrotz, trotzdem, nichtsdestoweniger

	area of modern literary studies and, as such, it is decidedly one of the better books on the subject. *Although John is poor, he is* ***nevertheless*** *happy.*	
While, whilst and ***whereas*** are used to point out a difference or a contrast. (***while*** and ***whilst*** may also imply a concession; see the next chapter)	*11 per cent of those surveyed said they were in favour,* ***while*** *the overwhelming majority did not support the government.* *Vic Wine's appropriately named 1993 Cinquaint Cabernet is buttery and pleasant,* ***whilst*** *the 1993 Cinquainte Cabernet and Merlot delivers finer, softer juicy plum fruit.* ***Whereas*** *dieting may cause your metabolism to slow down, exercise will speed it up.*	während, wo(hin)gegen; zwar … aber
Where can sometimes be used in a similar sense.	*Sometimes a teacher will be listened to,* ***where*** *a parent might not.* *What business is it of the state if someone now wishes to be known as a woman,* ***where*** *previously she was considered a man?* ***Where*** *Ayto's paper offers semantic analysis, Stock presents corpus evidence.*	~ wohingegen; in Fällen, wo
On the contrary is used to introduce a sharp contrast with, or a correction of, the main idea of the previous statement, which is usually in the negative; in other words, it expresses contradiction or complete disagreement and should not be confused with ***by/in contrast.***	*It emerged that not only was there no reliable evidence of guilt, but,* ***on the contrary****, there was considerable proof of innocence.*	im Gegenteil
On the other hand usually introduces a contrast between two different 'sides' or qualities of the same thing or person.	*When the idea of twelve was reached, the number became a favourite because it was so pleasantly divisible by five of the first six digits; and that duo-*	~ dagegen; auf der anderen Seite

It often co-occurs with ***and, and yet, but*** and ***while***. It is sometimes, but by no means always, preceded by ***on the one hand.***	*decimal system was born- which obstinately survives in English measurements today. Thirteen,* ***on the other hand****, refused to be divided and became disreputable and unlucky forever.* *(+ while) We cannot properly estimate the achievements of prehistoric men, for we must guard against describing their life with imagination which transcends the evidence,* ***while on the other hand*** *we suspect that time has destroyed remains that would have narrowed the gap between primeval and modern man.*	
In contrast, by way of contrast, in *(adjective)* ***contrast*** *[e.g. in dramatic contrast, in apparent contrast, in striking contrast]* suggest various degrees of difference. They introduce sentences which must be interpreted as a contrast with something explicitly stated in the previous sentence.	*When human beings let their conditioning interfere with their reasoning, they will make wrong judgements.* ***In contrast****, when they base their reasoning on values, they tend to make right judgements.* *Short, straightforward relative clauses pose no problems for the translator in that they can normally be rendered literally into English.* ***By way of contrast****, lengthy and complex sentential relative clauses seem contrary to accepted modern English usage and must be translated using a variety of linking devices.* *The 1970s had been a time of agressively asserted economic nationalism, a decade peppered with nationalizations and swepping indigenization programs.* ***In dramatic contrast****, the beginning of the 1980s found Africa at a developmental impasse.*	im Gegensatz dazu, im (krassen) Widerspruch dazu (usw.)

Contrariwise is a formal word indicating that the argument is moving in a new direction.	*In any case in which one penetrates beyond the directives or the rules to their underlying justifications one has to discount the independent weight of the rule or the directive as a reason for action. Whatever force they have is completely exhausted by those underlying considerations.* ***Contrariwise,*** *whenever one takes a rule or a directive as a reason one cannot add to it as additional independent factors the reasons which justify it.* *If the marginal cost of any output (y) is less than the price, sales revenues will increase more than costs if output is increased by one unit (or even a few more), and profits will rise.* ***Contrariwise****, if the marginal cost is greater than the price, profits will be increased by cutting back output by at least one unit.*	umgekehrt, im Gegenteil, andererseits
Conversely is a formal word which introduces a sentence expressing the opposite of the statement made in the previous sentence.	*An alien woman does not, as formerly, automatically assume British citizenship on marriage to a British citizen.* ***Conversely****, a woman who is a British citizen does not automatically lose her citizenship on marriage to an alien.* *If the climate changes, then obviously the weather changes. But* ***conversely,*** *each day's weather affects the climate, however infinitesimally, either maintaining the status quo or helping to tip the balance towards climatic change.*	umgekehrt

	In the immediate aftermath of any suddenly bearish sentiment, share prices in the two property sector giants Land Securities, which alone accounts for a fifth of the property sector, and MEPC tend to bear the brunt. ***Conversely,*** *though, they recover sooner than other property stocks.*	
Instead proposes an alternative to, or an alternative interpretation of, what has gone before.	*Nevertheless, pressure lightened on the pound yesterday as financial markets decided to wait for the Chancellor's speech later today. But there are few expectations that policy changes will be announced.* ***Instead****, the Chancellor is expected to offer a reaffirmation of the Government's commitment to a 'firm pound', which might provide temporary support for sterling.*	stattdessen, eher (noch)
rather	*There is no such thing as the definitive interpretation of a text;* ***rather,*** *texts are of a plural nature …*	vielmehr
in fact/in reality help the writer to deny something which has just been explicitly stated.	*In the temple at Karnak there was now a large harem, supposedly the concubines of Amon, but* ***in reality*** *serving to amuse the clergy.*	in Wirklichkeit, in Wahrheit
The following patterns are used to say that what has just been stated about one person or thing is not necessarily true of another one: • ***The same cannot/could not be said of/for/about + NP*** • ***The same is not the case for/is not true for (or: of, with) + NP***	*The exact purpose of Bristol's earliest Atlantic explorations remains uncertain, but* ***the same cannot be said of*** *the projects of John Cabot.* *Matthew Arnold, like his father before him, was strongly opposed to slavery;* ***the same could not be said of*** *Thomas Carlyle.* *In a market economy, investments in physical capi-*	Anders verhält es sich mit …

• ***It/the situation/the position/the picture/the case (etc.) is different/otherwise (obsolesc.) with/in + NP; NP is different*** • ***Not so (with) NP*** • ***it is a different/another story/matter with/for/ in + NP*** • ***It is a different story/matter when/if + CLAUSE; it/the case (etc.) is different/otherwise (obsolesc.) when/ if + CLAUSE*** • ***NP is (quite/entirely/ altogether) another/a (very) different matter; another/a (very) different story (entirely/altogether)*** • ***The same considerations/conclusion(s)/remark(s) do not hold for/ are not valid for + NP***	*tal that can be expected to yield more than the normal market return will always be made.* ***The same is not true for*** *investments in human capital. They will be made only if the human in question (or his parents or someone else who values his future welfare or trusts him to pay back loans) can provide the necessary capital.* *For white South Africans, rugby is as much an obsession as it is for New Zealanders.* ***It is different with*** *blacks. Outside the Eastern Cape Province, most black South Africans do not give a fig for rugby ...*	

4.8 Concession

A concessive string of sentences helps you to indicate that one part of what you are trying to say is wrong or surprising in the light of the other part. More precisely put, concession indicates a reversal in outlook or result despite an adverse condition. In hypotactic constructions (i.e. main clause + subordinate clause), this means that the content of the main clause runs counter to expectation given what is said in the concessive clause.

If the whole paragraph is concessive, there is a constant shift between thesis and antithesis, usually leading to a synthesis in the concluding sentence:

> To be able to drive is undoubtedly a useful accomplishment, and the ownership of a car is for many people a fact of life that reaches beyond convenience into sheer necessity. On the other hand, all possessions are a burden, and a car may rank among the heaviest. It is expensive to maintain, it makes the owner a prey to vandals, thieves and pedestrian acquaintances, and it exposes him to the risk of accident. Against these considerations he has to weigh the privilege of travelling in door-to-door comfort, the freedom of deciding when he will travel, the value of time saved, and (if he cares for such things) the pride and joy of property. (Nash 1980)

Table 48 provides a brief overview of concession; Table 49 presents a detailed survey.

Table 48: An overview of concession

An overview of concession	
Although 1956 is the earliest stated date for entries, the program will accept a date as early as 1951. **Although** I disagree with the author, I must admit that such statements are out of place here.	obwohl, obgleich
This is an interesting argument**, even if** I find it unpersuasive. Is there a sense in which we are morally responsible for our dreams **even if** we cannot control them?	auch wenn; obwohl
11 per cent of those surveyed said they were in favour, **while** the overwhelming majority did not support the government.	während, wohingegen
In spite of all their troubles, the royal family still believes they can count on us.	trotz
It is very old-fashioned to use such Latin contractions as *ibid.* (lit. 'the same place') or *op.cit.* (lit. 'the work cited (above)'). **However**, the Latin *passim* (meaning 'throughout') is a useful way of indicating that the subject matter is found regularly throughout the work you are referring to, and not on particular pages.	jedoch, hingegen, dagegen, indes (**contrast between aspects of the same thing or between different things**)
In the time period covered by this collection, few if any women were acknowledged as scholars. **Nonetheless/Nevertheless** women read, discussed, acted in and wrote about the plays of Shakespeare.	trotzdem, dennoch, nichtsdestotrotz, nichtsdestoweniger (**contrast between aspects of the same thing only**)
It has often been said that if Parliament ceased to talk for 12 months, the country would suffer no inconvenience, and many people would probably be glad. **On the other hand**, if the LCC ceased to work for a few days, indescribable chaos would result, and the health of London be seriously jeopardised.	auf der anderen Seite, dagegen
This is, **of course**, a minor mystery, but an interesting one. This is a very patchy book, **certainly; but** it contains writing of vividness, wit and colour.	zwar – aber

Table 49: A detailed survey of concession

	Group 1: Conjuncts and other sentence connectors	
but	(cf. the preceding section)	aber, jedoch
although, though	*In this regard, I have been guided principally by Finegan (1994), which* ***although intended*** *as an introductory linguistics text, provides a very useful overview of the interaction of pragmatics with syntax.* *Gullestead found, in a 1984 study, that friendships between women*, ***although perceived*** *by the husbands as undermining, often were found to strenghten the marriages.* *Declarative statements are rare in this book –* ***although*** *less rare than in the earlier versions.* *Much of the material in this book has appeared in articles,* ***though*** *apparently in significantly different form.* *… proved to be a more efficient –* ***although*** *less flashy – alternative method for transferring files.* ***Although*** *not necessarily so, it is probably true that nowadays corpora are stored in machine-readable form.* ***Although*** *not significant, there was a trend for earlier detection of HSV in rolling diploid cell cultures.* ***Though*** *a Myndian outlander, he has gained access to the elite Greek world.* *Ling's illustration,* ***though*** *a detail, has the virtue of including a portion of the elaborate florals that frame the figural composition.* *He provides,* ***though*** *again only in translation, a fascinating papyrus text explaining …* *Somehow to see through this veil to 'what was actually happening',* ***though indeed*** *an historian's credo, is a feat which, in this case, requires endurance with singularly recalcitrant source materials.*	obwohl, obgleich; allerdings
Strictly speaking, ***even if*** is used to introduce conditions rather than concessions; however, in conjunction with lexical phrases such as 'one assumes', it can express concessive meanings.	***Even if*** *one assumes that interactive fiction is a novelty, that does not negate its significance for the future study of writing.* ***Even if*** *a college is not connected to a major network, the asynchronous peer-critiquing network presented here can be replicated by using a modem to dial directly into schools' mainframe computers.* *And for the pantheist the fact that 'X is wrong' will be explained, and partially analysed, in terms of (****even if*** *not reducible to) non-natural facts about the divine Unity.*	auch wenn, selbst wenn; wenn auch; obwohl

even though	***Even though** human minds are different from AM in many ways, some broadly similar questions would be relevant in deciding whether to call a human mathematician creative.*	obwohl; wenn auch; selbst wenn
while, whilst, whereas	*11 per cent of those surveyed said they were in favour, **while** the overwhelming majority did not support the government.* *Vic Wine's appropriately named 1993 Cinquaint Cabernet is buttery and pleasant, **whilst** the 1993 Cinquante Cabernet and Merlot delivers finer, softer juicy plum fruit.* ***Whereas** dieting may cause your metabolism to slow down, exercise will speed it up.*	während, wo(hin)gegen, zwar … aber
where	*Sometimes a teacher will be listened to, **where** a parent might not.* *What business is it of the state if someone now wishes to be known as a woman, **where** previously she was considered a man?*	~ wohingegen; in Fällen, wo
granted (that) has a similar meaning to ***'it is true that'.*** It often adds a valid afterthought.	*I refer frequently to Montaigne because he was available to Shakespeare in translation and because he is such a good witness to the impact of Stoicism in Europe at this time, **granted that** (= although it is true that) he repudiates some of its teachings in his later essays.* ***Granted**, success feeds on success and publishers who pay fabulous sums for rights tend to throw the weight of their publicity machines behind a book. **But still**, sight unseen, why have people who rarely buy books scrabbled to buy this one?*	auch wenn (man bedenken muss, dass) zugegeben(ermaßen), natürlich
but then	*To begin with, there should be no doubt that slips of the tongue often reveal one's hidden thoughts and feelings. However, it seems equally obvious that people might be unable to control or avoid making Freudian slips. **But then** if slips of the tongue are outside the agent's control, in what sense can we justifiably hold someone responsible for them?*	allerdings
but then again	*Credibility might be a problem. **But then again**, credibility has always been a problem.* *He asks whether the worship of such personifications represents 'in any way a new phenomenon, as has often been supposed' (235). The answer is no, and yes. Abstractions are common in archaic (and I would add, poetic) thought, but now in the 330s 'were claiming a substantial share of the public ritual budget' (236), **but then again** figures such as Demokratia are 'givers of blessings', much like traditional gods.*	allerdings; aber andererseits

however As can be seen from the example sentences, ***however*** can occupy a large number of different positions in a sentence.	***However****, there were no adverse effects.* *... was,* ***however****, a little publicised event ...* *policy has* ***however*** *been dogged by an excessive fear of* *In private,* ***however****, all are making judgements about the ...* *... managed to rectify this omission,* ***however****, by playing a hitman ...* *... sounded a little attenuated,* ***however****, and the general attack ...* *Some bankers,* ***however****, are beginning to have doubts about ...* *The rewards,* ***however****, are worthwhile.* *Sir Leon stressed,* ***however****, that ...* *The fact remains,* ***however****, that ...*	jedoch, aber
Placed at the end of a clause, ***though*** is similar to *however* in meaning but more informal.	*There is a case for saying that you rarely see much growth in US real estate and the profit is in developing. Analysts have long wanted Martins to do something 'more exciting',* ***though****.*	jedoch
nevertheless, nonetheless (none the less)	*In the time period covered by this collection, few if any women were acknowledged as scholars.* ***Nonetheless*** *women read, discussed, acted in and wrote about the plays of Shakespeare.* *Most particularly he has often been quick in the past to fend off moves against his own country, especially against its car industry. He has,* ***nonetheless****, authorised a state capital injection of Fr1bn into the plant.* ***(+ but****) Lamont thus reiterates C.H. George's warning about relating Puritanism to modern abstractions* ***but nevertheless*** *concludes the book by arguing that there are certain interconnections between Puritan dilemmas and those of twentieth-century society, citing the works of John Updike to support this claim.* ***(+ concessive participle construction****) Less varied in pace than Uncle Vanya, at times even slightly funereal, the production* ***nevertheless*** *displays the same wonderful precision of performance and, even within rather abstract action, some of the same depths of emotion.* ***(+ while****)* ***While*** *his book is more interested in crime, it seems, than in poverty, it is,* ***nevertheless****, a welcome contribution to an area of modern literary studies and, as such, it is decidedly one of the better books on the subject.* ***(+ although****) Although John is poor, he is nevertheless happy.*	nichtsdestotrotz, nichtsdestoweniger

	The England he represents is not so much irrelevant as antithetical to any modern image of Britain. ***Nevertheless****, he has saddled up the old warhorse and given it new colours.* *Weller dovetails the angles of available interpretation like a true craftsman, and rightly refuses to run off a reductive thesis.* ***None the less****, the emotional energy of the piece moves all in favour of the mother, whose communist idealism may have proved a 'pipe-dream' but was nobler than an empty heart.*	
in spite of that	*Analyst Mike Atkinson points out that there are currently some worries on the advertising revenue front, and that some television people have seen a bit of pressure.* ***In spite of that****, he believes: 'These times seem a good opportunity for long-term investors to get hold of stock.'*	trotzdem
still	*The film repeatedly cut away to police raids on criminal hideaways; and the setting was not the Korean War, but the present-day crack war in Washington DC.* ***Still****, resemblances to MASH were not fortuitous.*	dennoch
Yet often introduces a surprising fact or idea.	*That would make it extremely painful to have gone short of sterling.* ***Yet****, however great the pain, the effect of a technical approach may fail to have a lasting impact in such a bear market.*	dennoch, trotzdem, aber
on the other hand	*It has often been said that if Parliament ceased to talk for 12 months, the country would suffer no inconvenience, and many people would probably be glad.* ***On the other hand****, if the LCC ceased to work for a few days, indescribable chaos would result, and the health of London be seriously jeopardised.*	jedoch; andererseits; dagegen
all the same	*Yet only weeks ago he was saying that existing derelict land was needed for greening the cities, and providing amenities for citizens.* ***All the same****, the decision can be seen as sound enough.*	dennoch
notwithstanding	*Attempts at post office reform have brought down French ministers of state before now, notably Pierre Lelong, who held the posts and telecommunications portfolio in Jacques Chirac's government but was forced to resign after a long and bitter strike in 1974.* ***Notwithstanding****, Mr Quiles commissioned a report into strategies for reform and its controversial recommendations, made public at the beginning of last month, immediately drew the wrath of the unions.*	dennoch

that/(with) this said and ***having said that*** also imply concession, meaning 'although I agree' or 'although what I have just said is true'.	*Most serious-minded of all are the very few professional electronic journals, which are as selective and jealous of their standards as any professional paper journal.* ***That said****, some of the material on the Internet is scurrilous, biased, denigrating, abusive, lavatorial, indecent, pornographic, actionable and generally disgraceful.* *... there may be important material lurking outside the portions of text that B. did collate.* [end of paragraph] ***With this said****, it is best to go directly to Part III. Brockmann is a remarkably accurate collator.*	allerdings; dies vorausgeschickt
all right – but	*The majority rules,* ***all right****,* ***but*** *in a way which makes some people more equal than others.*	zwar ... aber
true – but	***True****, the mind is a neural net.* ***But*** *it is also a symbolic processor at a higher and more abstract level of description.*	zwar ... aber
certainly/undoubtedly/admittedly/of course ... but/yet/however	*This is a very patchy book,* ***certainly****;* ***but*** *it contains writing of vividness, wit and colour.* ***Certainly*** *composition scholars should be rewarded with tenure.* ***But*** *the movement in our profession to imitate the literature people – to prove to them that we, too, are scholars – is leading us, the compositionists, to devalue our teaching in favour of research.* *... 1994 will* ***undoubtedly*** *reveal negative growth.* ***However****, a stabilisation package announced in April of last year set out to steady markets and reassure creditors.* *This is,* ***of course****, a minor mystery,* ***but*** *an interesting one.* *Earth's organisms have not, of course, remained unchanged over their existence,* ***but*** *have evolved in response to new environmental and biotic challenges.*	zwar/sicherlich/ohne Frage ... aber/jedoch (usw.)
officially/outwardly/technically/... [– actually/really/in (actual) fact/in reality/the reality is that/the truth is that (etc.)]	***Outwardly*** *a respectable businessman, he is involved in big city crime.* *He had* ***formally*** *acknowledged,* ***actually*** *ignored, the Eastern Emperors.* *Some of the overlapping effects and voice exchanges are* ***superficially*** *quite interesting.* ***But*** *the piece remains effect-music ...* *It was clear that the order of the day, although* ***formally*** *adressed to the men, was* ***actually*** *aimed at the officers.* *In 1094 he left Bagdhad,* ***ostensibly*** *on a pilgrimage to Mecca;* ***actually*** *he went into seclusion, seeking silence, contemplation and peace.*	offiziell/von außen betrachtet (usw.) ... tatsächlich/in Wirklichkeit (usw.)

	*Then he left her, **ostensibly** to become a monk. (**In fact**, he took up with a friend of hers and fathered a child.)*	
Some conjunctions co-occur with connectors in one sentence or across two or more sentences. The conjunctions ***although/(even) though/while/ whilst/granted (that)/even if*** may thus be followed by the connectors ***yet/but/still/ however/nevertheless/nonetheless/anyway/ anyhow.***	***Though** I was sympathetic to P's case, it **still** seemed to me …* ***While** not a dualist, Chomsky **nonetheless** epitomized his conception of human nature in terms of free creation within a system of rule.* *The limiting factor is not availability of frequencies, but rather, the existence of enough listeners to justify a particular programming format. **Granted**, there may not be adequate listeners to justify accommodating every fringe or splinter faction. **However**, is it really necessary for the proper functioning of a democracy that the federal government assure platforms in every medium, in every community, for the rantings of bizarre conspiracy theorists, paranoid delusionists, flat-earthers, anarchists and others without any significant constituency?*	obwohl … doch (usw.)
although – in fact	***Although** Derrida claims to describe historical Christianity, **in fact**, his argument is based on a serious distortion of Christian practice and theology.*	zwar … aber
however/whatever/whenever/wherever	***However** international sport may be, the interest of its devotees is often narrowly national.* (cf. ADJ + as + NP + may be [see Group 3 below]: *International as sport may be, the interest of its devotees is often narrowly national.)*	So international Sport auch sein mag: das Publikumsinteresse ist häufig auf das eigene Land begrenzt.
no matter how + adjective (sometimes followed by a clause***), no matter what*** + noun (sometimes followed by a clause)	***Now matter how** fine is the attention to detail, eventually visitor sleuths will detect faults in the fakes.* *Dispositions, **now matter how** conceptualized, are key aspects of the personality construct.* *Computer software, however, **no matter what** flexibility it may claim, can never escape the instructional attitudes of its programmers.*	gleichviel, …; egal, …
regardless of + wh-word	*It defines Palestinians as refugees **regardless of whether** they left out of a "well-founded fear of persecution" …*	unabhängig davon, …; egal, …
albeit	*… we will here follow convention and treat these writings as a unit, **albeit** a not necessarily homogeneous one.*	obgleich, wenn auch

	Group 2: Prepositions	
in spite of	***In spite of** all their troubles, the royal family still believes they can count on us.*	trotz
despite	*By demonstrating that **despite** twenty years of a welfare state, poverty still persisted, especially among children and the elderly, the book challenged the social and political complacency of the day.* ***Despite** a weakening of the mark against the dollar this year, the German currency is still considered too strong.* *The occasion, **despite** be**ing** a friendly international, was marred by 47 arrests in the city before the game.* ***Despite** admitt**ing** that he is an opportunist, willing to sell in the afternoon what he bought in the morning, Soros seems to want to take a long-term stake in Blake.* ***Despite all this** some companies do offer properties catering for eight or more people …* **Despite the fact that** … (try using *although* or *even though* instead) *Despite widespread doubts that …* *Despite allegations/evidence/worries that …*	trotz
regardless of	*Poets traditionally capitalize the first letter of each line, **regardless of** punctuation.*	ungeachtet (+ Gen.)
***for + all* + NP**	*For all its length, there is not much here**, although it must be granted that** R. compares it to an Oxo cube.*	trotz
	Group 3: Multi-word Discourse Markers and Other Devices	
it is true that/ there is no doubt that/it cannot be denied that/there is no denying the fact that … but/yet/against that …	***True**, Granada TV made pounds 69.4 billion profit last year, **but** the poor lamb is forced by shareholders to 'increase profits by 15 per cent each year'.* *… **All true**, but there is often some fire behind the ideological smoke …* *Yet two years later John Major led them to victory with an eight-point lead over Labour. **True**, there was a change of leadership along the way, and Neil Kinnock was a less formidable opponent than Tony Blair looks likely to be. **Against** that, the economy was heading into recession.* ***While it is true that** a business phone-call, a lawyer's speech, a math equation and a sexual encounter are all rhythmic events, this fact tells us nothing of significance about them.*	zwar … aber (usw.)

ADJ + *as* + NP + *be*	***Trivial as the story is,*** *its idyllic charm is ingratiating.* ***Correct as Catford may be*** *in considering ..., the general assumption of ... appears problematic.*	**So** trivial die Geschichte auch ist, **so** anheimelnd ist ihre zauberhafte Idylle.
The position of the NP and the verb in the above construction may be inverted.	*Original and unique as was Novalis'* Experience of Death, ***how original and historically unique are also*** *the* Hymnen an die Nacht, *the first four poems of which we have hitherto spoken exclusively.*	So originell und in seiner Art einzig das *Todeserlebnis* des Novalis war, so originell und einsam in der Geschichte sind auch ...
much as	***Much as I admired their heroism,*** *I could not too strongly condemn their indiscipline. (or: While confessing my admiration for their heroism, I condemned in no uncertain terms their indiscipline ...)*	so ..., so
may ... but	*Rumanians* ***may be*** *jubilant,* ***but*** *they are also fearful of the uncharted world into which they have been pitched.*	so ..., so
even though ... equally (well)	***Even though*** *Seutel is romantically, almost incurably attached to his own childhood and youth, he is* ***equally well*** *aware of the dangers of the childish and adolescent mind.*	so ..., so
yet if ... equally	***Yet if*** *an adequate linguistic framework is indispensable for stylistic analysis,* ***there is equally no doubt that*** *linguistic and critical terminology is forbidding in its apparent technicality.*	so ..., so
on the surface ... careful analysis shows ***on the surface – on inspection/on closer examination***	***Though on the surface,*** *Beck's criticisms may seem valid,* ***closer analysis shows that*** *her claims often lack sufficient grounds and raise disturbing ethical questions.*	oberflächlich betrachtet ... bei genauerem Hinsehen (usw.)

4.9 Cause, reason and explanation

Cause, reason and explanation play a dual role in academic text. Writers may simply describe causal or other relations between people and things in the real world, or they may support their arguments by providing reasons and explanations that originate in their minds. Both types of causal relationships may, however, be described by means of identical or similar linguistic patterns. Thus, the prepositional phrase *as a result of* can be used to indicate causes in real life, but it can also help the writer build an argument. This is why we do not treat text-external and text-internal types of relationship separately, although some marker words, such as *therefore* and *hence*, exclusively describe text-internal relations. Table 50 presents a brief overview of cause, reason and explanation; Table 51 offers a detailed survey.

Table 50: Cause, Reason and Explanation

Cause, reason and explanation		
Since and *as* introduce the logical reason or reasons for the statement in the main clause. Someone who uses *since* or *as* invites us to follow their line of thought attentively in the hope that we will arrive at the same conclusions as they did. Put more simply, *as* and *since* often suggest that the reason given in the subordinate clause is obvious or can be taken for granted. *Since* often combines with other conjunctions at the beginning of a sentence, and it is sometimes used in elliptical subordinate clauses (*since not restricted to set form*).	***Since** morality is an expression of one's rational nature, it is essentially self-determined.* *It is felt, however, that **since** Clyne's view has been called into question (Stöckel 1984:283), such an interview would not necessarily have settled the matter.* *A trust, **since** not restricted to set form, can be construed where the law allows and the testator's intentions demand it.* *But **since** we know that y < fy, it follows that the Dice (X,Y) is never less than the true value of the Dice coefficient between X and Y.* *And since … / But since … / However, since … / Yet, since …* *… all the more so since …* ***As** these elements constitute 99 per cent of all living things, including plants, they are obviously of prime importance.*	da, weil
Because stresses the importance of the reason given in the subordinate clause. *Because* is only used at the beginning of a sentence if it refers to the cause of something described later in the clause.	*Imports of finished dairy products represent only a small proportion of total imports of dairy products **because** almost all are produced locally using imported ingredients.* ***Because** innovation will play a greater role than efficiencies, market leaders will come and go.*	weil
As a result of and its less frequent variant *as a consequence of* indicate that one action is the single, direct cause of another. These phrases often occur with the gerund (V-*ing*).	***As a result of** a contraction in Korean beef production, feed imports for cattle are expected to decline.* *Many of the women mentioned internal changes they have experienced **as a result of** parent**ing** boys.* *Occupational and recreational overuse injuries frequently occur **as a consequence of** the physical activities associated with military training an.*	wegen, aufgrund

Because of suggests a less direct link between two actions than *as a result of;* the gerund is not normally used with *because of.*	***Because of** space limitations, the passages to which comments are directed are not included in this article.* ***Because of** some glitch, the teacher was unable to run the class he or she had intended to run.*	wegen, aufgrund
This is because and *the reason is that* introduce the reason for something.	*Even if all five of the campaign elements outlined above and discussed in detail below were put into place, some number of unintended pregnancies would probably continue to occur. **This is because/The reason (for this) is that** many contraceptive methods have appreciable failure rates even under the best circumstances …*	der Grund dafür ist, dass; dies liegt daran, dass; dies ist darin begründet, dass
Therefore has very complicated position rules. It rarely occurs at the beginning or the end of the clause. More commonly, it appears in the middle of the clause, where it may occupy several different positions, such as the following: (a) after auxiliaries such as *can* or *may*; (b) between the noun subject and the verb; (c) after *and*.	*He is inconsistent and **therefore** unreliable throughout.* *This search took six minutes. It is **therefore** necessary to make the search as specific as possible.* *In normal times **therefore** a measure such as a work-to-rule does not attract much notice.* *It follows **therefore** that a measure such as a work-to-rule does not attract much notice.* *It is important **therefore** that …* *This Smaller Dictionary, intended for general consumption, can **therefore** go into any home, any school, any library.* *The Administration, **therefore**, will have to lean heavily on its new 'jawbone' policy.* ***Therefore** we have found it helpful to include …*	daher, deshalb
In academic writing *so* is rarely used at the beginning of a sentence. It is far less common than *therefore*. *Because of this* is only moderately frequent in academic writing.	*Very little material was available, and **so** in the last few years the class has been taught using student essays.* *The toilets were not properly maintained. **Because of this** we used the other building.*	daher, deshalb
Lead to and *result in* are neutral in meaning and can be followed by nouns denoting positive (e.g. *creation, integration, diploma*) or negative things (e.g. *clash, chaos, death, fall*).	*… a scheme that will **lead to** the creation of thousands of new jobs.* *Another simple command by the writer **resulted in** a printed version of the test.*	führen zu, auslösen, hervorbringen

Cause is normally followed by nouns denoting negative effects, such as *accident, addiction, agony, alarm, bloodshed, cancer, concern*, etc., but there are also exceptions to this rule: you can also cause *amusement* or a *boom*. *Cause* implies a more direct cause-effect relationship than *lead to* or *result in*.	*President Eisenhower's heart attack on September 26, 1955,* ***caused*** *a 6.54 percent decline in the Dow Jones Index.*	verursachen, auslösen, führen zu
bring with it is typically used with nouns such as the following: *redefinition, prospect(s), advances, problems*, etc.	*In the conservative world of the countryside, marriage* ***brought with it*** *expectations of a stable family life.*	mit sich bringen
stem is typically used with abstract nouns such as *fact (stem from the fact that), principles, conditions, problems, desire, inability, observation, recognition.*	*… social violence* ***stems from*** *human nature …*	herrühren von, entstehen durch
A *reason* is something suggested as the cause of an event or which provides an explanation or excuse.	*One* ***reason*** *for positing this is … Another/A second* ***reason*** *is that … A third* ***reason*** *is that …* *…* ***for*** *these* ***reasons*** *machine code is now seldom used* *Adultery was a ground* ***for*** *divorce.* *there are good grounds* ***for*** *doubt****ing*** *that* *for the* ***grounds*** *advanced in …* ***on*** *humanitarian* ***grounds***	Grund
A *cause* is the reason why something happens.	*the main* ***cause/root cause*** *of violence*	Ursache
A *motive* is a reason. It is typically used with nouns such as *behaviour, action, crime, attack, murder*, etc.	*the* ***motive*** *for their behaviour*	Motiv
An *explanation* is a statement that tells us why something happened.	*there is only one* ***explanation*** *for this*	Erklärung

Table 51: A detailed survey of cause, reason and explanation

	Group 1: Conjuncts	
since, as	***Since*** *today is a special day you may play in my study while I work there.* ***As*** *these elements constitute 99 per cent of all living things, including plants, they are obviously of prime importance.*	da, weil
especially since, especially as	*The superlative praise of Antony's description of Brutus has a powerful effect on our minds,* ***especially since*** *it comes so close to the climax of the action.*	zumal
For is rather formal and slightly old-fashioned. A ***for***-clause can only follow the main clause.	*This point is an important one for language teaching,* ***for****, as Pawley and Syder note, formulaics are ubiquitous.*	denn
Thus is often used in formal, academic writing; it is similar in meaning to *therefore*. It may occupy front-position or mid-position in a main clause. It may be placed immediately after the subordinator in a sub-clause, and may also introduce a participial clause.	***Thus****, formerly, at the Customary Court of a manor, events relating to the copyhold lands were presented by the tenants for the information of the Lord.* *Purely external history, so admirably treated in other books, is* ***thus*** *purposely kept to a minimum.* *It is believed that* ***thus*** *all pupils will be enabled to read some Latin author with understanding in the shortest possible time.* *He gets his promotion after punching the agency's biggest client,* ***thus*** *proving his honesty in a town of yes-men.*	daher, deshalb wodurch
accordingly	*... Michael discovered that the source of his difficulties was organization.* ***Accordingly****, he concentrated on work with the organization of his thesis statement.*	folglich, dementsprechend, entsprechend
consequently	*... it encourages us to view the characters as idealized, and* ***consequently*** *rather remote from the social realities of Cicero's day.*	folglich
Just like *thus*, ***hence*** can introduce main clauses and participial clauses. It is frequently preceded by *and* and followed by adjective phrases or noun phrases forming independent units.	*"Etic" (as opposed to "emic") studies engage their objects from the outside.* ***Hence*** *there is, contrastively, a "phonemics," if not a "genemics."* *In interactions involving only second-language speakers this would raise the importance of solidarity considerations,* ***hence*** *favouring BSAE as the stronger conveyor of solidarity.*	daher; deshalb wodurch

	*... the historical tendency to regard women as "other" or deviant **and hence** in need of control (see, e.g., Rothman 1982).* *... the supposedly greater proclivity towards volatile emotions to disorders of the womb (**hence** "uterus" as the root of "hysteria") ...* *For Joyce, she argues, the whole of art resides in the use of language to thwart the authority of the Father. **Hence** the importance in his work of language-play in the form of puns, irony, parody and pastiche, which recognise the rule of Law in discourse only in order to knock it down.*	
thereby	*Competition among producers always benefits consumers, who **thereby** are always winners.* *Finally, feminist perspectives tend to value the importance of narrative, **thereby** challenging the traditionally "objective" approach to case law reporting.*	dadurch, damit, auf diese Weise wodurch
with that	*English has achieved a uniquely wide spread throughout the world and, **with that**, a unique importance.*	damit
this/that is why, which is why	*The biggest yielders of revenue in underdeveloped countries are the taxes on commodities ... These are easiest to collect, administratively, when commodities pass through the hands of a few wholesalers in a small number of places. **This is why** the countries which raise the most in taxes are those which depend most on foreign trade.*	deshalb, daher, darum; weshalb
after all	*But that is not the whole story. **After all**, Mr Major has taken pride in the fact that recorded inflation is coming down, which makes it difficult to explain to the Tory party conference why interest rates have to follow the Germans up.* *His success in the competition had drawn world attention – he was the first Soviet to have won what was, **after all**, intended to put Soviet achievement on display.*	schließlich, im Grunde, eigentlich
at any rate, in any case	*These concerns in turn took their toll of equities, which **in any case** are increasingly being supported by institutional cashflow rather than expectations of company profits.*	jedenfalls; sowieso, ohnehin

anyway, anyhow	*But it would leave the Government exposed to the full force of house-buyers' fury, with no international excuse for forcing an increase in mortgage rates that would probably have occurred* ***anyway****.* *As far as I can judge, she has also more than her share of intellect.* ***Anyhow*** *she began to compose dramas at nine years of age.*	ohnehin, sowieso
	Group 2: Prepositions and prepositional phrases	
As a result of (often + V-ing) indicates that one action is the single, direct cause of another.	***As a result of a contraction*** *in Korean beef production, feed imports for cattle are expected to decline.* *Many of the women mentioned internal changes they have experienced* ***as a result of parenting*** *boys.*	aufgrund von, wegen, infolge von
Because of suggests a less direct link between two actions than ***as a result of*** (the gerund cannot be used with because of). It often co-occurs with adverbs such as *chiefly, especially, largely, mainly, mostly, (not) only, partially, partly, particularly, possibly, precisely, primarily, probably* and *simply*. ***Because of this*** has become a fixed expression.	***Because of*** *space limitations, the passages to which comments are directed are not included in this article.* ***Because of*** *some glitch, the teacher was unable to run the class he or she had intended to run.* *Parent involvement with homework appears to be an effective way to raise student achievement, primarily* ***because of*** *its influence on time.* *Different versions of pantheism offer different accounts of 'unity' and 'diversity'. There is no one meaning in all forms of pantheism, and within some forms several types are found.* ***Because of this****, the central problem of pantheism, unlike theism, is to determine just what pantheism means.*	wegen, aufgrund von daher, deshalb
Owing to is similar to ***because of*** in meaning, but more formal.	*Those examined here are environmentally significant,* ***owing to*** *their association with human or environmental health.*	wegen
Due to means the same as ***because of***, but is usually used after a form of *be*. It collocates with a large number of adverbs such as *chiefly, largely, mostly, partly, primarily* and *wholly*.	*The loss* ***was due to*** *his own poor initial planning.* *The progress of the race* ***is due to*** *a much greater extent than appears at first sight to the descendants of a few exceptionally large and vigorous families.*	zurückführbar auf

	The intricacy of the passage ***is partly due to*** *its odd construction.* *After 1988,* ***due to*** *a shortage of public funds, the MPP was used to compensate farmers for the increase in market interest rates.*	aufgrund, wegen
on account of	*In future,* ***on account of*** *restrictive budgetary policies, less support from public funds and less protection through trade barriers is to be expected for agriculture as a whole.*	wegen
in view of	*Collation of the five surviving copies has produced no variants.* ***In view of*** *the small sample, these results hardly seem anomalous.*	angesichts
considering	*Critics have differed greatly in their interpretations of Twain's intentions in writing* A Connecticut Yankee. *This is not surprising,* ***considering*** *the mixed messages that seem to mingle in the tale.*	angesichts, in Anbetracht von, eingedenk
by virtue of (often + V-*ing*)	*Agathon is allowed a voice in public affairs* ***by virtue of*** *his natural sex.* ***By virtue of*** *his monarchy, Augustus prevented petty rivalry from developing between generals.* *No priority is given to intellectualism and each person,* ***by virtue of being*** *a Muslim, is assumed to be a potential participant worthy of respect.*	qua, kraft, vermöge, wegen
in response to	*Earth's organisms have not, of course, remained unchanged over their existence, but have evolved* ***in response to*** *new environmental and biotic challenges.*	als Antwort auf, als Reaktion auf
Behind combines with a number of nouns to indicate source or cause.	*the architect / genius / brains / force / mastermind / moving spirit / voice* ***behind*** *the project* *the agenda / aim / inspiration / philosophy / strategy / rationale / reasoning / thinking* ***behind*** *the campaign* *the mechanism / principle / science / technology* ***behind*** *the process*	der (usw.) hinter etw. steht
with … justification, with justice, with reason, with … truth	*Mao believed,* ***with substantial justification,*** *that his highly personalized revolution would be rejected by his successors.*	mit (einigem) Recht

	Poeck and Orgass (1971) argued, ***with reason****, that Pick's descriptions were far too generic.* cf. ***with ample justification, with equal justification, with some justification***	
without justification, without reason, without precedent, without obligation	*Later observers sometimes argued,* ***without reason****, that immorality, lust and deviance counted among the causes of the fall of Rome.* *Stoker's monster was not born* ***without precedent****; there was already a vampire tradition not only in folklore but in literature as well.*	ohne Grund, grundlos (nicht) aus dem Nichts
to the extent that	*There is a serious risk of it being watered down* ***to the extent that*** *it will be unrecognisable.*	so weit … dass
	Group 3: Verbs	
	A: Cause → Effect	
lead to, result in	*… a scheme that* ***will lead to*** *the creation of thousands of new jobs.* *Another simple command by the writer* ***resulted in*** *a printed version of the test.* *The crash* ***resulted in*** *the death of more than half the passengers.*	führen zu
bring about (+ change, collapse, conclusion, cure, fall, overthrow, reconciliation, redistribution, etc.)	*Computers* ***have brought about many changes*** *in the workplace.* *Each node is connected to other nodes where it can* ***bring about increases or decreases*** *in the level of activation of those other nodes.*	hervorrufen, mit sich bringen, nach sich ziehen
bring in its wake/bring with it (+ redefinition, prospect(s), advances, problems, etc.)	*In the conservative world of the countryside,* ***marriage brought with it expectations*** *of a stable family life.* ***Reality brings with it the recognition*** *that the other may not be able to meet all of the partner's needs.* *Reinvention* ***brings downsizing in its wake****.*	mit sich bringen, nach sich ziehen
spark (off) (+ controversy, demonstration, reform, riot, uprising); ***trigger*** (+ alarm, alert, explosion, migraine, etc.)	***s.th. triggers/sparks (off) a rise in interest rates*** *the incident that* ***sparked (off) the strike***	auslösen

give rise to (+ controversy, misunderstanding, questions, speculation, uncertainty, violence)	*The restrictions applied to automobile imports* ***gave rise to several criticisms*** *from Argentina.*	auslösen, hervorrufen, provozieren
spawn (+ offspring, social practices)	*In 1990, a sunflower motif was so popular that it* ***spawned a teen "sunflower culture,"*** *…*	hervorbringen, erzeugen
arouse, awaken (+ anxiety, curiosity, doubt, interest, passion, suspicion), ***excite*** (+ admiration, attention, comment, controversy, criticism, interest)	*It* ***aroused strong emotions*** *and violent* ***controversy****.*	wachrufen, wecken, hervorrufen, erregen
bring back (+ memories, recollections)	*In his great novel* Remembrance of Things Past, *Marcel Proust told how a taste* ***had brought back recollections of earlier events****.*	wecken
evoke (+ association, feeling, memories, nostalgia, spectre)	*But popular culture no longer* ***evokes agrarian nostalgia*** *against modern machines …* ***Only the first chapter evokes the spectre of death*** *when Piri watches the bodies of Ukrainian soldiers floating down the Rika River.*	heraufbeschwören, wecken
make for (+ a happy marriage, inefficiency, optimism, easier reading)	*What* ***makes for good writing instruction*** *– frequent writing, discussion of writing in progress, revision, thoughtful responses from peers – does not need to change.*	fördern, förderlich sein; beitragen zu
cause, produce, create, engender, generate (+ effect) These verbs have a fairly wide meaning. Their participial forms are often found in compounds.	*… the view that mental events* ***are caused by physical events*** *in the brain* *… their teachings* ***caused a sensation*** *…* *This* ***caused*** *him to interfere.* *… P1 is a physical state* ***produced by the taste of*** *Vegemite …* *… a multi-layered story* ***capable of engendering*** *a number of conflicting readings …* *… the kind of religious practice* ***that pantheism engenders …*** *… story-writing programs can* ***generate plausible stories …*** ***human-caused pollution*** ***computer-generated protocols***	verursachen, hervorrufen, auslösen, generieren, hervorbringen

be motivated (+ by fear, envy, etc.)	*This experiment **was motivated by conflicting** L2 research …* *The degree to which sexual activity **is motivated by affection needs** seems to be higher in females.*	seinen Ausgangspunkt haben in, motiviert sein durch
prompt (+ action, move, retaliation, etc.), ***provoke*** (+ alarm, antagonism, anxiety, conflict, outrage), ***occasion, give occasion to*** (+ anxiety, debate, reaction, etc.)	***This phenomenon was prompted** by desktop publishing.* *This **prompted** another student **to 'interface'** with his critic.* ***the emotional and relational impoverishment occasioned** by the struggle against appetite* ***… has occasioned long** and sometimes heated **debates**.*	auslösen, hervorrufen
stir (up) (+ emotions, curiosity, imagination, interest, memories), ***fire*** (imagination)	*No subsequent action of the Socialist ministers **stirred up** the party as had the Panzerkreuzer decision.* *Poor Law reform was never going to **fire the imagination** of the general public.*	aufheizen; aufstacheln; aufwiegeln anregen
incite, kindle (+ desire, hatred, passions, violence)	*… his zeal for Catholic freedom **kindled widespread hatred** of the Papacy …* *In Chalons **a riot was incited** by 'the great and rich persons' of the town against the royal ordinance prescribing the return to strong money.*	schüren aufhetzen zu
Contribute to implies that the cause denoted by the subject noun is one of several causes.	*Various factors **contributed to** his victory.*	beitragen zu
precipitate	*… the fall in real incomes **precipitated** a sharp decline in demand for agricultural products …*	beschleunigen
foment (+ discord, rebellion, revolution, trouble)	*The Church **had fomented religious wars** that had almost ruined France.* ***… the intellectual revolution** which it helped **to foment** …* *Conservative elements in the university **deliberately fomented student discord** leading to the infamous Gospel riots …*	anfachen, schüren
yield (+ clue, crop, dividend, insight, profit, revenue, tax)	*… this experiment **yielded results** which satisfactorily corroborated well-established data obtained by other observers …*	liefern, produzieren
induce (+ hypnosis, reaction, sleep), ***bring on*** (+ headache, heart attack, migraine, nausea),	*The change in degree **induced a change** in kind.* *George Steiner **describes the 'profound crisis of confidence in language brought***	auslösen, erzeugen, verursachen

breed (+ discontent, violence), ***beget*** (rare)	***on** by the ruin of classic humanist values after 1914'.* *Violence **breeds violence**.* *… the moods and forms of one age are repudiated by the next, which tires of tradition and lusts for novelty; classicism **begets** romanticism, which **begets** realism, which **begets** impressionism …* *Authority **begets** the resistance that transforms it.*	
inspire (+ confidence, feeling, hope, reverence, trust)	*However, Marx's ideas have **also inspired great works of fiction**.*	inspirieren; einflößen, erwecken
account for	*The January sale **accounts for** 30 per cent of their annual turnover.* *The causal theory of reference for proper names has many advantages over the Fregian view that the use of a proper name presupposes a criterion of identity for the name's referent. **It accounts for** the fact that different speakers can and do use the same name to refer to an entity without these speakers sharing some common definite description.*	ausmachen erklären, motivieren
	B: Effect → Cause	
arise from/out of	*In the realm of experience, however, everything is known **to arise from** antecedent causes and thus to be subject to the laws of nature.*	entstehen aus
stem (from), originate from, have one's origins in, have one's roots in, follow from, emerge from, derive from	*… social violence **stems from** human nature …* *The principal limitation of these arguments **stems from** their attempt to repackage capital as a social phenomenon.* *Anger **has its origins** in anxiety that arises from feeling frustrated, humiliated or threatened at work.* *What consequences **follow from** that fact?* *Shame **emerges from** addiction.* *The value of a gold coin **derives from** the gold.*	herrühren von, seinen Ausgangspunkt haben in, folgen aus, seinen Ursprung haben in, herkommen von, sich herleiten von, sich ableiten von
appear from (often + pre-posed or post-posed that-clause)	***That** the function is adverbial **appears from** the possibility of omission, substitution by adverbs and postposition.* *It **appears from** the data **that** in BSAE …*	sich ergeben aus

be ascribed (to), be attributed (to), be traced (back) (to)	*Influenza* ***was ascribed to*** *celestial influences.* *A theory of plant development usually* ***ascribed/attributed to*** *Goethe.* *Beauty* ***is ascribed to*** *the symmetry, not to the various parts severally.* *Much of the recent Spinozism can* ***be traced to*** *Lacan.* *Regional differences in capital can* ***be traced back to*** *the Middle Ages.*	zurückführbar sein auf, zugeschrieben werden (+ Dat.), zurückgehen auf
relate to	*There are a variety of types of learning which* ***relate to*** *different neurological levels of the brain.* *The fifth characteristic of sounds is the way they* ***relate to*** *each other – forming patterns based on duration and contrast in a time sequence, that is to say, 'rhythm'.* *… the degree of development of private brands and how they* ***relate to*** *national brands …* *This study is based in part on these research objectives as they* ***relate to*** *Lake Macquarie, NSW, …*	bedingt sein durch, abhängen von; zusammenhängen mit, in einem Verhältnis stehen zu
correlate with	*… the extent of asbestosis does not* ***correlate with*** *the magnitude of D1CO reduction, though this also has been debated.*	korrelieren mit
mean	*Does more vocabulary* ***mean*** *greater fluency?*	bedeuten
argue	*And this limitation of view* ***argues*** *inadequacy of penetrative imagination.*	nachweisen, zeugen von, verraten
rest on	*The case that AM was himself an apostate is not implausible, but hardly proven. It* ***rests on*** *two arguments.*	beruhen auf
underlie	*… factors* ***underlying*** *the restructuring of the electric power industry …*	zugrundeliegen
	Group 4: Nouns	
reason	*One* ***reason for*** *positing this is … Another/****A*** *second* ***reason*** *is that …* ***A*** *third* ***reason*** *is that …* *For these* ***reasons*** *machine code is now seldom used.* *… and precisely* ***for that reason***	Grund

cause	*the root **cause** of violence*	Ursache
motive	*the **motive** for their behaviour*	Motiv
ground(s)	*Adultery was **a ground for** divorce.* *There are good **grounds for** doubting that...* *For **the grounds** advanced in ...* ***On** humanitarian **grounds**.* ***On grounds** of principle.*	Grund, Gründe
explanation	*There is only one **explanation for** this.*	Erklärung
rationale	***The rationale behind** this policy is ...*	grundlegendes Prinzip, (logische) Basis, Hauptbegründung
factor	*Cognitive styles are **a major factor** contributing to the success of learning.* *Cognitive styles may **be a contributory factor**.*	Faktor
determinant	***the determinant of/for s.th.** (= factor determining s.th.)*	Bestimmungsfaktor
influence	*... are subject to **influences** of various kinds ...*	Einfluss
the whys and wherefores	*Some journalists were free with their comments as to the **whys and wherefores** of the matter.*	das Warum und Weshalb
justification	*One **justification for** decomposing categories into feature sets is that it enables us to capture supercategorial generalisations.*	Rechtfertigung, Grund
warrant	*Although psychoanalysts often invoke Freudian theory to explain works of art, jokes, etc., do they **have warrant for** doing so?*	Berechtigung
motivation	*Thus, we have morphological **motivation for** drawing a distinction between 'black bird' and 'blackbird'.*	Grund, Begründung, Motivation
occasion	*The school ball was **an occasion for** debauchery.*	Anlass, Gelegenheit
pretext	*as a **pretext for** (doing) s.th./under the **pretext of** s.th./on an ideological **pretext***	Vorwand, Ausrede

excuse	*to find an excuse not to do s.th. / an excuse for doing s.th.*	Ausrede, Entschuldigung
inducement	*Cable operators may offer subscribers a month's worth of free HBO as an* ***inducement to*** *subscribe to the pay television service.*	Anreiz
incentive	*There is limited fear and maximal* ***incentive*** *to try hard.*	Anreiz
germ	*the* ***germ*** *of an idea*	Keim
encouragement	*She has to accept responsibility for her government's failings in the* ***encouragement of*** *selfishness and individualism which has undermined joint responsibility and the role of the family.* *Parental* ***encouragement to*** *enter a math or science field.*	Unterstützung, Bestärkung
mainspring	*Had solidarity provided* ***the mainspring of*** *union membership, the story of the past 15 years would surely have been different.*	Triebfeder, treibende Kraft
driving force	*He has been* ***a driving force behind*** *the firm's rise to power.*	treibende Kraft
inspiration	*He was* ***the inspiration for*** *this character.*	Inspiration
stimulus	*This is a powerful* ***stimulus to*** *the world economy.*	Anreiz, Antrieb
impetus	*Yesterday's announcement has provided enormous* ***impetus for*** *change.*	Anstoß, Impuls, Antrieb
source	***a source of*** *continued tensions / job growth / satisfaction*	Quelle
fount	***the fount of*** *French culture and identity / a* ***fount of*** *wisdom*	Quelle
fountainhead	*He argued that the classless society would remain a mirage as long as the monarchy survived as the* ***fountainhead of*** *falseness and snobbery.* *Writers are returning to* ***the fountainhead*** *– the 19th century novel.*	Urquell, Quelle, Ursprung
product	*She is* ***a product of*** *our education system.*	Produkt
cradle	*the* ***cradle of*** *the industrial revolution*	Wiege

seed bed	*a* ***seed bed of*** *strife / the* ***seed bed*** *from which these great men emerged*	Pflanzstätte; Brutstätte
breeding ground	*the* ***breeding ground of*** *violence /* ***a breeding ground for*** *charities*	Brutstätte, Nährboden; fruchtbarer Boden
hotbed	*The traditional* ***hotbed of*** *French nationalism / a* ***hotbed of*** *violence*	Brutstätte
genesis	*The* ***genesis of*** *this book was in my work on translation.* *He was the jewel in the England team, the* ***genesis of*** *so many of Lineker's goals.*	Ursprung
origin	*the* ***origin of*** *the universe*	Ursprung
ancestry	*These political groupings may not even recognize their religious* ***ancestry****.*	Herkunft
root	*the* ***root of*** *all evil / the* ***root of*** *the problem*	Wurzel
culprit	*the* ***main culprit in*** *fostering this decline is television.*	Übeltäter, Schuldiger
motor, engine (of growth)	*Economic recovery in America was* ***the main motor of*** *growth last year.* *an* ***engine of*** *growth*	(Wachstums-) Motor
pivot	*One* ***pivot of*** *future progress is the degree of consumer optimism.*	Dreh- und Angelpunkt
lever	*He uses it as a* ***lever to*** *get business.*	Hebel, Druckmittel
seeds	*... to plant* ***the seeds of*** *revolution.*	Keim
embryo	*an* ***embryo of*** *an idea*	Keim
raw material	*This provided the* ***raw material for*** *the book.*	Rohmaterial
benefits	*the* ***benefits of*** *our actions*	Nutzen
fruits	*the* ***fruits of*** *our labour*	Früchte
aftermath	*during* ***the*** *immediate* ***aftermath of*** *the French revolution*	Folgen, Nachwirkungen, Zeit danach
implications	*the environmental* ***implications of*** *climate change*	Folgen

author	*the **author of** a book/a scheme*	Autor
agent	*an **agent of** change.*	Verursacher, Mittel
inventor	*the **inventor of** a technology*	Erfinder
originator	*the **originator of** a new style*	Begründer
prime mover	*He has emerged as **a prime mover** in a drive to create in Britain what the French call the 'économie sociale'.*	Hauptfigur
founder	*the **founder of** the Club of Rome*	Gründer
generator	*The burden of proving that a waste stream is nonhazardous always falls on the **generator of** the waste.*	Erzeuger
legacy	*the **legacy of** Roman architecture/the **legacy of** divorce*	Vermächtnis, Erbe; Hinterlassenschaft; das, was zurückbleibt/übrigbleibt
architect	*the **architect of** the revolution* *Everyone is the architect of their own fate.*	Architekt; Gründer; (fig.) Schmied
mastermind	*the **mastermind behind** the organization*	Kopf, führender Kopf, kluger Kopf

4.10 Consequence and result

It is difficult to establish clear-cut distinctions between this functional category and the preceding one. We therefore list only some essential items here which were not mentioned in the previous section (see Table 52).

Table 52: An overview of consequence and result markers

Consequence and Result: The Essentials	
*Mice die **so that** cats may live.* *In the following study, the general word frequency has been factored out **so that** the effect of frequency in the current context can be assessed.*	damit
*... instead we seem to carry out all the operations all at once, **so that** phenomenal objects come up spontaneously to consciousness.*	so dass

These workers are not entitled to paid holidays, ***so (that)*** *most of them have to stay at home in summer.* *Less sleep is needed by the elderly, but the habits of a lifetime might not be changed easily,* ***with the result that*** *individuals retire earlier than necessary and too much time is spent in bed.*	so dass; wodurch
His knowledge is ***so*** *extensive* ***that*** *he can answer any question.*	*so* + adjective … *that*
These people had ***such*** *awful experiences during the war* ***that*** *they still cannot talk about them.* *He has* ***such*** *a great sense of humour* ***that*** *everybody loves him.*	*such* + adjective + noun … *that*
… these methods are developed and refined ***such that*** *the lecture format is augmented or replaced …* *Interest was* ***such that*** *the libretto of La maga fulminata quickly sold out …*	verb + *such that* (= in such a way that) noun + *such that*
In German, however, such expressions are usually compounded; ***consequently/as a consequence/as a result*** *the German language is very rich in compound nouns.*	folglich, daher, deshalb, deswegen
the ***consequences*** *(of s.th. for s.th.)* *the economic/political* ***consequences***	die Folgen/die Auswirkungen
the ***effect*** *(of s.th. on s.th./s.o.)* *to have/produce an* ***effect*** *on s.th./s.o.* *to have little effect* *the* ***impact*** *(of s.th. on s.th./s.o.)* *to have/make little* ***impact***	die (Aus-)Wirkung
the ***outcome****/the* ***result***	das Ergebnis
There are many important themes that ***arise from*** *the study of this play.*	entstehen, sich ergeben aus
Whether all the planetary nebulae have ***developed from*** *new stars is uncertain.* *This industry had been* ***developed from*** *a patented scientific invention.*	(sich) entwickeln, entstehen
charged with/loaded with *consequences/significance/assumptions and meanings*	(auf)geladen mit

fraught with *controversy/danger/difficulties/meaning/problems/uncertainties/worry and anxiety* *a ballad* ***heavy with*** *pathos*	voll(er) voll(er)
Liberationists were ***pivotal in*** *shaping this intellectual culture. (+ in N/V-ing)* *Enjoyment at one time may be* ***instrumental in*** *causing enjoyment at another time. (+ in N/V-ing)*	zentral, entscheidend
It follows (from this) that … *It is clear from this that …*	daraus ergibt sich, dass
Given Marx's reputation as a class theorist, ***one could be forgiven for thinking/believing/concluding that*** *the second sense of human must relate to class …*	es könnte der Eindruck entstehen, dass; man könnte meinen, dass (often followed by *but* or *however*)

4.11 Static relations

The precedings sections have presented a great deal of vocabulary that can be used in the description of dynamic relations and processes, such as cause-effect relations. This section is devoted to static relations. These are of five major types (cf. Meyer & Heidrich 1990: 46):

- the relationship between a symbol, name or term and the entity it designates; common verbs used to indicate such relations are *represent, stand for, mean, denote* and *indicate*:

  P **indicates** peak, T **indicates** trough
  the subscript 'm' **denotes** a given 'meaning' or 'word'
  Titles **denoted** by an asterisk are set for various Cambridge Overseas Examinations.

When statements of this kind are made after the relevant symbol has already been used, they are often introduced by the conjunction *where*:

> Find (move cursor to) next occurrence of x in the line, **where** x stands for any character.

The 'relational' verbs may be made passive and be followed by a gerund; this often means that reference is made either to a general convention or to the result of one's own work:

> For a particular thermodynamic quantity, such as free energy, the standard state **is denoted** by placing a zero or a degree mark as a superscript to the right of the symbol.

- the relationship between a whole and its constituent parts; common verbs employed to describe such relations include *consist of, include, comprise (umfassen), be comprised of, contain (enthalten), be made up of, break down into, be organized into, fall into, divide into, be divided into*:

  The trachea **divides into** two branches, and each of these branches **divides into** smaller and smaller branches or bronchi (air passages).
  The curriculum **comprises** 10 subjects.
  The chronicle **breaks down into** three large parts.
  The novel **falls into** three sections.
  Are all galaxies **made up of** similar stellar populations?

Some of these verbs, such as *break down into* and *divide into*, can also be used in descriptions of dynamic part-whole relations:

  On distillation the acid **breaks down into** phenol, hydroquinone, benzoic acid and salicylaldehyde.

- the relationship between an element and the class it belongs to; there are numerous ways of expressing such relations, the simplest being the use of verbs like *be* and *include*:

  Three of these lineages of symbionts **are** microbes.
  Atomic particles **include** electrons and protons.
  The policy and mix, the type of tactics to be used, and the criteria for judging success, all **come under the heading of** strategy.
  Cather's novel **falls into the category of** the Künstlerroman or 'artist novel', a subset of the Bildungsroman or novel of formation.
  Palatals **can be classified as** either [high, front] Dorsal sounds or as complex segments that are both Coronal and Dorsal.
  Intangible assets **can be classified into** three categories: ...

Nouns such as *category, head* or *group* can be used to make other collocations such as

  Poverty falling under this **head** may be described as 'primary' poverty.
  ... in which 'lilac' and 'roses' are assigned to the **category** of names ...
  They **constitute** a group of languages with features that together have been described as belonging to the 'Philippine type'.

- the relationship between a quality and the person or object which has this quality; this can be expressed in a wide variety of ways, notably through use of the verbs *have, display, exhibit, act as, show, possess, lack, characterize* and *serve as*:

A significant percentage of the high school graduates **display** a low degree of proficiency in the use of Jamaican Standard English.
The growth of children is so sensitive to the environment that it **serves as** a reliable indicator of the quality of that environment.
Medieval romances are filled with herbs that **possess** wonderful qualities.
But since all virtues have one root, those who **possess** wisdom **possess** all virtue, and those who **lack** it **lack** all.
Upon the development of the primordial root, its cells **possess** no nuclei at all.
The Balkan Peninsula **is characterized by** mountainous terrain.

If several entities exhibit the same characteristics, the verb *share* can be used (see also Chapter 4.7):

Objects that do not **share** the same class or superclass may still be members of the same type by virtue of implementing the same interface.

If one entity possesses two properties whose combined effect you wish to stress, you may use *combine* (s.th. with s.th.):

Programmed Palletizer, providing an infinite variety of load patterns, **combines** reliability **with** simple continuous operation.

- relations of dependence; these can be expressed by means of verbs such as *influence, affect (= beeinflussen), depend on, hinge on, separate* (*s.th. from s.th.*), *be associated with (= zusammenhängen mit, in Verbindung stehen mit), be related to (= zusammenhängen mit, verursacht werden durch), be based on* (*beruhen auf*), *rest on, carry with it, bring with it*:

... poorer perceived health status is **significantly (or: clearly/only slightly/seriously) affected** by negative emotions ...
... divorce **adversely affects** children's grades and achievement test scores ...
It is still not quite evident that fracture initiation **is critically (or: crucially/decisively/significantly) influenced** by these surface conditions.
Each of Shakespeare's plays **brings with it** a discrete set of textual problems.
Being a son or daughter or parent **carries with it** the idea of a set of obligations and interests.
One point of view **rests on** the questions and methods of science.

Bibliography

Adamson, Donald 1995. *Practise your conjunctions and linkers*. London: Longman.
Arnaudet, Martin L. & Mary Ellen Barrett 1990. *Paragraph development: A guide for students of English*. New York: Prentice Hall.
Biber, Douglas, Stig Johansson, Geoffrey Leech, Susan Conrad & Edward Finnegan 1999. *Longman grammar of spoken and written English*. Harlow: Pearson.

Blumenthal, Peter 2007. Sciences de l'homme vs. sciences exactes: combinatoire des mots dans la vulgarisation scientifique. *Revue française de linguistique appliquée* 12(2): 15–28.

Chalker, Sylvia 1996. *Collins Cobuild English guides 9: Linking words*. London: Harper Collins.

Coxhead, Averil 2000. The new Academic Word List. *TESOL Quarterly* 34(2): 213–238.

Crystal, David 2003. *A dictionary of linguistics and phonetics*. 5th edn. Oxford: Blackwell.

Francis, Gill 1994. Labelling discourse: An aspect of nominal-group cohesion. In Malcolm Coulthard (ed.), *Advances in written text analysis*. London: Routledge. 83–101.

Francis, Gill, Susan Hunston & Elizabeth Manning 1996. *Grammar patterns 1: Verbs*. London: Harper Collins.

Francis, Gill, Susan Hunston & Elizabeth Manning 1998. *Grammar patterns 2: Nouns and adjectives*. London: Harper Collins.

Friederich, Wolf 1969. *Technik des Übersetzens*. Munich: Hueber.

Gallagher, John D. 1996. *German-English translation. Deutsch-englische Übersetzungsübungen: Texts of politics and economics*. 4th edn. Munich: Oldenbourg.

Gerzymisch-Arbogast, Heidrun 1994. *Übersetzungswissenschaftliches Propädeutikum*. Tübingen: Francke.

Granger, Sylviane 2006. Lexico-grammatical patterns of EAP verbs: How do learners cope? Talk given at ELGI, Hanover, 5–7 October 2006.

Herbst, Thomas et al. 2004. *A valency dictionary of English: A corpus-based analysis of the complementation patterns of English verbs, nouns and adjectives*. Berlin: Mouton de Gruyter.

Hinkel, Eli 2002. *Second language writers' text*. Mahwah, NJ: Lawrence Erlbaum Associates.

Hinkel, Eli 2004. *Teaching academic ESL writing: Practical techniques in vocabulary and grammar*. Mahwah, NJ: Lawrence Erlbaum Associates.

Hoey, Michael 2005. *Lexical priming: A new theory of words and language*. London: Routledge.

Hrdina, Christian & Robert Hrdina 2006. *Langenscheidt* Scientific English *für Mediziner und Naturwissenschaftler: Wortschatz und Formulierungshilfe für wissenschaftliche Publikationen und Vorträge*. Munich: Langenscheidt.

Hyland, Ken & Polly Tse 2007. Is there an 'academic vocabulary'? *TESOL Quarterly* 41(2): 235–253.

Klotz, Michael 1999. Word complementation in English learners' dictionaries – A quantitative study of CIDE, COBUILD2, LDOCE3 and OALD5. In Herbst T. & K. Popp (eds), *The Perfect Learners' Dictionary?*. Tübingen: Niemeyer, 33–43.

Königs, Karen 2004. *Übersetzen Englisch – Deutsch*. 2nd, rev. edn. Munich: Oldenbourg.

Kraus, Roland 1978. *Die Präposition „bei" in technischen Texten: Ihre Wiedergabe im Englischen*. Mannheim: Verlag Sprache und Technik.

Kraus, Roland 1989. *Die Präpositionen in deutschen technischen Texten und ihre Übersetzungsmöglichkeiten im Englischen. Lebende Sprachen* 34: 12–14.

Kraus, Roland 1999. *Wörterbuch und Satzlexikon: Gemeinsprachlicher Wortschatz in technisch-wissenschaftlichen Texten. Teil 1: Deutsch-Englisch*. Heddesheim: Verlag Sprache + Technik.

Kraus, Roland & Peter Baumgartner 2002. *Phraseological dictionary: General vocabulary in technical and scientific texts. Part 2: English-German*. Heddesheim: Verlag Sprache + Technik.

Laufer, Batia & Paul Nation 1995. Vocabulary size and use: Lexical richness in L2 written production. *Applied Linguistics* 16(3): 307–322.

Leech, Geoffrey, Paul Rayson & Andrew Wilson 2001. *Word frequencies in written and spoken English. Based on the British National Corpus*. London: Longman.

Legler, Bernd & Guy Moore 2001. *Science English*. Bad Honnef: Bock.

Leisi, Ernst 2008. *Das heutige Englisch. Wesenszüge und Probleme*. Heidelberg: Winter.

Lewis, Michael 2000. *Teaching collocation*. Hove: LTP.

Meldau, Rudolf 1981. *Sinnverwandte Wörter der englischen Sprache*. Heidelberg: Winter.

Nash, Walter 1980. *Designs in prose*. London: Longman.

Reum, Albrecht 1931. *A dictionary of English style*. Leipzig: Weber.

Römer, Ute 2005. This seems somewhat counterintuitive, though ... – Negative evaluation in linguistic book reviews by male and female authors. In Tognini Bonelli, Elena & Gabriella Del Lungo Camiciotti (eds), *Strategies in Academic Discourse*. Amsterdam: John Benjamins, 97–115.

Rotter, Wilfried & Hermann Bendl 1978. *Your companion to English texts*. 3 vols. Munich: Manz.

Santos, Terry 1988. Professors' reactions to the academic writing of nonnative-speaking students. *TESOL Quarterly* 22(1): 69–90.

Schmitt, Diane & Norbert Schmitt 2005. *Focus on vocabulary: Mastering the Academic Word List*. London: Longman.

Siepmann, Dirk 2001. Determinants of zero article use with abstract nouns: a corpus-informed study of academic and journalistic English. *Zeitschrift für Anglistik und Amerikanistik* 49(2): 105–120.

Siepmann, Dirk 2005. *Discourse markers across languages. A contrastive study of second-level discourse markers in native and non-native text with implications for general and pedagogic lexicography*. Abingdon: Routledge.

Sinclair, John 1991. *Corpus, concordance, collocation*. Oxford: Blackwell.

Smith, Edward L. & Stephen A. Bernhardt 1997. *Writing at work. Professional writing skills for people on the job*. New York: McGraw Hill.

Soler, Viviana 2002. Analysing adjectives in scientific discourse: an exploratory study with educational applications for Spanish speakers at advanced university level. *English for Specific Purposes* 21(2): 145–165.

Speight, Stephen 1998. *Right or wrong? Spotting mistakes and borderline cases*. Berlin: Cornelsen.

Stevens, John 1999. *Englischer Sprachgebrauch: Ein Ratgeber für Zweifelsfälle*. Stuttgart: Klett.

Thompson, Geoff 1994. *Collins Cobuild English guides 5: Reporting*. London: Collins.

Thompson, Geoff 1996. *Introducing functional grammar*. London: Arnold.

Werlich, Egon 1969. *Wörterbuch der Textinterpretation Englisch. The field system dictionary for text analysis*. Dortmund: Lensing.

West, Michael P. 1953. *A general service list of English words*. Longman: London.

Wilhoit, Stephen W. 1997. *A brief guide to writing from readings*. Boston: Allyn and Bacon.

Wilss, Wolfram 1996. *Übersetzungsunterricht: Eine Einführung*. Tübingen: Narr.

Module IV

Style

Introduction

Modules I–III have equipped you with an extensive vocabulary as well as detailed knowledge of word grammar, sentence building and text organization. Such knowledge will enable you to write with idiomatic assurance; yet this is not enough. You also need to learn how to use language to best effect.

This is the subject of the present module, which discusses questions of style. You will learn that the production of a stylistically acceptable text depends crucially on general discourse competence, observance of shifting linguistic trends and the use of various devices for achieving reader appeal.

There are two chapters. Chapter 1 gives some background to the notion of style, introduces a distinction between academic and personal style, and discusses various steps involved in acquiring stylistic competence. It then goes on to explore key features of academic and personal style. Chapter 2 gives advice on how to use language to best effect and shows how traditional stylistic principles can be applied to modern academic texts.

Chapter 1

Style and stylistic competence

This chapter defines style and stylistic competence and makes some suggestions concerning the acquisition of stylistic skills. We make a basic distinction between academic and personal style and discuss these concepts in turn.

The main points of this chapter are these:

- Stylistic competence is the ability to make informed decisions about the communicative adequacy and effectiveness of variant forms.
- Stylistic choices are conditioned primarily by the nature of the subject under discussion and by the potential readers' expectations.
- Academic style is characterized by specific linguistic features, such as technical terms, nominalizations and impersonality.
- Academic writers can give a personal touch to their prose as long as they respect academic conventions and maintain unity of tone.

1.1 What is style?

Style is too complex a phenomenon to be forced into a simple definition. It has been defined as "a distinctive, formal, or characteristic manner of expression in words, music, painting, etc." (cf. Hanks 1979, under 'style'). For our present purpose, however, this definition is too loose.

In academic writing two distinct kinds of style coexist, often uneasily. The first kind is characteristic of academic text types in general; the second is characteristic of individuals. The first kind of style offers little scope for creativity. Academic writers are expected to conform to fairly rigid norms by using standard vocabulary, formal syntax, conventionalized fixed phrases, headings and subheadings, diagrams, tables, footnotes, and the like. We shall call this 'academic style'. The second kind of style, by contrast, arises from the recurrence of certain linguistic elements characteristic of an author. We shall call this 'personal style'. Personal style may be plain or sophisticated, brisk or leisurely, wholly impersonal or consciously individual. To what extent stylistic decisions are deliberate is often difficult to say, but individuality in style is undoubtedly unavoidable.

Good academic style is a must, whereas the cultivation of a distinctively individual style is merely a matter of personal preference. Constant interaction between academic and personal style gives rise to tensions which are not always easy to resolve, but the stylistic toolkit offered in this chapter will enable you to cope with most of the stylistic problems which are likely to arise during the writing process.

It remains for us to clear up two common misconceptions. The first concerns the relationship between style and substance, or manner and matter; the second, the importance accorded to style:

- Style is often opposed to substance and described as the dress of thought (cf. *O.E.D.*, under 'style' 14; Hough 1969: 2–4). Admittedly, some stylistic qualities (e.g. variety and elegance) are comparatively superficial, but it is undoubtedly a mistake to equate style with purely formal features of composition, for style and substance are always closely interrelated (cf. Quirk 1982: vii), and well-ordered thought constitutes the basis of formal perfection.
- Since we read academic prose primarily for its meaning, the use of stylistic devices in this kind of prose is often regarded as an inessential luxury – like icing on a cake or a vase of flowers on a drawing room table. Yet stylistic devices may have a useful role to play in achieving a personalized and appealing style. This is because they kindle the reader's emotions to such an extent that a fine piece of writing may be a source of intense pleasure, while a badly written text may trigger negative reactions ranging from irritation to contempt.

It is quite sufficient for beginners to focus on the basic requirements of academic style (see Chapter 1.3), for most academic writers are content to cast their ideas in traditional formulaic moulds (as we saw in Module III). Advanced students, however, may wish to experiment with subtle stylistic devices (cf. Section 1.5 and Chapter 2).

1.2 How to achieve stylistic competence

It is a well-known fact that good craftsmanship forms the basis of art. The kind of craftsmanship we have in mind has been discussed in Modules I–III, whose main purpose is to help you to shape text in such a way as to achieve basic communicative aims. In some sections of these modules, however, attention has been drawn to areas where writers can choose among several options. Consider again the following example, which was discussed in the Introduction, p. 11:

> The purpose of this paper is to examine in depth the impact of Berlin's home care programs for the elderly. Here the degree to which functionally disabled elderly people receive badly needed help is a central question.

This excerpt is acceptable as it stands. However, if we are correct in assuming that the writer wishes to give prominence to the idea expressed by the word group *the degree [...] help*, it might be preferable to begin the second sentence with a presentative device, which would move the subject into clause-final position:

> → Of central concern here is the degree to which functionally disabled elderly people receive badly needed help.

In order to be able to modify a text in this way, you have to possess a high degree of stylistic competence (i.e. the ability to make informed decisions about the communicative adequacy and effectiveness of variant forms). This involves balancing a variety of communicative factors such as the subject-matter of the text, the genre to which the text belongs, and the readers for whom the text is intended.

The most important among these factors are your readers; it is their needs and expectations that will determine a large number of stylistic decisions. Since these people are your contemporaries, you will have to exercise particular care when presenting anything that might be considered outmoded, strange or exotic. Your entire text should proceed from the familiar to the unfamiliar, from the known to the unknown, from the given to the new. Wherever possible, you should try to breathe life into shadowy abstractions by giving concrete examples, using vivid metaphors or inserting diagrams and the like. This will lighten your reader's task considerably.

Here are eight recommendations for achieving good style (both academic and personal):

1. Know your subject.
2. Think of your reader.
3. Choose appropriate word combinations for the given context (see also Module III).

4. Vary your sentence patterns (see also Module II, Chapter 3.7).
5. Structure your text clearly and logically.
6. Do not digress (see also Module I, Chapter 4.1).
7. Use one variety of present-day English.
8. Use the same tone and style level throughout your text.

These recommendations will not help you acquire stylistic competence unless you have sufficient time and perseverance to perfect your English through extensive writing practice and close observation of authentic language. To this end, we suggest a stepwise procedure:

Step 1: Observe. The best way to acquire a feel for style is by looking at the largest possible number of examples. Start by working carefully through this section, noting how we comment on more or less successful pieces of text. Read good novelists as well as distinguished academic authors. Read English before and during the writing process, and read some more English before revising your text. Make a habit of reading for style as well as for content. This will enable you to discover all kinds of stylistic variants that you would not otherwise have thought of.

Step 2: Choose. As you become more experienced, you will probably develop personal preferences. You will begin to read more selectively, focusing for example on your favourite authors or on certain stylistic traits or patterns. When you borrow such features from other authors, you should take care to ensure that your text is not merely a hotchpotch of stylistic idiosyncrasies.

Step 3: Control. You are now well on your way to developing a sophisticated style. The essential thing to bear in mind at this stage is stylistic consistency: make controlled and uniform use of the stylistic patterns that you consider most effective and most pleasing.

Some learners tend to become obsessed with style, and this kind of obsession is not without risks. You will probably find it easier to develop a pleasing style if you concentrate on the purpose, the subject matter and the potential readers of your text.

1.3 Academic style

This section seeks to bring out some fundamental differences between academic and non-academic style. Academic style is characterized by specific lexical, nominal, verbal and textual features, which we shall deal with in turn.

1.3.1 Vocabulary

Perhaps the most striking feature of academic texts is their technicality. Since academic texts are intended for specialist readers or, in the case of the term paper, may at least be considered as training exercises in writing for a specialist audience (see Module I, Chapter 1), technical terms should be employed for the sake of precision, as in the following quotation:

> In our attempt to categorize the different approaches to the analysis of inflation, let us start with the two polar extremes, namely the *monetarist* and *cost-push* theories. (Trevithick 1977: 12, italics in original)

It is important to be consistent in one's use of technical terms. In other words, the principle of stylistic variety (see Chapter 2) does not apply to this area; once you have introduced and defined a technical term such as *intersentential linkage*, make sure you stick to that term rather than using synonyms such as *links between sentences, sentence connection*, etc. The practice of varying vocabulary is common in journalistic texts, but may confuse academic readers, since they might assume that when you talk about *sentence connection*, you mean something different from *intersentential linkage*.

Academic texts are also characterized by a high degree of formality. In addition to technical terms, academic writers employ a great many words and expressions which would sound inappropriate in spontaneous informal conversation. Here are some examples:

> It is only just to point out that new lines of inquiry into the nature of the inventive faculty in Balzac are not likely to surprise the recipient of this volume since they owe their impetus in great part to his labours. (Moore 1972: 192)
>
> It is very noticeable that Continental students are far more inclined to hypostatize that abstraction, the style of a period, than we are in the English-speaking world. (Hough 1969: 50)
>
> A host of illustrations could be given of this [...]. (Kelly 1972: 3)
>
> In order to furnish satisfactory answers to these questions, it is customary to introduce the equation of exchange made famous by Professor Irving Fisher. (Trevithick 1977: 19)

There are several formal items in the first example: *recipient, labours, owe + impetus*, and *in great part*; the second example contains a very learned word – the verb *hypostatize*, which means 'to regard or treat as real'; *a host of*, in the third sentence, is the formal equivalent of *a lot of*; and in the last example the formal verb *furnish* could be replaced by *provide*.

Some style guides (e.g. http://elc.polyu.edu.hk/cill/eap/academicstyle.htm) suggest that in academic texts phrasal verbs should be replaced with single, more formal verbs. This recommendation should not be taken too literally. True, phrasal verbs tend to be less formal than their one-word equivalents, but they are becoming increasingly common in written English and are frequently used by well-qualified academic authors. Here are a few examples:

> […] no extension of vocabulary or ingenuity in definition ever seems to **clear away** all the difficulties attached to this perfectly common notion of probability. (Moroney 1970: 4)
> Moreover, we should not be misled into thinking that we can and should **tidy up** our terminology by seeking the advice of the scientist. (Palmer 1976: 23)
> The style of imaginative prose in the early nineteenth century **goes through** many and rapid changes […]. (Hough 1969: 53)
> Both comment on how differences of language may seem to **break through** stereotypes […]. (Fairlie 1972: 223)

In the first example *clear away* could be replaced by *remove*. In the next example *tidy up our terminology* means 'make our terminology more consistent'. In this instance there is no other verb that could be substituted for *tidy up*. In the third example *goes through* could be replaced by *undergoes*, but there is nothing wrong with the phrasal verb *go through*. In the last example *overcome* could be substituted for *break through*, but *break through* sounds perfectly natural here.

It should also be noted that academic writers use a large number of routine formulae. For instance, if you want to explain an abstraction in more concrete terms, you can say *as a simple illustration, let us suppose that […]*; if you want to dispel possible misunderstandings or warn the reader about possible pitfalls, you can say *a word of warning should be sounded*; and if you would like to apologise for not treating a subject in more detail, you can use expressions like *space precludes exhaustive treatment of* + NP or *space prevents us from examining* + NP:

> **As a simple illustration, let us suppose that** bananas cost 2s. per dozen. (Moroney 1970: 271)
> At this stage **a word of warning should be sounded**. (Trevithick 1977: 24)
> **Space** in the present article **precludes exhaustive treatment of** Balzac's attitude to Constant […]. (Fairlie 1972: 210)
> **Space prevents us from examining** Goldberg's model of argument linking in detail […]. (Croft & Cruse 2004: 272)

1.3.2 Nominal constructions

English makes considerable use of nominal constructions, some of which differ from German. The first point to note is that in academic style you can easily recast a more informal formulation by nominalizing clauses and then linking them by means of 'relational' verbs (cf. Forner 1998; see below). Here is an invented example:

> He could not drive because he was tired. → His inability to drive was caused by fatigue.

The clause *he couldn't drive* has been turned into the noun phrase *his inability to drive* and the clause *because he was tired* has been converted into the simplex noun *fatigue*; the two nominal expressions have been linked by the relational verb *cause* (for an extensive list of relational verbs, see Table 51 in Module III). The resultant construction is not only more formal, but also more elegant than the verbal formulation. This gives us the basic format for this kind of construction:

> state of affairs A (inability to drive) – relational verb (cause) – state of affairs B (fatigue)

Here are a few more examples:

> Incomes policy alone, however, will not be enough to **bring about** the requisite changes. (Hawkins 1979: 103)
> Structural unemployment does not **result from** an overall deficiency of demand [...]. (Bannock et al. 1992: 410)

We shall now consider two more specific nominal constructions. First consider the following sentences:

> **The genesis** of this book **was in** my research on industrial economics. (Porter 1980: ix)
> **His natural sympathy is all with** the heroic age of expanding capitalism. (Robinson 1980: 141)
> **Popper's preference is for** programmes of 'piecemeal social engineering' [...]. (Bullock & Stallybrass 1983: 486)
> **Their conclusions were** that materials should be recycled where possible [...]. (Seldon & Pennance 1976: 104)

These sentences exemplify an English construction which has no nominal counterpart in German (cf. Gallagher 1986, 1989) and which can be represented diagrammatically as follows:

ABSTRACT NOUN + *to be* + PP/*that*-clause/*wh*-clause

This allows the writer to present the idea normally expressed by a verb as the subject and topic of the clause:

This book **originated** in [...] → The **genesis** of this book was in [...]
He **is** entirely **in favour of** [...] → His natural **sympathy** is all with [...]

In German the abstract noun usually has to be rendered by a verb:

The **genesis** of this book was in [...] → Das Buch ging aus [...] hervor
His natural **sympathy** is all with [...] → Er fühlt sich [...] verbunden

Here are some additional examples of this construction:

my concern is with + NP
our/the aim/concern/idea/intention is to + INF
their plea/preference (etc.) is for + NP
my feeling/judgement/point/suggestion/suspicion/conviction/position (etc.) is that ... (as well as *it is my conviction/contention/experience/suggestion/view/understanding/position (etc.) that ...*)

Another kind of nominalization can be found in 'support verb constructions' (*Funktionsverbgefüge*). In the constructions we have just discussed the nominal element invariably occurs in subject position (e.g. ***our aim*** *is to* [...]), but in support verb constructions the nominalized expression functions as a grammatical object, thereby giving more weight to the idea expressed by the noun and providing more scope for adjectival qualification. Here are some examples:

He **makes sporadic attempts** to escape from his dilemma [...]. (Grimsley 1972: 323)
Although the Don Juan theme **receives detailed treatment** in only one section of the long poem, it occasionally emerges in other parts. (Grimsley 1972: 326)
Namouna [...] also suggests the influence of Byron's *Don Juan*, a work **for which** Musset **had a particular admiration**. (Grimsley 1972: 326–327)

As the examples show, the adjectives used in support verb constructions cannot always be replaced by adverbials:

makes sporadic attempts → ?sporadically attempts
makes an interesting attempt (not: *attempts interestingly)
receives a timely boost (not: *be boosted timely)

Nominal constructions can fulfil a variety of purposes in academic English. For instance, they often enable the author to be more concise:

> Most of those who advocate or expect the **supersession** of capitalism by socialism have a strong sympathy with the idea of socialism and, indeed, call themselves socialists. (Robinson 1980: 141)
> Rafaël's **instability** is largely due to his **fear** of **boredom** [...]. (Grimsley 1972: 322)
> [...] the watchful husband suspects his wife's **infidelity** with Mardoche [...]. (Grimsley 1972: 322)

If you delete the abstract nouns here you will find that the sentences tend to become longer and syntactically more complex. The first example is very hard to rephrase because the noun *supersession* is governed by verbs which enter into different patterns: (1) *advocate that capitalism* ***should be superseded*** *by socialism*; (2a) *expect that capitalism* ***will be superseded*** *by socialism*; (2b) *expect capitalism* ***to be superseded*** *by socialism*. The second example offers less resistance to transformation. We could say: *The main reason why Rafaël is so unstable is because he is afraid of being bored*. This would be equally acceptable, but Grimsley's sentence is more compact and more formal. If we delete the noun *infidelity* in the last example, we shall have to say: *the watchful husband suspects his wife is having an affair with Mardoche*. The expression *have an affair with sb* makes the sentence sound much less formal. In colloquial English we would drop the formal adjective *watchful* and say something like: *the husband suspects his wife is messing around with Mardoche*.

In many cases the sole purpose of nominal constructions is to enhance the formality of a text:

> At times Ghil **evokes comparison with** Claudel [...]. (Daniel 1972: 363)
> [...] although the fables of the two stories differ as profoundly as their techniques, they **invite comparison** at various levels. (Gordon & Tate 1960)
> And this assumption **derives support from** his opening remarks [...]. (Atkins 1966: 167)
> [...] M. Galichet's statement **finds support in** the following passage [...]. (Harmer 1979: 2)
> The first assumption **receives support from** the fact that medial short vowels in Latin underwent a lesser degree of prehistoric weakening in heavy syllables than in light [...]. (Allen 1969: 197)
> The idea that Siegfried's power is a threat to Gunther **receives no support from** the poem [...]. (Hatto 1965: 306)

As in the previous examples, VERB + NOUN combinations have been used here as an alternative to verbs.[1] Both wordings are fine, but the VERB + NOUN collocations may sound more sophisticated:

1 This kind of device has been termed 'grammatical metaphor' (cf. Halliday 1994: 342–367; Thompson 1996: 163–178).

Ghil **resembles** Claudel → Ghil **evokes comparison** with Claudel
they **resemble each other** → they **invite comparison**
this assumption **is supported** by [...] → this assumption **derives support** from [...]
M. Galichet's statement **is supported** by [...] → M. Galichet's statement **finds support** in [...]
The first assumption **is supported** by [...] → The first assumption **receives support** from [...]
The idea [...] **is** not **supported** by [...] → The idea [...] **receives** no **support** from [...]

1.3.3 Verbal constructions

We come now to verbal constructions. We shall focus on two aspects of verbal style which are relevant for academic writing: passives and certain impersonal constructions. Another verbal type, involving participle constructions, was considered in detail in Module II, Chapter 3.2.3, and is looked at again later in this module (see Chapter 2.3) in the context of concision.

Passives are particularly frequent in academic prose because they can be used to depersonalize statements. Examples:

[...] **it must be admitted** that he does not appear to have in mind anything instantaneous or in any way strictly bounded. (Smith 1972: 197)
It should also be noted that quantity theorists did not confine price increases to a change in the value of final output (wheat). (Trevithick 1977: 23)
Nevertheless **it should not be deduced** that money serves no useful purpose in an economy. (Trevithick 1977: 24)
For example **it was** often **recognized** that during periods of inflation individuals would develop a certain reluctance to hold money [...]. (Trevithick 1977: 21)
Moreover **it was also conceded** that, as the financial infrastructure of advancing economies became more and more complex and specialized, the need to hold money for transaction purposes might diminish progressively. (Trevithick 1977: 21)

It is worth noting that academic authors sometimes use passive constructions in order to avoid addressing the reader directly as *you*. Examples:

It will be recalled that we calculate the variance of a set of data as the mean square deviation of the several items from their grand average. (Moroney 1970: 371)
The reader is asked to study the left-hand pages only, in order to see the formation of the different tables [...]. (Moroney 1970: 399)

In the first example *it will be recalled* means 'you will remember', and in the second example *the reader is asked to study* corresponds to 'you should study'.

We shall now consider passive constructions from a contrastive angle in order to help you to avoid errors due to interference between German and English. In English academic texts passive constructions are often considered appropriate in contexts where German authors normally use active constructions (cf. Kirkwood 1969: 93–98). Here are a few examples:

> A comprehensive survey of market structure and applications to the study of industrial organization can be found in Scherer (1970). (Varian 1978: 79)
> Einen guten Überblick [...] über Zusammenhänge zwischen diesen Disziplinen bietet B. Spillner, *Linguistik und Literaturwissenschaft. Stilforschung, Rhetorik, Textlinguistik*, Stuttgart; Kohlhammer, 1974. (Dressler 1978: 2)
> The view is increasingly held that Keynesian solutions are appropriate in particular circumstances, not of general application in all circumstances. (Gilpin 1977: 128)
> Zunehmend setzt sich die Ansicht durch, dass es sich bei symbolischer KI und Neuronalen Netzen eher um komplementäre als um gegensätzliche Ansätze handelt. (Meyer 2004: 27)

If you compare the first pair of examples, you will notice that the sentences have the same thematic structure. *Survey*, like its German equivalent *Überblick*, occupies sentence-initial position. In the second pair, however, the information structures are different. In English it is normally the subject that takes front position, while in German this position is often occupied by an adverb like *zunehmend*. *Zunehmend setzt sich die Ansicht durch, dass* corresponds exactly in meaning to *the view is increasingly held that*. In this instance it would be equally correct to write: 'There is an increasing number of economists who believe that [...]',[2] but the construction used by Gilpin has the double advantage of reducing the number of subordinate clauses (*who* + *that* → *that*) and giving particular emphasis to the idea expressed by the noun *view*.

Passive constructions are also a convenient way of avoiding the indefinite pronoun *one*. True, *one* is not yet defunct, but in recent years it has dropped out of general use. Curiously, its frequency varies from one discipline to another. Thus, for instance, it is still fairly well represented in philosophical writing, but less frequent in sociology. German-speaking scholars from all disciplines tend to overuse *one* because of its similarity to German *man*.

---

2 Cf. the following quotation from a newspaper article: The City still pushes companies to look to the short term, though there is an increasing number of fund managers who take a long-term view. (*The Guardian* 21.12.1996: 20)

One can be used as an equivalent of *man* in contexts like the following:

languages one already knows (variant: languages the speaker already knows)
one has to admit that (variant: it has to be admitted that)

In describing a general process, however, it may be preferable to use a passive construction, especially with verbs such as *assume, view, know* or *believe*:

There may be some disagreement as to whether one should view the assessment in a positive or a negative light. → There may be some disagreement as to whether the assessment should be viewed in a positive or negative light.
One knows that LTP takes place in different cortical areas. → LTP is known to take place in different cortical areas.

One is overused by Germans in such constructions as the following:

Having a look at the listening and speaking skill **one can say that** the listening skill plays even a more important role [...] → As for listening and speaking, **it is fair to say that/it is clear that/it is reasonable to assume that** the skill of listening is more important [...]

If you wish to portray yourself as part of a group (you and your readers, society at large), it is preferable to use *we* rather than *one*:

But **one** cannot ban the drug scene. They just move to another club. → But **we** cannot ban the drug trade altogether since dealers are likely to move from one location to another.
Only if **we** realise all this will further development be possible. (= nur wenn **man** all dies erkennt [...])

When reporting the work of other authors, *they* or an impersonal construction are usually the best options:

Physicists have now found that while **they** can reasonably predict the average reactions of great numbers of electrons in an experiment, **they** cannot predict what a single electron will do. (Lukasc 1994: 279) (= obwohl man mit einiger Sicherheit [...] voraussagen kann)
Further, it was found that the preference for a route was strongly determined by 'distance', 'time loss caused by traffic lights and queues' (Michon 1993: 115) (= darüber hinaus stellte man fest, dass [...])
There is evidence for and against religious beliefs. (Barbour 1974: 129) (= man findet Belege [...])
However, **it is well known that** [...] (= man weiß aber, dass)
I hope, however, that **it will be understood that** [...] (= ich hoffe jedoch, dass man versteht)

Despite the success of this action, **the fact is that** [...] (= trotz [...] muss man feststellen, dass)

This is only possible within a university context. (= das kann man aber nur in einem universitären Kontext)

Finally, in textbook style, *you* is more common than *one*.

But **when you consider that** [...] (bedenkt man aber, dass)

1.4 From non-specialist to specialist text

So far we have chosen to focus on lexical and syntactic features of academic texts intended for specialist readers. Now we would like to show how the various strategies we have discussed in Sections 1.1–1.3 can be deployed to transform non-specialist into specialist, and hence more formal, text. Consider the following example from a book by a distinguished British linguist:

> There are a remarkable number of words in standard English that are very easy to confuse. Some pairs of words are pronounced the same, but spelt differently. Others are quite different in pronunciation and spelling, but very similar in meaning. If you want to produce acceptable, standard English, you've got to get the distinctions right. You have to choose the right word for the right context. (Crystal 1984: 33)

This is a good example of popular scientific writing. The author avoids technical terms and addresses his readers directly as if he were speaking to them. In order to translate this passage into academic style, we have to make a number of radical changes. Some technical terms need to be used, and the tone has to be rendered more formal.

An academic version of our excerpt might look like this:

> There are a remarkable number of words in standard English that are very easily confused. Some homophones are spelt differently, while some near-synonyms are quite different in pronunciation and spelling. In order to produce acceptable, standard English, it is essential to make clear-cut distinctions and contextually appropriate lexical choices.

Explanations:

- *Easily confused* is slightly more formal than *easy to confuse*.
- *Make clear-cut distinctions* is much more formal than *get the distinctions right*; the same goes for *choose the right word for the right context* vs. *make [...] contextually appropriate lexical choices*.
- The use of technical terms (*homophones* and *near-synonyms*) brings about a considerable increase in information density.

- The conjunction *while* creates a logical link between sentences 2 and 3.
- Three devices have been used in order to avoid the informal and personal *you*. First, the *if* clause has been replaced by a purpose clause introduced by *in order to*. Second, the impersonal construction *it is essential to* + INF. has been used to express the idea of necessity. Third, *you have to* has been left out. This omission makes it possible to connect the last two statements by means of the conjunction *and*. In the revised version of the text the word groups *make clear-cut distinctions* and *[make] contextually appropriate lexical choices* are both dependent on the same introductory expression (*it is essential to*). Hence the ellipsis of *make* before *contextually*.

Our reworking of the above paragraph has entailed a shift from a personal to an impersonal style. The main stylistic changes involved in this shift have already been discussed at some length:

verbal formulations → nominalizations
subordinate clauses → relational verbs
active voice → passive voice
circumlocutions → technical terms
direct reader address using *you* → impersonal expressions introduced by *it* or *there*.

Whether you opt for a personal or an impersonal style will depend to a large extent on the field of activity in which you have specialized. Most scientists and engineers write in an impersonal style, while literary scholars and art historians generally prefer a more personal style. As a result, works devoted to subjects like science and engineering are often dry and austere, while books about arts subjects tend to be much more engaging.

Regardless of whether you choose to write in a personal or an impersonal style, the use of the first person pronouns (*I* and *we*) is likely to pose problems at some stage in the writing process. In formal English texts the use of these pronouns generally conveys an impression of authority, confidence and professionalism. If you are a recognized authority in your area of research, the use of *I* and *we* will appear perfectly natural, but it is advisable to avoid these words if your authority is doubtful or without relevance to the subject under discussion.

1.5 Personal style

As noted in Section 1.1, the recurrence of certain stylistic elements in an author's writings inevitably produces a kind of stylistic fingerprint. Every author's style is more or less overtly personal, and every author has the right to imprint the stamp of his/her personality on what s/he writes. Nonetheless, it would be an error to assume that it does not matter what kind of style you choose to write in. You should not confuse self-expression with wordy pretentiousness, unrestrained directness or an open display of emotion; nor should you assume that you can carve out an individual style by striving for originality at all cost. You should conform to academic conventions and do your utmost to maintain unity of tone throughout your text. Any stylistic inconsistency will detract from the value of your work.

As we pointed out at the end of the previous section, people who write about literary subjects have more opportunities to give a personal touch to their prose by using rhetorical questions, metaphors, similes, and the like. The frequency of such figures of speech in the works of literary scholars is hardly surprising since these authors are often steeped in classical literature.

It should, however, be noted that even scientists and mathematicians sometimes produce beautifully crafted prose. A good example is provided by the writings of M.J. Moroney, a mathematician who had an excellent knowledge of world literature, a rich and varied vocabulary and a genuine feeling for style.

The following quotations illustrate the interplay of individual and genre-specific factors in academic writing:

> We coax reverie into logic, and create in writing a simulacrum of speech. (Nash 1998: 43)
>
> There is perhaps a certain fittingness in this, for one of the professor's characteristic, and also most attractive, traits is his embarrassed reluctance to be classified as a *savant* and his preference for being assessed, if assessed he must be, by wider criteria. (Kelly 1972: 1)
>
> When the event proves us wrong, we keep a discreet silence. (Moroney 1970: 217)

The first example demonstrates a literary device known as personification. *Coax* is normally used with a personal object. Thus, for instance, you can coax someone into doing something, you can coax someone into acceptance (i.e. persuade them to accept something), or you can coax someone into a chair (i.e. persuade them to sit down in a chair). The word combination *coax reverie* implicitly compares reverie to a person who has to be persuaded to do something, so the first half of Nash's sentence could be paraphrased as follows: 'We give a logical form to reverie in spite of all the difficulties that this entails.' The flatness of this paraphrase contrasts sharply with the sophisticated elegance of Nash's formulation.

In the second example the word combination *embarrassed reluctance* deserves special attention. In this instance *embarrassed* is what is known as a transferred epithet, i.e. an adjective modifying a noun to which it cannot logically be applied, but which appears acceptable because the meaning is clear. It is the professor, not his reluctance, who is embarrassed. If you run a Google search you will discover that in modern English the word combination *embarrassed reluctance* is by no means uncommon, but it has to be used with great caution because of its literary overtones.

By employing a transferred epithet Kelly has compressed a great deal of information into a few words. In conversational English it would be impossible to reproduce this information with the same degree of concision. We would have to say something like this: 'The professor always felt embarrassed when people described him as a scholar.' or 'The professor didn't like to be described as a scholar. That word always made him feel embarrassed.'

Similar remarks apply to the third example. Like Kelly, Moroney uses a transferred epithet. Logically, the adjective *discreet* refers to *we* although it has been placed before the noun *silence*. A Google search shows that *discreet silence* is even more common than *embarrassed reluctance*. In this case there is some scope for variation, for the verb *maintain* may be substituted for *keep*. In naturally occurring conversation we would normally avoid statements like *he maintained discreet silence*. We would say *he discreetly kept his mouth shut* or – less politely – *he kept his trap shut* (without *discreetly*).

Such graces of style must be employed with discretion, for they may sound ridiculous in a text written by someone who is still struggling with elementary language problems. If used judiciously, however, they can embellish the sober style typical of academic prose.

We now move on to consider the interplay of formal and informal style, for even in highly specialized texts you will often come across echoes of speech – expressions which are somewhere on the dividing line between formal and informal usage. There is a considerable margin of uncertainty in using such expressions in academic prose, but the academic texts in which colloquial language is used most freely tend to be non-literary rather than literary. Consider the following examples:

> But while there is something in this, it is obviously not the whole story. (Halliday 1994: 393)
>
> But this gets us nowhere. (Palmer 1976: 25)
>
> The thing to be clear about here is that we are not dealing with a functional relationship, but a correlation. (Moroney 1970: 294)

In the first of these sentences Halliday uses two relatively informal idiomatic expressions. *There is something in this* means 'there is some truth in this', and *it is not the whole story* could be paraphrased as 'it is not entirely true'. In the second sentence *this gets us nowhere* could be replaced by a more formal expression like *nothing is gained by this*. In the third sentence Moroney uses a turn of phrase which is very common in everyday spoken English. *To be clear about something* means 'to have a clear understanding of something'. If we wanted to make Moroney's sentence sound more formal, we would have to say 'it is important to be aware that [...]' or 'it is important to realise that [...]'.

Sometimes formal and informal language can be blended, as in the following example:

> Money burns a larger hole in one's pocket when the rate of inflation is 50 per cent than when it is 5 per cent because of the more rapid rate of decline of its purchasing power. (Trevithick 1977: 21)

The tone is unmistakably formal (note the use of *one* instead of *you*), but the author skilfully adapts an idiom which is often employed in everyday speech. If you say money burns a hole in somebody's pocket, you mean they want to spend it as soon as they have it. In this instance Trevithick simply means that people spend a lot more money when there is an exceptionally high inflation rate.

Since the middle of the twentieth century, the boundaries between formal and informal language registers have become increasingly blurred (cf. Gallagher 2006: 35–40). As a result, colloquialisms occasionally crop up even in the most learned of journals, witness the following quotations from the *Journal of Linguistics*:

> In addition, this is not the only sense in which the proposal hangs by the skin of its teeth. (Matthews 1967: 130)
>
> At any rate, the point is worth discussing as a substantive issue – i.e. as an issue to be decided BEFORE, not AFTER, one plumps for a specific notational solution. (Matthews 1967: 131)
>
> This will be helpful, not only to English-speaking linguists, but also to many French-speaking linguists too who, like Ruwet himself, cut their generative teeth on the work of Chomsky, Lees, Postal, Bach, etc. (Lyons 1969: 190)

These quotations contain three colloquialisms which a German reader would probably not expect to find in a high-prestige academic journal: *to hang by the skin of one's teeth, to plump for sth,* and *to cut one's teeth on sth*. Since Matthews and Lyons are both highly competent writers, there is no reason to assume that the expressions in question are mere accidents of language. They are, in all probability, deliberate stylistic choices, for British academics not infrequently lapse into a mildly informal style when they are anxious to put their views across forcefully without sounding unduly stuffy.

Unfortunately, there are no hard and fast rules for the use of colloquialisms in academic texts. As a rule of thumb, you should use such expressions sparingly. If you read a great deal of academic prose written by native speakers, you will gradually acquire an intuitive sense of stylistic appropriateness and learn how to handle stylistic variants such as *opt for* (a relatively formal synonym of *plump for*) and *a barely feasible proposal* (a markedly formal equivalent of *a proposal that hangs by the skin of its teeth*). Idioms like *to cut one's teeth on sth* may prove rather more difficult for various reasons. One reason is that this colourful expression can be paraphrased in many different ways (e.g. *he cut his teeth on Chomsky* might be paraphrased as 'he read Chomsky at an early stage of his career', 'he started reading Chomsky early on in his career', etc.). Another reason is that an adjective – more precisely, a transferred epithet – is frequently inserted before the word *teeth*. This is the case in the example from Lyons' review, where *generative* refers to generative linguistics. The adjectives that can be combined with *teeth* in this idiom include *journalistic, linguistic, literary,* and *scientific*. It remains to add that *to cut one's teeth on sth*, which is labelled as 'informal' in Hanks (1979), seems rather less casual when it is expanded by means of a technical adjective like *generative*.

To conclude this section, we would like to stress once more that in order to develop an individual style you need first to find out what you like or dislike about the prose produced by other writers. Once you feel certain of your personal preferences, you can try to make regular and controlled use of the kind of language that you consider worthy of imitation.

Chapter 2

The principles of style

The main points of the chapter are these:

- Academic writers need to learn how to use language to best effect.
- In order to obtain optimal results, they have to observe five principles: aptness, clarity, concision, variety, and elegance.

The present chapter is based on the assumption that novice writers can benefit from an acquaintance with the time-honoured stylistic principles expounded by classical rhetoricians. However, our reliance on classical rhetoric should not be mistaken to mean that we underestimate the role of linguistic and social change. As we pointed out in Chapter 1, you need to keep abreast of the latest developments in the English language. Reliable information about such developments can be found in recently published dictionaries and grammars.

Such reference works usually reflect a general consensus on what is right or wrong, but they do not enable us to differentiate between good and bad style. There is a clear-cut dividing line between the often vague and fluid principles of style and the comparatively rigid rules that govern spelling and grammatical usage. Statements about spelling and grammar may lay claim to objectivity, while judgements about personal style are essentially subjective.

In this chapter the spotlight will be turned successively on the problems associated with aptness, clarity, concision, variety, and elegance. Since linguistic phenomena do not occur in isolation, a certain amount of overlapping is unavoidable. Thus, for instance, there is a strong probability that a concise text will be elegant.

Let us begin by considering two German examples which will help you understand what many people see as the difference between good and bad style:

> Immerhin wollen wir hier einleitend unter Bezug auf C. Hernández Sacristán 1994 und T. Sáez Hermosilla 1994, die beide – wenn auch partiell von unterschiedlichen Ansätzen aus – die Diskursbezogenheit der übersetzerischen Aktivität zum Ausgangspunkt sehr anregender detaillierter Ausführungen machen, unterstreichen, daß auch wir das Übersetzen durchaus als Bestandteil eines Dialogs (vgl. Hernández mit seiner dialogical intentionality, S. 31), des durch die Ego-Hic-Nunc-Deixis charakterisierten Diskurses, betrachten, was im einzelnen noch detaillierter zu beleuchtende Konsequenzen für deren Beschreibung hat. (Wotjak 1997: 135)
>
> Im heutigen wissenschaftlichen Sprachgebrauch versteht man unter Romania die Gesamtheit der Länder, in denen romanische Sprachen geredet werden. Diese Sprachen sind auf dem Boden des Römerreiches entstanden – vom Schwarzen Meer bis zum Atlantik. (Curtius 1993: 40)

Wotjak's style is laboured and graceless. Most readers will probably be tempted to give up before they get to the end of his tortured and unwieldy sentence. Curtius, by contrast, writes with engaging clarity and economy, and his syntax is aptly tailored to his thought.

Here is an example of what we consider to be good English style:

> If you are looking for comfortable reassurance in a world of headlong heedless change, there is always the English dictionary. There are few more firmly established and dependably stable institutions. Some of the reasons for this are less reassuring. (Quirk 1982: 86)

This example is from an article by a distinguished British linguist. The style is clear, fluent, and unpretentious. Among the points to notice here are the use of alliteration (*headlong heedless*) and the creation of inter-sentence links by means of words such as *reassurance, reassuring, more* and *this.*

2.1 Aptness

The classical concept of aptness (cf. Latin 'aptum'), which is virtually synonymous with 'communicative adequacy', encompasses both matter and manner. It is the most important of all stylistic qualities. Briefly stated, 'aptness' means that your communicative choices must be in conformity with the norms of contemporary academic style, which is characterized first and foremost by objectivity, economy and precision of expression, and by a comparatively high degree of formality (cf. Chapter 1.3.1). In other words, academic writers focus their attention unswervingly on the purpose and the subject matter of their texts rather than on their own personality and feelings (objectivity); they say as much as possible in as little space as possible (economy);

they try to avoid anything vague, equivocal or uncertain (precision); and they adopt a rather formal register (formality).

In order to produce a text characterized by aptness, you have to give due consideration to every facet of the communicative situation (e.g. the subject matter and the nature of your relationship with the reader). Avoid abrupt shifts in style; do your utmost to maintain unity of tone; make an effort to fulfil your reader's expectations; and try to achieve congruence between substance and form. An essay that fails to get to the point cannot be 'apt', even if it is written in an appropriate style; nor can an article be 'apt' if it contains interesting subject matter, but adopts the wrong tone.

We shall exemplify the difficulties involved in achieving aptness at several levels, beginning with problems arising at word and phrase level. These problems are mainly concerned with register. By 'register' we mean a variety of language which is appropriate to a particular kind of situation (cf. Raban 1968: 145–146). To take just one example: in a casual conversation it might be acceptable to say, 'She had a bit on the side'; in a formal situation it would be preferable to say, 'She was unfaithful to her husband' (cf. Dexter 1999: 40); and a comic effect could be created by means of a euphemism such as 'She forgot her marriage vows' (cf. Dexter 1999: 53). Our three variants may therefore be classified as follows:

Table 53

Informal Register	Formal Register	Comic Register
to have a bit on the side	to be unfaithful to one's wife/husband	to forget one's marriage vows

When writing an academic text (e.g. a term paper, a thesis for a master's degree, a conference paper, or a journal article), you ought to adopt a formal or technical register. Whenever appropriate, you should use technical terms and formal expressions (e.g. *inter-glacial period, marginal utility, tribrach, phoneme, to be in the ascendancy,* etc.). You should also conform closely to academic convention by using multi-word routine formulae such as the following (cf. Module III, Chapter 4; Siepmann 2005):

Table 54

English phrase	German equivalent
It is interesting to note that [...].	Interessant zu vermerken ist, dass [...].
It should be further noted that [...].	Weiter ist zu beachten, dass [...].

It would take us too far afield now to consider + NP.	Es würde zu weit führen, wollte der Verfasser [...] berücksichtigen.
It follows from what has been said so far that [...].	Aus dem Gesagten ergibt sich, dass [...].

Another area of difficulty at the lexical level is the use of adjectives. Since academic texts aim to provide an objective account, there is little room for purely 'decorative' epithets, as exemplified in the following excerpt from a student text:

> This passage shows that Robinson is not really a true, fervent, passionate believer. (Anon.)

Here one adjective (e.g. 'true') would have been sufficient.

Metaphors may also give rise to difficulties. If you use figurative language, you must beware of mixed metaphors like the bizarre image in the following quotation:

> A crime wave festers in cyberspace (*International Herald Tribune* 28.1.2003)

This headline sounds ridiculous because a wave cannot fester. When *fester* is used in its literal sense, it is normally combined with nouns like *sore* and *wound* (cf. Ger. *eitern*).

The syntactic features of style which make for aptness have already been discussed in Chapter 1. The features in question include nominal, passive and other impersonal constructions. Another interesting feature, which has received detailed treatment in Module II, Chapter 2.3.6, is the placement of circumstantial elements in subject position:

> **The thirteenth century saw** the establishment of six universities in Spain. (Durant 1994: s.p.)
> **The policy found** its advocates in Adam Smith (1723–1790), David Ricardo (1772–1823), Thomas Robert Malthus (1766–1834), John Stuart Mill (1806–1873) and John Locke (1623–1704). (Gilpin 1977, under 'laissez-faire')
> He returned to Britain in 1766, retired to Kircaldy and set about revising and finishing his work. **It** was finally published in 1776, and **brought** him considerable fame. (Seldon and Pennance 1976, under 'Smith, Adam')

All these constructions are extremely formal.[3] In everyday spoken English they would be replaced by completely different patterns: *in the thirteenth cen-*

[3] Like *derive support from* and many other similar expressions, they could be classified as grammatical metaphors.

tury six universities were established [...], the policy was advocated by [...], when it was finally published in 1776 he became quite famous. If you are a native speaker of German, you will probably find it hard to imitate the construction in the first example, for in German you have no choice but to say: *im dreizehnten Jahrhundert wurden sechs Universitäten in Spanien gegründet.* However, you will have less trouble with the expressions used in the other two examples. *To find advocates in* + NOUN PHRASE corresponds to *Befürworter in* + NOUN PHRASE + *finden,* just as *to bring sb considerable fame* corresponds to *jmdm beträchtlichen Ruhm bescheren/bringen.*

Finally, let us consider the text level. When you set about writing an academic paper, you are bound by a number of well-established conventions, the most important of which were outlined in Modules I and II. The conventions in question concern the overall structure of, say, a quantitative linguistics paper, the organization of individual paragraphs, preferred ways of formulating titles and introductory sections, etc. Writing appropriately at the text level is therefore chiefly a matter of copying the models provided by the representatives of your academic discipline.

In order to achieve aptness at the text level, German-speaking writers of English will be well advised to write with more qualifications than is usual in German. Nash & Stacey (1997) have brilliantly caricatured the Anglo-American tendency to academic prudence in the following excerpt, which may serve as a blueprint for abstracts and first paragraphs:

> There are *two* ways, *provisionally,* of diddling a dum. *One, probably* the simpler, is to begin the diddle on the North side and work Southward, avoiding the distortion, *if any,* of the hi-de-ho. *The other,* used by some but by no means all experienced dum-diddlers, is to proceed from South to North. A *third* method, of diddling the dum from East to West, and *in certain circumstances* vice-versa, lies beyond the scope of the present discussion, which will be confined, *in the main,* to dum-diddling of the first kind, with *some* reference to *the principal* findings of *relatively* advanced research into diddling technology. (Nash & Stacey 1997: 22; italics theirs)

By using words and phrases such as *two, probably, if any* and *in the main,* the authors introduce a notion of imprecision and qualification. It is their way of fending off potential criticisms to the effect that they appear certain of more things than is humanly possible or that they have overlooked some aspects of research.

Closely related to academic prudence, and of equal value in achieving aptness, is academic modesty. The following example will serve to illustrate what is meant:

> The present study has been a valuable contribution to research into tag questions. (Anon.)

Here the author has used an evaluative adjective (cf. Module III, Chapter 2.2) to describe his own work. In Anglo-American academic circles, such statements are felt to be immodest, and you should avoid them. What you may do is express the hope that your work may make a valuable contribution, open up new avenues for research, etc. We suggest you might write something like this:

> → It is hoped that the present study may be a valuable contribution to research into tag questions./(with a different meaning) I hope to have shown that tag questions are an area of investigation that may well repay further study.

If you want to ensure that your text will be considered apt, you should take the following precautions:

1. If you are planning to publish an article in a scholarly journal, you should have a look at some back issues in order to find out about the formal and linguistic conventions of the journal in question.
2. Check logical and inter-sentential relations to make sure that everything in your text fits perfectly together.
3. Weed out informal words and phrases that might sound inappropriate. Consult a monolingual dictionary if you are not sure how a particular vocabulary item might be perceived by a native speaker of English.
4. Check all the technical terms to make sure that you have used them correctly. Consult monolingual technical dictionaries to check meanings and carry out corpus investigations to check collocations (e.g. *to perform diagnostic radiology, to carry out amniocentesis,* etc.).
5. Do not use mixed metaphors and decorative adjectives.
6. Show academic prudence and modesty.

2.2 Clarity

The problems connected with clarity fall into three broad categories: (1) lexical choice, (2) syntax, and (3) beyond-the-sentence phenomena. It is true that these problem areas are closely interrelated, but we would only confuse our readers if we were to attempt to deal with all of them at the same time.

It will be convenient to begin with the difficulties associated with lexical choices. The following example is from a text written by a native speaker of German. It shows how an infelicitous choice of words can result in obscurity:

> Many respectable families and individuals were ready to risk the circulating library's ambiguous space. (Anon.)

How, one wonders, can anyone risk a space? What is an ambiguous space? And where can one find an ambiguous space in a library? In order to solve these mysteries, one has to look more closely at the term paper from which the sentence has been extracted, and which, for considerations of space, cannot be reproduced here. If we try to reconstruct the meaning, we may arrive at something like this:

> Many respectable families and individuals were ready to risk going to circulating libraries even though these establishments had a rather dubious reputation.

In order to render the student's sentence grammatically acceptable, one needs to know that the verb *risk* is often used with an *-ing* form (*to risk doing sth*), and in order to resolve the problem posed by *ambiguous space* one needs to know that the noun *reputation* collocates with the verb *have* as well as with adjectives like *dubious*. The noun *space*, which is probably intended as as a fashionable sociological term (cf. *a male-dominated space*) in the incriminated sentence, may be replaced by a more appropriate noun such as *establishment*.

The following sentence also exhibits a high degree of imprecision and obscurity.

> Herewith PPT broadens the view from a disorder perspective to that one on the individual personality of the patient. (Anon.)

There is nothing wrong with *PPT*, which stands for 'personality-oriented psychotherapy'. But what does the author mean by *broadens the view*, and what is a *disorder perspective*? As in the preceding case, one has to submit the text to detailed examination in order to elucidate the meaning of the sentence under discussion. The aim of the sentence in question is to show that PPT allows one to take a broader view of something and to highlight a contrast between two approaches – one centred on the patient, the other on the patient's disorder. This gives us the following sentence:

> By shifting the focus from the disorder to the patient, PPT enables us to view the individual patient's personality in a broader perspective.

The use of the collocation *shift the focus* allows us to use the simple nouns *disorder* and *patient*; we can do without opaque compounds such as *disorder perspective*. In order to draw attention to another difference between PTT and other approaches to psychotherapy, the author uses the word sequence *broadens the view*. Unfortunately, the noun *view* is inappropriate here. If, instead of *view*, she had chosen *perspective* (a word she reserved for another part of the sentence), she could have employed a typically English word combination: *to view something in a broader perspective*.

A good way of noting useful vocabulary is to look for constructions before literally or metaphorically putting pen to paper. Let us suppose you want to write an English text about monetary integration in Europe. Instead of sifting through German source material, you can dip into monographs written by British economists. Do not focus on isolated words such as *difference, system, discipline* or *objective*. Instead, look for constructions like *pronounced differences of view, there is a widespread consensus that* + clause or *to set up a system* (cf. Module III, Chapter 1). The following examples will show you what can be done with the word combinations we have just mentioned:

Table 55

Collocations	Sentences
pronounced differences of view	When politicians began to discuss the problems posed by monetary integration, it soon became evident that there were pronounced differences of view between the member states./Pronounced differences of view existed among the member states from the outset.
to set up a system	They decided they would have to set up an entirely new system./The system that was set up the following year was far from perfect.

So much for lexical problems. Let us now turn to syntax. The syntactic defect that most frequently results in obscurity is the separation of sentence elements that belong together. The greater the distance between these elements, the greater the probability that the reader will have difficulty in understanding the sentence.

Separating closely linked elements will not detract from the clarity of a sentence unless the writer exceeds a certain limit. A few examples will show you where that limit lies. Let us begin by examining a sentence in which a relative pronoun has been separated from its antecedent:

> A number of shorter poems survive which belong like *Beowulf* to the stories of the Germanic peoples. (Evans 1970: 15)

Evans has made use of a discontinuous structure by separating the relative clause (*which belong* ...) from the noun phrase to which it refers (*a number of shorter poems*). The meaning is perfectly clear because there is only one word (*survive*) between *poems* and *which*, and because the relative clause is in focus (cf. Module II, Chapter 2.5.2).

Similar observations apply to the following sentence, where the verb has been separated from its direct object (i.e. a case of object postponement; see Module II, Chapter 2.5.4):

> [...] Shakespeare's skill is seen by his elimination of Falstaff at the very opening, so that he shall not delay with his great bulk the action which is to follow. (Evans 1970: 151)

Evans had to choose between at least three options:

Table 56

	Description of option	Text
(1)	main clause + relative clause with prepositional phrase in end position	he shall not delay the action which is to follow **with his great bulk**
(2)	main clause with prepositional phrase in mid-position + relative clause	he shall not delay **with his great bulk** the action which is to follow
(3)	main clause with prepositional phrase inserted after the auxiliary	he shall not **with his great bulk** delay the action which is to follow

Options (2) and (3) are acceptable, but option (1) is unsatisfactory because there are too many words between *delay* and *with his great bulk*. The reader gets the impression that *with his great bulk* belongs to *follow*. Since Evans decided to put a relative clause after *action*, he chose to insert the prepositional phrase *with his great bulk* between the verb *delay* and its direct object (*the action*). His sentence is clear and elegant.

Now let us consider a much longer sentence where over 20 words have been placed between a verb and its preposition:

> He might well have joined those who contrasted the speed with which tyranny disappears in the modern world when it is based upon the rule of only one man with its apparent unshakability when fed on an ideology and sustained by a self-perpetuating oligarchy. (Thody 1989: 7)

The odds are that most people will have to read this sentence twice before they grasp the author's meaning. The main obstacle to comprehension is the inordinate length of the word group *the speed with which tyranny disappears in the modern world when it is based upon the rule of only one man.*

When you use the verb *contrast* and the preposition *with* in the active voice, you have no choice but to separate the verb from the preposition. Thus, for instance, you will say *to contrast France with Spain* or *to contrast literature with the pictorial arts*. Such word combinations are perfectly clear as long as there are only one or two words between *contrast* and *with*, but serious problems arise once a certain limit has been exceeded.

Look again at Thody's sentence. When you get as far as the prepositional phrase *with its apparent unshakability*, you will no doubt assume that the preposition *with* belongs to the noun *man*, and you will expect to find a noun phrase introduced by the indefinite article (e.g. *a man with an unnatural lust for power*). When you suddenly encounter the pronoun *its*, you will probably feel rather like someone who has just run headlong into a glass door that looked as if it was wide open. Realizing that *its* cannot possibly refer back to *man*, you will begin to retrace your steps, and a few seconds may elapse before you become aware that *with* belongs to *contrasted*.

Another obstacle to comprehension is the fact that the noun phrase *the modern world* has been placed between *it* and *tyranny*. It may be surmised that most readers will hesitate for a couple of seconds before they realize that the pronoun *it* refers to *tyranny*, not *the modern world*.

In order to make Thody's sentence more readable, we have to recast it completely. The contrast between transience and unshakability can be expressed by means of the conjunction *but*, which may be set off by a comma to highlight the adversative relation (cf. Module III, Chapter 4.7); *tyranny* and *it* can be brought closer together if we move *in the modern world* out of the way; the noun *speed* can be converted to an adverb (*quickly* or *soon*); and the word group *apparent unshakability* can be replaced by *seems to be unshakable*:

> He might well have joined those who were struck by the fact that in the modern world tyranny quickly disappears when it is based upon the rule of only one man, but seems to be unshakable when it is fed on an ideology and sustained by a self-perpetuating oligarchy.

The management of sentence structure is often intimately related to textual fit, which we discussed in Module II, Chapter 2. Considerable importance attaches to the initial part of the sentence, for the fronting of sentence elements is a useful device for establishing a stronger link with the previous context. This can be seen from the following examples, where syntactic structures have been adjusted in order to create clear inter-sentence links (cf. Module II, Chapters 2.3.2, 2.4, 2.5.5):

> The fashion is to despise Sir James Barrie (1860–1937), but it is dangerous to dismiss one who invented a mythology in a play of permanent popularity. **This** Barrie did in *Peter Pan* (1904). (Evans 1970: 191)
> The values contrast with the heroic standards of Shakespeare's *Othello*; **for high tragedy**, Heywood substituted sentiment and introspective morality. (Evans 1970: 167)
> The curious can turn to such a play as Cumberland's *The West Indian* (1771) to find how every human issue can be obscured in the welter of emotion. **From such depths** the drama was rescued by Goldsmith and Sheridan. (Evans 1970: 182)
> W.B. Yeats (1865–1939) brought his poetical gift to the service of the movement, and though he remained a lyrical writer rather than a dramatist, in *The Countess Cathleen* (1892) and *The Land of Heart's Desire* (1894), he evoked the mysticism and folk-lore of the Irish imagination. **Greater as a dramatist** was John Millington Synge (1871–1909), who had travelled widely on the Continent before he was encouraged by Yeats to seek in the Aran Islands the rhythms of a simple and unadulterated language for drama. (Evans 1970: 190)

In the first example Evans establishes a close link with the preceding sentence by fronting the demonstrative pronoun *this*, which refers to the word group *invented a mythology in a play of permanent popularity*. If we 'normalise' the word order in the second sentence (*Barrie did this*) the meaning is still sufficiently clear, but the link with the preceding sentence is less apparent and therefore less effective. In the second example the verb *substituted* has two complements. One of them (*for high tragedy*) has been fronted in order to forge a stronger link with the word group *Shakespeare's Othello*. In the third example the adverbial complement *from such depths* could have been placed after *rescued*, but it has been moved to clause-initial position in order to strengthen the link with the author's critical appraisal of Cumberland's play. In the last example the use of a presentative construction has been triggered by two factors: (1) the desire to reinforce the link with the preceding sentence, (2) the desire to afford focal prominence to the long and complex subject.

The fronting of sentence elements is only one of many devices which can be used to achieve or enhance clarity on the text level. These devices include anaphoric linkage, sentence connectors, the presentation of facts in chronological order, a gradual progression from the abstract to the concrete, and a combination of parallelism and antithesis. In order to show how these devices function, we shall analyse a few brief excerpts from well-written academic texts.

Our first example is from a biographical note on H.G. Wells:

> During his years as a biology tutor Wells slowly began making his way as a writer and journalist. He wrote for the *Educational Times*, edited the *University Correspondent*, and in 1891 published a philosophical essay, 'The Rediscovery of the Unique', in the prestigious *Fortnightly Review*. His first book was a *Textbook of Biology* (1893). But no sooner was it published than his health again collapsed, forcing him to give up teaching and rely entirely on his literary earnings. His future seemed highly precarious, yet soon he was in regular demand as a writer of short stories and humorous essays for the burgeoning newspapers and magazines of the period. He became a fiction reviewer and, for a short period in 1895, a theatre critic. (Wells 2005: viii–ix)

This paragraph is very loosely constructed, but the author has achieved clarity by using two very effective sentence-linking devices:

- First, he presents facts in chronological order (*1891, 1893, 1895*).
- Second, nearly all the sentence subjects (*Wells, he, his first book, his health, his future, he, he*) refer directly or indirectly to Wells. The only exception is the pronoun *it*, which refers back to *his first book*.

Our second example is from a book about statistics:

> Statistics is no more than State Arithmetic, a system of computation by which differences between individuals are eliminated by the taking of an average. It has been used – indeed, still is used – to enable rulers to know just how far they may safely go in picking the pockets of their subjects. A king going to war wishes to know what reserves of manpower and money he can call on. How many men need he put in the field to defeat the enemy? How many guns and shirts, how much food, will they need? How much will all this cost? Have the citizens the necessary money to pay for the king's war? (Moroney 1970: 1)

In this passage the author proceeds from the abstract to the concrete. The opening sentence is a definition of the term *statistics*; the second sentence concerns the uses to which rulers put this science; and the rest of the paragraph exemplifies the assertion made in the second sentence. The first sentence is purely abstract; the second sentence provides a transition from the abstract to the concrete; and the remaining sentences are essentially concrete.

Our third example is the first section of a relatively long paragraph from the introductory chapter of a history book. It highlights the value of structural parallels to express contrast.

> The history of civilized man in our country is very old; it begins long before the reign of Alfred. But the history of Britain as a leader in the world's affairs is of

much shorter date; it begins with the reign of Elizabeth. The reason can be read upon the map. (Trevelyan 1964: xiii)

This passage conveys an impression of exceptional clarity because of the adversative conjunction *but*, the structural parallels and contrasts between the first two sentences, and the brevity and directness of the final statement. The structural parallels and contrasts are shown in tables 57 and 58:

Table 57: Parallels

(1)	The history of + NP	is + COMPLEMENT	it begins	the reign of + NAME OF MONARCH
(2)	the history of + NP	is + COMPLEMENT	it begins	the reign of + NAME OF MONARCH

Table 58: Contrasts

(1)	civilized man	in our country	very old	long before
(2)	Britain	as a leader in the world's affairs	of much shorter date	with

Our fourth example is a tightly constructed paragraph from a book review:

The two women tell the story in their diaries. Margaret's is full of descriptive detail, reports on her moods and feelings, and the conversations she has with friends and family. Selina, by contrast, sticks to the bare bones, concealing as much as she reveals. (*World and Press*, 1st October issue, 2006: 7)

The opening sentence is the topic sentence, i.e. it tells us what the paragraph is about. The other statements expand on the topic sentence: they provide more information about the two women mentioned in sentence (1). Sentence (2) is about Margaret, while sentence (3) focuses on Selina.

The links between the three sentences are so clear that they will be immediately apparent to most readers. The author, however, has inserted an additional link between sentence (2) and sentence (3). In order to underline the differences between Margaret and Selina, she uses the conjunctive adverbial *by contrast* (cf. Module II, Chapters 3.4.1 and 3.5.1 and Module III, Chapter 4.7).

A word of warning must be added here: even in texts written by native speakers of English, one occasionally comes across passages which are lacking in clarity because pronouns have not been used with sufficient care. Consider the following example:

There is a simple explanation for this: in mid-twentieth-century France, as in Europe in general, the **police** were often required to play a political role. Quite

> a lot of **people** therefore came to think that this was all **they** did. Camus's lifelong enthusiasm for revolutionary syndicalism led him to be one of **them**. (Thody 1989: 101)

In this passage it is not always clear what the personal pronouns *they* and *them* are meant to refer to. The pronoun *they* refers back to *police*. Unfortunately, however, the noun *people* has been placed between *police* and *they*. This can create confusion because both *people* and *police* can be replaced by a plural pronoun. The problem is further complicated by the presence of the pronoun *them*, which refers to *people*, not *police*. We can remedy such deficiencies by replacing pronouns by noun phrases: *this was all* ***the police*** *did, one of* ***these people***.

If you are anxious to ensure that your text will be sufficiently clear, you should proceed as follows:

1. Draw up a list of the principal word combinations you wish to use in your text. All these word groups should be taken from monolingual reference books and published texts written by native speakers of English.
2. If you want to use words you have found in a bilingual dictionary, you should look for example sentences in monolingual reference works or authentic texts. A Google search may throw up some useful collocations.
3. If the word combination you have chosen does not fit easily into your sentence, you should change the construction or look for another word combination that belongs to the same conceptual field. In such cases you may find what you are looking for in a book like the *Longman Language Activator* (Summers 1993).
4. Try to avoid separating sentence elements that belong together (e.g. relative pronouns and their antecedents, verbs and their prepositions).
5. If such sentence elements are separated, check whether the sentence is easy to interpret.
6. Make sure that the grammatical relationships between the various parts of each sentence are perfectly clear. Words like *to* and *that* deserve special attention.
7. Check all the inter-sentence links in your text. Particular attention needs to be paid to pronouns (especially *it* and *this*), sentence connectors (e.g. *but, however, nonetheless*), generalizations, illustrative examples, parallels and contrasts.

2.3 Concision

We now turn to the question of concision. Concision concerns both form and substance and is greatly appreciated in academic circles since it contributes in no small measure to clarity. In order to achieve concision, you have to eliminate irrelevancies and compress a great deal of information into a few words.

Let us begin with the problems posed by the substance of the text. Needless repetitions and irrelevancies convey an impression of flabbiness and are likely to exasperate readers who are pressed for time. In the following example an inexperienced writer repeats information from the immediately preceding context. The propositional content of the first sentence is reproduced more or less verbatim in the second one:

> A lie can improve one's status. A very famous lie which had to do with the improvement of status was made up by a man called Carl Schwietert.

The same idea can be expressed in less laboured fashion by a word such as *example*:

> → A lie can improve one's status. One very famous example is due to a man called Carl Schwietert.

We come now to the language problems associated with concision. These problems may be brought under the following heads: (1) lack of vocabulary, (2) imitation of German constructions (3) superfluous adverbs, (4) sentence-shortening devices (e.g. paired postmodifying adjectives, participial constructions, ellipsis).

The problems associated with a limited vocabulary are frequently compounded by a lack of familiarity with the norms governing formal written communication (cf. Chapter 2.1). Let us consider a sentence which sounds awkward and inappropriately informal, especially since the conjunction *and* is repeated three times:

> The company lost a lot of money, and its debts got higher and higher, and it couldn't pay these debts, and so it went bankrupt. (Anon.) [25 words]

Here is a more concise formulation:

> Heavy losses and mounting debts drove the company into bankruptcy. [10 words]

If we compare the two versions, we find that 15 words have been eliminated. Table 59 pinpoints the main changes.

Table 59: Revising an awkward formulation

Original Sentence	Revised Version
The company lost a lot of money	heavy losses
its debts got higher and higher	mounting debts
it couldn't pay these debts, and so it went bankrupt	drove the company into bankruptcy

Almost all the constituents of the original have undergone some kind of transformation: *lost* → *losses* (nominalization), *a lot of money* → *heavy* (more precise adjective), *debts got higher and higher* → *mounting debts* (nominalization), *went bankrupt* → *drove [...] into bankruptcy* (relational verb) (cf. Chapter 1.3.2 on the interplay between nominalization and relational verbs). A careful examination of these transformations shows that a sentence similar to the reworked version can be generated only if the writer possesses two types of information: (1) information about collocations (*heavy* + *loss, mounting* + *debts, drive [...] into bankruptcy*), (2) information about the norms governing written as opposed to spoken language.

Information about the aforementioned collocations can easily be gleaned from the *Oxford Collocations Dictionary for Students of English* (cf. Module III, Chapter 1), but it is much more difficult to obtain reliable information about the differences between spoken and written English. This is because the norms governing the written language are often very subtle and have to be inferred from sentences such as the following:

> Meanwhile, steeply rising social costs were driving the dormitory town into bankruptcy. (*The Economist* 22.10.1994)

This example shows that in written English the expression *drive sth into bankruptcy* can be used with an inanimate subject like *costs*.[4] Most readers, however, will fail to notice this construction unless their attention has already been drawn to the fact that transitive verbs with inanimate subjects are a recurrent feature of academic English (cf. Chapter 2.1).

True, it might be argued that *heavy losses and mounting debts drove the company into bankruptcy* (10 words) is not much shorter than *the company went bankrupt because of heavy losses and mounting debts* (11 words), but one should not overlook the fact that all the lexical choices in our reworked version are interdependent. If one knows that in formal written English transitive verbs

4 The same goes for the expressions *to force a company into bankruptcy* and *to push a company into bankruptcy*.

are often used with inanimate subjects, the formulation process will evolve in ways that would not otherwise be possible. For instance, one may think of Ger. *ein Unternehmen in den Konkurs treiben* or one of its English equivalents (*to drive a company into bankruptcy*), then one may start casting around for abstract nouns that might be placed in clause-initial position; the search for such words may well trigger a chain reaction, the verb *lose* suggesting the noun *loss*, and the noun *loss* linking up automatically with *debts*.

Learners who read widely and devote a sufficient amount of time to vocabulary work gradually become aware of the rich possibilities offered by the English language. As their vocabulary expands, they find it increasingly easy to express themselves concisely without recourse to lengthy periphrases like those listed in the left-hand columns of Tables 60 and 61. If you are unsure how to express yourself concisely, you may skim through such vocabulary aids as *Longman Language Activator* (Summers 1993) or the thesauri which come with the electronic versions of the *Cambridge Advanced Learner's Dictionary* (Walter 2006) and the *Macmillan English Dictionary* (Rundell 2005). The word *buff*, for example, can be found in the section entitled *know* of the *Longman Language Activator*.

Table 60: Compounds formed with *buff*

Periphrases	Compounds
a person who is very interested in computers and knows a lot about these machines	a computer buff
a person who is very interested in wine and knows a lot about this kind of alcoholic drink	a wine buff
a person who is very interested in films and knows a lot about them	a film buff
a person who is very interested in history and knows a lot about this subject	a history buff
a person who is very interested in science and knows a lot about this area of knowledge	a science buff

Table 61: Typical Collocations Used in Academic Texts

Periphrases	Collocations
repetitions *which have no useful purpose*	*otiose* repetitions
information *that is not directly connected with the subject the author is dealing with*	*extraneous* information
to *make* prose *more interesting*	to *vivify* prose

Since German academics writing in English tend to be strongly influenced by their mother tongue, they often use wordy expressions like *within the framework of this article* or *an authority in the field of microbiology. Within the framework of* + NP and *in the field of* + NP admittedly do occur in texts written by native speakers of English, but they are much less common than German phrases such as *im Rahmen* + NP, *im Bereich* + NP or *auf dem Gebiet* + NP. The normal English equivalent of *im Rahmen dieser Untersuchung* is ***in** this article, im Rahmen der modernen Gesellschaft* is ***in** modern society,* and *eine Autorität auf dem Gebiet der Quantenphysik* can be rendered as *an authority **on** quantum physics.*

At this point it may be appropriate to say something about superfluous adverbs. Native speakers of English often pad out their sentences with overworked words like *actually, basically, obviously,* and *literally.* Here are a few typical examples:

> Though Rupert Murdoch probably never did **actually** say that only three national daily papers would eventually survive, he had a point. (*The Guardian* 28.12.1998: 17)
> He certainly looks quite fit and perky – what I can see of him anyway, which is **basically** just his head. (*The Observer* 13.12.1998: 4)
> Liberal Democrat leader Paddy Ashdown said: "It sounds as if it was a bungled operation. **Obviously** this is a tragic outcome and we have had a few of these outcomes." (*The Guardian* 30.12.1998: 1)
> As deputy chief executive, his door was **literally** always open and even the most junior member of staff was welcome to come and air his or her woes. (*The Guardian* 1.12.1998: 22)

The adverbs in boldface type are so popular with German students that a naïve observer might be tempted to hypothesize that Germans are directly influenced by the linguistic behaviour of native English speakers. However, there are good grounds for assuming that German students deliberately lengthen their English texts with the aid of meaningless modifiers because they are afraid that their texts may not be long enough to satisfy their teachers. This assumption has been confirmed by many students we have interviewed over the past few years.

Let us now turn our attention to three artful sentence-shortening devices: paired postmodifying adjectives, participial constructions, and ellipsis. The following examples show how greater economy of expression can be achieved by using paired postmodifying adjectives instead of relative clauses or noun phrases in apposition (cf. Broughton 1990: 223–224):

In *Grandeur Nature* the relationship is that of a mediocre, unsuccessful actor and his wife: the husband, **selfish and self-centred**, is content as long as he can monopolize the attention and admiration of his wife [...]. (Troyat 1954: 9)

This man, who a dozen years before had been a Wicklow country gentleman, **moody and reserved**, known outside his own family chiefly as a cricketer, had become the touchstone of the whole British Empire and the arbiter of fate to its Ministers. (Trevelyan 1965: 382)

The author of the first example could have used a relative clause (*who is selfish and self-centred*), but the formulation he opted for is more concise.[5] Our second example is rather different, for if we wanted to turn *moody and reserved* into a relative clause we would have to insert a conjunction before *known*: *[...] a Wicklow country gentleman who was moody and reserved* ***and*** *known [...]*. The sentence would be grammatically correct, but the repetition of *and* would be somewhat infelicitous. The word group *moody and reserved* might also be placed before *Wicklow*, but *moody and reserved Wicklow country gentleman* would be unduly long and would sound rather clumsy. It follows therefore that the only really acceptable substitute for Trevelyan's paired adjectives would be a noun phrase in apposition (*a moody and reserved fellow*).

Like paired postmodifying adjectives, participial constructions (cf. Module II, Chapter 3.2.3; Wilss 1971) are often substituted for relative clauses. A few examples will suffice:

Europe had been the centre of yet another devastating war **arising** out of the unbridled ambitions of nation states. (Swann 1992: 1–2)

But what if, in the century now **dawning**, the air became a pathway of attack? (Trevelyan 1965: 410)

The contemporary newsreels **showing** the demonstrators sweeping down the Champs Elysées are a terrifying reminder of how powerful the right was at the time. (Thody 1992: 74–75)

The quotation also invites the reader to see the artist as **forced** into a kind of inner exile by the pressures which society exerts on him. (Thody 1989: 100)

Most academic economists, even when writing for large popular audiences, cannot resist hinting at their rigorous scholarly ways: an assumption here, an equation there, a remark '**proved**' by reference to a theory too complicated to explain to the lesser mortals **reading** their books. (*The Economist* 11.4.1992)

All these sentences become somewhat longer when the participles in boldface type are replaced by finite verb forms: *arising* → *that had arisen, dawning*

---

[5] It is interesting to note that the word-group *selfish and self-centred* might also have been placed before the noun: *[...] selfish and self-centred, the husband [...]*.

→ *that was now dawning, showing* → *which show, forced* → *someone who is forced, 'proved'* → *which is 'proved', reading* → *who are reading.*

Turning now to ellipsis, we find that this device can take on a great variety of forms. The following examples will convey to you some appreciation of that extraordinary diversity:

Table 62: Ellipsis

Types of Ellipsis	Examples
Ellipsis of a verb	a) Each art **had** its own medium: the painter Δ his pigments, the musician Δ his sounds, and the writer, Δ words. (Evans 1970: 23) b) True scholarship **is** incommunicable, true scholars Δ rare. (Forster 1960: 13) c) There is a progession in the way the elements **nourish** plants, the fruits of plants Δ beasts, and the flesh of beasts Δ men. (Tillyard 1998: 36) d) But times **were changing**, and Gladstone Δ with them. (Trevelyan 1965: 369)
Ellipsis of a noun-phrase head	e) Both **men** were pioneers in the statistical, theoretical, and mathematical advances of the modern generation. Yet each Δ was also passionately concerned with economic policy, within his own country and for the world at large. (Samuelson 1980: 5) f) Naturally, most **students** do not expect to specialize in economics. Most Δ will study it only for a term or two […]. (Samuelson 1980: 4) g) There is not one **theory of economics** for Republicans and one Δ for Democrats; one Δ for workers and one Δ for employers; one Δ for the Russians and still another Δ for the Chinese. (Samuelson 1980: 6)
Ellipsis of a subject and a verb	h) Though Δ familiar with the concept of natural law […], the rabbis objected to making nature the basis of law. (*Encyclopaedia Britannica*, s.v. Judaism) i) Although Δ born in extreme poverty, his inherent ability enabled him to attend the lycée, and later the university, in Algiers. (Thorlby 1969: 156)
Ellipsis of a noun-phrase head and a verb	j) The first **part was published** in 1604 and the second Δ in 1630. (Evans 1970: 167)
Ellipsis of a verb and its complement	k) This doesn't mean that we do not **have great amounts of accurate statistical knowledge available**. We do Δ. (Samuelson 1980: 7)
Ellipsis of a direct object, a subject and a verb	l) Let us briefly ask ourselves what **part they play** in our lives, and what Δ in novels. (Forster 1960: 47)

Ellipsis of a relative pronoun and a verb	m) As far as medieval literature is concerned this is well illustrated in R.M. Wilson's *The Lost Literature of Medieval England* (1952) which shows how many references there are to poems Δ no longer extant, to heroes Δ unknown, and to stories Δ now unrecorded. (Evans 1970: 12)

This table calls for a few comments:

- Sentence elements which are subsequently omitted are in boldface type. The symbol Δ has been inserted wherever a word or word group has been deliberately left out.
- In some cases only one constituent is ellipted (e.g. a); in others two or three constituents are omitted (e.g. l).
- The examples fall into two clearly recognizable groups: (1) examples in which the ellipted expression is visible, (2) examples in which the ellipted expression is invisible. Example j) belongs to the first group, while i) may be assigned to the second group. Example j) contains both an antecedent construction (*the first part was published in 1604*) and an elliptical construction (*the second in 1630*). Example i), by contrast, has no antecedent construction. *Although born* means *although he was born*, but the ellipted sentence elements (*he* and *was*) are invisible.

That said, concision is sometimes purchased at the expense of clarity. Consider the following example:

> So far, poachers have not exercised their right to export ivory, but if they are offered no compromises, they **may start** looking for ways of resuming the ivory trade with countries that have not signed the CITES agreement, **or leave** the convention altogether. (Anon.)

Because of the great distance separating the verbs *start* and *leave*, it might be preferable to repeat *may* in front of *leave* or to resort to more radical expansion (*otherwise they may*). The greater the distance, the more you have to repeat.

If you are anxious to pare down your style, you should proceed as follows:

1. Re-read your text carefully to make sure you have not wandered off the subject.
2. Avoid needless repetition.
3. Look for specific lexical items that might be substituted for long-winded periphrases. If you are looking for words and expressions which are not

yet part of your active vocabulary, you can use the *Longman Language Activator* (Summers 1993) or the thesaurus which comes with the *Cambridge Advanced Learner's Dictionary* (Walters 2006).

4. Look for clauses that might be replaced by noun phrases (e.g. *inflation was rising* → *rising inflation*).
5. Make sure you have not used the conjunction *and* more often than necessary.
6. Look for relative clauses that might be replaced by paired postmodifying adjectives or participial constructions.
7. Look for structures that might be tightened up by means of ellipsis.

2.4 Variety

Now it is time to examine the question of variety. The primary focus will be on the artistry involved in composing texts which are free from unpleasant verbal or structural repetitions. Four problem areas will command our attention: (1) lexical variation, (2) variations of syntax, (3) variations in sentence length, and (4) variations in the organizational patterns of paragraphs.

Let us look first at the problems germane to lexical variation. Consider the following extract:

> **Notification**, or rather the lack of **it**, also poses a problem. It cannot be said that lack of **notification** of, for example, international cartels totally inhibits antitrust control since those who are adversely affected may none the less be able to assemble unmistakable proof of the existence of such a cartel by reference to the pattern of prices and supplies. (Swann 1979: 254)

This passage illustrates two complementary phenomena: lexical variation and repetition. *Notification* is replaced by the pronoun *it* in the first sentence, but not in the second. *Lack of it* is possible, but **lack of it of* is not.

The pronoun *it* is often used wrongly by German students to refer back to an entire stretch of text rather than a noun phrase. This is probably due to interference with German *es* or *das*:

> It would be senseless to attempt a comparative analysis of bilingualism in Canada and other countries without being aware of the internal structure of language across the country. **It** may be analogous to a comparison between two glasses of red wine → There would be little point in trying to compare bilingualism in Canada and other countries without an awareness of the situation in Canada itself. **This/Such a procedure** would be analogous to a comparison between two glasses of red wine.

In both studies, no change was found in the period between 1900 and 1950. **It** may be explained by several factors. → In both studies no change was found in the period between 1900 and 1950. **This (result)** may be due to several factors.

As can be seen from the revised versions, this overuse of *it* correlates with an underuse of 'retrospective labels'[6] such as *result* (cf. Module III, Chapter 2.1). The writer should have used the pronoun *this* or, preferably, *this* plus an abstract noun such as *finding* or *result*.

In the following sentence *it* is used correctly to refer back to the noun *book*. However, the sentence introduced by *it* is so short that it can be profitably merged with the preceding one by means of a relative clause:

He seems to have been a practical man because he wrote a book called 'Physica et Mystica' (title of the Latin translation). **It** contains a number of rather obscure recipes for the making of gold and colouring of metals. → [...] since he wrote a book called 'Physica et Mystica' **which** contains [...]

The word *it* is by no means the only pro-form used in contemporary English, nor are pro-forms the only device we can employ in order to avoid the needless repetition of a lexical item. Witness the following examples:

Table 63

Linguistic devices	Examples
Other pro-forms	Contributors of more permanence were those serious **authors** who wrestled with the 'inadequacy' of English. Of **these** the most important was Sir Thomas Elyot. (Gordon 1980: 76) All South African rivers are obstructed by silt, and as sheltered bays are **rare, so** also are good harbours. (Suggate 1957: 386–387) On 25 March 1957 the governments of France, West Germany, Italy, the Netherlands, Belgium and Luxembourg **signed the Rome Treaty**. In **so doing** they agreed to create what is now known as the Common Market, or, more accurately, the European Economic Community. (Swann 1992: ix) Let us begin by taking a simple **case** – virtually a non-literary **one** – the **case** of a scientific paper reporting the results of an experiment. (Hough 1969: 9) Only if God existed could there be complete knowledge of any **event**, especially as complex and complicated **a one** as a world war. (Thody 1992: 146)
Compound nouns	**Agreements about prices** in respect of sales to third-country markets may well be accompanied by quotas applicable to individual enterprises or to national groups. Such **price arrangements** may also be accompanied by agreements not to lay down additional capacity. (Swann 1979: 237)

6 By 'retrospective labels' we mean general nouns that summarize the previous context.

Synonyms	The third reaction is to say that if you can keep believing in God only by **abandoning** all normal rational criteria, it might be a better idea to **give up** religious belief altogether. (Thody 1989: 55–56)
Partial synonyms	Only a few years back their **soldiers** had been represented by our comic artists as funny **little** men strutting about under the weight of enormous helmets. In 1870 these **diminutive warriors** shot up, in the English prints, into genial giants with bushy beards, singing Luther's hymns round Christmas-trees before Paris. (Trevelyan 1965: 352)
Hypernyms replaced by hyponyms	People grew tired of his spirited foreign and Imperial policy when they found themselves involved in prolonged **operations** against the Afghans and Zulus. Yet both these **wars,** after a period of reverses, ended successfully [...]. (Trevelyan 1965: 369)
Hyponyms replaced by hypernyms	The **letter**, if genuine, would have killed the Home Rule movement in Britain. Nearly two years later the **document** was proved to have been forged by a needy Irish journalist named Pigott, and to have been accepted without scrutiny as to its origin. (Trevelyan 1965: 393) The word appears again, and with a new supporting quotation, in the 1933 **supplement** – a **volume** that had to be added because of the sheer weight of new words and new evidence of new meanings that had accumulated during the decades when the original Dictionary was being compiled. (Winchester 1999: 28)
Gerundial expressions	Although the actual steps which have been taken to **achieve economic and political unity in Europe** are mostly, if not all, post 1945 in origin, the idea of such a **coming together** is not unique to the last forty or so years. (Swann 1992: 1)

If you are anxious to introduce more variety into your English prose, you will have to build up an extensive vocabulary through wide reading and systematic study. The kind of vocabulary you acquire will depend to a large extent on the subject(s) you want to write about (history, literature, sociology, economics, law, medicine, etc.).

Your ability to use your vocabulary effectively will depend largely on the way you store and organize your information. All your lexical material should be stored in computer files (e.g. Excel files); the entries should be cross-referenced in such a way that you will be able to find synonyms, antonyms, hyponyms and hypernyms in a matter of seconds; and particular attention will have to be paid to word groups which constitute reusable linguistic units.

Recognizing these units is going to be one of your major problems, especially if, like most readers, you are accustomed to skimming through texts merely in order to glean non-linguistic information from them. If you want to find out more about the mechanics of language, you will have to read more slowly, and you will have to know what to look for. Here are a few example sentences which may serve to sharpen your awareness of the problems with which we are concerned here:

> The second point is that there is really very little justification for the selection of WILL and SHALL as the markers of future tense in English, even if we rely heavily upon time reference. (Palmer 1974: 37)
> Will you miss much of a movie dialogue heavily laced with slang? (Burke 1988: vii)

Notice how the adverb *heavily* is used by Palmer and Burke. In the first example *heavily* is synonymous with *a lot,* and in the second it could be replaced by *a lot of* (*a movie dialogue with a lot of slang*). It follows therefore that *heavily* and *a lot of* should be linked by cross-references in your computer files and stored in the same recess of your brain so that both expressions can be retrieved rapidly and effortlessly whenever you need them.

Here are two further examples:

> The central character of *L'Etranger*, he wrote, was a man 'without humanity, without human value, and even, in spite of the ambition to be realistic which provides the sole framework to the book, without any kind of human truth', and other critics took a similar line. (Thody 1989: 18–19)
> Camus expressed the same idea when he wrote in one of the essays in *Noces*: [...]. (Thody 1989: 25)

If you look closely at these examples you will discover two linguistic units which are very similar in meaning: *took a similar line* and *expressed the same idea. Take a similar line* and *express the same idea* are particularly useful expressions because they can be used as stylistic variants in order to avoid needless repetition in passages where you are discussing research literature and summarizing the findings reported by various scholars.[7] You can set up a link between two stretches of discourse by writing something like *Wilson expressed the same idea in an article about genetic fingerprinting;* then, in another part of your survey, you can write: *In recent years several other researchers have taken a similar line.*

Our next step is to consider how greater variety can be achieved at the sentence level without infringing Anglo-Saxon norms for theme-focus progression (cf. Module II, Chapter 2.2). Let us begin by examining a few extracts, all of which display typical features of German English, for example the underuse of subordinate clauses and the overuse of *and* as a clause or

7 There are similar expressions in German: *Den gleichen Standpunkt vertritt X, Ähnliche Ansichten entwickelt X in [TITLE OF A BOOK]* (cf. Gallagher 1994: 68–69).

sentence connector. In order to knock these extracts into shape, we have to make numerous adjustments of vocabulary and syntax. Our suggestions are given in Table 64 below. You will probably agree that our lexical and syntactic adjustments make a significant difference in writing quality. However, since space precludes a detailed discussion of all our emendations, we shall content ourselves with a few comments on syntactic structures and the semantic configurations which they express. The focus of our analysis will be on causal and temporal relationships, choice between two possibilities, and purpose.

Table 64: Improving variety at sentence level

Student version	Revised version	Commentary
The advantages of the introduction of Euro far outweigh the drawbacks. Finally, the new currency is accepted by most of the EU-citizens. Some became even europhoric and waited in the New Year's Eve before the cash machines to get the new currency. (Anon.)	Since it soon became clear that the advantages of the euro would far outweigh its drawbacks, the new currency had been accepted by most EU citizens by December 2001. Indeed, some people were so eager to get the new banknotes that they queued up in front of cash machines on New Year's Eve.	The first two sentences can be coalesced into a single statement if sentence 1 is transformed into a causal clause (*Since it soon…*). There is also a cause-effect relationship between the two facts reported in the sentence beginning with the words *Some became even*. However, instead of making this relationship clear, the student simply uses the coordinator *and* to link two independent clauses. In this instance it would have been preferable to recast the first independent clause and turn the second one into a result clause (*that they queued…*).
In June 1999 I had made my final examination at the Otto-Hahn-Gymnasium and then I had to absolve the civilian service as a paramedic at the "german red cross" (DRK) lasting on 10 months. (Anon.)	After taking the Abitur examination in June 1999, I opted for community service as an alternative to military service and spent ten months working as a paramedic for the German Red Cross.	In the original sentence a student has attempted, not very successfully, to verbalize two temporal relationships. The first of these is expressed by *and then*, the second by the participle clause *lasting on ten months.* The word combination *and then* is grammatically correct, but it can be replaced by a time clause introduced by *after* (*after taking the Abitur examination…*). *Lasting on 10 months*, however, is grammatically incorrect. The student has confused the prepositions *on* and *for*, and he has separated the participle *lasting* from the noun phrase to which it refers. In order to express the second temporal relationship correctly, we have to recast the second clause completely and use a

		construction which German students of English seem to find difficult (*to spend* + TIME INDICATOR + *-ing* form).
Do not worry about the use of capital and small initial letters, both will be accepted. (Anon.)	It does not matter whether you use upper- or lower-case letters.	The student who produced the original sentence was apparently unaware that a choice between two possibilities can be expressed by a dependent clause introduced by *whether* (*it does not matter whether...*). Since his syntactic repertoire was severely limited, he juxtaposed an imperative and an assertive main clause.
Click below and the quiz will start immediately. (Anon.)	Click on the following link in order to access the quiz.	As in the previous example, the student has juxtaposed an imperative and an assertive main clause. In the present instance, however, the semantic relationship between the two parts of the sentence is quite different and can be expressed by means of a purpose clause (*in order to access the quiz*).

The excerpts we have just discussed are typical of the English written by native speakers of German. They show that in order to produce better texts foreign students of English need to expand their syntactic repertoire. The best way to do this is to study grammatical structures and writing techniques simultaneously.[8]

Our analysis above shows that independent clauses, which tend to be overrepresented in English texts written by Germans, can often be combined by means of subordinators such as *since, that, whether* and *in order to*. In what now follows, we would like to bring attention to bear on some other syntactic structures which are rarely, if ever, used by German learners, and which might be adopted by advanced students who are anxious to give more variety to their English prose. The following examples will repay study:

8 Recent research has shown that students do not benefit from grammar study in isolation from writing, but there is evidence to suggest that sentence-combining exercises and sentence-imitating activities can help learners to produce texts which are syntactically more sophisticated and rhetorically more effective (Weaver et al. 2001).

Table 65: Improving variety with the aid of subordination

Construction	Examples	Commentary
Concessive clauses	The trial scene, **magnificent though it is**, does not form the climax of the play. (Evans 1970: 170) **Great novelist though she was,** – exquisite in her descriptions, tolerant in her judgments, ingenious in her incidents, advanced in her morality, vivid in her delineations of character, expert in her knowledge of three Oriental capitals – it was yet on none of these gifts that she relied when trying to save her life from her intolerable husband. (Forster 1960: 28)	Experienced writers employ concessive clauses where *though* occurs in non-initial position after the subject complement. This special type of concessive clause, which is very formal in tone, is comparatively common in academic texts written by English-speaking historians and literary critics.
interruptive adverbial clauses	**The Romans, after they** had conquered the island, made the fortune of London Bridge by concentrating upon it one half of their great roads, from both north and south. (Trevelyan 1964: 18)	Here again we have a rather unusual syntactic ordering (cf. Module II, Chapter 3.5.1). If we were to place the subordinator *after* at the beginning of the sentence, we would have to say *after conquering the island, the Romans […]* or *after they had conquered the island, the Romans […]*. Trevelyan, however, has transferred *the Romans* from the time clause to the main clause (*the Romans […] made the fortune […]*). This syntactic sleight-of-hand brings *the Romans* into prominence and serves as a topic-shifting device. It indicates that the author is moving on to a new topic, namely the intensive road building that followed the conquest of Britain.
It-clefts	**It was under the Emperor Claudius**, a century after Caesar's exploring expeditions, **that** the actual conquest of the island took place. (Trevelyan 1964: 18) In *much as I would like to help*, on the other hand, **it is an adverb alone that** is fronted. (Quirk et al. 1979: 750)	These cleft sentences are similar to some of the examples cited in Module II, Chapter 2. Instead of writing *the actual conquest of the island took place under the emperor Claudius*, Trevelyan has broken up the sentence into two clauses, each with its own verb (*was, took place*). The *it*-cleft gives exceptional prominence to the prepositional phrase *under the emperor Claudius*. In the second example Quirk et al. have used

		exactly the same device in order to bring the word group *an adverb alone* into focus (*an adverb alone is fronted → it is an adverb alone that is fronted*).
Non-restrictive appositions	In the common-sense **world** of modern English – the **world** which, after all, the great Dictionary was designed to fix and define – it is surely quite reasonable to have two or more leading players in any story. (Winchester 1999: 29) First, the Six were **preoccupied** with the problems of creating the kind of Community envisaged by the Rome Treaty, a **preoccupation** which was made no easier by internal dissension over matters such as majority voting and the continuing French rebuff to the U.K.'s membership aspirations. (Swann 1992: 189–190)	The first example shows how a sentence can be expanded by means of a simple appositive construction. The units in apposition are the noun phrases *the world* and *the common-sense world of modern English*. Although the antecedent of the relative pronoun *which* is the noun phrase *the common-sense world of modern English*, the pronoun *which* cannot be placed immediately after *English*, for if we were to write *the common-sense world of modern English which […]*, the sentence would almost certainly give rise to misinterpretations. Readers would not be sure whether *which* referred to the entire noun phrase or only to its last element (*modern English*). It is in order to avoid this kind of misunderstanding that Winchester repeats *the world*. The second example illustrates a much more complex kind of apposition. Two points need to be made here. First, the units in apposition do not belong to the same syntactic class, for the appositive noun phrase *a preoccupation* refers back not to another noun phrase, but to an entire clause: *the Six were preoccupied with the problems of creating the kind of Community envisaged by the Rome Treaty*. Second, instead of repeating the noun *preoccupation*, Swann uses two lexical items belonging to the same word family but different word classes (*preoccupied, preoccupation*).

We may now turn to a consideration of variations in sentence length. If all your sentences are the same length, your text will sound dull. The following extract will show you how a supremely accomplished stylist keeps his readers awake by means of skilful variations in rhythm:

> The net result was that the Liberals outnumbered the Conservatives by more than eighty, but the Conservatives and Home Rulers together outnumbered the Liberals by four. It would therefore be useless for anyone to form an administration without coming to terms with Parnell. This man, who a dozen years before had been a Wicklow country gentleman, moody and reserved, known outside his own family chiefly as a cricketer, had become the touchstone of the whole British Empire and the arbiter of fate to its Ministers. Such control over the Parliament at Westminster was to all appearance the summit of good fortune for the Irish cause. **Actually it led to disaster**. When Gladstone had asked the electors for a majority over Conservatives and Home Rulers together, so that he could settle the Irish question without Irish dictation, he had not been far wrong. **But he had asked in vain**. (Trevelyan 1965: 382)

The dominant impression conveyed by this finely written passage is one of irrefutable logic and intellectual vigour. The two shortest sentences are in boldface type (our emphasis). They stand in sharp contrast to the rest of the passage, which consists mainly of medium-length sentences. Each short, snappy sentence creates a surprise effect. In each case an abrupt change in rhythm is highlighted by a clause-initial element implying opposition or contrast (*actually, but*).

If you use too many short sentences in succession, your prose may sound awkward or childish. However, as you can see from the passage we have just discussed, a few well-placed short sentences can be extremely effective in a paragraph consisting mainly of long or medium-length sentences (cf. also Module II, Chapters 1.1 and 3.7).

This conveniently brings us to the problems associated with variations in the organizational patterns of paragraphs. Little in the restricted space here available can be said about this formidably difficult subject (but see Module I, Chapter 3.3). Nonetheless, it may be instructive to compare and contrast two short paragraphs from a monograph by a British economist. The first of these paragraphs reads as follows:

> The purpose of this chapter is twofold. First, we shall review the basic phenomena and identify some of the particular problems which arise at the international level. Secondly, we shall consider some of the approaches which have already been adopted, and may conceivably be adopted in the future, in dealing with that collection of issues which we may for convenience term the international antitrust problem. (Swann 1979: 233)

This is a highly organized piece of writing. It displays a tightly knit tripartite structure which is not uncommon in academic prose. The idea presented in the opening sentence (the twofold purpose of the chapter) is developed with unerring precision in two sentences introduced by enumerative terms (*first, secondly*).

Now let us look at another paragraph from the same book:

> The central concern of this book is market power, its causes, consequences and the state policy which is concerned with it. The latter is often referred to as competition policy. In North America, on the other hand, such a policy would be referred to as antitrust policy. In this book, these two terms are used quite interchangeably. Competition policy (antitrust policy) addresses itself not only to the market power arising from monopolies and mergers, but also to that which proceeds from agreements between otherwise legally independent enterprises. Such a policy is almost invariably based on specific laws and is, indeed, often executed through judicial institutions. It constitutes a fascinating field of study on the boundary between economics and the law. (Swann 1979: 9)

This paragraph is less sharply focused and more loosely structured than the passage we have just discussed. In the opening sentence Swann not only indicates the central theme of his book; he pinpoints three aspects of this theme which he intends to examine in detail ('its causes, consequences and the state policy which is concerned with it'). Rather surprisingly, he says no more about the first two aspects, but devotes the rest of the paragraph to the third aspect (competition policy).

Competition and Consumer Protection (the work from which our two specimen paragraphs have been borrowed) displays an extraordinarily wide range of organizational patterns, and these patterns are not infrequently characterized by a randomness of development that challenges description. In this respect, Swann's monograph is not unlike other academic treatises published by English-speaking academics. Paragraph-patterning is – and indeed must be – varied and flexible. This is because it has to be adapted to constantly changing patterns of thought.

You can observe the principle of variety by following a few simple rules:

1. Do not repeat words or expressions unless repetition is the only means of ensuring clarity or producing a rhetorical effect. Read a few pages of academic English before and during the writing process, and read some more English before revising your text. This will enable you to discover all kinds of stylistic variants that you would not otherwise have thought of. During the revision process you can borrow stereotyped expressions from the English texts you have just read (e.g. *As an illustration, we could cite [...], The list could be greatly lengthened, The reason for this lies partly in the fact that [...]*). Beware, however, of committing plagiarism (cf. Mod-

ule I, Chapter 1.4). Sentences which are more than mere stereotypes are the intellectual property of their authors.

2. Subject your syntactic structures to critical scrutiny. If you discover that nearly all your sentences are constructed on the same model (e.g. subject-verb-object), you should try to introduce more variety into your prose by using rhetorical questions, clefting, ellipsis, fronted complements, and the like. Before revising your syntax, you should try to relax and read a few pages of academic English. During the reading process, you will probably come across syntactic structures which you can incorporate into your own text.
3. Vary the length of sentences within the body of each paragraph. Make sure your sentences are not too long, and use short sentences sparingly in order to highlight important ideas.
4. You may have the impression that one of your paragraphs sounds dull or disjointed, yet you may not be sure how to make it sound more interesting. Before attempting to reorder your sentences, you might stop writing in order to read a few pages from an English text. Interrupting the writing process may help you to relax, and reading a few pages of good English may enable you to find a solution to your problem(s). The best solutions are often discovered by chance.

2.5 Elegance

It remains now for us to consider how formal elegance can be attained. Elegance is a vague and elusive concept which has been defined as 'tasteful correctness', 'ingenious simplicity', and 'refined grace or propriety' (cf. *SOED*, under 'elegance'). It is the most superficial of all stylistic qualities, but it can assume crucial importance in situations where the writer is anxious to please and impress the reader.

It is often claimed that the ability to write with elegance in a foreign language is an unattainable goal. That this claim is unduly pessimistic should be evident from the following quotations:

> Friedman tried to make clear to them that they could not outrun the inevitable. (Anon.)
>
> It [*sc.* the text] deals with the desperate (or arrogant) efforts that were taken in order to keep the economy on course artificially. (Anon.)

These examples are from an exam script handed in by a German economics student who was not allowed to consult any reference works during the examination. The student's English displays a real sense of style and structure.

The sentences are well-built, and all the word combinations (including the somewhat rare *efforts [...] taken*)[9] can be found in texts written by native speakers of English. One is immediately struck by two phrases: *outrun the inevitable* and *keep the economy on course*. These expressions reveal a kind of linguistic sophistication which is extremely rare in the English prose of German language learners who are not specializing in English language and literature.

Stylistic elegance is a quality which depends on the interplay of three factors: lexical choice, syntactic ordering, and the overall organization of the text. For clarity of exposition we shall try to deal separately with each of these factors, but it will sometimes be difficult to keep them apart.

We shall begin by drawing a distinction between two types of lexical choice which we shall term 'standard' and 'rhetorical'.[10] By 'standard' we mean choices of vocabulary which conform closely to linguistic norms (e.g. collocations such as *to foster economic growth* and *a stinging defeat*). By 'rhetorical' we mean lexical choices which are in some way unusual, but not incorrect (e.g. *sclerotic growth*), i.e. choices which are intended to produce rhetorical effects.

Most foreign learners can content themselves with standard lexical choices, for the vast majority of their stylistic errors can be corrected by substituting standard English collocations for word combinations of doubtful acceptability. We can illustrate this point with the aid of two inelegantly worded sentences from examination scripts written by German students. Our first example reads as follows:

> During the war the Serbs **did a lot of bad things**. (Anon.)

This sentence is grammatically correct, and all the word combinations occur in conversational utterances produced by native speakers of English. *Did a lot of bad things*, however, is inappropriate here. It should therefore be replaced by a more sophisticated word combination such as *committed numerous atrocities*. Our second example is much more seriously flawed:

> Friedman's advice to the government is to take account of market realities and to stop **acting in a wrong way just to be more accepted by the people**. (Anon.)

This sentence contains two very inelegant expressions (*acting in a wrong way* and *to be more accepted by the people*); it could be reformulated as follows:

---

9 *Make efforts* is much more common than *take efforts*.

10 This distinction corresponds to the one we made in Chapter 1 between academic and personal style.

> Friedman's advice to the government is to take account of market realities and stop **pursuing misguided policies merely in order to curry favour with electors**.

We can now examine some lexical choices which are distinctly rhetorical in character, but not at all unusual in polished academic English.[11] In the following sentence *veiled in euphemism* is an elegant way of saying that some lexical fields contain a large number of euphemistic terms:

> Certain fields may be taboo, and veiled in euphemism [...]. (Wise 1997: 1)

Word combinations like *veiled in euphemism* are generated by metaphorical processes which strain language in various directions in order to fuse dissimilar objects into a new unity. The following quotation will shed further light on one of these processes:

> Goethe soon slipped into easy intimacy with his fellow-diners, who were mostly medical students [...]. (Robertson 1973: 23)

Easy intimacy is a standard collocation,[12] yet it assumes a rhetorical character when it is combined with the verb *slip*, which often denotes a purely physical process, but here suggests a gradual transition from one state to another.

Metaphors belong to the stock-in-trade of the literary artist, yet it would be a mistake to imagine that in academic texts such tricks of rhetoric are used only by professional linguists and literary scholars like Wise and Robertson. Texts dealing with economic subjects, for instance, are full of metaphorical expressions, many of which could easily be borrowed or adapted by foreign students of English. Typical examples are afforded by *the wilting dollar, the creaking economy, aged and creaking factories, the wheezing public transport system* and *wheezing state-run industries*. Just as *the wilting dollar* can easily be transformed into *the wilting local currency*, so *the creaking economy* can be transmuted into *the creaking global economy, the creaking Soviet economy* or *the country's creaking economy*. Such examples could be multiplied indefinitely.

Since metaphors combine abstractions with concrete images and appeal strongly to the imagination, they present several substantial advantages. First, they can add a dash of welcome colour to prose which might other-

---

11 This is one of the most interesting stylistic differences between academic English and academic German. In the first half of the twentieth century German academics used a great deal of metaphorical language, but contemporary German scholars tend to favour a more abstract style of writing.

12 A typical example can be found in Burrough's introduction to Storm's *Schimmelreiter*: Of the two, the father [...] influenced Storm more, though Storm was never on terms of easy intimacy with either. (Storm 1953: vii)

wise be unduly dry and abstract. Second, they can sustain and reinforce the author's theme. Third, they can facilitate memorization (cf. Draaisma 2000: 17). Fourth, they can bring complex ideas within the reach of a wide readership. A particularly elaborate example can be found in Module III, Chapter 4.7, where we quote from a text in which brain activity is likened to the working of a company. The following example is much simpler, but equally effective:

> Now here is a piece of exposition – 'exposition' signifying the laying-out of a topic, the setting-up of the market stall – that presents to the reader something more subtle, more *ingratiating*, than the blunt professional-functional prose of passage A: [...] (Nash & Stacey 1997: 23)

Instead of giving a lengthy formal definition of the term 'exposition', Nash and Stacey opt for a metaphorical reworking of the phrase *the laying-out of the topic*, comparing the writer's work to that of a market trader. We believe this kind of image is within the reach of student writers. If you wish to make imaginative comparisons for purposes of explanation or ornament, you should get into the habit of looking at one thing in terms of another. Thus, for instance, you might liken the study of a foreign language to a voyage of discovery, or a foreign culture to a shrine where none but the initiated may enter.

Abstract ideas can also be presented imaginatively with the aid of similes. Such comparisons should always appear unforced and spontaneous, like the image of the moth and the candle in the following passage, where a literary historian tries to account for the persistent role played by Berlin in the history of German Romanticism:

> And yet, throughout the whole history of the movement, Berlin would seem to have had a fascination for the younger writers like that of the candle for the moth. (Robertson 1959: 393)

In addition to metaphors and similes, many other rhetorical devices can be used to embellish academic texts. These devices include litotes (e.g. *in no small measure, not inconsiderably*), hyperbole (e.g. *sky-high prices, a skyrocketing yen*), polyptoton (*essentially inessential*), and archaisms (e.g. *at sb's behest*). Such tricks of style should, however, be used sparingly and distributed more or less evenly across a text.

We must now bring our minds to bear on the subject of syntactic ordering, the second of the three factors which condition stylistic elegance. The first point that needs to be made here concerns syntactic complexity. Many German academics write in a complex style in their mother tongue and try to reproduce this style in English. There is nothing inherently wrong with this, for a complex style – often a reflection of intellectual subtlety – can be just as elegant as a simple style. The trouble is that long and overly complex sentences are difficult to handle. In the hands of an inexperienced writer they tend to get out of control, and they become extremely inelegant when they are overloaded with complicated noun phrases, adjectives, adverbials, parentheses, and embedded subordinate clauses.

Constructing long sentences is rather like performing a balancing act. You have to strike a balance between complexity and simplicity, and in order to strike this kind of balance you need to observe four rules of thumb:

- First, avoid long word groups at the beginning or in the middle of your sentence.
- Second, avoid unnecessary adverbials and parentheses. Adverbials and parentheses are unnecessary when they assert the obvious or distract the reader's attention from the main idea.
- Third, avoid unnecessary subordinate clauses by using adjectives and nominalizations. Examples: *students* ***who come from other countries →*** ***foreign*** *students – workers* ***who are employed in the public sector → public sector*** *workers* – **When prices go up**, workers ask their employers for more money → **Price increases** trigger demands for higher wages.
- Fourth, keep interruptions as short as possible by using devices such as ellipsis (cf. Chapter 2.3). Examples: '[…] and tragedy herself, **though not excluded**, will have a fortuitous air as if a word would disarm her.' (Forster 1960: 104) – Speculations, **whether sad or lively**, always have a large air about them […]. (*Ibid*: 156)

If you are not sure whether you have made the right syntactic choices, you should read your text aloud to someone who has a good command of English (preferably a native speaker). If you get out of breath, or if your listener shows signs of strain or disinterest, the odds are that your text will have to be rewritten. Even if you cannot find anyone who is prepared to help you, you can assess the effectiveness of your prose by reading your text aloud to an imaginary audience. If word groups are excessively long you will soon get out of breath.

The second point we would like to make here concerns syntactic figures of style which can give pattern and rhythm to your prose. The most basic of these figures is parallelism, which can assume a wide variety of forms. Here are some relatively simple examples:

> **Social distinctions** and **political power** are of primary importance in language. (Burchfield 1985: 3)
>
> It takes the sharpened insights of the experienced communicator to acquire a full respect for the linguistic instrument by which man both **releases his fancy** and **reflects his mythologies**. (Quirk 1982: 16)
>
> Despite the fact that it [i.e. the English language] seems to be **less conscientiously taught** and **less successfully mastered** by many people than once was the case, its inner power remains undisturbed. (Burchfield 1985: vii)

In all these sentences identical syntactic structures are linked by the conjunction *and*: ADJECTIVE + NOUN (*social distinctions, political power*), VERB + POSSESSIVE ADJECTIVE + NOUN (*releases his fancy, reflects his mythologies*), *less* + ADVERB + PAST PARTICIPLE (*less conscientiously taught, less successfully mastered*).

Parallelism is often combined with antithesis. Examples:

> The French were invited to think much of their duties and little of their rights. (Thody 1989: 28)
>
> To invade Britain was singularly easy before the Norman Conquest, singularly difficult afterwards. (Trevelyan 1964: 1)
>
> Against the beasts they could fight; against the dim, impalpable unknown they were helpless. (Sampson 1972: 4)

In the first sentence the syntactic parallel between *much of their duties* and *little of their rights* is reinforced by a double semantic contrast: *little* is the opposite of *much,* and rights are opposed to duties. In the second sentence *singularly easy before* corresponds to *singularly difficult afterwards*; the adjective *easy* is brought into contrast with *difficult,* and *before* is set against *afterwards.* In the third sentence *against the beasts they could fight* corresponds to *against the dim, impalpable unknown they were helpless*; beasts are contrasted with the unknown and the ability to fight is contrasted with helplessness.

Note that parallel word groups can be elegantly linked by ellipsis (cf. Chapter 2.3) if their initial elements are identical. Here is an example from an article by an American economist:

> Time will tell if the course corrections already put in place will work to keep the economy on course and inflation at bay. (Zaretsky 2000: s.p.)

Since the word groups *keep the economy on course* and *keep inflation at bay* both begin with the verb *keep, keep* has been ellipted before the noun *inflation*. In this instance there is a significant degree of overlap between the problems posed by lexical choice and syntactic ordering.

It remains to add that certain patterns are used exclusively for the purpose of underscoring parallels. Such is the case with *as […] so, just as […] so too,* and the like (cf. Module III, Chapter 4.7).

Before leaving the subject of syntacic ordering, we would like to add a few words about rhythm as a stylistic device. The effectiveness of rhythmic devices can be demonstrated by a brief quotation:

> History shows that men have endeavoured, with extraordinary unevenness and sometimes at great intervals of time, to represent 'trains of words' in a written form for greater **convenience, instruction, or imaginative enjoyment**. (Burchfield 1985: 1)

Burchfield's sentence is elegantly rounded off with a rhythmic group consisting of three main elements: (1) *convenience,* (2) *instruction* and (3) *imaginative enjoyment*. An adjective (*imaginative*) has been attached to the third noun to give it greater weight. The rhythmic device in question is known as a ternary sentence ending.

Let us conclude this chapter with a few remarks about the third factor which conditions stylistic elegance, viz. the overall organization of the text. In a sense things have come full circle, for text organization is the subject of Module I. Suffice it to remind the reader that an elegant text in the English style moves resolutely to achieve its aim. The entire text, and the sections within it, and the paragraphs within them should all have forward dynamics. Topic sentences are placed at or near the start of each paragraph; discussion moves briskly with no unnecessary digression or repetition; and assertions are clearly and cogently supported by evidence.

Bibliography

a) Sources of examples

Allen, W. Sidney 1969. The Latin accent: A restatement. *Journal of Linguistics* 5: 193–203.
Atkins, J.W.H. 1966. *English literary criticism. 17th & 18th centuries*. London: Methuen.
Bannock, Graham et al. 1992. *The Penguin dictionary of economics*. London: Penguin.
Barbour, Ian G. 1974. *Myths, models and paradigms: A comparative study in science and religion*. New York: Harper and Row.
Bullock, Alan & Stallybrass, Oliver (eds) 1983. *The Fontana dictionary of modern thought*. London: Fontana.
Burchfield, Robert 1985. *The English language*. Oxford: Oxford University Press.
Burke, David 1988. *Street French*. New York: Wiley.
Croft, William & Cruse, D. Alan 2004. *Cognitive linguistics*. Cambridge: Cambridge University Press.

Crystal, David 1984. *Who cares about English usage?* London: Penguin.

Curtius, Ernst Robert 1993. *Europäische Literatur und Lateinisches Mittelalter*. Tübingen: Francke.

Daniel, Vera J. 1972. Courage – c'est du René Ghil. In D.G. Charlton et al. (eds), *Balzac and the nineteenth century*. Leicester: Leicester University Press, 353–364.

Dexter, Colin 1999. *The remorseful day*. London: Macmillan.

Dressler, Wolfgang 1978. Wege der Textlinguistik. In Wolfgang Dressler (ed.), *Textlinguistik*. Darmstadt: Wissenschaftliche Buchgesellschaft, 1–14.

Durant, Will 1994. *The age of faith*. In *The story of civilization* (CD-ROM). Irvine: World Library, Inc.

Encyclopaedia Britannica on Compact Disc. 1997. Chicago: Encyclopaedia Britannica.

Evans, Ifor 1970. *A short history of English literature*. Harmondsworth: Penguin.

Fairlie, Alison 1972. Constant's *Adolphe* read by Balzac and Nerval. In D.G. Charlton et al. (eds), *Balzac and the Nineteenth Century*. Leicester: Leicester University Press, 209–224.

Forster, Edward Morgan 1960. *Aspects of the Novel*. London: Arnold.

Gilpin, Alan 1977. *Dictionary of Economic Terms*. London: Butterworth.

Gordon, Caroline & Tate, Allen 1960. *The house of fiction*. New York: Charles Scribner's Sons.

Gordon, Ian A. 1980. *The movement of English prose*. London: Longman.

Grimsley, Ronald 1972. Alfred de Musset and Don Juan. In D.G. Charlton et al. (eds), *Balzac and the nineteenth century*. Leicester: Leicester University Press, 321–334.

Halliday, M.A.K. 1994. *An introduction to functional grammar*. London: Arnold.

Harmer, Lewis C. 1979. *Uncertainties in French grammar*. Cambridge: Cambridge University Press.

Hatto, A.T. 1965. *The Niebelungenlied*. Harmondsworth: Penguin.

Hawkins, Kevin 1979. *Unemployment*. Harmondsworth: Penguin.

Hough, Graham 1969. *Style and stylistics*. London: Routledge & Kegan Paul.

International Herald Tribune.

Kelly, J.N.D. 1972. Herbert J. Hunt: career and influence. In D.G. Charlton et al. (eds), *Balzac and the nineteenth century*. Leicester: Leicester University Press, 1–5.

Lucasc, John 1994. *Historical consciousness: The remembered past*. London: Transaction Publishers.

Lyons, John 1969. Review of Nicolas Ruwet, *Introduction à la grammaire générative*. *Journal of Linguistics* 5: 189–190.

Matthews, Peter H. 1967. Review of Noam Chomsky, *Aspects of the theory of syntax*. *Journal of Linguistics* 3: 119–152.

Meyer, Uli 2004. *Die Kontroverse um Neuronale Netze*. Wiesbaden: DUV.

Michon, John Albertus 1993. *Generic intelligent driver support*. Boca Raton: CRC Press.

Moore, W.G. 1972. The changing study of Balzac. In D.G. Charlton et al. (eds), *Balzac and the nineteenth century*. Leicester: Leicester University Press, 187–192.

Moroney, M.J. 1970. *Facts from figures*. Harmondsworth: Penguin.

Nash, Walter & Stacey, David 1997. *Creating texts*. London: Longman.

Nash, Walter 1998. *Language and creative illusion*. London: Longman.

Palmer, Frank R. 1974. *The English verb*. London: Longman.

Palmer, Frank R. 1976. *Semantics*. Cambridge: Cambridge University Press.

Porter, Michael E. 1980. *Competitive strategy*. London: Collier Macmillan.

Quirk, Randolph et al. 1979. *A grammar of contemporary English*. London: Longman.
Quirk, Randolph 1982. *Style and communication in the English language*. London: Arnold.
Robertson, J.G. 1959. *A history of German literature*. Edinburgh: Blackwood.
Robertson, J.G. 1973. *The life and work of Goethe*. New York: Haskell House.
Robinson, Joan 1980. *Further contributions to modern economics*. Oxford: Blackwell.
Sampson, George 1972. *The concise Cambridge history of English literature*. Cambridge: Cambridge University Press.
Samuelson, Paul A. 1980. *Economics*. Tokyo: McGraw-Hill Kogakusha.
Seldon, Arthur & Pennance, F.G. 1976. *Everyman's dictionary of economics*. London: Dent.
Smith, Colin 1972. Destutt de Tracy and the bankruptcy of sensationalism. In D.G. Charlton et al. (eds), *Balzac and the nineteenth century*. Leicester: Leicester University Press, 195–207.
Storm, Theodor 1953. *Der Schimmelreiter*, edited with an introduction and notes by E.H. Burrough. London: Harrap.
Suggate, L.S. 1957. *Africa*. London: Harrap.
Swann, Dennis 1979. *Competition and consumer protection*. Harmondsworth: Penguin.
Swann, Dennis 1992. *The economics of the Common Market*. London: Penguin.
The Economist.
The Guardian.
Thody, Philip 1989. *Albert Camus*. London: Macmillan.
Thody, Philip 1992. *Jean-Paul Sartre*. London: Macmillan.
Thorlby, Anthony (ed.) 1969. *The Penguin companion to literature*, vol. 2: European Literature. Harmondsworth: Penguin.
Tillyard, Eustace M.W. 1998. *The Elizabethan world picture*. London: Pimlico.
Trevelyan, George Macaulay 1964. *History of England*. London: Longmans.
Trevelyan, George Macaulay 1965. *British History in the nineteenth century and after: 1782–1919*. Harmondsworth: Penguin.
Trevithick, James A. 1977. *Inflation*. Harmondsworth: Penguin.
Troyat, Henri 1954. *La neige en deuil*, edited by W.D. Howarth. London: Harrap.
Varian, Hal R. 1978. *Microeconomic analysis*. New York: Norton.
Wells, Herbert George 2005. *The time machine*, edited by Patrick Parrinder, with an introduction by Marina Warner and notes by Steven McLean. London: Penguin.
Winchester, Simon 1999. *The surgeon of Crowthorne*. London: Penguin.
Wise, Hilary 1997. *The vocabulary of modern French: Origins, structure and function*. London: Routledge.
World and Press.
Wotjak, Gerd 1997. Äquivalenz und kein Ende? Nochmals zur semantischen, kommunikativen und translatorisch-diskursiven Äquivalenz. In Gerd Wotjak & Heide Schmidt (eds), *Modelle der Translation/Models of translation*. Frankfurt am Main: Vervuert, 133–170.
Zaretsky, Adam M. 2000. Was that a soft landing or have we not touched down yet? In *Federal Reserve Bank of St. Louis, The Regional Economist*. Available: http://stlouisfed.org/publications/re/2000/d/pages/national-overview.html. (Retrieved 15 July 2008)

b) References

Broughton, Geoffrey 1990. *The Penguin English grammar A–Z for advanced students*. London: Penguin.

Draaisma, Douwe 2000. *Metaphors of memory: A history of ideas about the mind*, tr. Paul Vincent. Cambridge: Cambridge University Press.
Forner, Werner 1998. *Fachsprachliche Aufbaugrammatik Französisch*. Wilhelmsfeld: Egert.
Gallagher, John Desmond 1986. English nominal constructions. A problem for the translator and the lexicographer. *Lebende Sprachen* 31(3): 108–113.
Gallagher, John Desmond 1989. English nominal constructions revisited. *Lebende Sprachen* 34(2): 60–67.
Gallagher, John Desmond 1994. Ressemblances et dissemblances: les ressources stylistiques du français et de l'allemand. *Lebende Sprachen* 39(2): 66–70.
Gallagher, John Desmond 2006. Foreign language vocabulary learning. In Dirk Siepmann (ed.), *Wortschatz und Fremdsprachenlernen* (special issue of *Beiträge zur Fremdsprachenvermittlung*, vol. 9). Landau: Empirische Pädagogik, 11–95.
Halliday, M.A.K. 1994. *An introduction to functional grammar*. London: Arnold.
Hanks, Patrick (ed.) 1979. *Collins dictionary of the English language*. London: Collins.
Nash, Walter & Stacey, David 1997. *Creating texts*. London: Longman.
Quirk, Randolph 1982. *Style and communication in the English language*. London: Arnold.
Raban, Jonathan 1968. *The technique of modern fiction*. London: Arnold.
Rundell, Michael (ed.) 2005. *Macmillan English dictionary (with CD-ROM)*. London: Palgrave Macmillan.
Siepmann, Dirk 2005. *Discourse markers across languages*. Abingdon: Routledge.
Summers, Della (ed.) 1993. *Longman language activator*. Harlow: Longman.
Summers, Della (ed.) 1995. *Longman dictionary of contemporary English*. Munich: Langenscheidt-Longman.
The Oxford English dictionary on compact disc. 2nd edition. (1996). Oxford: Oxford University Press.
The shorter Oxford English dictionary, 2 vols. 3rd edition (1978). Oxford: Clarendon Press.
Thompson, Geoff 1996. *Introducing functional grammar*. London: Arnold.
Walter, Elizabeth (ed.) 2006. *Cambridge advanced learner's dictionary (with CD-ROM)*. Cambridge: Cambridge University Press.
Weaver, Constance et al. 2001. To grammar or not to grammar: That is *not* the question! *Voices from the middle* 8(3): 17–33.
Wilss, Wolfram 1971. Englische Partizipialkonstruktionen und ihre Wiedergabe im Deutschen. In Karl-Richard Bausch & Hans-Martin Gauger (eds), *Interlinguistica. Sprachvergleich und Übersetzung*. Tübingen: Niemeyer, 555–568.

A final word

The purpose of this book has been to help you as a native speaker of German to produce well-structured, persuasive, accurate and stylistically appropriate argued texts in English. Inevitably, we have had to present you with an abundance of rules, instructions, principles, advice and suggestions as well as alerting you to countless ways in which English surprisingly differs from German. Rather than just expecting you to take this information on trust, however, we have provided instances of good writing that exemplify our precepts and have always tried to explain their underlying rationale. We have also asked you to accept that writing is a creative business and that it is impossible to give hard and fast rules for every imaginable writing situation. Our hope is that by helping you to understand why certain solutions may have some advantages and why others may have certain drawbacks, we have prepared you to make your own independent intelligent decisions as a writer.

The last Module focused on style. Although the book as a whole aims to equip you as a writer of academic prose (hence the focus on academic style), we very much encourage you to develop your own individual writing style (called personal style in Module IV) as an academic writer. Just as you want to be recognized for who you are by the way you dress, by the way you sign your name, and indeed by the way you speak, so you will also wish to have a particular way of writing that is unmistakably yours, is admired by your readers and conforms to the image of yourself that you wish to project. You should therefore read this book as defining a domain (that of the academic argued text) within which you can express your thoughts and your research findings freely while still respecting the norms required by publishers, editors and university tutors.

Every writer falls prey from time to time to writer's block, that horrible feeling of being unable to write anything, often despite a looming deadline. We are aware that all the many rules and regulations given in this book may actually seem to make things worse. "How can I possibly bear them all in mind and also write interestingly about my subject?", you may wonder. Yet this is exactly why we have divided the book into separate Modules, and within these Modules have broken down the writing task into separate processes. In particular in Module I, we have emphasized how you should give yourself time for the three stages of planning, writing proper and editing (even allowing yourself to cycle back to earlier stages when necessary); and we have separated each of these stages into smaller tasks. As your experience with writing grows, you will learn to handle a number of writing processes at one and the same time, and will then learn to write more quickly and efficiently. As long as your skills are less developed, however, the best answer to writer's block is to break your assignment up into doable tasks and subtasks. Deal with them in succession until things begin to flow again.

A theme of Modules I and II has been that all units of text display a tripartite structure. The well-known trio "Introduction – Body – Conclusion", which of course gives structure to the text as a whole, is reflected, too, in the sections of which the entire text is composed, but also in the paragraphs within those sections, in the sentences that make up the paragraphs, and even in the clauses that go together to form those sentences. What is common to all these levels of discourse is that there should be forward dynamics: the introductory part whets your reader's appetite for what is to come, and the quality of the concluding part determines whether what you have written will leave a lasting impression. Module II, which also emphasizes the crucial role of punctuation, has given you a wealth of techniques for ensuring that your clauses and sentences will be formed to achieve communicative effectiveness in exactly this way.

Module III has given you insight into the lexical riches of English, concentrating on the fact that many combinations which seem logically plausible are unacceptable, since they do not take account of collocation, the "company words keep", as it has been called. The best guide to how to put words together is to discover how they have been put together before, and this Module both draws on the abundance of data now available in corpora and shows you how to derive pertinent information from corpora yourself. This part of the book contains so much information that you should have it open by your elbow as you write; it is a treasure house of useful expressions.

Our hope is that this book has persuaded you that an analytical attitude to the task of writing, although it initially may seem to slow things down, actually soon comes to pay dividends. The understanding that you develop from a more conscious approach to writing gives you the confidence and control that will make you proficient and effective in your communication. We wish you well with your writing.

Glossary

Words in the definitions that are in bold are themselves defined in the glossary.

Adjective a word that is used to modify, restrict or add to the meaning of a **noun**.

Adverbial an element of the **clause** – a single adverb, a **phrase** or a **clause** – that typically serves to modify the state of affairs expressed by the **verb**.

Adverbial clause a **subordinate clause** used to indicate time, place, reason, condition, etc.

Apposition a construction consisting of two adjacent units that give different information about the same thing; *Smith the butcher* gives information about the man's name and his profession.

Archaism an old-fashioned word or **phrase** (e.g. *betimes*). In legal and liturgical texts the use of archaisms is often inevitable, but in most academic texts the deliberate use of archaisms is a stylistic device.

Argued text any text that both presents information and takes a stand on that information, providing justification for the positions it adopts.

Backgrounded information at the level of the **sentence** or paragraph, information which is relatively unimportant given the writer's communicative goals.

Clause a grammatical unit, usually containing a **subject** and a **verb,** which expresses a state of affairs and is the basic building block of the **sentence**.

Climax sentence the final **sentence** in many paragraphs in **argued text**; it indicates the culmination of the argument in the preceding **elaboration**.

Collocation a sequence of **lexemes** which commonly occur together; the most common types of collocation are described in Module III, Chapter 3.

Collusion presenting written work as your own although some or all of the work has been written by a fellow student or other person; a serious offence.

Comma splice the incorrect use of a comma to combine two independent **clauses**.

Compound word a word consisting of a combination of two or more forms which behave grammatically as one word (e.g. *optimality-theoretic, inflation rate, brother-in-law, double-cross*).

Constituent an element that is part of a larger structure (a **noun** is a constituent of a **noun phrase**).

Construction a pairing of form and meaning, including morphemes (e.g. *pre-*), **lexemes** (*shape, institute*), **collocations**, idioms (*blind spot*) and partially lexically filled patterns (*there is a* ADJ *case for* + V-*ing*).

Coordinated clause the second or later clause in a string of **clauses** connected by *and, or, but* or *for*.

Editing the essential process of producing the final version of a text by correcting its shortcomings.

Elaboration (1) the central part of any paragraph in an **argued text**; it develops the **topic sentence** and typically leads to a **climax sentence**; (2) the process of adding various grammatical devices following the main **clause** of a **sentence** in order to develop an idea expressed by the **main clause.**

Embedded clause a **clause** which serves as a **constituent** of another **clause**.

Extraposition a construction where either the subject or the object is placed at the end of the **clause**, and the dummy element *it* is placed in the position where the subject or object would normally have been.

Figure of speech an expressive linguistic device (e.g. a metaphor).

Focus the informational high point of a **clause**.

Foregrounded information at the level of the **sentence** or paragraph, information which is relatively important given the writer's communicative goals.

Formatting the process of preparing a text for submission according to specified requirements for layout.

Forward dynamics the reader's sense that each part of a text has direction, leading from a starting point to a conclusion.

Framing placing elements at the beginning of the **clause** or **sentence** in order to provide a framework for the understanding of the information that follows.

Fronting placing **constituents** such as direct objects before the subject.

Given information information which the writer assumes can be retrieved by the reader from the prior context, or from general knowledge.

Head the most characteristic word in a **phrase**; thus the **noun** is head of a **noun phrase**.

Hyperbole a deliberate exaggeration used to produce a vivid effect. For instance, instead of saying that somebody is very rich you can say that they are 'rolling in money'.

Hypernym a general term whose meaning includes the meanings of other, more specific words. *Vegetable*, for instance, is the hypernym of *onion* and *carrot*, just as *plant* is the hypernym of *vegetable*.

Hyponym a specific term whose meaning is included in that of another, more general word. *Cat* and *dog*, for instance, are hyponyms of *animal*.

Information packaging making grammatical choices which allow you to place **constituents** in a position which accords with their informational status, given your communicative aims.

Interruption the process of breaking the flow of a **clause** in order to insert information which in some way modifies the immediately previous information.

Lexeme an individual item of vocabulary which may have several forms (e.g. *give/gives/giving/gave/given*).

Litotes an understatement. In academic publications this device is often used to tone down statements. Thus, for instance, scholars can say that they have learnt 'not a little' (i.e. a great deal) in the course of their research work.

Main clause a grammatically independent **clause** which forms the communicative core of a **sentence**.

Message what is communicated by an information unit, typically expressed by means of a **clause**.

Metaphor a **figure of speech** whereby two unlike objects are implicitly compared to one another. Unlike **similes**, metaphors rely on the substitution of one element for another. 'Life **is like** a walking shadow' is a simile. 'Life **is** a walking shadow' is a metaphor.

New information information which the writer assumes cannot be retrieved by the reader from the prior context, or from general knowledge.

Non-finite clause a **clause** containing a non-finite **verb,** i.e. a **participial** form or the infinitive (as in *to be*).

Non-restrictive pertaining to an **apposition**, a **relative clause** or an **adverbial clause** which adds extra information about the element which it modifies in the form of a separate information unit.

Noun a word that names a person, place, thing or idea.

Noun phrase a **sentence constituent** which functions exactly like a **noun** and often has a noun as its **head**; in ***An old woman*** *crossed* ***the street*** the heads of the noun phrases are *woman* and *street.*

Paraphrase the reformulation, accompanied by a reference to the source, of a scholar's work in your own words; an alternative to **quotation**.

Participial pertaining to a **participle**.

Participle a form of the **verb** which ends in -ing (*present participle*) or -ed (*past participle*).

Pattern the way in which elements of language combine to form larger units; more specifically, the ways in which **verbs**, **nouns** and **adjectives** occur with particular grammatical structures (e.g. *different from* + **noun phrase**, *give* + **noun phrase + noun phrase**).

Phrase a grouping of words smaller than a **clause**; phrases are named for the word that is their **head**, cf. **noun phrase**.

Plagiarism the wilful or careless incorporation of a scholar's work into your text without **quotation** marks or reformulation and without a reference to the source; a serious offence.

Polyphony the observation that **argued text** typically contains several 'voices': those of the author, other academics, the writer of the primary literature, the characters in primary literature, etc.

Polyptoton the deliberate repetition of a word in various grammatical forms (e.g. *telling, told*) or the bringing together of two or more words derived from the same root (e.g. *strength, strengthen, stronger, strongly*). Polyptoton is particularly effective when the elements that are repeated are in the same **sentence** (e.g. *What's* ***done*** *cannot be* ***undone***.).

Postponed object a direct object in **clause**-final position that is separated from its **verb** by one or more **adverbial** elements.

Pragmatic pertaining to aspects of meaning that have to do with how language is used in a specific context.

Presentative construction a construction whereby the subject is placed in **clause**-final position because it is in **focus**, usually being introduced into the discourse for the first time.

Primary literature in literary essays, the work under analysis and any other relevant literary works.

Quotation the incorporation of a scholar's work into your text; all quotations are surrounded by quotation marks and accompanied by a reference to the source.

Relative clause a **subordinate clause** which typically modifies a **noun** or **noun phrase**.

Secondary literature in literary essays, published non-literary work by critics, literary theoreticians and other academics.

Semantic pertaining to the meaning of linguistic expressions.

Semantic feature a minimal unit of meaning; thus, the word *bachelor* may be said to be imbued with the features /+ man/, /+ unmarried/.

Sentence orthographically, a unit of text whose first word typically starts with a capital letter and which ends with a full stop; rhetorically, the basic building block of a paragraph.

Simile a **figure of speech** whereby two unlike objects are explicitly compared to each other. For instance, if we say that somebody is 'as white as a sheet', we use the word *as* to establish a relationship between the whiteness of that person's face and the whiteness of (clean) bed linen.

Subordinate clause a **clause** which is grammatically dependent on another **clause**.

Theme the initial **constituent** of the **clause**.

Thesis statement a statement, towards the end of the Introduction, which delimits the scope of the text that will follow.

Topic sentence the (usually) initial **sentence** of a paragraph in an **argued text**; it sets out the scope of the paragraph.

Verb a word that expresses action or a state of being.

Verbless clause a shortened **clause** structure without a **verb**.

Wh-clause a **clause** beginning with the word *when, where, why, who* or *how*.

Index